Towards a Sociology
of Pedagogy

Alan R. Sadovnik and Susan F. Semel
General Editors

Vol. 23

PETER LANG
New York • Washington, D.C./Baltimore • Bern
Frankfurt am Main • Berlin • Brussels • Vienna • Oxford

Towards a Sociology of Pedagogy

The Contribution of Basil Bernstein to Research

EDITED BY
Ana Morais, Isabel Neves,
Brian Davies, Harry Daniels

PETER LANG
New York • Washington, D.C./Baltimore • Bern
Frankfurt am Main • Berlin • Brussels • Vienna • Oxford

Library of Congress Cataloging-in-Publication Data

Towards a sociology of pedagogy: the contribution
of Basil Bernstein to research / edited by Ana Morais ... [et al.].
p. cm. — (History of schools and schooling; vol. 23)
Includes bibliographical references and index.
1. Bernstein, Basil B. 2. Educational sociology. 3. Education—
Philosophy. I. Bernstein, Basil B. II. Morais, Ana.
III. History of schools and schooling; v. 23.
LB880.B462 T69   306.43—dc21   2001029248
ISBN 978-0-8204-5585-3
ISSN 1089-0678

Die Deutsche Bibliothek-CIP-Einheitsaufnahme

Towards a sociology of pedagogy: the contribution
of Basil Bernstein to research / ed. by: Ana Morais....
–New York; Washington, D.C./Baltimore; Bern;
Frankfurt am Main; Berlin; Brussels; Vienna; Oxford: Lang.
(History of schools and schooling; Vol. 23)
ISBN 978-0-8204-5585-3

Cover art and design by Joni Holst

© 2001, 2010 Peter Lang Publishing, Inc., New York

All rights reserved.
Reprint or reproduction, even partially, in all forms such as microfilm,
xerography, microfiche, microcard, and offset strictly prohibited.

In memory of Basil Bernstein

Contents

Series Editor's Introduction.. xiii
Acknowledgments xvii

Introduction 1
Brian Davies

PART 1
Literacy and Schooling 15

Chapter 1
Literacy Pedagogy Prior to Schooling: Relations Between
Social Positioning and Semantic Variation 17
Geoff Williams
    Introduction 17
    The Children and Their Families 20
    The "Same" Context 22
    Reading Difference in Family Readings of *The Three Little Pigs* ... 25
    Joint Book-Reading as Situation-Type 34
    Finale: Evidence From Reading at Home in the Early School Years 40

Chapter 2
The Ontogenesis of Decontextualised Language: Some
Achievements of Classification and Framing 47
Ruqaiya Hasan
    Conjectures About Decontextualised Language 47
    Where, When, and How Do They Learn It? 50
    Decontextualised Language and the Classroom 72

PART 2
Pedagogic Discourse and Curriculum Organization 81

Chapter 3
Subject, Power, and Pedagogic Discourse 83
Mario Diaz
- Introduction 83
- Bernstein's Program 83
- Power, Boundaries, and the Subject 84
- Power, Subjects, and Voice 86
- The Subject and Meanings 88
- Subjects and Code 89
- Subjects and Pedagogic Discourse 92
- Final Comments: The De-Centred Subject in Bernstein 94

Chapter 4
Bernstein and Activity Theory 99
Harry Daniels

Chapter 5
The Teaching of Sociology: Towards a European Comparison of Curricula 113
Philippe Vitale
- Introduction 113
- Teaching Content and What Is at Stake 114
- The Structure of Sociology Instruction 115
- In Search of Koïnè(s) 124

Chapter 6
Intimations of Boundlessness 129
Johan Muller
- "Déréglement" 129
- Sacred and Profane 132
- Vertical and Horizontal 138
- Prometheus Unbound, or What Does It Mean to Be Literate? 141

Chapter 7
Founding the Sociology of Knowledge: Basil Bernstein,
Intellectual Fields, and the Epistemic Device 153
Rob Moore
Karl Maton
   Introduction.. 153
   Conceptualising Intellectual Fields 156
   Illustrating the Switch Event: From "Perspectives"
   to "Paradigms" 162
   Grammars, Modes, and Communities: The Cases of
   Literary Criticism and Mathematics.. 166
   Conclusion: Devices and the Sociology of Knowledge............................ 176

PART 3
Classroom Contexts and Pedagogic Practices 183

Chapter 8
Pedagogic Social Contexts: Studies for a Sociology of Learning 185
Ana Morais
Isabel Neves
   Introduction.. 185
   Pedagogic Social Contexts 188
   Research Methodology: Developing an
   External Language of Description... 191
   Final Considerations 212

Chapter 9
Texts and Contexts in Educational Systems: Studies of
Recontextualising Spaces 223
Isabel Neves
Ana Morais
   Introduction.. 223
   Theoretical Framework 225
   Application of the Pedagogic Discourse Model in the Analysis of
   Science Curriculum Reforms: Exemplar Research Studies 227
   Final Considerations 241

Chapter 10
Pedagogic Discourses and Student Resistance
in Australian Secondary Schools 251
Parlo Singh
    Introduction.. 251
    Theoretical Framework: Analysis of the Structure of Pedagogic
    Discourse 252
    Interview data: Samoan Members of Para-Educational Networks
    and Students 256
    Classroom Data: Analyses of Pedagogic Discourses in English
    Classroom Lessons 263
    Discussion.. 276

Chapter 11
Educational Evaluation: The Social Production of Texts and
Practices 287
Joseph Solomon
Anna Tsatsaroni
    Introduction.. 287
    The IEP Project and Its Contexts 288
    Theoretical Considerations 294
    Research Questions and Methodology................................... 296
    The Analysis of Transmitters' Texts 298
    Critical Reflections 308

PART 4
Bernstein's Sociology of Education:
Looking Backward and Forward 317

Chapter 12
Classification Strength and Power Relations 319
Magnus Haavelsrud
    Language Codes, Class, and Power Relations 319
    Curriculum, Class, and Power Relations 325
    The Pedagogic Device and Power Relations 326
    Power Relations and Relative Autonomy.............................. 330

Chapter 13
Crosswired: Hypertext, Critical Theory,
and Pedagogic Discourse 339
William Tyler
    Developing an Online Educational Resource: A tertiary
    Education example 342
    Open Textualities, Closed Technologies:
    Two Faces of Online Learning 344
    Pedagogic Discourse and Post-modernity 347
    Dimensions of the Virtual: Hypertext as Pedagogic Device 351
    Conclusion 356

EPILOGUE
Coda: Basil Bernstein Speaks 361

From Pedagogies to Knowledges 363
Basil Bernstein

Video Conference with Basil Bernstein 369

List of Contributors 385
Index 391

Series Editor's Introduction

Alan Sadovnik

It gives Susan Semel and me great pleasure to include this book in the *History of Schools and Schooling* series. Although at first glance it might not appear that a volume in the sociology of education fits in a history series, we believe that this book has important historical significance. Almost all of the chapters in *Towards a Sociology of Pedagogy: The Contribution of Basil Bernstein to Research* were originally commissioned for presentation in June 2000 at a symposium organised by the editors, Ana Morais, Isabel Neves, Harry Daniels, and Brian Davies, in Lisbon. Although Bernstein could not attend because of illness, it did mark his final appearance at a conference, as he participated via video link from his home in London. As the record of the conference, this book represents a contribution to the history of sociological theory and the sociology of education, including important theoretical and empirical papers on the work of one of the preeminent sociologists of the twentieth century alongside his own final public statements.

Basil Bernstein, Karl Mannheim Emeritus Professor of the Sociology of Education at the Institute of Education, University of London, died on September 24, 2000, after a prolonged battle with cancer of the larynx. Professor Bernstein was one of the leading sociologists in the world, and his pioneering work over the past four decades illuminated our understanding of the relationships between political economy, family, language, and schooling. Although committed to equity and social justice, or in his own words, "preventing the wastage of working class educational potential" (1961, p. 288), as Davies suggests in his "Introduction" to this volume, Bernstein's work was often misunderstood and incorrectly labelled a form of "cultural deficit" theory. Nothing could be more inaccurate.

Raised in London's East End, the son of Jewish immigrant parents, Bernstein's career reflected his concern for understanding and eliminating the barriers to upward social mobility. After serving as an underage bombardier in Africa in World War II, he worked in the Stepney Settlement Boys' Club for underprivileged Jewish children. He put himself through the

London School of Economics by working various menial jobs and earned a degree in sociology. He completed teacher education at Westminster College of Education in 1954. From then until 1960 he taught a variety of subjects, including English, civics, and physical education, at City Day College in Shoreditch. In pure Goffmanesque style, he also taught elementary vehicle maintenance although he did not drive, a fact that he claimed to have successfully concealed from his students.

By 1963, following a period of research work at University College, London, he had moved to the Institute of Education as head of its Department of the Sociology of Education, where he stayed for the remainder of his career, rising from senior lecturer to reader, to professor, to Mannheim Chair. From 1963 to 1974 he also served as head of the Institute of Education's influential Sociological Research Unit and later as Pro-Director of Research.

For over four decades, Bernstein has been a centrally important and controversial sociologist, whose work has influenced a generation in education and socio-linguistics. From his early work on language and schooling to his later work on pedagogic discourse, Bernstein elaborated a theory of social and educational codes, drawing on the essential theoretical orientations in the field: Durkheimian, Weberian, Marxist, and interactionist. Karabel and Halsey (1977, p. 62), in their review of the literature on the sociology of education, called Bernstein's work the "harbinger of a new synthesis", a view entirely justified by subsequent events. Whatever the criticisms of Bernstein's work, it represents one of the most sustained and powerful attempts to investigate significant issues in the sociology of education. Bernstein's project has provided the most systematic analysis that we have of the role of schooling in social reproduction.

I first met Basil Bernstein in 1978 at New York University, when I was a doctoral student and he was a visiting professor. He took an interest in a paper I wrote for him, applying his work to Bowles and Gintis' *Schooling in Capitalist America*. For the next 22 years, he was my mentor, colleague, and, most of all, beloved friend. His impact on my career (as well as the careers of dozens of his other students now in prestigious university positions all over the world) was enormous. When I told him that I had received the American Sociological Association's Willard Waller Award for my article on his work, he replied with his usual sense of humour, "My dear boy, I *have* made your career, haven't I?"

Professor Bernstein was no narrow academic. He was an arts aficionado, an audiophile, and an expert photographer. As a conversationalist he was ironic, creative, clever, amusing, knowledgeable, and, at times, cryptic and sardonic. Whether it was applying code theory to the exploitation of South American farmers, at one of his favourite Bloomsbury haunts or, with Eliot Freidson, entertaining us with tales of 1968 at Berkeley, he was one of a kind.

Basil was married to his wife, Marion, for 45 years and they had two sons, Saul and Francis. His dedication to the fifth volume of *Class, Codes and Control* in 1996, as to the first in 1971, reads simply, *For Marion*, summing up the incredible devotion they had for each other, partners in every sense of the word.

The last time I saw Basil was in June 2000, when I journeyed to London from the conference in Lisbon. Too ill to attend as planned, Basil had participated for its last hour via video link to his home in London. Despite being weak from treatment, he was vintage Basil, witty and creative. His brief written contribution had already provided us with significant food for thought. Upon termination of the link, there was not a dry eye among us. We all knew that this might have been his last public appearance and we all knew how much we would miss him. Two days later, here he was, telling Susan Semel and me about finishing *Class, Codes and Control, Volume 6*, about applying code theory to the Internet and technology, and about New Labour's educational policy, which was still, in his view, like Thatcher's, "a new pedagogical janus" reproducing the old inequalities. Although I left hoping it was not a final goodbye, I knew that it might well be. When he died on September 24, the world of sociology lost a giant, while I lost a mentor and friend, to whom I will always be grateful.

Fortunately, Bernstein has left us his legacy through his research and, just as importantly, through dozens of former students and researchers who continue to refine and test his theories. The Lisbon conference was the first in what are planned as bi-annual meetings to continue Bernstein's project, especially through empirical research. In 1991, although otherwise supportive, Bernstein was critical of my claim that there had been little empirical testing of his theories. In his last book, *Pedagogy, Symbolic Control and Identity* (1996), he reviewed a significant number of empirical studies through which his theories had been developed and refined, albeit most of them hitherto unavailable in the United States of America. With the publication of this book, a set of new theoretical and empirical papers testing, advancing, and extending those theories is now available, alongside the growing body of work in the journals, in the United States, Canada, the UK, and the rest of Europe, as well as in Australia, New Zealand, South Africa, and

Taiwan. These papers will contribute to the history of the sociology of education and provide valuable insights for further empirical research. Above all else, Bernstein believed that his contribution to theory had been possible only through the efforts of others, not least his former students who, for the past 25 years, had provided the empirical basis in which it was grounded. He would have been proud of Ana Morais, Isabel Neves, Harry Daniels, and Brian Davies, as well as all the other contributors to this volume, for furthering his project.

Bibliography

Bernstein, B. (1961). Social structure, language and learning. *Journal of Educational Research, 3*, 163–176.

———. (1971). *Class, codes and control: Vol. I, Theoretical studies towards a sociology of language.* London: Routledge & Kegan Paul. (Rev. ed. 1973, 2nd ed. 1974)

———. (1973). *Class, codes and control: Vol. II, Applied studies towards a sociology of language.* London: Routledge & Kegan Paul.

———. (1975). *Class, codes and control: Vol. III, Towards a theory of educational transmissions.* London: Routledge & Kegan Paul. (2nd ed. 1977)

———. (1990). *Class, codes and control: Vol. IV, The structuring of pedagogic discourse.* London: Routledge.

———. (1996). *Class, codes and control: Vol. V, Pedagogy, symbolic control and identity: Theory, research, critique.* London: Taylor & Francis.

Bowles, S., & Gintis, H. (1976). *Schooling in capitalist America.* New York: Basic Books.

Karabel, J., & Halsey, A. H. (Eds.). (1977). *Power and ideology in education.* New York: Oxford University Press.

Sadovnik, A. R. (1991). Basil Bernstein's theory of pedagogic practices: A structuralist approach. *Sociology of Education, 64* (1), 48–63.

Acknowledgments

The commissioning of these papers and the arrangements for the meeting that followed in Lisbon in June 2000 were only made possible with the support of the Institute for Educational Innovation, Foundation for Science and Technology, Centre for Educational Research of the School of Science, University of Lisbon, and the wisdom and funding of the Gulbenkian Foundation.

We are grateful to Fernanda Freire and Joana Guimarães who did the administrative work for the symposium and on this volume.

This volume is dedicated to Basil Bernstein, with whom we all worked closely and from whom we learned so much and, as we are sure that he would wish, to Marion.

The publisher and the authors would like to thank the following for permission to reprint material in this volume:

Johan Muller, *Reclaiming Knowledge: Social Theory, Curriculum, and Education Policy* (chapter 5), (London: Routledge Falmer, 2000). Reprinted by permission of the publisher.

Introduction

Brian Davies

The more or less organised form of hindsight known as history tells us that it was round about the time that Basil Bernstein was conducting his early socio-linguistic studies that education first lost its innocence. This was a matter of correlation rather than causation. Uneven though its incidence and form was, at least a decade or more of universal and extended secondary education in the West had begun to look less like a guarantee of individual and system improvement than the same old story of class, gender, and ethnic differentiation. While experience of schooling palpably did good, it did more for some than for others, and progress in attempts to provide "more equal" forms of access was halting. To be trained to teach in the late fifties and early sixties was to be given a dose of Rousseau's idealism, the technology of Piaget's stages and the absolution in advance of class cultural differences. To work in education beyond the early years of schooling was to risk the realisation that, although we had willed the end, we had neither willed nor discovered the means to achieve effective mass education. To be a social scientist researching education was, almost inevitably, to choose one's location in the opportunity and educability industries.

Basil Bernstein's publications started here, in 1958, and flowed continuously until 2000. He was both the most interesting and the most important British sociologist of recent times, internationally better known for longer than any other. There are certainly those who have published more, especially among those not burdened with the necessity of carrying out empirical work. Bernstein never sought to create a band of followers, choosing to become an analyst of power rather than a prescriber of policy. His ideas have measured the change that has taken place in our systems and they offer the most developed grammar for understanding the shape and character of our current educational practice. He attempted, with some scrupulousness, to offer a commentary on the evolution of his ideas across the period of publication of five volumes referred to collectively as *Class, Codes and Control, I–V*. The first edition of *Volume I* was published in 1971 and the second edition of the last volume in 2000. The first four volumes were published by Routledge, for whom he also edited the *Primary Socialisation, Language and Education* series in which most of the work of his Sociological Research Unit (SRU) appeared. *Volume V* first appeared in 1996, published by Taylor & Francis. In each of the volumes he wrote an introductory essay that revealed the background of his thinking *ad interim*, his motives for offering a further book, and a guide to the changes that had taken place in his corpus, with a word to his critics. All the introductions are excellent guides to his thinking and were written with great clarity, even if the introduction to *Volume IV*, the shortest, was overly given to the slaying of his "recontextualisers". These were much the same people that he referred to in the video conference that serves as an endpiece to this volume as "people who not only won't read but can't read" (p. 371). Bernstein was a constant reviser of his ideas between editions and books, arguing always that this was necessitated by the relationship between the empirical and the theoretical in his work.

In much of the educational and social science world, that work is still identified with his early socio-linguistic studies[1] and, even more particularly, its earliest formulations which, he freely admitted, were relatively crude. Briefly, Bernstein's earliest ideas on the interactions between class, language, cognition, control, and social structure, initially evidenced by studies of young workers on day-release courses and public (i.e., private) school boys, prefaced 12 years of further study by the SRU, the largest single educational research group of its day or probably any day, at the Institute of Education, London. Bernstein had moved from further education college teaching, through a brief but crucially formative interlude of full-time research with Dr. Frieda Goldman-Eisler at University College, London, to become the founder and head of the SRU within a Sociology Department whose leadership he inherited from Jean Floud in January 1963. The work could hardly have been hotter or heavier. An enormous amount of funding was provided for the Unit by government and the Nuffield and Ford Foundations for the investigation of a number of socio-linguistic and educational problems by to 15 full-time researchers. At the same time, the change and ferment taking place in British academic sociology racked his department.[2] Though he taught a good deal and, notwithstanding his protestations to the contrary, in inspirational manner, most of his energy went into the management and conduct of the Unit's work.

Its complex and highly nuanced studies, on the boundaries of linguistics, sociology, and psychology, showed evidence of class related differences in the social functions of communication. Given certain assumptions underlying educational practice, including those prevailing then and now, these differences were transformed into inequalities. But not for the first or last time in educational discourse, both politicians and professionals appeared to hear only what they were ready for. The findings of the studies were steadfastly misread as indicating black and working class language deficit and inevitable relative failure. Working with Bernstein at the time, I well remember the depth of his indignation that more than a decade of work should have such calumny heaped upon it by those who claimed to see it as an obstacle to more egalitarian educational reforms. No irony could have been greater with respect to a man driven to understand both how people were and how they might be. The squabble with Labov hurt, for Bernstein thought it "a travesty to relate the concepts of elaborated or restricted codes to superficial stylistics of middle class and working class forms of conversational behaviour", adding,

> I have difficulty in understanding, and I have very little sympathy with, complaints that the socio-linguistic thesis of 1958 is in some respects different from the thesis in 1972. Such a critique is based upon a complete misunderstanding of the nature of research. (Bernstein, 1974, pp. 241–242)

There was a scary persistence to the criticism from a Right that accused Bernstein of romanticising "the working class" and its language and a Left that saw him as confirming its deficit and underplaying class in power relations. The view of the Left is represented in this volume by Haavelsrud's re-rehearsal of Bisseret's (1979) accusations of essentialism and partiality. Bernstein was damned if he did and damned if he didn't and noted the irony, then and now, claiming that

> I couldn't stand the romanticising of everyday language, anymore than I can stand the romanticising of the working class, or anymore than I could stand, you know, the double indemnities of the middle class [...] all this is just radical chic that I can't be bothered with. (Video conference, p. 373)

In addition, it cannot be said too often that Bernstein always saw himself as a researcher and that techniques elaborated and questions raised were more important than "answers". Yet his "question" remained remarkable, focused upon "fitting it all together" around an increasingly refined code theory to produce work on pedagogic practice that spanned social institutions and involved the deepest questions of the relationship between knowledge and power, identity and communication, consciousness and change.

He looked back at the point where he disengaged from socio-linguistic research and disbanded the SRU in the early seventies as a crucial move, freeing him from the "daily necessities of empirical research on a vast program" (Video conference, p. 370) and giving himself time to attend to

> the imperfections of the socio-linguistic theorising, make distinctions between power and control [...] show that you could have modalities of elaborated codes [...] what were the principles selecting why a particular modality was institutionalised for particular groups of children. (Video conference, p. 371)

The first public evidence of this change came at the British Sociological Association (BSA) Conference on the sociology of education in 1970, the first and only one with education as its theme. Bernstein presented a closing address, "On the Classification and Framing of Educational Knowledge" (1971b), that captivated and astonished his audience, promising an approach to analysis that dealt directly with issues of curriculum, teaching, evaluation, and social relations (collectively, pedagogy) that transcended our narrow preoccupation with educability. In part, its impact was due to his wit and skill as a communicator. Although he claimed not to have been "a born teacher" of day-release youth, several generations of higher education students have experienced epiphanies in his presence. However, many of them in the early seventies were all too easily drawn to the utopia promised by the "new directions" in the sociology of education associated with Bernstein's former student and departmental colleague Michael F. D. Young. Bernstein was contemptuous of this movement's "radical chic" and incensed when held to be associated with it, having generously allowed Young to publish his BSA paper in *New Directions* before it appeared elsewhere.[3] The easy liaison of soft Marxism and phenomenology that constituted the core of Young's paper was anathema to one aiming to forge the links between Durkheim, Mead, Luria freed of the necessities of his Marxism, and, later Althusser and Foucault, that enabled movement from "Classification and Framing" (1971b) through successive versions of "Visible and Invisible" (1973b) and "Education and Production" (1977a).

The development of this process took place across a decade of teaching and research supervision in London and around the world during which "Code, Modalities" (1981) and "On Pedagogic Discourse" (1986) established the notion of the pedagogic device. For Bernstein these were crucial steps along the way to his final work, "Vertical and Horizontal Discourse"

(1999). This dealt with aspects of the internal properties of forms of knowledge and their social context, providing him with the opportunity both to restate the relations between knowledge form, content, and identity and to exemplify them with respect to the character of the social science within which he had spent his working life.

This volume is replete with cameos involving various aspects of his corpus that the individual researchers represented here have regarded as particularly important both for themselves and their analyses. They came together by invitation, precisely to show how these developments had taken place. Basil Bernstein, as a researcher, was to have been present to receive and comment upon papers whose aims were to use, extend, test, and critique various aspects of the ideas he was developing. Our contributors fall into many categories. Some are former colleagues (Hasan, myself), many are ex-students from Bernstein's department (Daniels, Diaz, Morais, Tsatsaroni) and others are scholars who made strong working connections with Bernstein and these scholars' students (Moore and Maton, Muller, Singh, Haavelsrud, Neves, Solomon, Tyler, Vitale, Williams). Some of the papers present the work of young scholars at the very beginning of their academic careers (Maton, Vitale); others represent many years of empirical endeavour. All are similar in arising out of research and being oriented to its continuation. In that sense, they celebrate a joint dedication to "developing a more systematic and general language of description" in the belief that

> their view would be markedly improved if the discursive centre of gravity shifted from the specialised languages to issues of empirical description, a shift from commitment to a language to dedication to a problem and its vicissitudes [...] a repositioning of the role of specialised languages. (Bernstein, 1999, pp. 169–170)

Bernstein frequently complained about the difficulty and irony of having to introduce new, specialised vocabulary in order to do so. And one of the least endearing commentaries on his own disciplinary community is that many have managed to do no more than find his work unconventional or difficult, failing, despite its inspirational character, to provide accessible routes to its theories and empirical insights. This is amazing in face of the fact that Bernstein has so scrupulously attempted to chart his own intellectual odyssey and has invited others, like Donald MacRae in *Volume I* and Michael Halliday in *Volume II*, to further introduce his writings.

It is also interesting and important that very few of our contributors are British; the long-standing, now post-modernism refreshed, British suspicion of those continental Johnnys who aspire to fit it all together has, until very recently, marginalised Bernstein's contribution to their predominantly "relations to" rather than "relations within" sociology of education. Moreover, expelled from their patrimony by governments bent on putting "progressivism" into reverse, Bernstein has not endeared himself in recent years to British sociologists in their dash for cover in policy or curriculum studies. Whereas they have, by and large, had to bite the bullet of providing news that forms an acceptable base for "evidence"-based practice, Bernstein has insisted on the importance of the research text being not so much a source of instant (including policy) gratification, as a theory-led, carefully won means of connecting problem and reality levels. Perhaps even more profoundly, many years ago he required us to engage with the notion that pedagogy had no voice of its own, that it served merely as a relay for other voices. I well remember the shock to my own thinking that this idea provided, before the ideas of knowledge and policy production, recontextualisation, and reproduction had been elaborated and detailed work on the character of the struggle for control and the operation of the pedagogic device had appeared. As a teacher who had been drawn in to teacher training and, hence, to classroom and organisational studies (I also well remember Basil's advice in September 1971 that classrooms were the graveyard of researcher intentions), I found the beauty of the revelation that the instrumental was embedded in the regulative to be stunning. Like all necessities, once revealed, it had always been there, in this case in the code theory that ran from Bernstein's London East End youth, through the day-college teaching where he pan-handled for survival, through the family control and language and cognition patterns, and into my puzzlement as to why teachers were least clever at encompassing the heart of their trade—why they were doing what they were doing in the way they were doing it with these students, here and now, and what it presupposed and led to. In teachers' answers, more often than not, it was disciplinary and motivation management that came first. Accounts that reduced the problem either to correlates of student or teacher histories or necessary features of knowledge were not enough. Yet the ubiquity of ID/RD is still ignored in almost every plan or policy for public education with which we live.[4]

Everyone in this volume has a story about "taking something" of importance from Bernstein. In the short chapter and the video conference that comprise our epilogue, Bernstein recognises his matching debt to Hasan in particular and his research students in general, who, along with colleagues, carried out the empirical work over most of the last 30 years "at the micro-sociological level" that shifted the focus of his code theory "more and more into the modalities of the elaborated codes institutionalised in education, the principles of their description and their social assumptions", leading his theory to become

> a more general account of the social structuring of pedagogic discourse and the shaping of various practices as relays of a society's distribution of power and principles of control. In this way the theory returned to its partly Durkheimian origins in the nature of symbolic control. (Bernstein, 1996, p. 92)

At its various points, Bernstein's emerging corpus has offered a combination of connectedness and openness. This has appealed to those keen to problematise not only the crucial social categories of class, gender, and ethnicity through which pedagogic power was seen to be mediated but also the character and effects of its practice. Many of our contributors are not easily assigned to particular aspects of Bernstein's corpus and their work and interests ought to be considered under one or more headings.

The two that most obviously belong together are Hasan and Williams, both of whom look at aspects of pedagogic discourse in terms of the orientation to meanings revealed in mother-child interactions. In their chapters, which constitute Part 1, Williams focuses specifically upon parental practices in developing pre-school literacy, while Hasan's broader canvas explores children's participation in certain forms of classification and framing and the ontogenesis of children's orientations to decontextualised meanings. Both Williams and Hasan offer detailed analysis of concrete instances of verbal interactions. Williams (chap. 1) reports how, in three families where the breadwinners differed in relation to their relative workplace autonomy, in the context of reading *Three Little Pigs* there were "significantly different means of semiotic mediation through which the children's orientation to literacy was built up", with important consequences for the early years of education. Hasan (chap. 2) claims "that the environment hospitable to the ontogenesis of orientation to disembedded talk is furnished by social praxis of the kind that displays relatively weak classification and framing". Her close study of mother-child and school linguistic contexts lead her to highlight the "interplay of the material and semiotic aspects as typical of the environment in which decontextualised language can and does occur". She comes to the view that "it seems very unlikely that schools would provide the best environment for learning how to use such language for those who do not possess the expertise to some extent before they enter". When Bernstein was reminding us in 1969 that schools cannot compensate for society he was, apparently, offering us a text for the twenty-first century as well as the twentieth.

Among the chapters in Part 2, the focus is upon the social formation of persons and minds. Neither Diaz nor Daniels directly reports empirical work. Daniels (chap. 4) is driven to further clarify the intellectual basis upon which his analyses of Emotionally and Behaviourally Disturbed (EBD) children may rest by suggesting that a Vygotskyan tradition that is neither reductionist, or determinist, represented by the work on cognition in context of Engestrom and other activity theorists, can usefully sit alongside Bernstein's sociological account of cultural transmission, in which the social formation of mind is underdeveloped. Having been instrumental in the research processes that clarified code modalities as "the principles for distinguishing between contexts (recognition rules) *and* the creation and production of specialised communication within contexts (realisation rules)", Daniels sees "Vertical and Horizontal Discourse" as providing "research with an enhanced capacity to provide description that captures the delicacy" of the form and interrelation of everyday and scientific concepts, as outlined by Vygotsky.

Diaz (chap. 3) contends that there is no explicit theory of the subject in Bernstein, whose "basic and empirical unit [...] is not an individual subject but a pedagogical relationship through which the subject emerges". The subject is socially constituted in meanings that create and reproduce unequal relations that "not only serve as relays for communication and interaction but for investing power and class relations in subjects and positions [...] it is not the subject that produces meaning [...] but meanings which produce subjects" and both "are structured in the position-opposition created by power relations", existing "in a play of differences within and between spaces (fields and contexts)"; they are relational. More specifically, pedagogic discourse is "decisive for the understanding of the dialectic between power, knowledge and the subject".

Boundaries and the urge to abandon or transcend them are also Muller's topic (chap. 6), centred around the "new literacy studies" and an account of some of the practices of a non-literate worker. Muller sees Bernstein, an "exemplary neo-Durkheimian", paying Durkheim, our exemplary modernist, the "ultimate compliment" of re-theorising "the sacred by delineating invisible alignments" in his binaries. For Bernstein, a way of talking about knowledge that avoids Durkheim's commitment to the arbitrariness of social valuations of cultural forms and Bourdieu's contention that cultural contents are historically arbitrary must be found. Bernstein does this by distinguishing between horizontal and vertical discourse and then, within vertical discourse, between hierarchical and horizontal knowledge structures. The first has no recontextualising principle; it is simply common. Hierarchical knowledge structures within vertical discourse give us physics, horizontal structures with strong grammars give us economics, and weak ones give us sociology, learnt by acquiring a "gaze". For Muller, Bernstein's main point

> is that only after we have understood the internal structuring of symbolic systems, and the way in which that structuring creates rules of distribution which shape possibilities for positionality within that system, can we come to a complete understanding of social positionality in relation to cultural formations. (p. 140)

If the view from the Cape, RSA is much the same as from Cali, Colombia, it is also the same from Cambridge, England. Moore and Maton (chap. 7) substitute mathematic and literary criticism for physics and sociology and boldly propose the discovery of the "epistemic device" to go where, they claim, Bernstein's enterprising pedagogic device could not. Accepting Bernstein's distinctions between knowledge production, recontextualisation, and reproduction, they focus on sites of production; they seek "a means of conceptualising their generating principles, that is, an analogue of the pedagogic device, but focused on the question of the basis of claims to new knowledge" in Moore and Maton's principles of legitimisation, which distinguish between arbitrary and non-arbitrary dimensions of knowledge. The epistemic device is a means whereby actors or groups of actors or institutions may alter their reactions; it is the object and means of struggle in intellectual fields, the key to symbolic domination. Just as Bernstein extended our notion of the pedagogical well beyond school, Moore and Maton claim that "the epistemological nature of social relations is similarly universal and ubiquitous".

The third chapter in this group, by Vitale, shares concern about the sociological nature of knowledge, addressing the issue of what pass for university courses of sociology across Europe. Vitale takes Bernstein's vertical and horizontal knowledge structures as his starting point. Like Moore and Maton, he explores the variety of weak grammars in sociology and the humanities, following Bernstein's distinction between general approach and specific problem planes, discovering that epistemic devisers live in "Köinè", groups sharing language and meaning in a common epistemological space.

Whereas all the chapters in Part 2 deal with aspects of the relationship between self and identity, knowledge forms and wider aspects of power, those in Part 3 come closest to the conventions of school-based empirical enquiry. Those presented by Morais and Neves (chaps. 8 and 9) set out to summarise many years of work in classrooms and on curriculum, predominantly in the science area, where they follow Bernstein's injunction as to the necessity of developing languages of description which are adequate to the sort of realities that he set forth for theory and data collection and which also respect and leave space for the voices of the "researched". Both Morais and Neves and Solomon and Tsatsaroni (chap. 11) claim to be action researchers, though not in a form that would be recognisable to the broad church of classroom reflexologists (Davies, 2001). Solomon and Tsatsaroni's study of the chequered early career of the Internal Evaluation and Planning (IEP) school project in Greece, whose teachers were drawn into partnership with university researchers in examining their own and their schools' practices, raises serious issues about how far the researcher injunction "to engage in co-operative and collective action presupposes knowledge, skills and research values" if they are to avoid "populist and radical-emancipation modes of competence models". Both sets of researchers are determined to combine theoretical and research rigour with improvement goals, believing that

> Pedagogic innovation is possible whenever teachers undergo a process of professional development where they have access to an education which promotes the acquisition of recognition and realisation rules and socio-affective dispositions appropriate to implementing such acquisition. (chap. 8, p. 217)

The remaining school chapter, by Parlo Singh (chap. 10), focused on educational disadvantage, is prefaced by as clear an outline of the structure of pedagogic discourse as one could wish. This chapter focuses upon Samoan high school students from a newly established diasporic community in Queensland. Thirty-six of them and 35 Samoan community members working in the schools' para-educational networks were interviewed, and their discourses, along with those of two secondary school English teachers, are compared. Misrecognition and collapse of respect engendering disadvantage in relation to the acquisition of school knowledge characterises one classroom, while literacy-focused, procedurally explicit instructional discourse, combined with strong teacher control over regulative discourse, in a context of mutual respect, characterises the other. The implications for improving policy and practice are readily apparent.

Our final section might have been entitled "Back to the Future". Haavelsrud (chap. 12) expresses northern European *angst* that Bernstein might not have given sufficient attention to

> how new power relations could be created with the help of education or at least how knowledge could be *translated* into new power relations [...] dealing with the conditions necessary for the development of an alternative pedagogic device. (p. 331)

so as to produce dialogic devices for dialogic democracy. However, Haavelsrud welcomes Bernstein's contribution "to the theory of how education can be understood in the context of the overall development of society in which equitable and democratic developments are at stake".

From his vantage point in the Australian outback, Tyler (chap. 13) brings an analysis of hypertext to bear on what we might call Bernstein's last theorem, the apparent inexorability of a totally pedagogised society. Once more invoking necessity as the mother of invention, Tyler tells us how he harnessed the Web in resourcing a compulsory first year Australian studies course at the Northern Territories University, available on and off campus. He asks whether the new totalising technologies have the potential to deconstruct, if not completely undermine Bernstein's entire project of development of the theoretical framework of pedagogic discourse. He believes that Bernstein's "identification of the recontextualising principle as constitutive of pedagogic discourse", suitably augmented, is up to it in its convergence with the semiotic field of hypertextuality, and he proposes the term "hypervocality" to capture its "interactional and organisational equivalent" as text is mobilised and shaped for use. These are issues very close to the concerns of Bernstein's epilogue. Bernstein shows deep concern, in his note prepared in advance of the conference and in his reply to Tyler's question in the video conference, as to the issue of "segmentation" and "navigation" implicit in Tyler's work.

The notions of direction and voyage are, indeed, the right places to both start and end with Basil Bernstein. It is only in the last 10 or so policy-besotted years that increasingly serious attention has been paid to his mature ideas, not least to the vicissitudes of policy itself, where he believed that, for the first time, "pedagogic panic has masked moral panic" (Video conference, p. 377). No doubt, as with other thinkers of his importance, the real dissemination and elaboration of his ideas is to be left to followers who gladly accept the task.

Notes

1. Even a number of his obituarists, who ought to have known better, seemed to believe that his intellectual life ended in the seventies.

2. I tried to outline some of this in Davies (1994). A useful resource on Bernstein's early intellectual biography is Atkinson (1985), while the festschrifts produced by Atkinson, Davies, and Delamont (1995) and Sadovnik (1995) also provide numerous insights on his work from those who, in a variety of ways, have used and enjoyed it.

3. The publication of the conference's official proceedings was delayed until 1973 when they appeared as edited by Richard Brown. "Classification and Framing" not only appeared here but also in *Volume IV* and widely in reprints and translations. Almost all Bernstein's papers published elsewhere were eventually included in the next *Volume*, sometimes to be modified in subsequent editions.

4. There continues to be extraordinary ignorance of the implication of Bernstein's work for understanding classrooms and other sites of learning (Davies, 1995), nowhere better exemplified than in the route taken in the past 3 years in England to the imposition of "literacy" and "numeracy" hours in primary schools, based on the putative superiority of classroom life on the Pacific Rim where regulative discourse is rather different. Alexander (1996) comments tartly on the dangers of such transplants.

Bibliography

Alexander, R. (1996). *Other primary schools and ours: Hazards of international comparison.* Warwick, England: Centre for Research in Elementary and Primary Education.

Atkinson, P. A. (1985). *Language, structure and reproduction: An introduction to the sociology of Basil Bernstein.* London: Methuen.

———, Davies, B., & Delamont, S. (Eds.). (1995). *Discourse and reproduction: Essays in honor of Basil Bernstein.* Creskill, NJ: Hampton Press.

Bernstein, B. (1958). Some sociological determinants of perception. *British Journal of Sociology, 9,* 159–174.

———. (1969). *A critique of the concept of compensatory education.* Paper given at the Work Conference at the Teachers College, Columbia University, Columbia, New York.

———. (1971a). *Class, codes and control: Vol. I, Theoretical studies towards a sociology of language.* London: Routledge & Kegan Paul.

———. (1971b). On the classification and framing of educational knowledge. In M. F. D. Young (Ed.), *Knowledge and control. New directions for the sociology of education.* London: Collier Macmillan.

———. (1973a). *Class, codes and control: Vol. I, Theoretical studies towards a sociology of language* (Rev. ed.). Oxford: Paladin Books.

———. (1973b). *Class and pedagogy visible and invisible.* Paris: OECD (CERI).

———. (1973c). *Class, codes and control: Vol. II, Applied studies towards a sociology of language.* London: Routledge & Kegan Paul.

———. (1974). *Class, codes and control: Vol. I, Theoretical studies towards a sociology of language* (2nd ed.). London: Routledge & Kegan Paul.

———. (1975). *Class, codes and control: Vol. III, Towards a theory of educational transmissions.* London: Routledge & Kegan Paul.

———. (1977a). Aspects of the relation between education and production. In *Class, codes and control: Vol. III, Towards a theory of educational transmissions* (2nd ed.). London: Routledge & Kegan Paul.

———. (1977b). *Class, codes and control: Vol. III, Towards a theory of educational transmissions* (2nd ed.). London: Routledge & Kegan Paul.

———. (1981). Code, modalities and the process of cultural production: A model. *Language and Society, 10,* 327–363.

———. (1986). On pedagogic discourse. In J. G. Richardson (Ed.), *Handbook of theory and research for the sociology of education.* New York: Greenwood Press.

———. (1990). *Class, codes and control: Vol. IV, The structuring of pedagogic discourse.* London: Routledge.

———. (1996). *Class, codes and control: Vol. V, Pedagogy, symbolic control and identity: Theory, research, critique.* London: Taylor & Francis.

———. (1999). Vertical and horizontal discourse: An essay. *British Journal of Sociology of Education, 20* (2), 157–173.

———. (2000). *Class, codes and control: Vol. V, Pedagogy, symbolic control and identity: Theory, research, critique* (Rev. ed.). Oxford: Rowman & Littlefield.

Bisseret, N. (1979). *Education, class, language and ideology.* London: Routledge & Kegan Paul.

Brown, R. (Ed.). (1993). *Knowledge, education and cultural change*. London: Tavistock.

Davies, B. (1994). Durkheim and the sociology of education in Britain. *British Journal of Sociology of Education, 15* (1), 3–26.

———. (1995). Bernstein on classrooms. In P. Atkinson, B. Davies, & S. Delamont (Eds.), *Discourse and reproduction*. Creskill, NJ: Hampton Press.

———. (2001). Is action research good for us? In L. Pugsley & T. Welland (Eds.), *Ethical dilemmas in qualitative research*. Salisbury, England: Avebury Press.

Halliday, M. (1973). Foreword. In B. Bernstein, *Class, codes and control: Vol. II, Applied studies towards a sociology of language*. London: Routledge & Kegan Paul.

Labov, W. (1970). The logic of non-standard English. In F. Williams (Ed.), *Language and poverty*. Chicago, IL: Markham Press.

MacRae, D. G. (1971). Foreword. In B. Bernstein, *Class, codes and control: Vol. I, Theoretical studies towards a sociology of language*. London: Routledge & Kegan Paul.

Sadovnik, A. (Ed.). (1995). *Knowledge and pedagogy: The sociology of Basil Bernstein*. Norwood, NJ: Ablex Publishing Corporation.

Young, M. (Ed.). (1971). *Knowledge and control. New directions for the sociology of education*. London: Collier Macmillan.

PART 1

Literacy and Schooling

Chapter 1

Literacy Pedagogy Prior to Schooling: Relations Between Social Positioning and Semantic Variation

Geoff Williams

Introduction

The focus of this chapter is an attempt to explore aspects of one of the most long-standing of Bernstein's interests in pedagogic discourse, the relations between local pedagogic sites in families and the modalities of pedagogic discourse in schools. More specifically, the problematic is semantic variation in interaction between mothers and young children in which the goal, from the perspective of parents, is the development of children's literacy in preparation for school entry.

It appears, at first sight, a benign enough question. There is, after all, an extensive research corpus demonstrating that interaction during literacy events does vary (Heath, 1983) and that certain kinds of interaction are closely associated with precocious literacy development, particularly through family joint book-reading (Moon & Wells, 1979; Wells, 1985, 1987). So why pursue the question further? There are several reasons to do so. First, though the function of interaction in the ontogenesis of literacy has been explored, and variation between families noted quite frequently, none of this work has involved very detailed linguistic analysis of interaction, either in families or in schools. Precisely what kind of variation in interactive language is involved? Are some mothers, as has been suggested, more "sensitive" than others to the educational needs of their children and therefore use language differently from those who are "less sensitive"? If so, what are the linguistic realisations of this sensitivity, and why are these particular features apparently associated with desired forms of linguistic response from children? Are some parents more accomplished at providing appropriate "scaffolding" than others? What does this "scaffolding" comprise, so far as interactive language is concerned, and how, precisely, do "scaffolding" practices vary?

A second reason to return to this question is a directly practical one, having to do with pedagogic practice. Looking at early literacy education from an international perspective, it is striking to notice how many education authorities have been influenced by research describing the correlates of precocious reading development in formulating literacy development policy. This research, selectively recontextualised in pedagogic handbooks, has supported the use of the metaphor of a necessary partnership between homes and schools, through which families are encouraged to adopt the particular interactive practices thought to be associated with precocious development in schools and through which school literacy pedagogy mirrors certain family interactive practices thought to lead to precocious reading development (Williams, 1999). But what are the major social prerequisites that enable families to enter such a partnership (or preclude them from it) and, consequently, what are the likely effects, both intended and unintended, of its use in educational policy?

A further key reason to pursue the question is to reconsider arguments commonly advanced in pedagogic literature about relations between variants of "literacy events" and the social positioning of families. In most research the correlate of such variation is the "socio-economic status" of the family. In other studies the correlate is "different cultures". In Heath, where the relation between family social positioning and variation is most carefully considered, it is the socio-historical development of different literacy practices in three communities (Roadville, Trackton, and Gateway/Maintown) which is the correlate. The question is, then, is there an arbitrary relation between variants and their "socio-historical" location or, following Bernstein, is this unlikely to be so?

To address this question I examine interaction in three families which formed part of a larger set of participants in a study of interaction during joint book-reading and in the first year of schooling. The participants were selected on the basis of differences in positioning in the social division of labour, using Bernstein's concepts of classification, framing, and field, and following the approach developed by Hasan and her colleagues in their explorations of semantic variation in casual conversations between mothers and pre-school children in the home.[1] A key criterion for selection was the relative autonomy of the family breadwinners to exercise power in the workplace. Use of this criterion yielded two contrasted groups, one of lower autonomy and one of higher autonomy (hereafter LAP and HAP, respectively). The children were between 3.5 and 4.5 years old. (The participating kindergarten classes were drawn from the schools which these pre-school children would normally attend the following year, though I do not discuss interaction in the school environment further in this chapter.)

The basis of the selection of these occasions of interaction, two involving families from the LAP group and one from the HAP, is that all three families happened to read the same narrative, which was the familiar traditional story *The Three Little Pigs*. The mothers and children talk about the referential "world" of the story, and it happens that on these particular occasions they do not refer to very much outside this fictive world. Here, because the referential domain of talk is held more or less constant but other regions of meaning are able to vary quite freely, there is an unusual opportunity in natural conversational data to explore the possibility of systematic variation in the exchange of *non-referential* meanings. Casual conversation in families does not often present opportunities for this type of comparison.

Selecting specific occasions of interaction in just three families also enables me to describe some specific features of social positioning more fully than can be achieved by a list of occupational comparisons (cf. Williams, 1995b), thus approximating a similar delicacy of description as in the well-known studies reported in Heath (1983), Tizard and Hughes (1984), and Wells (1985, 1987), which are the immediate dialogic background to this chapter. I present this description in the second section. In the third section, features of the linguistic interaction common to all three occasions of joint book-reading are presented, supporting the argument that these occasions are appropriately regarded as tokens of the one general type of context of situation (Halliday, 1978). In the fourth section, I contrast other features of linguistic interaction and describe commonalities between the two LAP dyads in contrast with the HAP dyad. The comparisons indicate semantic variation, which obliges me to elaborate the argument. In the fifth section, therefore, I discuss how semantic variation in this interaction might be understood in relation to a description of contextual variables recently advanced by Hasan (1995) and to Bernstein's coding orientation theory, contra the interpretations advanced by the scholars cited above. Finally, I present some evidence from a current research project about interaction in family joint book-reading during children's first years in school to further exemplify the argument developed in the fifth section. Since the three preschool occasions take up approximately 12 pages of transcript, they cannot be presented in full here. The transcripts are, however, available in Williams (1996).

The Children and Their Families

The focus here is the social positioning of the families and their approaches to early literacy education. I will attempt to provide a similar level of delicacy of description to that presented by Heath, Wells, and Tizard and Hughes in order support the journey to a different conclusion.

Since the research was designed to study intra-cultural variation, it needs to be said that there are some commonalities between the families, given the selection processes. Each parent was born of English-speaking parents, each parent was educated in Australia, and English was used exclusively in family communication in the home.

The two LAP children were Paul and Ashley. It happened that the two families lived in the same suburb of Sydney, though they did not know each other. The boys attended the same state-funded early childhood education centre, built in the grounds of the local primary school because the area is identified as "educationally disadvantaged". This suburb is on the northern edge of the main western axis of Sydney's suburban development. It was formerly a quite distinct community, built around a large factory with a set of small businesses servicing local needs, but technological changes have resulted in the factory's closure and there are few businesses left. The suburb now provides cheap private and rental housing for workers who travel some distance to an air force base, a naval repair facility, or an urban centre nearby. As the community has been incorporated into metropolitan development, housing has extended into the surrounding farmland.

Paul was 3.7 years old at the time of the study. His family rented a small "fibro" house on the outer edge of the suburb, surrounded by large stretches of farmland. His mother was not in paid employment but his father worked as a boilermaker at the naval facility. Before the birth of her first child, the mother had worked as a shop assistant, having left school in Queensland at the minimum leaving age. She did not undertake any post-school study. The father had completed a boilermaker's certificate. Paul's mother indicated that it was she who read to him, almost exclusively, and that she typically did so once a day. For Paul's mother, the primary reasons for reading were to share an activity which Paul enjoyed very much, to create an interest in reading, and to teach him new vocabulary. Generally, books were obtained through purchases at a supermarket or as gifts from relatives and friends.

Ashley's family lived several kilometres away, on the opposite edge of the suburb, in a small brick house which the family was purchasing. Both he and his younger sister, aged 2, were adopted. Ashley was also 3.7 years old at the commencement of the study. He had been physically abused as a baby and taken permanently from his biological parent by the State at one year of age, moving more or less directly to his adoptive family. His mother mentioned this background to me briefly in Ashley's presence, following her comments by saying, "But you're OK now, aren't you mate?" (We see a trace of this background in the interaction while they were reading *The Three Little Pigs*.) Ashley was firmly committed to becoming a train driver, but his mother joked that she felt equally strongly that he would be a brain surgeon because he seemed very bright. His mother stressed that their joint book-reading was one of his favourite activities. The major purposes, she said, were to engage him in an enjoyable activity, to get him ready for school work, and to help him to recognise some basic written words. Like Paul's family, this family primarily obtained books from a supermarket or through gifts, though they sometimes also bought texts through mail order catalogues. The mother commented that they read picture story books almost exclusively, and this was the case on each occasion of reading audiorecorded for this project.

Ashley's mother left school as soon as she was able, at the end of Year 9, and had not completed any further formal education. She worked some evenings as a part-time waitress at a Pizza Hut. Ashley's father finished school at Year 10 and completed a blacksmith's certificate at a technical college. At the time of the study, he was employed as a welder by a rail authority.

Rachel, the child of the HAP family, had just turned 4 at the time of the study. Her family lived in a suburb on the edge of natural bushland, close to the coast on the northeastern perimeter of Sydney. The family had only recently moved into a newly constructed house, which they were purchasing. Their street was a cul-de-sac and all the houses were large double-storied brick constructions less than 5 years old. Rachel attended the fee-paying early childhood centre housed in the hall of a local church.

Her mother worked part-time as secretary to a private company, supervising the preparation of accounts and business reports. Her work also involved making business contacts by phone from the home. She completed secondary education to Year 12, then studied both shorthand/typing and surveying/drafting at a technical college. The father held a law degree and worked as a sales manager and company director.

Rachel and her mother usually read a book before bedtime. Rachel's mother's major purposes were very similar to those stated by the other mothers. She aimed to create an interest in reading and to engage in an activity which was very enjoyable for the child. Additionally, she stressed the importance of the activity's role in "creating Rachel's imagination". She and Rachel usually read picture story books, information books, or religious stories obtained through their local church. The family obtained titles from a wider range of sources than the two LAP families. Though, as with those families, books were received as gifts and purchased from a supermarket, they were also purchased from newsagencies and a local bookshop, and borrowed from a local library. These sources were close by in the large shopping centre about 5 minutes drive away from their home, whereas for the two LAP families there was no local suburban bookshop or library. For them, the nearest children's bookshop and library was about half an hour away by car.

This, then, is a brief introduction to the home situations of the three children who happen to have read *The Three Little Pigs* with their mothers at the time of audiorecording. Growing up in the same city and about to enter the same education system, they were already enthusiastic about reading, partly because their families invested a lot of time in the activity and, more generally, informally encouraged them to read the written code. In many ways they quite closely resemble the children whom Wells (e.g., 1985, 1987) identified as making strong early progress in school.

There are also some striking commonalities in the linguistic interaction between them and their mothers, as the discussion in the following section shows.

The "Same" Context

There is a marked tendency in literacy ontogenesis research to talk about variation in joint book-reading practices as though these differences were about as clear as the difference in shopping for vegetables in Karachi and Copenhagen. In these data, they are not, and to understand the subtlety of semantic variation and some of its effects it is important to see how similar, in many respects, the practices are.

There is, first, the basic similarity of the material setting in which the interaction occurs. It was each mother's habit to sit with the child next to her, typically on the child's bed or in Ashley's case on the lounge, with the text visible to both interactants. This is precisely the configuration in family joint book-reading which has been so influential in early school literacy education, so when these children commence school they will be likely to readily "recognise" the context (Holdaway, 1979). Precisely, also of course, there is here a key basis for misrecognition.

Each of the three children was already very familiar with the story so they were able to spontaneously accompany their mother's reading of the wolf's chant, and occasionally anticipate the plot. In other words, they actively predicted the development of the writing. Paul, for example, identified the building materials well before the relevant passage was read:[2]

Example 1
Mother – (READING) *Soon the little pigs met a peddler, hauling straw. The first little pig said,*
Please *sir.
Paul – *That's straw and that's sticks.
Mother – (READING) *Please, sir, give me some straw.*

All three children also appeared to enjoy the story intensely. Their contributions were often animated, on occasion contributing dialogically to the reading of the story. Paul was very eager as his mother read, "Little pig, little pig, let me come in!" and called out, "No! Silly, silly thing!" Similarly, Ashley called out enthusiastically as his mother read:

Example 2
Mother – (READING) *Away raced the little pigs, straight to the third little pig's house of bricks.*
*Don't worry.
Ashley – *Look!
Mother – Yeah. He blew him all away, didn't he?

Rachel was not impressed when her mother playfully suggested that they not continue reading such a familiar story:

Example 3
Mother – Do you know this story already?
Rachel – *The Three Little Pigs.*
Mother – *The Three Little Pigs.* Do you know this story already? Well, maybe we shouldn't bother reading it.
Rachel – I want to.
Mother – You want to. Mm.

All the children spontaneously initiated conversation during the reading; they did not simply respond to questions or comments made by their mothers. Sometimes their initiating turn was a question, as when Paul asked, "Mum, why the wolf can't come up there?" or Rachel inquired, "What was he doing?" All three children commented directly on the events of the narrative, usually to predict what was about to happen, as Rachel did in Example 4 and Paul in Example 5.

Example 4
   Mother – (READING) *This made the big bad wolf perfectly furious.*
   Rachel – And he was in the chimney. Look at his feet in the chimney.
   Mother – Yeah.
          (RESUMING READING) *Not by the hair of my chinny chin chin, he roared* ...

Example 5
   Mother – (READING) *and I'll*
   Paul – No you
   Mother – *blow*
   Paul – no you doin' the walls because the wolf's climbing in and the pig's up in bed.
   Mother – Yeah.
   Paul – And he that little pig made him [?that burned the house].
   Mother – Oh.
          (RESUMING READING) *And I'll blow your house in, roared the wolf* ...

A relatively high degree of reciprocity is evident in the exchanges. Almost all demands for information, and for sharing of attention to some detail of the illustrations, were acknowledged linguistically in some way by the mothers and the children. Children and mothers clearly shared in the process of text construction.

Considering the interaction more from the perspective of the mothers, there are again many commonalities. It is evident from the audiorecording that all three mothers read fluently and dramatised their presentation of the object text. All three mothers addressed some questions to the children and all appeared to be concerned that adequate answers were given. When, for example, Ashley could not remember a specific term his mother wanted him to provide, she persevered until he appeared to understand.

Example 6
   Mother – (READING) *And off he danced down the road to see how his brothers were getting along.* What's he playing? What's he got in his mouth?
   Ashley – Umm ... a tar.
   Mother – A what?
   Ashley – *A t
   Mother – *It's a flute em flute.

Ashley – Flute.
Mother – Yeah.
(RESUMING READING) *The second little pig was building himself a house too.*

Similarly, Rachel's mother made sure that Rachel possessed the correct information at the beginning of the session, when she appeared confused to multiple references of "straw".

Example 7
Mother – (READING) *He quickly built himself a house of straw.*
Rachel – No, Um I want to call ...They're not straws.
Mother – What are they?
Rachel – They're sticks.
Mother – That's sticks. Straw is like grass.
Rachel – Oh.
Mother – It's funny sort of grass.
Rachel – Mm. They're straws.
Mother – Not straws like you drink out of. Did you think it was straws like you drink out of? Did you?
Rachel – No.
Mother – Drinking straws? You did, didn't you?
(MOTHER AND CHILD BOTH LAUGH)

This small incident is an evocative example of the warmth of relations evident between all three mothers and children. It also instances the mothers' ability to "track" the child's processing of information very closely, and to provide some relevant assistance as it is needed (cf. Ninio & Bruner, 1978).

Given the extent to which these and other obvious features of interaction are common to all three dyads there are strong grounds for arguing that the specific contexts of situation can be grouped as tokens of a general situation-type. However, that is only part of the story.

Reading Difference in Family Readings of *The Three Little Pigs*

Perhaps the most obvious difference between the three instances is the extent of linguistic interaction around the story, consistent with general findings reported previously (Williams, 1995a, 1999). Taking as the basic analytic unit "message", a semantic unit which is closely related to "clause" at the lexico-grammatical stratum (Hasan, 1983, 1989), from Table 1.1 it can be seen that between Ashley and his mother a total of 67 complete interactive messages were exchanged, between Paul and his mother, 41, and between Rachel and her mother, 187.

Table 1.1: *Distribution of punctuative and progressive messages in readings of "The Three Little Pigs"*

Message Type	Ashley's Interaction	Paul's Interaction	Rachel's Interaction
Progressive	54	27	136
Punctuative	13	14	51
Incomplete	2	2	10
Total	69	43	197

Table 1.1 also reports the data in terms of distributions between progressive and punctuative messages. In brief, progressive messages are those in which the exchange of information or goods and services is advanced, while punctuative messages are more routinised messages which may involve ritual exchanges (demands for attention, greetings, expletives, etc.) or perhaps attempts to clarify an inaudible message. The two types are illustrated in Example 8. (For fuller discussion, see Hasan, 1989; Williams, 1995a.)

Example 8
Child – Mum?   Punctuative
          Oh.   Punctuative
Mother – Yeah?   Punctuative
Child – What's that um ... heavy metal plates?   Progressive
Mother – Armour plates.   Progressive

The extent to which each partner contributed to the exchanges is obviously significant. It might perhaps be supposed, on the basis of commonly held views about the language of working class children, that such children would contribute a smaller share of the interaction. That was not the case on these occasions. Table 1.2 presents the relevant distributions.

All the children actively contributed a substantial proportion of progressive messages to the interaction, so difference in extent of interaction cannot be explained by a relative passivity of the children in the LAP group. A large proportion of the children's punctuative messages in all three dyads comprised chanting of the wolf's threats to blow in the houses.

Table 1.2: *Distribution of numbers of messages contributed to interaction by mothers and children*

Message Type	Ashley's Interaction		Paul's Interaction		Rachel's Interaction	
	Mother	Child	Mother	Child	Mother	Child
Progressive	33	21	9	18	73	63
Punctuative	7	6	3	11	20	31
Incomplete	0	2	0	2	1	9
Total	40	29	12	31	94	103

Probing the extent of interaction in progressive messages further makes it clear that one significant difference is to be found in the frequency of demands for information. In the interaction between Ashley and his mother, 15 demands for information were made by the mother and Ashley himself made none; between Paul and his mother 7 demands were made, of which Paul made 2; and between Rachel and her mother 43 demands were made, of which Rachel made 5.

Turning specifically to some of the qualities of this type of interaction, it is interesting to consider the results of Paul's two requests for information. In one case he appeared to enquire about some object in the material environment, asking, "That's yours?" His mother made no linguistic response; she continued reading the story. On the other occasion he asked for an explanation but his mother responded by disclaiming any knowledge, as the excerpt in Example 9 indicates.

Example 9
  Mother – (READING) *Quickly he scrambled up on the roof of the brick house and made his way to the chimney.*
  Paul – Mum, why the wolf can't come up there?
  Mother – Oh I don't know.
    (READING) *The smart little pig ran to the fireplace and whisked the lid off a pot of steaming water.*

It is unlikely that Paul's mother actually lacked the knowledge needed to answer his question, so why this reply? One interpretation might be that she somehow lacked "sensitivity" to his interests, but it is difficult to sustain that view in the light of so much other evidence of her solicitude and responsiveness during the four sessions. That she was responsive to his initiatives is evident in her reply to his initiative in Example 10.

Example 10
   Mother – (READING) *and I will show you the big apple tree in Merry Garden.*
   Paul – There's the apple tree.
   Mother – Yeah. Look at all the apples.
      (RESUMING READING) *The next morning the little pig got up at six o'clock and hurried to the tree.*

Adopting the explanation of a general psychological attribute of "insensitivity" would involve a further assumption of inconsistency. A different kind of explanation seems to be needed, which takes the analysis beyond an explanation based on an individual's idiosyncratic predispositions.

An interestingly contrastive moment occurred when Rachel asked her mother to explain an ambiguous illustration.

Example 11
   Mother – (READING) *but he had covered himself with a sheep's skin and was curled up in a big basket looking like a little lamb.*
      Oh ah, look!
   Rachel – What is it?
   Mother – He's pretending to be a sh a sheep. That's what you call a wolf in sheep's clothing.
      (THEY LAUGH TOGETHER)
   Mother – Isn't it? A wolf pretending to be a sheep.
      (READING) *Who's there? called the second little pig.*

Rachel's mother reacted enthusiastically to the illustration but Rachel was puzzled by it and sought clarification. The response to Rachel's question became more than just a textual site for providing information relevant to the point of her query. It also extended beyond this specific message, providing an additional semantic resource which gave the child contextualised access to the possibility of tracking allusion to other narrative texts. It is also a good example of a "text-to-life" move, such as is widely endorsed in the pedagogic discourse of literacy development, relating the textual instance to more general textual practices. It was a moment in which the child was apprenticed to particular literate ways of saying and meaning.

To use terminology from earlier research in this field, Rachel's mother could be regarded as sensitive to Rachel's interests because she directly responded to the question with relevant information. Specifically in terms of Tizard and Hughes' categories she gave a "full" answer (Tizard & Hughes, 1984, p. 151). However, this attribution does not perhaps fully capture the discursive resources which are accessed through her response, and these are a significant further difference requiring some theoretical interpretation.

Generally it was the mothers who led the dance in the question-answer exchanges, so it is important to enquire more closely into the kinds of questions they raised. More directly, we might ask, what kinds of information were demanded and, consequently, what kinds of interpretive work were the children asked to engage in? It is here, particularly, that one looks for assistance from a linguistic model which articulates a systematic relation between "langue" and "parole" beyond the traditional bifurcation which has dominated twentieth-century linguistics, so that, as a discourse analyst, one is neither trapped by the local particularities of "parole" nor debarred from the interpretative riches of a detailed account of the system. It is precisely this relation that has been of central interest to those who work with the systemic functional linguistic model (for example, Halliday, 1978; Hasan, 1995, 1996), and within their work, one significant sub-set of work has explored the writing of descriptions of the resources available to speakers for specific aspects of meaning-making. These are articulated as networks of semantic options, available as features of the system and realised through lexico-grammar. Halliday (1973) made a general proposal along these lines, and in Hasan's work on semantic variation the idea has been further developed. In relation to demands for information, Hasan (1983) proposed the network presented in Figure 1.1 as a description of the resources available to speakers across a fairly general set of situation-types, to a primary degree of delicacy. Each of the semantic options is described through statements of their realisation lexico-grammatically, though for space reasons these cannot be included here.

Reading the network from left to right, which is to say, from the primary features to more delicate systems dependent on these features, produces selection expressions such as [*demand; information: confirm: verify: reassure*]. An example of a message selecting these features is: "He's getting very cranky, isn't he?" The lexico-grammatical realisation statement for this option is [major: indicative: declarative: tagged: reversed]. In contrast, a message selecting [*demand; information: confirm: verify: probe*], exemplified by "He's getting very cranky, is he?" is realised lexico-grammatically by [major: indicative: declarative: tagged: constant]. To recapitulate, the analysis of each demand for information through the framework of the semantic network is based on an analysis of the lexico-grammar. So, when a mother asks a question, "But why why can the wolf blow houses down of sticks?" the semantic analysis of this message from the perspective of its role in the exchange of information is [*demand; information: apprise: precise: explain*]. The ground for this claim is the lexico-grammatical realisation [major: indicative: interrogative: non-polar: wh/ conflated with Adjunct and Circumstance of cause why^F^S^P].³

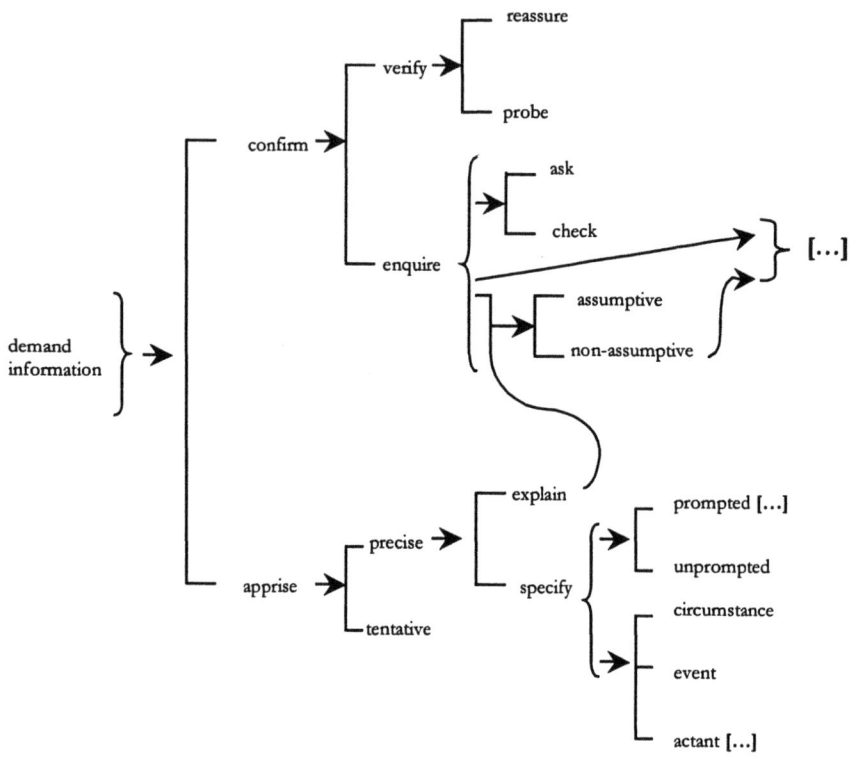

Figure 1.1—*An excerpt from Hasan's network of choices in making demands for information.*

Table 1.3 presents some findings about the distribution of types of questions asked by the mothers.

It is clear that there are considerable differences in the function played by demands for information in the mothers' talk. In the case of Paul's mother, though the number of progressive messages she spoke is small (a total of nine), more than half were demands for information. However, only one of these required Paul to apprise his mother of information. All of the mother's other questions selected the feature [*demand; information: confirm: enquire: ask*]. When these messages are further considered from the perspective of experiential meanings, it can also be seen that each is concerned with Paul's perception of some aspect of the visual images. Example 12 illustrates the typical fashion of this questioning.

Table 1.3: *Distribution of selection of options in demanding information*

demand; information: confirm:

Option	Ashley's Mother	Paul's Mother	Rachel's Mother
[reassure]	8	0	7
[probe]	0	0	1
[ask]	2	4	17
[check]	0	0	0
demand; information: apprise:			
[explain]	0	0	5
[circumstance]	0	0	0
[event]	0	0	1
[actant: specific]	0	0	2
[actant: non-specific]	5	1	5
[tentative]	0	0	0
Totals	**15**	**5**	**38**

Example 12
Mother – (READING) *One was a lively little pig, who liked to dance, and one was a happy little pig, who liked to sing, and one was a smart little pig, who remembered that the wolf was always about.*
See them three little piggies?
Paul – There's the first one, there's the happy one and there's the happy one.

The mother's main interest in asking questions seems to be to ensure that Paul noticed key features of the narrative encoded in the illustrations.

Ashley's mother also asked a high proportion of questions, 15 out of a progressive message total of 33. Of these, 5 selected [*demand; information: apprise: precise: specify: actant: non-specific*] but they were not really very significant in the overall interaction since three followed in quick succession and were concerned with one item, the name of the instrument played by one of the pigs.

Example 13
Mother – (READING) *And off he danced down the road to see how his brothers were getting along.*
What's he playing? What's he got in his mouth?
Ashley – Umm ... a tar.
Mother – A what?
Ashley – *A t

So in Ashley's case too, despite the apparent contrast with Paul's interaction, very little of the dialogue functioned to require him to display information explicitly. In fact, the more typical fashion of questioning was the mother's selection of [*demand; information: confirm: verify: reassure*]. The longest exchange in the transcript deployed this meaning resource extensively.

Example 14
Mother – (READING) *Ho, ho, ho, ha, ha, ha, laughed the two lazy little pigs, dancing along to the tune of the fiddle and the flute.*
He's getting very cranky, isn't he? Because he wants a very strong house, doesn't he?
Ashley – Yeah, cause fox can blow them sticks house down, and he doesn't blow the bricks house down.
Mother – Yeah, and the wolf can't blow bricks down, can he? And what what's your house made of?
Ashley – Umm, bricks.
Mother – Yeah, and no wolf no wolf can blow our house down, can he?
Ashley – No, cause it we haven't got no sticks.
Mother – That's right, we haven't got any sticks.

We turn to Rachel's interaction. Of the 73 progressive messages which the mother contributed to their interaction, 38 were demands for information. So from one perspective, that of their density through the whole interaction, their role in the exchange was approximately the same as with the other mothers. However, a difference in their significance is clear when the semantic choices are considered. Of the total 38, 13 select the feature [*apprise*]; of these 5 select the further options [*precise: specify: actant: non-specific*], 2 select [*precise: specify: actant: specific*] and 5 select [*precise: explain*]. Of the 25 questions which select [*confirm*], 17 select [*enquire: ask*].

The demand to explain phenomena is in complete contrast with the practice of the other two mothers. Neither Paul nor Ashley were asked, here or actually in any of the eight occasions of their talk about object texts recorded for this study, to provide an explanation. However, for Rachel, an overview of all the transcripts shows that requests for explanation were not an unusual experience. In total, she was asked 19 times to provide explanations, so the frequency here closely approximated the mean for all the occasions.

Providing an explanation was not an easy demand for Rachel to meet at this stage of her literacy development. She was still very much an apprentice in formulating her reasoning explicitly, as, for example, when her mother asked her to explain why a wolf could easily blow down a house made of sticks.

Example 15
Mother – (READING) *so he had decided to build a quick and easy house of?*
Sticks.
Rachel – Sticks.
Rachel – That's not easy house cause the wolf can blow it easily.
Mother – Can he? Why?
Rachel – Look ... See? ... It's all huffed in.
Mother – But why why can the wolf blow houses down of sticks?
Rachel – Here he comes. Look.
Mother – Wooah that's the next page. Wait a minute.
(RESUMING READING) *Soon it was finished too.*

On this specific point it is interesting to contrast the interaction with Tizard and Hughes' (1984) general notion of a passage of intellectual search. Rachel does seem to have been actively involved in interpreting the plot, and in formulating aspects of causality explicitly. She said, for example, "That's not easy house cause the wolf can blow it easily".

Nevertheless, it was the mother's consciousness of particular forms of interpretive activity which appears to be a primary resource for the development of these behaviours.

It is important, of course, that this aspect of the mother's agency was not exercised to the exclusion of the child's initiatives. Rather, as in this interaction, there was an intricate, complex arrangement of semantic point and counterpoint. The child's initiatives, and also on occasion her responses, were the point of origin for the mother's systematic moves to require her to construct a more extended explanation or set of observations. Throughout the transcript there was a sense of the mother explicating, requiring the child to go beyond the information immediately available. Rachel was learning through her talk what to attend to, how to say and how to mean in a very particular way.

One interesting aspect of the intricacy of the exchanges is the mother's role in developing the child's responses beyond an initial observation. In

Example 15, when Rachel commented, "Look ... See? ... It's all huffed in", the mother responded by asking, "But why why can the wolf blow houses down of sticks?" This option was selected by the mother on no less than 29 occasions throughout their conversation, whereas in Paul's mother's discourse it was not selected at all. Though Ashley's mother did select it 6 times, in 2 of these cases it actually followed his silence in response to a prior question and functioned more as a prompt than a development of his initial response.

The very strong impression one forms from detailed analysis of these data is of "sameness but difference": in some senses there is a familiar type of context, but in other senses there is something significantly different about the exchange of meanings in the interaction between the LAP and the HAP families. Of course, it can be argued that the variation to which I'm drawing attention is nothing more than local, momentary, and therefore inconsequential. After all, anybody who reads to young children knows occasions on which the whole point of the activity is to get them to sleep rather than to ask them to develop their ideas! The response to this obvious possibility has to come from the results of the whole study, in which the selection of a large number of semantic features by LAP and HAP families was compared statistically to assess the likelihood that the variation is explainable by chance. These results have been reported in Williams (1995a, 1999). From the statistical analyses there seems virtually no likelihood that the difference is attributable just to chance.

There may be considerable advantages in using these specific occasions to begin to re-theorise some implications of differences in interaction, precisely because the mothers were reading stories which, speaking informally, involved very similar "content". In the following section I present an initial exploration of how the observed differences might be interpreted within a systemic functional linguistic conceptualisation of context of situation, in dialogue with Bernstein's theory of coding orientation.

Joint Book-Reading as Situation-Type

How can these occasions be understood, then, to be at one and the same time instances of one situation-type yet variants of that situation-type? One of the distinctive features of a systemic functional linguistic account of language in use is that context of situation is built into the description. The most general features of contexts of situation, first described by Halliday, are *field*, *tenor*, and *mode* (Halliday, 1978; Halliday & Hasan, 1985). But from what actual features of the context, understood as constituted by field of activity, tenor of relation between interactants, and mode of language use, does the semantic variation derive? It is not possible, I think, to address this question using the general features of context as initially used in the systemic linguistic model. Some further refinement of the variables is required in order to tie down, as it were, the source of variation in the semantic realisations of these instances of interaction. I will draw here on refinements proposed by Hasan (1995).

From the perspective of *field*, an examination of the whole of each transcript shows that the kind of social activity in which the mothers and children engage is reflection on the object text. Here they are not at all concerned with the material environment in which the talk takes place (they don't, for example, fuss about cushions, food, heat, or the like) and they don't perceive any need to service the needs of their social relation in order to make reflection on the story possible. In short, they simply get on with the reading and talk about the story. In all three instances this appears to me to be unequivocally reflection-based activity in the sense Hasan (1995) has identified. The local goal-orientation adopted by the mothers is very similar, so far as one can judge from the interview protocols and their responses to preliminary questionnaires about their reasons for reading to the children. The three mothers indicated that one of their major purposes was to provide an enjoyable activity for their children, and they also specified creating an interest in reading for the child as an important long-term goal. The evidence from the transcripts is that they worked consistently to achieve this goal. Additionally, all the mothers commented that they were concerned to prepare the child well for entry to school literacy. (Remember, these children were all enrolled in early childhood centre programmes.)

From the perspective of *mode* of language, very little needs to be said. There is minimal difference between the occasions. In the three instances, language is obviously constitutive of the interaction, the medium is spoken, and each of the members of the dyads shares in the process of developing the interactive texts.

From the perspective of *tenor*, the interpretation is somewhat more complex. The key variables Hasan has elaborated in describing this contextual feature are the degree of social distance between interactants, the agentive role taken up by interactants, and the institutional status held by interactants. To illustrate this briefly, if I approach a head of department with a request for relief from teaching to complete a research article, the interaction will reflect the fact that there is some *social distance* between us (let's suppose that the two of us are not personal friends), that I have a *different institutional status* from the head of department and that I am the one exercising the *agency*. Now, let's suppose alternatively that, by the administrative quirks of which universities are sometimes capable, I have a different institutional status with respect to certain specific features of university activity (a faculty-level responsibility, maybe) and the head of department is obliged to approach me with a request to approve some overdue application to the faculty. The same individuals are involved, the same degree of social distance is implicated, but a different *tenor* of interaction is to be predicted because of the difference in institutional positioning, which defines the nature of the work we have to do.

To return to *tenor* in the joint book-reading. The social distance is obviously minimal in all three cases—there is no suggestion of reserve in the interaction or of lack of a long-standing personal intersubjectivity. The agentive role is largely with the mothers, as has been shown partly through an analysis of the distribution of demands for information, though all three children do exercise some degree of agency at various points in the talk.

The particularly interesting and complex feature is the social institutional status of the mothers. Obviously they are all "mothers" and there are, equally obviously, many aspects of this status which are equivalent. At the crudest level, the equivalence is indicated by the legal entitlements and obligations of these three women as mothers. But, as my introductory discussion has attempted to show, there are also important and relevant differences in their locations in social formations with respect to social institutional status. These appear to contribute to differences in their socially constructed roles as mothers, the pedagogic work mothers "do" in the local context of the family. This is to argue that the social category of "mother" is non-equivalent between the social groups, and that it is primarily (though obviously not exclusively) given by the location of the family in relations in the social division of labour.

Changes in the tenor variables may also affect the realisation of *field*. Using Hasan's argument that the contextual variables are not discrete but rather permeable, it is possible to argue that relevant conditions are established for two field variables, social activity: reflection-based activity and supra-local goal orientations to be realised differentially in the semantic choices. That is, aspects of the interaction represent variant realisations of the same contextual variables as discussed above. For example, though the social activity is, unequivocally here, "reflection-based" activity in all three cases, there is variance in its linguistic realisation between the LAP and HAP mothers. Similarly, though a significant long-term goal of joint book-reading is to prepare the child for school entry, this appears to be variantly realised in the interactive texts. That is to say, the configuration of contextual features "has" a potential for variant linguistic realisation and these possibilities are taken up systematically and differentially by the LAP and HAP mothers. But the key contextual feature through which the potential for variant realisations is mediated, arguing by elimination of other primary variables, appears to be the social institutional status of the mothers.

This reading suggests a rather different order of problem from analyses of variation in joint book-reading based on differences in socio-economic status or on the "sensitivity" of the mothers. Focusing just on practical pedagogical problems for a moment, it suggests not only that there will be real difficulty caused by adoption of the "partnership" metaphor in early literacy education, but that these difficulties will not be overcome by programmes designed to inform parents about ways to talk with their children during joint book-reading (cf. Cairney & Munsie, 1992; Dwyer, 1989; New South Wales Department of Education, n.d., and many similar "resource materials" for parents produced by state authorities and parent organisations). The problems with the metaphor are in the pedagogic assumptions about what these early literate contexts are *for*, not in the parents.

The difference in the social positioning of the mothers appears to result in different construals of the contextual relevance of using orders of meaning and relation beyond the specific instance (Bernstein, 1975, 1986, 1990). The moment at which Rachel's mother introduces an allusion to the biblical metaphor of wolves in sheep's clothing is apposite. Using a simple, playful illustration, the mother draws in a discursive resource at first glance somewhat remote from conversation with a 4 year-old, and in doing so extends for the child the range of the text's relations. But the pedagogic principle of showing a child the potential of a text to allude to other texts, important as it is in itself for school success, is significant for other reasons. It is also an instance of use of an orientation to orders of meaning and relation beyond the local, particular instance and, consequently, an opportunity for Rachel to learn this orientation. In this sense, the moment has a double significance: both as interpretive practice in itself, a way of saying and meaning commonly used in a type of pedagogic discourse, and as an abstract and powerful way of meaning commonly used by only a fraction of the population.

Consistent with this mode of argument, different principles appear to regulate the relevance of producing individuated meanings. This difference is evident in the co-variation of patterns of demands for information and metarepresentations of states of consciousness. Rachel, for example, is frequently asked to reveal what she as an individual thinks, but Paul and Ashley are never asked to do so. To use an evocative term from Bernstein's early writing, Rachel's conversation with her mother implicates an orientation to the individuation of her *person*.

The various semantic features can be interrelated by reference to a single factor regulating the relevance of meanings and of relations between contexts. This factor is the differential extent of individuation of experience. Once individuation of experience is a privileged principle in interaction, the explication of relations between events and entities becomes very important because the basis of action and belief in the particular instance cannot be taken as a given. Explanations are therefore required so that "reasonable" coherence in social relations can be maintained. Things must be negotiated explicitly, so demanding explanations, developing the bases of initial ideas and their implications, and explicitly stating causal relations between events are made necessary. Conversely, where individuation of experience is not the privileged practice, where instead the social similarity of experience forms the basis of action, then there is no need to make experience visible. When it is the shared similarity of experience which is the orienting basis for action, then things tend to be recognised as either being or not being the case.

Joint book-reading provides a particularly important, though not of course unique, locale for the specialisation of individuated literate consciousness. This is because object texts introduce such a potential for the elaboration of meaning relations beyond the specific instance of the linguistic interaction. Object texts can be read as interesting, entertaining, and more or less informative specific instances of written text. Or, they can be read additionally as a basis for establishing a wide range of intertextual relations between the focal texts, other object texts, and the interactive texts of the child's everyday life. Once intertextual relations begin to be elaborated beyond the specific and local environment, meaning relations become probabilistic and often ambiguous. They must therefore be explicated and clarified, and their significances teased out for contemplation.

The visibility to the care-giver of the child's learning is important in an environment of greater uncertainty, so certain interpersonal meanings such as responses to demands for information of the [*apprise: explain*] and [*apprise: specify: actant: non-specific*] type assume greater significance. In this register they are crucially involved in displaying the fact that meaning relations beyond the specific instance are being established by the child. It is not that such types of demand for information always "have" such a specific discursive function, but in the environment of joint book-reading in the HAP families these meaning relations have particular significance and they are therefore selected with differential frequency. Different semantic resources tend to be selected within the social groups as variant realisations of contextual variables because the orientations to meaning relations beyond the local instance of object text reading are non-equivalent.

I now extend the argument about meaning relations beyond the specific instance by drawing on a larger range of data from the research. On this occasion Rachel's mother does not happen to talk with her about her own experiences, but this is in fact unusual both for other occasions with this particular dyad and for all of the other HAP participants.[4] (Its absence here was temporarily functional to the general argument in enabling me to focus on the non-referential meaning exchanges.) More typical is the kind of interaction we see in Example 16 between Anne and her mother, reading a contemporary text, *The Three Little Wolves and the Big, Bad Pig*.

Example 16
  Mother – They worked very hard.
  Anne – Mm, I bet they're getting tired, do you?
  Mother – I bet they're getting tired, too, yes. Cause remember one day when we were going over to Grandma's?
  Anne – Mm.
  Mother – And you said you wouldn't like to be a housebuilder?
  Anne – Oh.
  Mother – Remember that? [?When] Uncle Joe and Aunt Betty's house was getting built?
  Anne – Oh yes.
  Mother – Remember? Why did you say that?
  Anne – Because they would get really tired.
  Mother – They would, wouldn't they?
  Anne – Mm.
  Mother – But they do go home, they have a break.

There is almost no similar interaction in any of the LAP dyads during joint book-reading, which suggests that different principles regulate the relevance of producing meanings about the individuated self in the two social environments. Ashley's interaction in Example 14 represents a rare exception, the motivation for which may be in features of his personal history noted earlier.

In this discussion I have drawn attention to the primary structuring effects of the mothers' institutional social status, but of course the children's institutional social status, which is in process of development, is not without its own influence at the age of 4. Coding orientation initially enters the situation-type "through", as it were, the mothers' institutional social status, but as the coding orientation becomes a child's "inside" world of orders of relevance of meanings, the child's institutional social status may also have an important effect on reflection-based activity. As a child enters schooling this is a crucial feature of her new social status as student.

Finale: Evidence From Reading at Home in the Early School Years

Finally, I offer a brief comment on mediating literacy practices in families during children's first years of schooling. Bernstein has often drawn attention to the significance of two sites of acquisition of official pedagogic discourse, especially under conditions of strong framing, on which the partnership metaphor is obviously predicated (Bernstein, 1990). In current work I have begun to look at reading and interaction during the year immediately prior to school entry and the year subsequent to school entry. In the Australian environment this means the children are 4 and 6 year olds respectively. In this research, the dyads discuss somewhat more abstract texts such as metafictive writing for the young (*The Stinky Cheeseman and Other Fairly Stupid Tales*), books of jokes, and rewritings of traditional stories, such as *The Three Little Wolves and the Big, Bad Pig*.

We have yet to formally contrast two sets of data drawn from LAP and HAP families, but fairly extensive informal contrasts have been possible in the exploratory work. It seems that the variants of literacy practices do extend into the first years of schooling: that is to say, variants of the local pedagogic work by the mothers are again evident. There is space just to illustrate this briefly through some excerpts from Tom's conversations with his mother in a HAP family while they read *The Three Little Wolves and the Big, Bad Pig*.

Example 17
Mother – (READING) *Then I'll huff and I'll puff and I'll blow your house down said the pig. So he huffed and he puffed and he puffed and he huffed and the house didn't fall down.*
Tom – Mum?

Mother – Mm?
Tom – Why does it have ... footprints of the wolf on the wall?
Mother – On the wall. I think that's meant to be the wallpaper pattern. It's a funny wallpaper pattern isn't it? Be like us having our footprints all over the wall.
Tom – Yeah.
Mother – Yeah, I wouldn't be surprised if some of them were in your room.
Tom – There's already my fingerprints in there.
Mother – Yeah, that's why. (MOTHER LAUGHS)

Here is the same ready movement between the fictive experience and Tom's personal experience. However, the mother additionally construes the reading as an occasion for Tom to learn about the general significances of the text, beyond the immediate occasion.

Example 18
Mother – This story's all—this story's all reversed, isn't it?
Tom – [?Why?]
Mother – Well normally this story's about what? The three little?
Tom – Pigs and the big bad wolf.
Mother – That's right. So that's reversed. This time it's the big bad pig. And normally the house that they built gets what?
Tom – [?   ]
Mother – No normally their houses get stronger don't they each time.
Tom – Yes.
Mother – First of all it's straw, and then it's a wood, and then it's a brick, and the houses have been strongest, but this time they build very strong houses, and he still manages to blow them up. He uses a drill.
Tom – A bomb.
Mother – A bomb. And they're pretty ugly looking houses anyhow. Look at that house. Would you want to live in that house with barbed wire all around it?
Tom – (INAUDIBLE) the pig bad pig I wouldn't go out I would just—Cause it's everywhere. If the big bad pig touched it he would get barbed.
Mother – Barbed wire in his fingers.
Tom – Mm.
Mother – Yeah, but it didn't work, did it?
Tom – Nup.
Mother – So the thing that worked the best was making a beautiful house.
Tom – Yep.
Mother – that smelled beautiful and then he became a good pig.

Not all of the HAP mothers engage children in quite such a direct discussion of a story's "meanings" but, so far as I have been able to ascertain, all of them do ensure that the children interpret the text beyond its status as one specific, local story. There is also consistently a low boundary strength between the classification of the fictive experience and the child's personal experience. There is a strong sense of the context readily acquiring other texts, whether they are other texts of fictive experience or of the child's own experience. This is in contrast with the parsimony of the interactive texts in the LAP environment, which are restricted (dedicated) to the specific object text. Of particular interest in subsequent analyses of these data will be the different modalities that these HAP mothers use to draw children's attention to features of the texts.

Notes

1. For further details of the selection process and of Hasan's concept of "relative autonomy" used in this research, see Hasan (1989) and Williams (1995a, 1999).

2. The conventions adopted for the transcription of the data are the following:
    * = simultaneous speech;
    [?] = a slightly uncertain transcription because of sound interference on the audiotape;
    ... = a lengthy pause, greater than 3 seconds;
    [CAPS] = Comment interpolated by the author.

3. Each message would also, of course, be analysed from the perspective of experiential meanings, its role in turn-taking, topic maintenance, and so on, through the various further network systems.

4. For transcripts of four occasions of interaction between Rachel and her mother, see Williams (1996).

Bibliography

Bernstein, B. (1975). *Class, codes and control: Vol. III, Towards a theory of educational transmissions.* London: Routledge & Kegan Paul.

———. (1986). On pedagogic discourse. In J. G. Richardson (Ed.), *Handbook of theory and research for the sociology of education.* New York: Greenwood Press.

———. (1990). *Class, codes and control: Vol. IV, The structuring of pedagogic discourse.* London: Routledge.

———. (1996). *Class, codes and control: Vol. V, Pedagogy, symbolic control and identity: Theory, research, critique.* London: Taylor & Francis.

Cairney, T. H., & Munsie, L. (1992). *Beyond tokenism: Parents as partners in literacy.* Carlton, VIC: Australian Reading Association.

Dwyer, B. (1989). *Parents, teachers, partners.* Rozelle, New South Wales: Primary English Teaching Association.

Goldfield, B. A., & Snow, C. E. (1984). Reading books with children: The mechanics of parental influence on children's reading achievement. In J. Flood (Ed.), *Promoting reading comprehension.* Newark, NJ: International Reading Association.

Halliday, M. (1973). *Explorations in the functions of language.* London: Edward Arnold.

———. (1978). *Language as social semiotic.* London: Edward Arnold.

Halliday, M., & Hasan, R. (1985). *Language, context and text.* Geelong, VIC, Australia: Deakin University Press.

Hasan, R. (1983). *A semantic network for the analysis of messages in everyday talk between mothers and their children.* Unpublished manuscript: Department of Linguistics, Macquarie University, New South Wales, Australia.

———. (1989). Semantic variation and sociolinguistics. *Australian Journal of Linguistics, 9,* 221–275.

———. (1991, March-April). Questions as a mode of learning in everyday talk. In T. Le & M. McCausland (Eds.), *Language education: Interaction and development. Proceedings of the International Conference held in Ho Chi Minh City.* Vietnam, Launceston: University of Tasmania.

———. (1992). Meaning in sociolinguistic theory. In K. Bolton & H. Kwok (Eds.), *Sociolinguistics today: International perspectives.* London: Routledge.

———. (1995). The conception of context in text. In P. H. Fries & M. Gregory (Eds.), *Discourse in society: Functional perspectives. Meaning and choice in language: Studies for Michael Halliday.* Norwood, NJ: Ablex Publishing Corporation.

———. (1996). The ontogenesis of ideology: An interpretation of mother child talk. In T. Threadgold, E. A. Grosz, G. Kress, & M. Halliday (Eds.), *Semiotics ideology language.* Sydney: Sydney Association for Studies in Society and Culture. Reprinted in *Ways of saying, ways of meaning: Selected papers of Ruqaiya Hasan,* C. Cloran, D. Butt, & G. Williams, Eds., 1996, London: Cassell.

Hasan, R., & Cloran, C. (1990, August). A sociolinguistic interpretation of everyday talk between mothers and children. In M. Halliday, J. Gibbons, & H. Nicholas (Eds.),

Learning, keeping and using language. Selected papers from the 8th World Congress of Applied Linguistics, Sydney. Amsterdam/Philadelphia: John Benjamins Publishing Company.

Heath, S. B. (1983). *Ways with words: Language, life and work in communities and classrooms.* Cambridge: Cambridge University Press.

Holdaway, D. (1979). *The foundations of literacy.* Sydney: Ashton Scholastic.

Moon, B. C., & Wells, C. G. (1979). The influence of home on learning to read. *Journal of Research in Reading, 2,* 53–62.

New South Wales Department of School of Education. (n.d.). *Reading with your child at home: Ideas for parents of young children.* Sydney: NSW Department of School of Education.

Ninio, A. Z., & Bruner, J. S. (1978). The achievements and antecedents of labelling. *Journal of Child Language, 5,* 1–15.

Scieszka, J., & Smith, L. (1993). *The stinky cheeseman and other fairly stupid tales.* London: Puffin Books.

Teale, W. H. (1986). Home background and young children's literacy development. In W. H. Teale & E. Sulzby (Eds.), *Emergent literacy: Writing and reading.* Norwood, NJ: Ablex Publishing Corporation.

Tizard, B., & Hughes, M. (1984). *Young children learning: Talking and thinking at home and at school.* London: Fontana Press.

Trivias, E., & Oxenbury, H. (1995). *The three little wolves and the big, bad pig.* London: Heinemann Young Books.

Wells, C. G. (1985). Pre-school literacy-related activities and success in school. In D. R. Olson, N. Torrance, & A. Hildyard (Eds.), *Literacy, language and learning: The nature and consequences of reading and writing.* Cambridge: Cambridge University Press.

———. (1987). *The meaning makers: Children learning language and using language to learn.* London: Hodder & Stoughton.

Williams, G. (1995a). *Joint book-reading and literacy pedagogy: A socio-semantic interpretation.* Ph.D. dissertation, School of English, Linguistics and Media, Macquarie University, Sydney. Also reproduced as:
———. (1995b). Joint book-reading and literacy pedagogy: A socio-semantic interpretation. Vol. I. *CORE, 19* (3); and
———. (1996). Joint book-reading and literacy pedagogy. A socio-semantic interpretation. Vol. II. *CORE, 20* (1).

———. (1999). The pedagogic device and the production of pedagogic discourse: A case example in early literacy education. In F. Christie (Ed.), *Pedagogy and the shaping of consciousness: Linguistic and social processes.* London: Cassell Academic.

Chapter 2

The Ontogenesis of Decontextualised Language: Some Achievements of Classification and Framing

Ruqaiya Hasan

Helen — Doesn't matter for you or me to do these [i.e., to wash these dishes. *RH*]
Mother — No.
Helen — Because we can do it the right way, God teaches us.
Mother — No, God doesn't teach us things like that. It's mummy's job to teach you things like that.

[Hasan, 1986, p. 144]

Every function in the child's cultural development [i.e., in the development of the child's higher mental functions, *RH*] appears twice: first, on the social level, and later on the individual level; first *between* people (*interpsychologically*), and then *inside* the child (*intra-psychologically*). [...] All the higher functions originate as actual relations between human individuals.

[Vygotsky, 1978, p. 57; emphasis in original]

Conjectures About Decontextualised Language

The natural condition for human discourse is to be situation dependent. It is natural both from the point of view of phylogeny and from that of ontogeny. Clearly, it is not possible to cite actual evidence for such language use from early human history, but on the assumption that language grows in the business of living one's life with others, one could reasonably believe this to be the case. Situation dependent discourse, after all, hugs pretty close to the material situational setting in which the interactants find themselves, and on the basis of what is known about the material conditions of social existence for early humans, it does not seem very possible for early language use to have taken any other form. With this close prehension of language and material situation as the defining criterion for context dependent[1] language, its purest condition perhaps is best represented in the initial linguistic processes of infants, especially those at the *proto-linguistic* stage as illustrated by the data presented by Halliday (1973, 1975), Painter (1984, 1985), and Torr (1997). But whatever the natural condition of human discourse, whatever the arguments for taking it as the original use of language phylogenetically or ontogenetically, the fact of the matter is that what is remarkably pervasive today is the kind of language use that is known as context independent, disembedded or decontextualised, especially in the sorts of societies spawned by the so-called *progressive* Western world. One might go so far as to say that decontextualised language enters the very fabric of these societies. Thus, in the absence of context independent forms of talk, the workings of Bernstein's *field of symbolic control* would be unimaginable; and Bourdieu's *symbolic violence* or *cultural field* would be qualitatively different phenomena. Violence, of course, is not unique to the human species, but its modes of exercising violence are unique to the species. Humans specialise in subtle ways of exploiting, controlling, and claiming power by imposing a particular kind of significance on certain events and actions, and this calls for the use of decontextualised language.

What might have been the impetus for this change which made context independent language so pervasive? It seems to me that in the battle for survival, somewhere in their history, the species *homo sapiens* chose to use social semiosis rather than bodily change for effecting adjustment to their environment. I would not use the metaphor of *social contract* to describe the way this choice might have prevailed, because invoking that metaphor creates more problems than it resolves. I would say, rather, that the early semiotic actions of our ancestors must have possessed an efficacy which argued in favour of the continued use of semiotic action. It is this continued use of language that created the condition whereby the management of environment *via* semiotic action became a *de facto* choice: instead of adapting *somatically* to the environment as other species had done, the species *homo sapiens* opted for *exo-somatic evolution* (Vygotsky, 1978; Popper, 1979)—an evolution which depended not on the body adapting itself physically to the environment but on the environment adapting to the body, underwriting its very obvious weaknesses, and this adaptation of the environment to the human body was achieved by the use of semiotic modalities. Thereafter the continued evolution of decontextualised talk and its pervasiveness became a necessity—a choice that is effectively no longer arbitrary, in the sense that its abandonment would involve a quite improbable reversal of direction for humanity.[2] It is certainly true that such a reversal can come to pass, but it is also just as true that for such a reversal to be propelled into existence, some kind of catastrophic event, such as a modern-day Noah's flood as a result of global warming, would be a necessary condition. On the basis of the behaviour of the pilots of industry and state, it would seem that decontextualised language use is a fact of modern life, and is probably here to stay for the foreseeable future: After all, among other things, decontextualised language is the voice *par excellence* of official ideology.

Yet the fact remains that the neonate does not come equipped with language of any kind, let alone language that is context independent. If the natural condition of human discourse is to be context dependent—and this is what children are good at in the very early stages of their life—then the question arises: At what point and by what means might children become inclined to use decontextualised, disembedded language? This is the central issue of my enquiry here. The question is of some interest because as Cloran (1994) points out, scholars such as Bernstein (1971), Bruner (1970), and Donaldson (1978), amongst others, have cited decontextualised language as essential to the creation of knowledge; it has been claimed that the absence of orientation to such language could be one of the reasons for educational failure.[3]

To the extent that the above claim is correct, it implies certain things. First, instead of talking about *children* as a completely homogeneous category which knows no variation, it would be more accurate to say that only *some* children become inclined to use decontextualised language: These are children that are likely to be amongst the educationally successful. Secondly, as pedagogic sites, schools themselves could not be said to be uniformly successful in *creating* the orientation to the use of decontextualised language: this is clear from the fact that the official pedagogic system fails some children. The children whom the system fails are, following this argument, precisely the ones whom it has not managed to initiate into the use of decontextualised language. Third, this situation raises the likelihood that the schools may in fact not be the initial site for the ontogenesis of decontextualised language; that instead of actually creating this inclination, schools may simply make use of it if they find it in their pupils. This would not be surprising since, as Vygotsky (1978, p. 84) points out, "Children's learning begins long before they attend school [...] Any learning a child encounters in school always has a previous history". In fact, with specific reference to decontextualised language, Bernstein has argued for nearly half a century that before children enter the school, the different experiences that they have in their everyday life already either predispose them to the "unnatural" use of decontextualised language or not, as the case may be: they come to school with distinct orientations. If Bernstein is right, then we should expect to come across examples of both kinds of language in young children's everyday talk, and, indeed, Cloran's research (Cloran, 1994, 1999b) provides strong indication that a specific category of children does experience decontextualised language at home. Cloran (1999b) has identified the kind of environment in which decontextualised talk between mothers and children typically occurs at home. My main aim here is to use her investigation as a point of departure for moving into a related but somewhat different area. The questions that I am primarily interested in exploring are, first, what shape exactly does the ontogenesis of decontextualised language take in the data of naturally occurring everyday talk between some mothers and their children? Second, what features of this ontogenesis might be said to attract the children to the continued use of this variety at home? In the course of answering these questions I also comment both on the crucial defining criterion of decontextualised talk and on the environment that favours this talk. These comments complement Cloran's findings. In the concluding section of this chapter I look briefly into the classroom as the site for the development of decontextualised language.

Where, When, and How Do They Learn It?

Let me first say a word about the origin of the data of mother-child interaction on which the enquiry reported below is based.[4] These interactions, covering some 100 hours of real time, were audiorecorded by the 24 mothers themselves in the privacy of their homes in and around Sydney suburbs; no outsiders were present. The children were 3 years 6 months to 4 years old. The mothers were requested to provide these data ostensibly to assist in a study which was said to be concerned with finding out what young children talk about of their own free will in their everyday life situations when no one is actually requiring them to talk this way or that. The mothers were also requested to record their talk with the child when they themselves were engaged in doing things that they normally did in the course of running their household. No restrictions or positive instructions were given regarding what to talk about except that mothers were not to prod their children to talk, and were to avoid recording while vacuuming or watching the TV. No individual microphones were worn; a powerful tape recorder was left running whenever the mother and the subject child were talking. Thus, any one spatio-temporally located interaction could be as short as a minute or two or it could be quite long, lasting some 20 minutes or more. The experience of managing a household while living with and attending to the needs of very small children exercises its own selective pressures as the care-giving adults very quickly discover. There are the household jobs of cooking, cleaning, washing, tidying up, and so on; and then there are specific care-giving duties, including that of keeping the child engaged and amused and/or out of trouble. Given such conditions, one may reasonably expect that the care-giving adult's talk with the child will be typically context dependent. And so it is—but not all the time, and certainly not in all 24 dyads.

A word now about the background to the extract presented as Dialogue 1 below.[5] Carol, 3 years 6 months old, her little sister, Annie, and her mother are having a snack outside in the garden. Suddenly Carol notices a cat that has wandered into their garden. "Oh, a pussy-cat!" says Carol. The mother has also noticed the cat: "It's up in the tree, isn't it?" she says. Carol and her mother discuss how it is acceptable for a strange cat to appear in their garden: "We don't mind, do we, mum?" Carol asks, and the mother confirms, "No, we don't". Carol then goes on to contrast their attitude with that of people who behave differently: They, it appears, would not like stray cats to come into their gardens. It is at this point that we pick up their dialogue:

Dialogue 1

1   *Carol*   – But sometimes when pussy-cat goes into people's garden some people say, "Come back, pussy-cat! Come back!"
2   *Mother*   – Do they? Is that what they do? (AMUSED TONE; MOTHER AND CHILD LAUGH)
3   *Carol*   – Mum, do pussy-cats die when people die?
4   *Mother*   – Do pussy-cats what, love?
5   *Carol*   – Die when people die?
6   *Mother*   – Well, pussy-cats die when their time comes ... everything dies one day.
7   *Carol*   – Do dogs do they one day ?
8   *Mother*   – Do what?
9   *Carol*   – Do dogs die one day when ...
10   *Mother*   – Yes, dogs die too ...
11   *Carol*   – Do fruit die?
12   *Mother*   – Fruit dies, yes, in a different sort of way.
13   *Carol*   – How?

14	*Mother*	– Well, see how the fruit up there on the tree's green?
15	*Carol*	– Mm.
16	*Mother*	– See how down here it's gone all yellow and squashy and horrible?
17	*Carol*	– Uhhu.
18	*Mother*	– That means it's died, it's ... well, we don't say (EMPHASIS ON "SAY") it's died, we say it's gone bad ...
19	*Carol*	– Mummy?
20	*Mother*	– Mm?
21	*Carol*	– Mum, see where the persimmons have dropped off the tree ... cos um cos they're sick and they've got germs.
22	*Mother*	– Yes, that's right.
23	*Carol*	– They're sick and they've got germs.

I believe that most readers will agree that the above dialogue makes some use of decontextualised language. Before beginning to look more closely into some of its properties, it is useful to make one general point. The binomial categories of context dependent versus context independent, embedded versus disembedded and so on are not an "all-or-none" affair: There are continuities between the two. One form of continuity is that these descriptive terms need not apply to the whole of a discourse. Even within the same spatio-temporally located interaction, different parts of the discourse may vary in the extent to which one segment consists of context independent language use and another does not. This situation has been well documented by Cloran (1994, 1999a). But there is another aspect of the continuities between the two, in which the drawing of clear lines between them is not so easy: I am referring here to the fact that one and the same segment of discourse may display characteristics of both types of language use. This calls for a further clarification of the nature of the two varieties. As we continue the examination of the data, we will note that decontextualisation is itself not a uniform phenomenon: There are different degrees of being disembedded, and the differences in ways of being disembedded appear to be significant from the point of view of the child learning how to engage in such discourse. Following this brief introduction, I turn to Dialogue 1. What continuities and discontinuities do we find here? What are the characteristics of the mother's talk, and what are those of her daughter's? How does this early *sortie* into disembeddedness occur for Carol? How does it relate to her "natural" mode of interaction—her discursive *terra firma*, namely, situationally dependent talk? I hope that asking these questions begins to reveal the complexity of what it means to claim orientation to decontextualised talk.

Continuities between actual and virtual contexts

Elsewhere (Hasan, 1984) I have referred to the discursive theme of the dialogue between Carol and her mother as the discourse of *mutability*—talk about life and death. But Carol is not really enquiring into mutability as an abstract idea: she is not concerned with the cosmic principle of death as the end of all life; she is concerned rather with the fate of cats. And the idea of the general category "pussy-cats" itself comes to her mind in the context of talking about "*a* pussy-cat"—the cat in the here and now of their immediate experience, the cat that has wandered into their garden. It is interesting to note also that before the child raises the question of pussy-cats dying, she introduces the general category "pussy-cats" as a class of entities that is habitually engaged in familiar everyday activities: pussy-cats come into and go away from people's houses and gardens. In other words, some generalisations based on the actual observation of what cats do are already on the table before we move to the topic of mutability, which obviously is not a familiar concept to the child. The child's disembedded discourse, her use of decontextualised language, has employed as its point of departure the discourse that was embedded within the immediate material situation; it relates to a phenomenon that has been physically sensed by the child, and that happens to be an element of her personal experience in the context of this talk. Equally, as the mother attempts to explain the difficult idea of death/decay as applicable to all organic things, she reaches out to what is actually present in the material situation: "the fruit up there on the tree, (the fruit) down here [...] all yellow and squashy and horrible [...] that means it's died."

There are thus two critical moments in this discourse, and I am suggesting that there is a continuity between them. To comment on the nature of this continuity, I want to introduce two terms, namely, *actual* and *virtual*, which describe the context to which language is referring. I shall say that a context (or some element of it) is actual, if it can be actually, that is, physically sensed by the interactant(s). For example, "the fruit on the tree" in Carol's garden and the fruit on the ground "all yellow and squashy and horrible" are instances of reference to actual (elements of) context: Carol and her mother have bodily experience of these phenomena. By contrast, a context (or some element of it) is virtual if no possibility exists for experiencing it physically: The phenomena are, in fact, not available to the senses. A discourse is decontextualised/disembedded, not because what it refers to is not physically present to the senses here and now, but because it refers to something that is by its very nature incapable of being present in any spatio-temporal location whatever: It is simply not sens-ible. The virtual context of situation is an entirely text-based reality, brought into existence by constitutive verbal action (Hasan, 1999). I believe it is important to emphasise here the fact that constitutive verbal action does not always and necessarily create a virtual context of situation: What is critical to the *virtual* nature of context is its distance from the *actual*. An actual context is rooted in experience that is essentially sensuous, or *sens-ible*, irrespective of whether it relates to an *immediate* situation or one that is *displaced* as in a narrative of personal experience. When I tell someone what happened to me the other day, my verbal action is constitutive; it re-creates an actual context that actually existed and that is now spatio-temporally displaced. This context, displaced in reality but invoked by constitutive language, is as actual as an immediate context in which I use my language as an ancillary tool for negotiating the performance of some ongoing physical action such as helping someone wash up. Whether verbal action is ancillary or constitutive, so long as it refers to some actual context, one thing is certain: Part of the source of my knowledge of such contexts goes beyond language to other modalities of knowing. Virtual contexts, I am suggesting, differ from both categories of actual context, the immediate and the displaced. Because virtual contexts are non-material and removed from situational realities, they simply cannot be directly and physically experienced: they are intellig-ible, not sens-ible. They reside only in a conceptual universe, and consist simply of the said and the imagined. Table 2.1 summarises these distinctions:

Table 2.1: *A classification of contexts for discourse*

Context type	Verbal action Ancillary	Constitutive	Context in relation to the speaker
Actual	Immediate	Displaced	Sensible
Virtual		Virtual	Intelligible

This discussion suggests that for a young child who is as yet an apprentice to a given culture, actual situations are far more accessible than virtual ones. And while much more can be said about the above categories of context, what is relevant here is really this quality of discourse, its capacity to construe a *virtual context of situation*, that characterises disembedded discourse: This is at the heart of the distinction between context dependent and context independent talk. At least some of us become so familiar with virtual contexts that we do not appreciate the strangeness of this universe. For the young child it may be a different experience. We will see how Carol treads hesitatingly as she tries to grasp the elements of this virtual context.

The cline of de/contextualisation

Cloran (1994, and elsewhere) set up a cline of decontextualised language. Using her concept of rhetorical unit (henceforth RU), she suggested that if *action* RU represents the most context dependent language use, then *generalisation* RU is the most context independent (Cloran, 1999b, p. 37, and elsewhere). An example of the former is "don't hit her" and of the latter, "boys don't play with dolls". Let me begin by considering the category of generalisation, which is akin to what I called *principle* in the structure of the reasoning game (Hasan, 1992). Using her metalanguage for the description of RU, Cloran would say that in generalisation, the Central Entity component of the message is a class exhaustive category: It refers not to a specific individual—not to *a* pussy-cat—but to a class of "pussy cats". At the same time, the Event Orientation is habitual: "die", not "has died", or "is dying", and so on. Speaking from observation, there is no doubt that generalisations typically instantiate decontextualised language use. I, however, want to draw attention to a statement such as "some people say", which to my mind already exemplifies a species of disembedded language although technically speaking it is not a generalisation, since the Central Entity "some people" refers to a sub-class, not to a whole class, such as "people". Relevant to my claim of "some people say" as already indicating some disembeddedness is the *actual* versus *virtual* distinction. The nominal group "some people" does not refer here to persons in the here and now of the actual immediate situation[6] as it might do in another message, such as, "I see some people at the gate". Instead, it refers to a category of persons that in Whorf's (1956) terms would never form a sensuously apprehended aggregate. It is thus a conceptual construct made possible by language; it has no *specific* material manifestation, just as most of the situations construed by the language of *Metamorphosis* or *Adventures in the Skin Trade* are incapable of material manifestation: They reside in the conceptual universe alone. In one respect, "some people say" is like "pussy cats die": The simple present tense in the verb "say" refers to a habitual and/or timeless event. The time to which a simple present tense refers is, again using Whorf's terminology, not time that is being sensed here and now by the speaker. The simple present tense[7] realising the meaning *habitual* invokes past time, which has been sensed by some person(s); it invokes future time, which exists as anticipation; and it also invokes present time, which is in the here and now of others at this very moment of speaking, though the occurrence of the event may not be being sensed by the speaker. In simplified language, "says" means "have said, are saying, will say". The invocation of the past, the future, and the present iconically spans all time: It has the effect of bestowing an aspect of timelessness on the event in question. A habitual event is thus an event that defies the boundaries we impose on time: And this, too, is a conceptual construct made possible by language. It is not a phenomenon that can ever be known sensuously.

I have deliberately emphasised the sensuous aspect of personal experience to differentiate it from the nature of knowledge—or information, if you like—that can *not* be based on bodily experience: bodily experienced phenomena constitute the quintessential context dependent information. One of the things that a generalisation does is to transform categories of referents which can be sensuously apprehended into categories whose referents cannot be sensed: it transports the *sens-ible* exclusively to the domain of the *intellig-ible* and that is one reason for maintaining that generalisations typically instantiate disembedded language. But by the same token, any message or RU which is capable of construing the virtual will be, to some extent, a case of disembeddedness. From the point of view under consideration, the further removed the referents of categories from primary, bodily experience, the more decontextualised the information, irrespective of whether or not there is any generalisation involved. It follows that given two or more cases of generalisation, the degree of their disembeddedness need not be the same. So while there is generalisation both in the message "pussy-cats die" and in the message "everything dies one day", nonetheless following the logic of my argument I maintain that the latter is more decontextualised than the former; and by the same token, the former is more decontextualised than an utterance such as "we don't mind", on the assumption that "we" here refers to Carol's immediate family: herself, her parents, and her sibling; the Central Entity of this message refers to a tight local group, and the Event refers to an occurrence in which Carol herself is implicated. For Carol, the message "everything dies one day" is considerably more decontextualised than her own message, "we don't mind". It should be noted in passing that the critical principle underlying variation in the degree of decontextualisation cannot be specified simply in terms of the presence or absence of some lexico-grammatical, *or* semantic, *or* contextual category: It must rest on a calibration of all three. The same first person plural pronoun, *we*, may refer to the interactants here and now, as in "shall we look at this picture book together"; or to a small group well known to the interactants such as their family, as in "we don't mind"; or to a group that extends to include friends and/or neighbours, as in "we keep our streets clean"; or to members of the interactant's speech fellowship, to use Firth's (1957) term, as in "we don't want to act like those fancy people"; or to the entire human race, as in "we owe it to our future generations", and so on. The referents thus construed discursively are realities of different orders. I am suggesting that differences in the orders of reality might be significant at the early stages of learning how to mean disembedded meanings. The more removed from personal experience a category is, perhaps the more problematic it is from the point of view of understanding its full meaning, and this naturally means lack of sure-footedness in building it into one's own discourse.

The mastery of disembedded language

The gist of my argument has been that the stranger, the less familiar the reality being construed, the more decontextualised the message. It follows that the mastery of disembedded language will consist in feeling at home with reality that is not sensuously mediated: This reality is a terrain that is navigated by the intellect alone. The problem that is posed for the child by the incommensurability of the various orders of reality is indicated by how Carol handles the issue of mutability. One way of describing Carol's response to the mother's "Everything dies one day" is to say that she is testing the referential scope of "everything": Does the reference of the word extend beyond people to whole classes of animals such as cats and dogs? Does it cover inanimate objects: "Do fruit die?" People dying is already a less familiar happening than cats coming and going; but mutability as a superordinate concept which subsumes all change, all decay, all death is certainly a very remote concept for the child. It is to this high degree of decontextualisation that the mother has moved the discourse by saying that "everything dies one day" and "fruit dies, yes, in a different sort of way". Note how she attempts to bridge this gap for the child by instantiations that refer to the here and now: the tree in the garden, the fruit on that tree, the colour of that fruit; the fruit on the ground in the garden, the colour of the fruit on the ground; the difference between the colour of the fruit on the tree and that of the fruit on the ground. Secure in the knowledge that the child can see all this, she builds her most abstract claim on it, and goes on to suggest that it is this *kind of* difference that we refer to as the death of the fruit; more specifically, "we say it's gone bad". The mother's explication is impressive both as a lesson in language and as a lesson in elements of reality: it shows in action the process of conceptualisation as a socio-genetic activity (Vygotsky, 1978). Which is not to say that in this one single step Carol will now master the virtual reality construed so carefully by her mother.

Carol enters this virtual universe hesitatingly: Note, for example, the pauses. It is obvious that her navigation of the terrain lacks the assurance the mother displayed. However, with all the experience of 3 years 6 months of living, Carol can show at least some tentative understanding of organic change. She most probably has knowledge of a particular kind of bodily change that in all likelihood she herself has experienced—having germs, being sick. Carol applies this understanding to the fruit in a halting kind of way: her key to the entry into the remote world of virtual reality is the certainty of the knowledge that most probably she has herself bodily experienced or at least witnessed in person. This halting entry cannot be equated with mastery, though of course it is a significant step in that direction. What is important is the trajectory of her entry into decontextualised forms of discourse.

Again and again, the data of mother-child talk shows us evidence of children's halting, hesitating entry into the unfamiliar conceptual universe construed by disembedded language. I present another such example below. In Dialogue 2, the mother is trying to get Kristy ready to go to a day-care centre. Kristy is more than reluctant to go: There are tears, tantrums, and arguments. Little fights keep erupting between Kristy and her baby sister, Ruth. Much of the mother's energy is devoted to diverting Kristy and to defusing the tension in the air. Through all this she is not only continuing to get Kristy dressed but she is also attending to Ruth. At the point when the following extract begins, the process of dressing Kristy is still continuing:

Dialogue 2a
1 Mother – This tee-shirt? Right! We'll have to make you some blouses, won't we?
2 Kristy – Yeah then everyday I can wear blouses. Mummy, I think I'm going to get cold today.

3	Mother –	I have no idea what the weather is going to be like today. I'll send your sweatshirt or your cardigan or your jumper or whatever you'd like over too.
4	Kristy –	I want—I want a short-sleeved cardigan—a long-sleeved one if it goes hot I'll have to wear a short-sleeved one so** —
5	Mother –	**Yep well see yesterday I thought it was going to be cold and you were really hot by the end of the day so I think the best thing is to put a short-sleeved tee-shirt on you and a cardigan.
6	Kristy –	Yeah I think we don't know what day it's going to be.
7	Mother –	No it's a bit [?] in spring and autumn, isn't it? Stand up straight so I can get your duds on. In winter it is cold and in the summer it's hot and in the spring and the autumn it's funny. (RUTH IS HEARD CRYING)
8	Mother –	Oh Ruth … she's jammed her fingers in the sewing box [? put] her hand on top of the [?lid]… silly monkey!
9	Kristy –	Silly monkey!
10	Mother –	She had her hand in [?the box].
11	Kristy –	Yeah.
12	Mother –	And she had the other hand on top pushing it down squashing her hand. (KRISTY LAUGHS)
13	Mother –	Oh you're a goose Ruth!
14	Kristy –	Oh you're a goose! Do goosies do that?
15	Mother –	No no but you often call people a goose if they're silly.
16	Kristy –	Hmm.
17	Mother –	You know if you eat too much I say you're a little pig you're a little piggy-wig.
18	Kristy –	Yeah. (LAUGHS)
19	Mother –	Well if people are silly you say "silly goose" and sometimes you can say they're a donkey (MIMICKING) you silly donkey!
20	Kristy –	Silly donkey! (LAUGHS)
21	Mother –	And if they are fussy what do you say?** I think you'd say they're a hen … or a mother hen.
22	Kristy –	[?].
23	Mother –	You haven't got your panties on, have we? Where are they? Goodness me, I put them out, there they are! The blue ones.
24	Kristy –	Hello [?fussy hen].
25	Mother –	OK Ruth … we've nearly got Kristy dressed, we'll get you dressed after her. Stand up pet, put your hands on my shoulders so you don't fall over.
26	Kristy –	Why is spring and **autumn —
27	Mother –	**[?Those Kristy's shoes].
28	Kristy –	Why is spring and autumn um is is funny?
29	Mother –	Well um it is less predictable you don't really know what it is going to be like.
30	Kristy –	Hmm.

31	*Mother* –	In spring the weather is changing from—no I haven't got your [?leg] in. The weather is changing from cold to hot and in the autumn the weather is changing from hot to cold and it's not just in the middle, it seems to um be **colder in the morning.
32	*Kristy* –	**Hmm.
33	*Mother* –	And gets warm later in the day.
34	*Kristy* –	Yeah why does it?
35	*Mother* –	I don't understand enough about the weather to be able to explain that.
		(RUTH SCREAMS)

Here the point of departure for the mother's comments on the unreliability of weather in spring and autumn is a practical consideration that has involved Kristy personally: what clothes should the mother send with Kristy so that the daughter will be comfortable, unlike yesterday when she was too hot. So the discourse of weather is initially embedded within something that the child can "relate to" directly. Note, though, how unsure Kristy's own control of the information concerning weather is as she says (in Turn 6) "yeah I think we don't know what day it's going to be". Although talk of weather is interrupted by the discussion of metaphors occasioned by Ruth's antics, Kristy later returns to it (see Turn 25 onwards) as if she had some inkling of her incomplete understanding of the matter. In response to Kristy's specific questions, the mother elaborates on the "funniness" of the current weather. As it happens the mother is not able to fully satisfy Kristy's curiosity. But at a later point in the same interaction it becomes obvious that Kristy did not grasp the conceptual world of changing weather even to the extent that the mother was able to explain. As Butt (1989) comments, what she grasps is some vague sense of things being not quite right with regard to mornings, evenings, days and nights—a sense that the uncertain condition of the weather, its "a-normality", calls for especial consideration. This becomes evident in the segment of the same dialogue presented below as Dialogue 2b.

As I pointed out in introducing this interaction, Kristy is more than reluctant to go to the day-care centre. Off and on, throughout this interaction, Kristy has made her disagreement with her mother clear. She has tried to dissuade her mother from sending her there, using all the strategies available to children of her age, from crying, to fighting with Ruth, to presenting "rational" reasons, to displaying aggression, but all to no avail.[8] Finally, in a pathetic move, she claims, "I want to be a baby" and complains, "I just feel crooked today". It is at this point that Kristy uses the uncertainties of the weather as presumably her last argument in her battle against being sent to the day-care centre. Here is the relevant segment of the dialogue:

Dialogue 2b
1 *Kristy* – Um I just feel crooked today. (COMPLAININGLY)
2 *Mother* – You just feel crooked?
3 *Kristy* – I can't help the weather—I don't have the weather—it's cold out here in the morning and then it comes hot—
4 *Mother* – Think you are probably crook just because you have been hanging around the house too long. As soon as we get out you'll feel better.
5 *Kristy* – Yeah and I don't know what to do. (TEARFUL)

The longer one stays in official pedagogic sites engaged in the business of re/producing knowledge, the greater grows one's familiarity with disembedded talk, until one comes to take most of its elements for granted. The question of the mastery of concepts such as Kristy and Carol are encountering for the first time in these dialogues does not present itself to us as a problem. We are even less aware of the fact that our thoughts move constantly between the actual and the virtual worlds—that there are continuities between embedded and disembedded language. But the situation is different for children starting off on this journey. On the whole, the children who participated in this research proved themselves impressively competent with language. So their hesitations and their "peculiar" formulations as they grappled with the virtual world construed by disembedded discourse are all the more noticeable. Learning how to use disembedded language is in fact learning to come to terms with a new reality; it is learning a new way of engaging with reality that is at best only partly familiar. This learning is something quite hard to accomplish on a piecemeal basis, from nine to five in packages of 45 minute "periods" in official pedagogic sites. The children who get oriented to such language are those whose life is pervaded with discourse of the kind exemplified above.

The environment for disembedded talk

This brings me to the last point to be discussed in this section on the ontogenesis of orientation to disembedded talk: The question is, where do the children learn it—those who actually get to do so? What discursive environment might be said to be most hospitable to the ontogenesis of such talk in the home? It is almost impossible to answer this question without appealing to Bernstein's notions of classification and framing, since it is not the "substantive" nature of the environment which is criterial: Disembedded talk may surface and actually establish itself in immediate contexts of different kinds as Cloran (1999b) has demonstrated. But although this can happen in almost any actual immediate context, it does not happen randomly: The establishment of disembedded talk is highly selective. The underlying principle guiding this selectivity can be stated very simply and succinctly by referring to Bernstein's concepts of classification and framing, once these concepts are seen within the theoretical framework which gives them their significance. Using these concepts, we may very simply claim that the environment hospitable to the ontogenesis of orientation to disembedded talk is furnished by social *praxis* of the kind that displays relatively weak classification and framing. Underlying this "simple" statement is a complex situation to which I shall return at the close of this section; here I offer just a few words on my "take" on the critical concepts themselves. I see classification and framing as inalienably linked to each other. Classification is a function of power, and framing is a function of control to maintain that classification: It is through framing that classification is maintained and altered; and it is one's relation to classification that furnishes the ground for specific forms of framing. Inextricably linked as the concepts are, my focus here will be on framing though mention of classification will necessarily arise.

Although I believe that Bernstein's account of framing is designed with an eye more to official pedagogic practice than to local practice, it is nonetheless useful to reproduce its essentials here for easy reference:

> Framing is about *who* controls *what*. What follows could be described as the *internal logic* of the pedagogic practice. Framing refers to the nature of the control over:
> - the selection of the communication;
> - its sequencing (what comes first, what comes second);
> - its pacing (the rate of expected acquisition);
> - the criteria; and
> - the control over the social base which makes this transmission possible.
>
> Where framing is strong, the transmitter has explicit control over selection, sequence, pacing, criteria and the social base. Where framing is weak, the acquirer has more *apparent* control (I want to stress apparent) over the communication and its social base. (Bernstein, 1996, p. 27)

Bernstein points out that the framing values, their strength or weakness, can vary independently for each element of the practice. I will presently touch upon some of these aspects of framing in the dialogues I have presented above. Let me begin here by saying that the Macquarie group of researches[9] on mother-child interaction found that mothers varied nonrandomly in respect of the strength/weakness of their classification of contexts (Williams, 1995; Cloran, 1994, 1999b; Hasan, 2000): Some acted on the principle that contexts must be kept apart, some on the principle that the natural condition for contexts is to permeate each other. Strong classification of context typically "goes with" strong framing; conversely, weak classification of context, the affirmation of its permeability, goes with weak framing. The dialogues presented in the last section belong to the latter category. I want to say a few words about what weak classification of context means, what is implied in saying that contexts are taken as permeable.

Consider Dialogues 1 and 2. If we wished to take the entire interaction in which they occur as one unit, how would we describe the context of that interaction? It seems to me that we must invoke some such notion as *con/textual shift* (Hasan, 1999, 2000), or the embedding of one context within another, as Cloran puts it (Cloran, 1994, 1999b). What I mean by con/textual shift is that on the one hand the speakers are shifting from an ongoing context, they are *reclassifying* the discursive situation, and on the other hand, the new context to which the shift has been made is still being integrated into the discursive contexts from which the shift is being indicated: every con/textual shift implies a (somewhat) new context with an identity of its own, and at the same time, a context that is contributing to the primary context (for details, see Hasan, 1999). Taken together, these interrelated contexts succeed in giving the discourse its overall character. So there is reclassification of context and there is integration of the reclassified contexts: both these aspects are important to the progress and character of the discourse.[10] Dialogues 1 and 2 did not begin as an explanation or exposition of any idea. For example, Carol and her mother were engaged in eating snacks; Kristy and her mother were engaged in getting Kristy ready for the day. In these specific respects, both these dialogues are indicative of the sorts of material actions that adults giving care to young children must attend to, and of the fact that at least some of their discourse must be embedded in the here and now of their actual immediate situation: Their verbal action must be *ancillary*. But, paradoxically, precisely because the activities are of this kind—providing food, dressing, playing some game with the child, and so on—that is to say, precisely because the action is primarily material (Hasan, 1999), the situation becomes a frame in which verbal action is free either to be ancillary to the activity or to disregard the material action altogether, turning away from it to become a resource for constituting a context that is, as it were, independent of the material situation itself.[11] Germane to this point is the fact that most material activities are capable of being carried out without words, though they are hardly ever accomplished without words when an other is present in the same situation; nonetheless, the *potential* for the reclassification of context only arises where the ongoing verbal action is ancillary: One of the sites where this condition can be found is in talking to very small children while giving them care or playing with them, and so on.

Because material action moves along the temporal axis, because the performance of its stages is visible, and because it has a projected end-point so that the achievement of this goal can be easily ascertained, we may be inclined to prioritise this element of the field:[12] We may think of the material action as the mother's *real* agenda; we may say, for example, that what the mother is *really* doing is dressing the children. But where classification and framing are weak, especially in the environment of local pedagogy, what the mother is really doing on any one occasion may be many things at once. In Dialogue 2a, I have deliberately reproduced a segment that goes some way towards illustrating this characteristic. In the first turn of Dialogue 2a, itself a segment of a longer dialogue, the mother begins with reference to the material action, then there is talk of the uncertainty of weather interspersed with talk of clothing, then we have a lesson in the meaning of metaphors, after which, in Turn 23, the mother verbally "returns" to the material activity which has been physically going on all the time anyway, but now the verbal action occurs with specific reference to the needs of dressing Kristy: "You haven't got your panties on, have we? where are they? goodness me, I put them out, there they are! the blue ones", but very soon there is a shift back to talk of weather, which after many other shifts reappears finally in what is shown here as the first turn of Dialogue 2a. There are, thus, many co n/textual shifts throughout this interaction in which the mother's verbal action "returns" to the material action only to move away from it again. But by far the greater part of this lengthy interaction consists of language that is "about" things other than getting dressed. What is important here from the point of view of framing is that the movement between contexts, the weaving in and out of contexts, is not unilateral. Throughout this interaction, the shifts are typically construed in partnership with the child as the following discussion documents.

As local pedagogy is "segmental", perhaps the aspect of framing concerning sequencing of activities has a different significance here. Note, however, the sequencing of what happens to Ruth and how the mother "exploits" it to draw Kristy into the world of metaphors. And in this connection it is significant that the discourse is provoked by the child's question, "do goosies do that?" It is difficult to give a good idea of the pacing of discourse without reproducing most of the interaction, but the mother takes time away from the business of dressing Kristy to comfort her, to "make her feel better", to engage with her reasons for not wanting to go to the day-care centre, to reassure her of her own return by the time the child is supposed to come back home.[13] What can be said and done while Kristy is being got ready to go to the day-care centre is not entirely up to the mother: The child has *some* say, even if she has no say in the matter of where she will spend that day. The selection of discourse topics is as much Kristy's prerogative as it is the mother's. The discourse between the two is a relatively shared negotiated activity. To be sure, this constantly peripatetic discourse has other purposes than just presenting new information to the child. In a way, the construction of knowledge which entrains the use of decontextualised language plays second fiddle to the mother's primary concern in this interaction. Note that throughout this discourse the mother chooses to develop topics which have the potential of humouring Kristy and diverting her attention from the contentious issue of having to go to the day-care centre against her inclination (see Hasan, 2000, for further discussion). Obviously the mother's relatively weak classification of contexts in no way implies an absence of a specific fixed agenda, which is, as it were, non-negotiable. To this extent, the weakness of the mother's framing would seem to be *apparent*. In fact it may be true as a general rule that weak framing is simply the ultimate device for disarming opposition by (*apparently*) entertaining the other's needs. You may describe this situation as showing respect for the other's individuality, but you may equally justifiably describe it as exercising control by stealth—that is to say, *invisible control*. Once this view is taken, the social universe presents itself as a network of relations defined by various strategies of control. That is to say, control is not something that can be elided from the social. Be that as it may, what is important in the context of this discussion is the fact that decontextualised language typically occurs in the environment of weak framing, and weak framing may imply a readiness to entertain weak classification of context. The trick is to remember that weak classification and framing are not synonymous with the absence of social power and control; they are simply indicative of a qualitatively different kind of power and a different mode of control.

Ancillary verbal action and reclassification of context. I have suggested that the *potential* for the reclassification of context only arises where the ongoing verbal action is ancillary. I want to emphasise the word *potential* here, because it is *by no means necessary* that speakers will be inclined to entertain con/textual shifts, to reclassify their context, whenever the verbal action in the field of discourse is ancillary. The etiology of this inclination and its underlying logic must be traced back by following the workings of Bernstein's theoretical framework, aspects of which will be briefly brought to attention below. But the upshot is that interaction at home between mothers and children does not uniformly display weak classification and framing of the kind exemplified by Dialogues 1 and 2. Below I reproduce segments of a dialogue which is remarkably different from those we have examined so far. This interaction took place at mealtime and the recording opens with Karen requesting first some sauce on her food, then some lemonade. The mother attends to these requests and reminds Karen of some "linguistic table manners", asking her to say "please!" and commenting, "I didn't hear a thank you from you." With these niceties observed, we come to the following point:

Dialogue 3.1
1 Mother – Come on, eat your tea please...
2 Karen – Could you put some more in there? ...
3 Mother – (WARNINGLY) Karen! ... give me it, eat your tea.
4 Karen – [?].
5 Mother – Mm?
6 Karen – [?put] lemon in it.
7 Mother – Well, eat some tea or you don't get nothing.
8 Karen – I see how many [?] there are. (TALKS TO HERSELF AS MOTHER POURS DRINK)
9 Mother – Quick ... Want the lid on it?
10 Karen – No.
11 Mother – Come on, eat your tea, less drink and more eat ... Did you hear what I said, Karen?
12 Karen – Mm.
13 Mother – Well, do it.

As I have pointed out elsewhere (Hasan, 2000), here the mother's primary concern is to maintain the boundary of the ongoing context—the context of "eating your tea": within a dialogue lasting some 20 minutes the mother produced her injunction to "eat your tea" over 20 times. It is relatively easy to specify the general condition under which—all else being equal—the speakers are able to reclassify their context; it is, however, not easy to say in precise terms where exactly such a shift will actually occur—

that is to say, this possibility is not open so long as we focus simply on the nature of the field of discourse (see discussion below). There is no doubt a time and a tide in the affairs of a discourse, which some interactants will grasp, thus producing a con/textual shift; but the occurrence of such occasions does not mean that they will be necessarily grasped for this purpose. Here is an example of, as it were, a nascent possibility for entertaining a con/textual shift, but the mother does not treat it as such:

Dialogue 3.2
1   Karen   – Mummy that haven't got no sauce on it.
2   Mother   – Oh you've got plenty of sauce, there now now eat it.
3   Karen   – On here.
4   Mother   – Oh there's plenty of sauce on your plate, Karen, you don't need it on every single drop of tea.
5   Karen   – Eh?
6   Mother   – You don't need it on every little bit.
7   Karen   – [? of tea]?
8   Mother   – Mm.
9   Karen   – Is that [?tea]?
10   Mother   – That's sauce.
11   Karen   – Mm hot sauce.
12   Mother   – No, mint sauce.
13   Karen   – Mince? ... why do you put mince sauce on here for?
14   Mother   – "Mint" not "mince".
15   Karen   – Mint this mint?
16   Mother   – Use your spoon or your fork.
17   Karen   – "Country Practice" is on now?
18   Mother   – No.
19   Karen   – "Sons and Daughters"?
20   Mother   – No, the news.
21   Karen   – Oh ...
22   Mother   – That's why I said use a spoon ... Now sit up, and use a spoon.

It is not easy to describe the exact delineations of an absence, but the reclassification of context is noticeably different from that in Dialogues 1 and 2. It also seems reasonable to suggest that some of the topics the child raises could have functioned as the point for departure into another context. Karen is probably getting a rise from the mother when she asks, "is that tea?" since the expression "eat your tea" is fairly common in some communities and the child is bound to have heard it often before. But the mint/mince question, the question of what programmes might be on the TV appear to be definite candidates for "diversion". The mother, however, displays a single-minded devotion to her own definition of the context: an occasion for tea eating. Whatever does not meet her recognition criteria for the internal attributes of this context she will resist, because the principle on which she is acting is: "Things must be kept apart". Williams (1995) found that in joint book-reading, a specifiable group of mothers acted in precisely the same manner: They protected their conception of what counts as book-reading; and they resisted any questions, any comments from the child as a "distraction" from the business of book-reading. Cloran (1999b) reports similar incidents where the insertion of a putative imaginary context is actively discouraged by some mothers. In Dialogue 3, the strength of Karen's mother's framing of the discourse is quite remarkable. The strength of what Bernstein calls the *social order* becomes specially evident in segments of the same dialogue, such as the following, which occurred some 10 minutes after the discussion quoted above:

Dialogue 3.3
1   Mother – Give me your spoon and I'll feed you, like a big baby, come on, baby! Give me your spoon.
2   Karen   – (SCANDALISED TONE) No.
3   Mother – Well sit up properly and eat your tea ... Karen! (WARNING TONE)
4   Karen   – I'm falling down. (OFF THE CHAIR)
5   Mother – You're not falling down.
6   Karen   – Yes I am I always fall down ... **I am falling down.
7   Mother – **Eat your tea.
8   Karen   – I am falling down.
9   Mother – Sit up before I get a stick and smack you.

Strictly speaking, though, it is not quite correct to say that no contextual shift has occurred in this interaction. It is already obvious that the mother is "escalating" her regulative strategies. Imperceptibly but surely, the context has moved from one of providing the necessities of tea to the child and supervising her eating of tea to one of exercising visible control to prevent her from doing things that are just not the right things to do when you are eating your tea. The occasion for nurturing the body becomes the occasion for creating a particular form of personal relation. The mother and daughter have seriously "threatened" each other with dire actions and some 8 minutes later, we encounter the following:

Dialogue 3.4
1   Mother – I'm bigger than you. I can hurt more.
2   Karen   – And I could too.
3   Mother – No you can't.

4	Karen	— Yes **I —
5	Mother	— **You are only a little girl who is becoming a very cheeky little girl.
6	Karen	— No I not.
7	Mother	— And if you don't stop ** it
8	Karen	— **Christine is a naughty girl and spiteful.
9	Mother	— And so are you, you're a spiteful little girl when you want to be, you can't talk about anybody else, if you don't stop it (DOING OTHER THINGS THAN EATING) you are going to go into bed and you'll never see anybody cause I won't let you see any of your friends.
10	Karen	— [?] I will sneak out.
11	Mother	— No you won't sneak out. Now sit up on that chair and eat your tea.
12	Karen	— Yes I will. (SNEAK OUT)
13	Mother	— Karen ... I am not playing games.
14	Karen	— Mum ... Oh Mummy. (CUDDLING UP TO THE MOTHER)
15	Mother	— No, go away, don't come crawling to me, go away go away. I don't want you until you sit down and eat your tea ... go away ... go away. Karen leave me alone please now sit down and eat your tea. I won't talk to you until you eat it. No I don't want no cuddles, no I don't want a cuddle off of you, no, no kisses either, no I don't want—oh you kiss me I am not kissing you back ... Karen. (WARNING TONE)
16	Karen	— It doesn't matter.
17	Mother	— It will matter in a minute, now stop crawling and sit down and eat your tea.

I will refrain from making further specific comments about this particular dialogue. It is obvious that the con/textual integration here has what I have called a tone-setting function of a particular kind that borders on the conflictual (Hasan, 1999). If invisible control, signified by the weaker framing of discourse, gives the impression of regard for the unique individuality of the child, visible control, signified by the stronger framing of social interaction, gives the impression of creating a relation of interpersonal dependence. It would be doing violence to the mother's intentions and the child's behaviour in Dialogue 3 to take their mutual threats "literally": They seem to me to be creating a particular kind of teasing, demanding, and controlling relation which differs quite remarkably from that which Dialogues 1 and 2 might be said to produce. I will return below to the significance of the creation of specific kinds of relation for the ontogenesis of contextualised language.

We are interested in the frequent and varied reclassification of context because of what it implies for framing; we are interested in weak framing because its examination permits us to make some generalisations about the ontogenesis of decontextualised language. When reclassification accompanies strong framing, it implies a struggle to maintain the speakers' definition of some class of context: Logically in this struggle the participant with greater power will exercise control over the other. This environment typically does not encourage decontextualised discourse; specifically, it does not create the higher reaches of disembedded discourse. The highest it goes is the enunciation of communal conventions such as "Don't be silly! Boys don't play with dolls" or "I told you, you don't hit girls", which present generalisations but of a different order of abstraction from "Everything dies one day", or "In the spring the weather is changing from cold to hot and in the autumn the weather is changing from hot to cold." While generalisations of the former kind enunciate a code of practical conduct, disembedded language of the latter kind "becomes" the knowledge base of a community, an instrument through which nature and man can both be subjugated or succoured. I am certainly not suggesting that there is nothing more to knowledge than language, but I am claiming that without language, these non-language foundations of knowledge would have been impossible to create.

Forms of classification and framing and forms of consciousness. We have seen that while it is easy to predict the potential of a switch to decontextualised use of language between mothers and children, it is not possible to specify what turns this potential into a preferred choice on the part of some mothers but not of others. Simplifying a complex situation, I would say that Bernstein's theory explains this situation in a two-step process. On the one hand, classification and framing enter into a dialectic relation with subjects' social positioning, as a subject comes to adopt a certain perspective on what counts as a legitimate and what as an illegitimate category. This perspective informs the subjects' social *praxis* both from the point of view of recognition and from the point of view of actual participation in that social practice, what Bernstein calls *realisation rules*. On the other hand, participation in social practices is precisely what enters into a dialectic with the subjects' form of consciousness: Social subjects are what they do and what they say to and with others. From this point of view, given a subject's social positioning we can infer a range of possible perspectives, and therefore possible forms of classification and framing practices that will appear desirable and legitimate. By the same token, given the evidence of a subject's habitual social practices we can recover the subject's orientation to certain orders of meaning. Bernstein points out that he uses *positioning* to "refer to the establishing of specific relations to other subjects and to the creating of specific relations within subjects" (1990, p. 13). In other words, to specify where the predisposition for the reclassification of contexts is likely to be found, where the decisions about the nature of framing come from, we should turn not to the nature of the social action, not to the field of discourse; rather, we should turn to the nature of the social relation being enacted in and through the social action—what is referred to as *tenor of discourse* in systemic functional linguistics. A particular kind of field offers the potential for the reclassification of contexts: I have argued that the critical properties of this field may be expressed as (1) *material action ongoing*, (2) *verbal action ancillary*; and (3) *the sphere of action quotidian* (Hasan, 1980, 1999). To actually exploit this potential, to actually engage in reclassification of contexts, we need interactants who are given to enacting a certain range of relations with their interactive other. This range of relations inheres in orientation to elaborated code.

The interplay of the material and the semiotic aspects identified as typical of the environment in which decontextualised language *can* and *does* occur are important from the point of view of the ontogenesis of this form of discursive behaviour. Earlier I raised a question: Why should children continue their engagement in such discourse? A common-sensical answer would be: Because children are programmed by nature to wish to learn; because they are curious. But this applies just as much to the children who do not get initiated at home into this kind of discourse. In my view, the answer to my question is to be found in the material and the semiotic action within the frame of a particular kind of interpersonal relation. The quotidian activities of care-givers and children tend to centre on the children's needs. The children are being fed or they are being dressed; in short, they are being looked after physically; this is largely achieved by material action. In addition, at the same time, they are being attended to intellectually and semiotically with the interaction displaying regard for the child's interests. Not conflict but co-operation characterises the interaction. The bodily satisfaction is thus combined with the satisfaction of companionship. The ontogenesis of decontextualised language becomes associated with the specific characteristics of such relaxed contexts. On the one hand, the weaker framing of the mother willing to reclassify con/text sets up a tone of mutual negotiation; on the other hand, the satisfaction of primary bodily needs must lead to a feeling of contentment. The instructional discourse of this variety of local pedagogy is then framed within contexts that most probably generate a positive affect in the child, and I speculate that this positive affect plays a crucial part in successfully orienting the children to decontextualised discourse—a form of discourse that I have described as essentially "unnatural".

Decontextualised Language and the Classroom

As the sites for official pedagogic practices, schools and higher educational institutions are the places where knowledge is re/produced. My concern here is not with how this is done; I wish simply to draw attention to what strikes me as a paradox in the framing of early pedagogic discourse. The data of classroom discourse to which I refer specifically here were collected for my research project from 24 schools in and around Sydney, and concerned only the kindergarten class. In fact, amongst other things, we wished to "follow" 8 of the 24 children from phase 1 of the project: We wished to find out if the experience of participating in different kinds of discourse made any systematic difference to how these children acted in the classroom. Recordings were made in each school on two separate occasions: during the first four weeks of the first year of schooling and during the last four weeks of the same year of schooling. The observations made here are based on the first set of data.

Although the strength of framing in classroom discourse can vary, as the discussion of progressive and traditional classroom has made abundantly clear, one must pay attention to Bernstein's emphasis on the word *apparent* (see quotation above). When the data of teacher-pupil talk was seen side by side with that of mother-child talk, what impressed most were the two respects in which it exaggerated maternal behaviour: The semantic orientation of classroom talk was an exaggerated version of middle class mothers' semantic orientation (Hasan, 1988), while the framing of classroom talk was an exaggerated version of the working class mothers' single minded devotion to one context. We found that most teachers began with a clear conception of what it was to participate in a teaching-learning context, and they exerted themselves to put that definition into practice with their young pupils, as early as the second or third week of schooling; in this connection it is relevant that the kindergarten class is the first real experience of schooling for the 5 year-old children. For example, as one teacher is conducting picture talk, a pupil calls out, "Mummy has got some shells". But this intervention gets nowhere: Like Karen's "mint/mince" or "Country Practice/Sons and Daughters", whatever potential the pupil's comment about her mother's shells might have had for a con/textual shift remains unexplored. When children call out an answer out of turn, they are either ignored or they're advised "Don't sing out until I call your name". The regulation of pupils' conduct is apparently one of the things that children learn pretty early on in the school. Having seen these same children at home with their mothers and in play group, having witnessed their freedom in coming and going, speaking or remaining silent, it comes as a surprise that within a matter of the first couple of weeks of their arrival at school the children have on the whole already become well schooled in how to conduct themselves. So far as schools are concerned there may be different kinds of reasons for maintaining a stronger classification of the classroom context. First, there is the pressure of time as measured by the curriculum needs, expressed informally as having to "get through" a certain amount of "material". Mercer (1993) also talks of teachers' fear of being perceived as unable to manage the classroom, which would be a source of serious loss of face. There is also the desirability of "order" where in a class of over 20 pupils, many might wish to claim the privilege of speaking at the same time. But perhaps an important issue centres around the notion of "self-discipline", an internalisation of standards of conduct as a sign of voluntary control of one's behaviour. Whatever the reason, it is clear that children's discourse is being "ordered" by the teacher.[14] There is no sense at least in my data that the teachers have negotiated with the children the selection of what is being done in the class. The pacing of the discourse is already such that those who get left out could remain out, if not for ever, then certainly for an appreciable amount of time. So in many respects, then, the framing value is strong rather than weak. It was most probably this aspect of classroom talk which persuaded Edwards (1976) to claim that classroom discourse is oriented to restricted code. Bernstein's (1975) description of pedagogic discourse as a discourse of competences embedded within the discourse of control clarifies the source of his critics' error in equating the framing aspect of classroom discourse with pedagogic discourse as a whole.

So having identified the respect in which classroom discourse presents an exaggerated version of working class mother-child discourse, we turn now to the discourse of competences. Here, most teachers are concerned to take the teaching from simple acts of naming to conjectures, hypotheses, inferential reasoning; in specific subject areas there will be talk of geometrical shapes, forms in nature, "language expression", and so on. What is more, as I have suggested elsewhere (1987), the goal seems to be the achievement of what Bateson (1972) described as deutero learning: an effort seems to be made to orient children toward such "desirable" characteristics as objectivity, citation of evidence, argumentation, and logical reasoning. A very simple episode may illustrate this: During a picture reading class, the teacher is talking about the picture of a little boy.

Dialogue 4

1	*Teacher*	– Do you think he's having fun?
2	*1st Pupil*	– Yes.
3	*2nd Pupil*	– Mummy's got some shells.
4	*Teacher*	– (IGNORING THE 2ND PUPIL) What tells you? What tells you he's having fun? He's enjoying himself?
5	*1st Pupil*	– My brain.
6	*Teacher*	– Your brain tells you (DISMISSIVE TONE)! Well, how can we tell by looking at the picture, that he's enjoying himself, having fun?
7	*Pupils*	– (MANY CALL OUT TOGETHER) Smile.
8	*Teacher*	– Good, he's got a smile on his face. Do you think he'd be enjoying himself if he didn't smile?
9	*Pupils*	– (MANY TOGETHER) No!
10	*Teacher*	– I don't think so either!

I take this as one insignificant-seeming but typical example of early inculcation of the principle that objective knowledge is superior to subjective knowledge (see also Butt, 1989), and distancing from primary actual experience is what I have suggested above to be the essence of disembedded talk. While the knowledge presented to the children at this stage is "diluted" for the benefit of their tender years, it is surprising how complex the requirements are and how much is taken for granted by teachers. The projected movement of the process of official pedagogy is unmistakably towards disembedded discourse. And yet if my reading of the data of mother-child interaction is correct—and I believe it is—then the best environment for learning to use disembedded language is one where a continuity is maintained from the actual to the virtual, from the familiar to the unfamiliar. And the best environment for this tends to be, as I have argued, a social interaction whose framing is relatively weak. With their stronger classification of context and their stronger framing of the discourse, with their greater emphasis on disembedded meanings, their distancing from the personal concerns of the children themselves, it seems very unlikely that schools provide the best environment for learning how to use such language for those children who do not already possess this expertise to some extent before they enter the school. For the children, the question of experiencing any bodily or intellectual satisfaction in classroom discourse is a problem that remains invisible, though it may be one of the most central. Teachers will often play the game of asking their pupils "what is the word for...?" Why should a 5-year-old have any interest in finding a single word for what happens to a wound if germs get into it, or the name of the place where you take people if they have an accident, and so on. True, Kristy is riveted by the lesson on the meaning of metaphors (see Dialogue 2a), but her relation to that problem is much more personal, much less an exercise in vocabulary development!

In the early 1970s, one heard complaints that there was very little actual data of classroom interaction; with the advent of Sinclair and Coulthard (1975) this situation changed dramatically: Now there is perhaps too much data of classroom interaction, but too little theory guiding the examination of that data, and decidedly too little understanding of the significant forms of systematic variation driven ideologically from the experience of living. So the data are in search of a searching, probing analysis, which goes beyond surface manifestations, even beyond the somewhat common-sensical explanations, to a review which is based on a deeper understanding of the nature of pedagogic discourse, its place in the mis/management of the affairs of humanity, its role in creating both what we cherish, namely, the material and technological advances, the new limitless horizons of the virtual world made possible by official pedagogy, and what we, or at least some of us, most abhor, namely, the unequal distribution of our social resources. Is there a field of research here in the linguistics of education which would be served well by paying attention to *The structuring of pedagogic discourse*?

Notes

*   The major part of the research on which this chapter is based was funded by Macquarie University Research Grant Scheme and the Australian Research Council. I would also like to thank Carmel Cloran for her comments on the first draft of this chapter.

1. I wish to acknowledge explicitly the contribution of Carmel Cloran to this debate. Her excellent discussion (see Cloran, 1994, 1999a, 1999b) of the terms *context dependent* and *context independent* and their synonyms within the systemic functional framework remains to date the most careful and detailed account.

2. To claim that the evolution of decontextualised language use is necessary to the exosomatic evolution of humanity is not to say that as a consequence humanity's relation to the natural and social environment could take only the form it has taken in modern industrialised societies; far less does it imply any approval of the form it has taken.

3. For a more detailed discussion of these views, and the controversy surrounding them, see Cloran (1994).

4. Details of this research may be found, for example, in Hasan (1989), and in Hasan and Cloran (1990).

5. The conventions adopted here for the transcription of the data are the following:

1st column of figures	= speaker turn counted consecutively for each extract from 1…;
(CAPITALS)	= situational comment, based on analyst's hearing of audiorecording;
[?go away]	= segment not intelligible; best guess on the basis of context;
[?]	= segment unintelligible; co-textual clues insufficient to allow guess;
?**	= no time allowed for response after this question;
abc —	= message *abc* left incomplete;
abc …	= a (longer than usual) pause;
**abc	= overlap in speaking
def**	= the speaker did not allow time for the addressee to respond.

6. I am ignoring here the use of "some people" to refer coyly to the addressee or to a third party, typically a single individual who is present in the actual immediate situation; this use is found typically in the context of making an adverse statement about the person in question, which is passed off as a non-serious comment by the use of this device, while it in fact brings the judgement within the orbit of attention.

7. Again, there are uses of the simple present tense which cannot be treated as habitual. One obvious example is the narrative present. For discussion, see Leech (1987), Halliday (1994), Quirk, Leech, and Svartvik (1985).

8. For a more elaborate discussion of these strategies, see Butt (1989).

9. The initial research project in this group was directed by me; my main co-researcher, Cloran, undertook an investigation of the semantic concept *rhetorical unit*—a major contribution which has made possible the study of reclassification in relation to discursive meanings. Williams conducted a study, under my supervision, of joint book-reading; in both these studies the data consisted of mother-child and kindergarten teacher-pupil interactions. Butt conducted a study of teacher-pupil interaction at the primary and secondary levels of education in certain subject areas. These researches, which spanned the mid-'80s to the mid-'90s, focused on context meaning and discourse and were inspired by the work of Vygotsky, Bernstein, and Halliday.

10. In speakers suffering from language disorders, there may be con/textual shift but no con/textual integration.

11. For a more detailed discussion of these issues, see Hasan (1999).

12. I use the term *field* here as it is used in systemic functional linguistics to refer to one parameter of the context of situation within which discourse is said to be embedded. It should not be confused with *field* as in Bernstein or in Bourdieu, which is more like *domain* in socio-linguistics.

13. Other parts of this dialogue, including those where Kristy is wailing and "whingeing" or having fisty-cuffs with her little sister, are discussed in Butt (1989) and Hasan (2000).

14. In pointing out this fact, I am not making a value judgement. While the evaluation of these practices is necessary, here my purpose is simply to describe, to record what we found.

Bibliography

Bateson, G. (1972). The logical categories of learning and communication. In *Steps to an ecology of mind*. New York: Ballantine.

Bernstein, B. (1971). *Class, codes and control: Vol. I, Theoretical studies towards a sociology of language*. London: Routledge & Kegan Paul.

———. (1975). *Class, codes and control: Vol. III, Towards a theory of educational transmissions*. London: Routledge & Kegan Paul.

———. (1990). *Class, codes and control: Vol. IV, The structuring of pedagogic discourse*. London: Routledge.

———. (1996). *Class, codes and control: Vol. V, Pedagogy, symbolic control and identity: Theory, research, critique*. London: Taylor & Francis.

Bruner, J. S. (1970). *Poverty and childhood*. Detroit: Merril-Palmer Institute.

Butt, D. (1989). The object of language. In R. Hasan & J. R. Martin (Eds.), *Language development: Learning language, learning culture: Studies for Michael Halliday*. Norwood, NJ: Ablex Publishing Corporation.

Cloran, C. (1994). *Rhetorical units and decontextualisation: An enquiry into some relations of context, meaning and grammar*. Monograph in Systemic Linguistics, No. 6. Nottingham, England: Department of English Studies, University of Nottingham.

———. (1999a). Context, material situation and text. In M. Ghadessy (Ed.), *Text & context in functional linguistics*. Amsterdam: John Benjamins.

———. (1999b). Contexts for learning. In F. Christie (Ed.), *Pedagogy and the shaping of consciousness: Linguistic and social processes*. London: Cassell.

Cole, M., John-Steiner, V., Scribner, S., & Souberman, E. (Eds.). (1978). *L. S. Vygotsky—Mind in society: The development of higher psychological processes.* Cambridge, MA: Harvard University Press.

Donaldson, M. (1978). *Children's minds.* London: Fontana.

Edwards, A. D. (1976). *Language in culture and class.* London: Heinemann.

Firth, J. R. (1957). *Papers in linguistics 1934–1951.* Oxford: Oxford University Press.

Halliday, M. (1973). *Explorations in the functions of language.* London: Edward Arnold.

———. (1975). *Learning how to mean: Explorations in the development of language.* London: Edward Arnold.

———. (1994). *Introduction to functional grammar* (2nd ed). London: Edward Arnold.

Hasan, R. (1980). What's going on? A dynamic view of context in language. In J. E. Copeland & P. W. Davies (Eds.), *The seventh LACUS forum.* Columbia, SC: Hornbeam Press.

———. (1984). What kind of resource is language? *Australian Review of Applied Linguistics, 7* (1), 57–85. Reprinted in *Ways of saying, ways of meaning: Selected papers of Ruqaiya Hasan,* C. Cloran, D. Butt, & G. Williams, Eds., 1996, London: Cassell.

———. (1986). The ontogenesis of ideology: An interpretation of mother child talk. In T. Threadgold, E. A. Grosz, G. Kress, & M. Halliday (Eds.), *Semiotics ideology language.* Sydney: Sydney Association for Studies in Society and Culture. Reprinted in *Ways of saying, ways of meaning: Selected papers of Ruqaiya Hasan,* C. Cloran, D. Butt, & G. Williams, Eds., 1996, London: Cassell.

———. (1987). Reading picture reading: Invisible instruction. *Proceedings of the 13th Australian Reading Association Conference,* Sydney.

———. (1988). Language and socialisation: Home and school. In L. Gerot, J. Oldenburg (Torr), & T. van Leeuwen (Eds.), *Proceedings from the Working Conference on Language in Education.* Sydney: Macquarie University.

———. (1989). Semantic variation and sociolinguistics. *Australian Journal of Linguistics, 9,* 221–275.

———. (1992). Rationality in everyday talk: From process to system. In J. Svartvik (Ed.), *Directions in corpus linguistics: Proceedings of Nobel symposium 82.* Berlin: Mouton de Gruyter.

———. (1999). Speaking with reference to context. In M. Ghadessy (Ed.), *Text & context in functional linguistics.* Amsterdam: Benjamins.

———. (2000). The uses of talk. In S. Sarangi, & M. Coulthard (Eds.), *Discourse and social life*. London: Longman.

Hasan, R., & Cloran, C. (1990). A sociolinguistic study of everyday talk between mothers and children. In M. Halliday, J. Gibbons, & N. Howard (Eds.), *Learning, keeping and using language: Vol. I*. Amsterdam: Benjamins.

Leech, G. (1987). *Meaning and the English verb*. London: Longman.

Mercer, N. (1993). *The guided construction of knowledge: Talk among teachers and learners*. Adelaide: Multilingual Matters.

Painter, C. (1984). *Into the mother tongue: A case study in early language development*. London: Pinter.

———. (1985). *Learning the mother tongue*. Geelong, VIC: Deakin University Press.

Popper, K. (1979). *Objective knowledge: An evolutionary approach*. Oxford: Oxford University Press.

Quirk, R., Leech, G., & Svartvik, J. (1985). *A comprehensive grammar of the English language*. London: Longman.

Sinclair, J. McH., & Coulthard, M. (1975). *The English the teachers speak*. Oxford: Oxford University Press.

Torr, J. (1997). *From child tongue to mother tongue: A case study of language development in the first two and a half years*. Monograph in Systemic Linguistics, No. 9. Nottingham, England: Department of English Studies, University of Nottingham.

Vygotsky, L. (1978). *Mind in society: The development of higher psychological processes*. Ed. M. Cole, V. John-Steiner, S. Scribner, & E. Souberman. Cambridge, MA: Harvard University Press.

Whorf, B. L. (1956). The relation of habitual thought and behaviour to language. In J. B. Carroll (Ed.), *Language, thought and reality*. Cambridge, MA: MIT Press.

Williams, G. (1995). *Joint book-reading and literacy pedagogy: A socio-semantic interpretation*. Ph.D. dissertation, School of English, Linguistics and Media, Macquarie University, Sydney.

PART 2

Pedagogic Discourse and Curriculum Organization

Chapter 3
Subject, Power, and Pedagogic Discourse

Mario Diaz

Introduction

People usually think of subjects as normal, conscious, and autonomous individuals, able to think, perceive, and behave by themselves or in interaction within social groups. This version of the subject is due to the heavily philosophical influence that, to some extent, has become the stereotypical view of human beings as individuals with a coherent, stable, unique, or unified identity. However, understanding subjects and subjectivity implies reflection on their political, social, and cultural foundations and positioning within different orders of meanings. This chapter analyses the importance of Bernstein's contribution to a social theory of the subject, providing an introduction to his analysis of difference, boundaries, power, language, and contexts which, from my point of view, reveals his complex nexus with structuralism and post-structuralism which, together with proto-structuralism and functionalism, are the major foundations of his theoretical developments.

Bernstein's Program

Bernstein's program can be seen as a search for a system of rules, which regulate relations between the external configurations of power (boundaries, classifications, and distributions) and the internally shaped means of recognition and realisation of such configurations as a semiotic system. Bernstein criticised the isolated, radical thought in British sociology of education. His assumptions about power, knowledge, and social experience, which led him to see social positioning through meanings as inseparable from power relations, have offered one of the most significant perspectives in recent times for analysis of the intellectual field of education. These assumptions are derived from the narratives of Durkheim, Marx, Weber, Mead, Parsons, Vygotsky, Bourdieu, and Foucault, amongst others, and bring together different perspectives, including functionalism, structuralism, Marxism, and post-structuralism, which were, at one time, regarded as simply contradictory. Bernstein's program contains and utilises these contradictions in what may be termed his semiotics or the semiotics of his model. This offers an extraordinary synthesis of major positions concerned with internal structures and principles and objectivist views that emphasise the role of social contexts and symbolic systems in the constitution of subjectivity and identity. Bernstein cuts across paradigmatic positions in his concern with how society is inscribed within the individual and how what is written becomes a grammar for society. For this reason, his writing was in permanent displacement and reconstruction and his model has potential for deconstruction.

Working at both micro and macro levels, Bernstein provided a model for the understanding of how social class and power distribution become internally shaped means of recognition and cognition. The logic intrinsic in this position is neither mechanic nor deterministic. What Bernstein saw as mediating these relations was a semiotic device that implies a socially produced potential of meanings, contexts of internalisation, and unequally distributed realisations.

We cannot understand the complex tasks of the semiotic process constituting the subject and subject positions in Bernstein without considering structured and structuring relations such as power-subject, subject-meanings, subject-code, and subject-pedagogic discourse. These involve problematic relations with the logic of post-modern modes of production and reproduction (Castells, 1996, 1997).

Power, Boundaries, and the Subject

Bernstein holds a relational notion of power. At different levels, power is inseparable from physical and symbolic boundaries of experience, meanings, and the contexts of interaction in which realisations of meanings take place. Boundaries provide possibilities, potential space for power positions, oppositions, and strategies. Boundaries are the object of struggles between unequal power positions. Boundaries create fields of struggle, a whole geography of positions. In essence, boundaries are the critical point for definitions of knowledge and practice, as well as for the subject. The more the boundaries, the more the distribution of unequal spaces and the more the distribution of inequalities between positions, discourses, and practices. Thus, there is a close relation in Bernstein between boundaries, power, social groups, and forms of identity. Bernstein's analysis of power and boundaries provokes questions about their force, duration of spacing, ordering of internal forms and sites for knowledge, flows of identity, and relations with changes in the collective basis of society. To what extent, under conditions of post-modernity, do boundaries become fluid, leading to a repositioning of power and identity?

What is the *locus* for the subject in this view? There is no explicit theory of subject in Bernstein. However, this category runs parallel to social structure and power relations and is a consequence of the principle of identity. The incorporation of power in subject production has an important meaning for the constitution of external and internal symbolic boundaries within and between subjects. The external symbolic order is to individuals the means for production within them of internal cultural and social structures. At the same time, this internal order is the means, perhaps the regulative principle, for constituting the principle of identity.[1]

The de-centring of subjects in Bernstein's theory is defined in relation to different categories of which class is the foremost. Class regulates the distribution of power, knowledge, and forms of consciousness. It reveals the extent to which new structures of power structure positions and identities. Class, in itself, is a principle of organization/disorganization of identity whose realisation Bernstein explores in the conflict arena between production and symbolic control. This arena becomes the complex space for the flows of differentiating pressures on identities. Through these flows, class becomes identity and identity the means of both legitimising and opposing class.

Power is the second most important category, introducing the possibility of understanding external and internal breaks, external and internal gaps. Within subjects, power regulates the principles of their relations to other subjects and objects. This means that power is external but also internal and unconscious to the individual.[2] For Bernstein, power is a force that structures spaces, relations, and positions. However, the mapping of power, in this view, demands different moves along the boundaries between categories and practices. The main feature of power in Bernstein is the structuring of a space whose limits make possible the legitimising of its purity, identity, and voice.

The third category is code, an unconscious principle internal to the individual. We could argue that the individual is subjected to the code that regulates meanings, realisations, and contexts. Code regulates structures but is not itself a structure, and provides a means for understanding the relations between the external and the internal to the subject, body, space, form, and content. Codes trace the dialectical forms of recognition and realisation.

Discourse (or discursive practice) is the final category used by Bernstein in explicating the de-centring of subjects. Discourse is a crucial field for struggles, territorialising and deterritorialising meanings and their realisations. Discourse is not words but structured/structuring devices for positioning subjects.

These four categories, class, power, code, and discourse, bring together the most important aspects of Bernstein's theory. His own discussion of these related/relational categories drew attention to crucial problems of de-centring of subject positions. Bernstein was always interested in the demonstration of the grammar of de-centring[3] present in these categories. He paid considerable attention to Foucault's arguments on discourse and power, to the horizontal and vertical structures produced by class relations, and to the semiotic operational mode of code. He interrogated and modelled the centring and de-centring economy of this grammar at the most abstract level of thought.

Power, Subjects, and Voice

It seems that the subject is constituted, for Bernstein, in the articulation voice-message. However, in understanding the dialectical relations between objective and subjective power, we need to understand that the de-centring of subjects in Bernstein is more than the relation voice-message. It is mediated by the code that articulates the voice in the message and introduces relational conditions for knowledge and practice. Power is a means of constitution of voice in the multidimensional set of social relations or social games that both integrate and fragment. These social relationships take place in contexts where the interests of "individuals" give rise to conscious actions and interactions, full of strategies. This is a crucial problem for the understanding of subject positions because voice becomes dispersed throughout the range of social practices and messages. In other words, practices and messages have to do with concrete events dispersed in space and time, however inscribed in the voice.

Voice is a semiotic category that introduces a symbolic dimension to the conception of subject. Voice is an expression of power but unmasks power in its realisations in various fields and contexts of practice. This means that power is hidden behind voice, behind discourse. Through the development of the notion of voice, Bernstein questions the supposed unity of the subject with an independent and individual consciousness. For Bernstein, the conditions for experience are not experience itself but the limits that locate or position individual experiences in fields of meanings and practices. This theoretical formulation requires description of the ways power is inscribed in the subject and realised through voice. We assume that these ways are, to some extent, the means of recognition of boundaries present in meanings and contexts.

Voice is a means of understanding the fracture between conscious practice and its regulative principle and belongs to the field of subjectivity. It emerges from social positions and boundary acquisitions within culture but also from the ruptures, discontinuities, and gaps inherent in such positioning, oppositioning, and transgressing. Here we can juxtapose Bernstein's fundamental issues of power and voice with the post-structuralist perspective. As Foucault (1977a, 1977b) noted, limits and transgressions are interdependent. In this view, it is possible to treat voice in terms of a dialectical relation between position and opposition in boundaries.

Thus, subject becomes a symbolic space for the realisation of power positions that fragment voice into voices internal to the individual. In opposition to individual unity and freedom, Bernstein thinks of a subject as limited by what power establishes in actual voices. Voice is, in this sense, difference, is identity. Power is translated into voice, voice is translated into difference, and difference creates identity. But the translation is not mechanical; it is realised through the fracturing, dispersing, and fragmenting of voice. The voice is, then, the living condition of power within the limits structured in and experienced by the subject.[4] This reminds us of Derrida's (1972) language on margins when he discusses the play of limits and its relation to voice and relates the "inner border" to its implied "outer border". From this view, we can understand Bernstein's thinking on the structuring power of the voice, that is, that instead of being the natural centre or *locus* of identity, voice is a function of identity. This means that voice, as power and discourse, is a field of multiple formations and transformations.

The Subject and Meanings

The subject in Bernstein is social. Subject is socially constituted in meanings and these are specific cultural orders produced on the basis of differential arrangements or differential distributions. Meanings create differences, that is, they create and reproduce unequal relations. This means that, in addition to the material, the symbolic supports of class and power relations, are meanings. Meanings not only serve as relays for communication and interaction but also for investing power and class relations in subjects and positions.

The constructed concept of subject cannot be isolated from categories of meanings. The subject in Bernstein is not an abstract founding category of meaning. It is not the Cartesian subject support of truth. Meanings are explicitly bound to subject constitution or production. The subject is produced by the setting of differences, oppositions, and locations, displacements and substitutions through which meanings are also produced. From this point of view, intrinsic to Bernstein's argument is the point that it is not the subject that produces meanings (the paradox of evidence in the Cartesian subject) but meanings that produce subjects. The subject becomes, in this view, a space for meaning realisations, and the meanings become spaces for subject positions. The circularity in this statement reminds us of the dialectical relations between objective structuring structures and the internal or subjective structured and structuring codes that regulate practices.

Bernstein's arguments implicitly position him in a structuralist perspective. For him, neither meanings nor the subject are *a priori* categories. They are structured in the positions-oppositions created by power relations. From this point of view, the subject and the meanings exist in a play of differences within and between spaces (fields and contexts). This view is not deterministic at all. The boundaries set by symbolic spaces can be opposed, rejected, and changed in time and space. These transformations are neither the correlate nor the product of original experiences. On the contrary, experience, even if it is viewed as original, is set by exclusions, limitations, oppositions, and distributions in a paradigmatic form.

A more interesting way of explaining Bernstein's position is to say that the subject is an inscription in the discontinuity of meanings drawn from oppositions within and between fields. The subject in Bernstein speaks, realises the voice, from a position such that there are no absolute meanings. A positioning in meanings is always a relational positioning which can be structured and deconstructed. Different symbolic positions arising from power relations are constitutive, consciously or unconsciously, of different forms of subjectivity.

Although positioning in and orientation to meanings involve a plurality of practices, the fundamental positioning takes place in the process of acquisition of culture and language, called socialization by Bernstein (1977). If in 1971, Bernstein saw objective positions as determinants of an orientation, in 1981, in the "Codes, Modalities" paper, he reconsidered this view and said that subject positioning can be deployed in the social relations created within the subject. He defines the code as being responsible for the structuring of social relations within the subject in terms of tacit and unconscious practices.

When dealing with meanings, Bernstein characterises their relational nature, the difference and the hierarchies between them. Meanings become structured both by the space created by the displacement of boundaries and by the relations this space generates between opposed orientations.

Subjects and Code

The most important explanatory principle of subject and meaning in Bernstein is the code. Understanding code involves analysis of meanings, contexts, and texts mediated through rules, principles, and values. Code allows us to understand relations between cognition/recognition and social practices. Two questions arise concerning Bernstein's views of the relation between codes and subjects. First, is code a principle external to the subject? If there is a theory of subjects in Bernstein, it involves the critical question of codes, but the more interesting problem is their constituting role in the formation of subjectivity and its forms of realisation. Code is also responsible for orientation to knowledge but is irreducible to internal subjective process. Second, in relation to codes, what is the space for subjects? Code is a critical point between the objective, unequal distribution of discourses, practices, and relations and the internal subjective processes of their recognition and realisation. Code rules act on subjects' orientations but are not the means of their subjection; rather, code principles determine, to some extent, boundaries between meanings to which subjects are oriented.

It is clear that Bernstein's interest in codes brings out the fundamental issue of the constitution of the subject. His work is a critical social analysis of monological positions. Codes give an account of the system of differences and similarities between subject positions and of the limits on orientations to positions and meanings. Codes and code modalities are responsible for the constitution of meaning, subjectivity, and identity. With the development of the theory of codes, Bernstein rejects the idea that meaning or language is the simple expression of a speaking subject. From this point of view, cognition is not a natural condition of subjects. Cognition is a social and culturally structured process in the fields of power.

If we assume Bernstein's position on this, we can argue that codes and code modalities are not only the means of knowledge but also the means of power. In terms of knowledge, codes set the limits to experience. Codes encode limits and boundaries of contents. They have paradigmatic and syntagmatic dimensions that act upon the system of meanings. In terms of power, codes legitimate boundaries, positions, and oppositions. This means that neither in the subject nor in society are there natural boundaries. If boundaries become a naturalised reality and are perceived as such, this is the effect of misrecognition produced by the code. This is the way to produce positions, oppositions, and displacements from which subjects act and realise their practices. Bernstein explains this process when saying that

> Codes are positioning devices culturally determined [...] class regulated codes position subjects with respect to dominant and dominated forms of communication [...] Ideology is constituted through this positioning process [...] Ideology is not a content but a form of relation between contents. (Bernstein, 1981, p. 2)

As we can see, the subject problem in Bernstein underlies the relations between codes and ideology. Codes set the means for the constitution of subject into meanings, and ideology is a structural grammar of relations between meanings. Although I do not go beyond this formulation here I will try to formulate some assumptions about these two notions.

Codes are very complex devices that operate to regulate subject practices at the reproduction and acquisition levels. At the reproduction level, code principles of classification and framing are concerned with the constitution of identities through demarcations, separations, and gaps between categories. Classification and framing principles create spaces for struggles over identities. At the production level, codes produce a system of differential relations (positions or distributions and oppositions) between categories and practices which can be found in different fields, such as production, education, culture, and agencies such as family, school, community, and region. Fields and agencies consist of spaces of relative positions that can be described in terms of forces that act upon their members to produce interactions mediated by power relations. Fields and agencies are regulated by code matrices characterised by oppositions, distributions, associations, contiguities, and interdependencies. The homological character of distributions allows correlation between different categories so that, for example, a distribution of agents will correlate with a distribution of agencies. Underlying these correlations we may discern a paradigmatic law.

At the reproduction level, code principles of classification and framing are concerned with the constitution of identities through demarcations, separations, and gaps between categories. At the acquisition level, codes are concerned with tacit and unconscious principles regulating practices. The acquisition level generates an indefinite variety of processes that have nothing to do with intentions but much to do with code regulations. At the acquisition level, there is no "pure knowing subject"; internalisation of meanings depends on what we may call the anatomy of code, that is, recognition and realisation rules. These rules are at the margins of conscious practice and invisible but they regulate and generate visible and intelligible practices. The regulating effect of rules and principles of conscious practices may differ from the effect of tacit and unconscious practices that are part of what I call "the shadow zone" in Bernstein's model, which can be considered a condition for the production of regularities in practices and texts. It also could be considered both a principle of production and a principle of subversion of those regularities because, unconscious as a level of operation of the semiotic grammar of the code (the same rules and principles), it becomes a semiotic means of displacement or dislocation. Being the fundamental space for the generation of conflict and struggles within the subject, the force of the unconscious is a condition that rules and regulates acquisition through tacit practice. The value of principles intrinsic to tacit practice may be related to the visible and invisible potential realisation of codes, that is, code modalities. This is the reason for saying that acquisition (internalisation) cannot be separated either from external boundaries regulating meanings or from the semiotic conditions which unconsciously dominate the potential forms of conflict, opposition to, and change in pedagogical penetration of the social.

To some extent, I could argue, Bernstein's question about the *locus* of subject presupposes an analysis of theories of the unconscious. I will not consider here these theories, though the presence of the unconscious in Bernstein is a preliminary contribution to the analysis of the device for the deployment of discursive practices. In this view, we cannot imagine a unitary subject but only a subject where exclusion is inclusion, and vice versa, articulating the division between legitimate and excluded, or dominant and dominated positions.

What, then, are the boundaries between tacit or unconscious practice and actual practices? We can think of this problem in terms of space. There is a fundamental space that creates tensions, contradictions, oppositions, and transformations between tacit/unconscious and actual practice. This space is far from actual practice but acts upon this practice. It is a strategic space for acquisition, rejection, and transformation. This means that even if at the actual practice level, the subject seems to be the *locus* of concrete, arbitrary, and contingent practices, that is, of opposition, strategies, and tactics, practice itself becomes regulated according to the limits, principles, and rules created for its generation. From this view, the subject depends upon the modality of code produced in the tensions between invisible principles and rules and visible practices. We could argue that here Bernstein is near to Foucault when he sees the relation between practices and rules in terms of a space (code modalities) in which social relations determine and do not determine what can and cannot be a legitimate text.[5]

Subjects and Pedagogic Discourse

Pedagogic discourse is the most interesting reconceptualisation by Bernstein of his own theory. Pedagogic discourse is the complex device that encapsulates the different regions in the mapping of his model. Stepping over from language, much of Bernstein's work over years was an attempt to make legible and explicit the logic intrinsic to reproduction. While in his early work he explored the surface features of reproduction through the study of language and education in agencies like family, school, and work, he later shifted his attention to the limits of language embedded in the logic of codes. The study of codes, which became his major preoccupation, opened the possibility of delving into the grammar of power and reproduction. This preoccupation drove his searches around discourse and, more explicitly, pedagogic discourse. To some extent, the complexity of his model became a means for developing a new picture of the reproduction of vertical and horizontal social structures.

The structuring of pedagogic discourse is, perhaps, Bernstein's most important theoretical contribution, decisive for the understanding of the dialectic between power, knowledge, and the subject. I am not interested in describing the proto-model of pedagogic discourse. My aim is basically to understand the network of relations underlying Bernstein's theory and model of pedagogic discourse and its realisations within subjects. According to Bernstein, earlier work on discourse and power provided neither a methodological language nor a model of thought for the discursive means of reproduction of power, culture, and class within the individual, through education. He argued that critical hegemonic discourses, such as those of Althusser, Gramsci, and Poulantzas, treated education in terms of the pathologies it generates. The language of their descriptions limited the discussion of fundamental issues of education as a device for production, reproduction, and transformation of identity. It is in Foucault[6] that Bernstein found a primary model for understanding and developing a model of pedagogic discourse. However, he did not totally agree with Foucault. In Bernstein's view, Foucault's discourse is "a discourse without social relations". This extreme position makes it difficult to establish a more explicit articulation between these two authors.[7] Whatever Foucault's exact influence over him was, Bernstein drew upon Foucault's ideas in providing us with the most elaborate effort available in search of the language of the pedagogic device and of pedagogic discourse, including the isolation of their specific rules, presenting them as a means to model knowledge, practice, and subjectivity. In analysing the structure of pedagogic discourse, he also examined its structuring power.

For Bernstein, pedagogic discourse is not related to the autonomous production of meanings but is a means to effect meanings or discursive practice, a device for generating "the meant" in the very logic of social relations or interactions. Pedagogic discourse is only a juncture, a principle in which power and discourse meet to regulate the "meant". For Bernstein, it is a semiotic in which discourse itself is not pure. Social, cultural, political, and economic relations are intrinsic to it, or at its margins. This means that discourse is not only a discourse but also a principle for controlling, selecting, organizing, and distributing discourses.

What mediates between the subject and pedagogic discourse? This is a crucial question for socio-cultural theory. When reading Bernstein we sometimes assume an overlap between the production of discourse and the production of subjectivity. There is a dialectic relationship that permits the generation of the subject in discourse but also discourse in the subject. In this respect, Foucault states that to know is to exercise the power of subjection; Bernstein would agree with this, referring to positioning devices and adding that to know is to exercise not only the power of subjectivity but also power over subjection. Both discourse and subject are spaces for power, but the dialectical view of the relations between these categories makes it possible for Bernstein to state that pedagogic discourse accounts for the existence of field of discourse and multidimensional social relations.[8] In Bernstein, these social relations are the material substratum for the incorporation of an individual subject into the social space of discourses and practices.

The dialectical relation between discourse and subject makes it possible to think of pedagogic discourse as a semiotic means that regulates or traces the generation of subject positions in discourse. The transformation of a discourse (or of a field of discourse) into new discourses (which in turn generate new discursive positions) is linked to a complex set of decontextualising and recontextualising rules. These transformations, regulated from outside discourse, affect its very nature and commonly take the form of a new production, creation, or social relation.

Bernstein (1981) explored pedagogic discourse not from the point of view of content or as an isolated set of meanings but from the point of view of generating and regulating principles and rules. It is a principle for appropriating other discourses and bringing them together in a special relation. Pedagogic discourse is also a principle for "creating imaginary subjects", so that the subject of knowledge in Bernstein can be considered to be a subject displaced in knowledge. This is the function of the pedagogic modalities of code: to produce subjects of knowledge, social (collective?) subjects able to deal with social structures and practices as individual subjects. Subjects become a relational space for practices.

Final Comments: The De-Centred Subject in Bernstein

The social and the individual are present in Bernstein's description of the subject. His analysis of codes and further development of pedagogic discourse inspired him to think of the subject as a de-centred category of self-determining positions and perspectives. In Bernstein, codes or, more specifically, code modalities, are a means for the constitution of relational subjects. Codes affect or act upon symbolic structures and produce, in specific context, meaning matrices in which and through which subjects recognise and realise their practices. Recognition marks the limits and space of realisation. The invisibility of power embedded in recognition is made visible in its realisation in interactional practices.

I agree with Bernstein that the basic empirical and conceptual unit of his work is not an individual subject but a relationship, a pedagogic relationship through which a subject emerges. Thus, the subject is contingent on the pedagogic relation, while the consequence of the pedagogic relation is contingent on the response of the subject to that relation. If we regard the pedagogic relation as a symbolic space for constitution, reproduction, and transformation, the subject is a potential of that space.

This directs attention to the regulation of multiple pedagogic relations and forms of constituting pedagogic subjects, and draws attention to the relational logic of pedagogic discourse and its modes of production and reproduction. If we think of the pedagogic device as a semiotic grammar able to act upon the universe of potential meanings in society and to produce pedagogic identities in different contexts, we can understand the potency of pedagogic discourse in selectively producing subjects and their identities in a temporal and spatial dimension. The semiotic grammar can describe spatial and temporal demarcations, displacements, and transformations of the modes of relational positioning of subjects within discourse and practices. We are here touching a crucial theoretical and methodological problem concerning the grammar of pedagogic discourse, especially its ability to condition and regulate multiple spatio-temporal fields and to be restructured by the multiple discontinuities and variations of the political economy of discourse and practice. How, for example, should we read the forms of dissemination and effects of power produced by the neo-liberal discourse of technology? Is what we might call "the will to virtuality" a new realisation of relations, boundaries, discourses, voices, and practice generated by the pedagogic device which has brought new ways of production, transmission, and acquisition of knowledge? Or is the virtual technological assemblage a revolution "with the potential to deconstruct" the pedagogic device? A way to understand the dialectics between the device and its realisations is to search for the multiplicity of dimensions in the relations between the structuring structures of the semiotic grammar of the device and the potential for conflicts in their realisations. Thus, the imaginary effect on the autonomous realisations of the rules of the device is post-modern deconstruction and flow which, in turn, seem to offer powerful recontextualising means for reproduction. *Plus ça change, plus c'est la même chose.*

Notes

1. Bernstein's perspective is more concerned with the means of production of subjectivity, that is, pedagogic relations. The developments of his model, especially those detailed in "Codes, Modalities and the Process of Cultural Reproduction: A Model" (1981), specify what permits the individual to realise meanings. This offers an account of the internalisation of the code and its classificatory and framing means through "recognition and realisation rules".

2. It is important to distinguish between "subject" and "individual". I agree with Lacan´s view. For Lacan, "individual" is related to the human animal, an organism which has characteristics different from those of other animals, and is able to apprehend the social world, to interact consciously with the external world, to adapt to his/her environment, and to be creative, autonomous. However, for Lacan, there is a factor that is not included in this description but that is opposed to all the purposes of the individual. This factor is the subject, that is, the unconscious (Lacan, 1977).

3. This interest was constantly reinforced in Bernstein's conversations with me.

4. To some extent, I accept the equation of identity and the classified space of a discursive practice. However, this relation is multidimensional. Different spaces for discursive practices cut across different identities.

5. Bernstein places strategies at the practice level. They emerge from practice. What is not clear is whether strategies are the breaking point between acquisition and reproduction and through this become a field of struggle between dominant and dominated positions. In the view presented here, strategies are also a space for struggles between what is internal and external to the subject. The argument is based on the assumption that if strategies appear at the level of actual practice as a means of subversion, they can also be considered as means of structuring positions in the structuring process of subjects. Strategies are forces included in practices, that is, forces for positioning (impositioning or dispositioning) but also forces for oppositioning. From this point of view, code modalities are not just means for regulating practices. They create spaces for acceptance but also for rejection. Let us take an example. It is common that what is not said is what is excluded in an interaction, in contrast to what is said. This "excluded in interaction" becomes excluded knowledge and a powerful means for controlling interaction.

6. Bernstein acknowledged the influence of Foucault in his approach to pedagogic discourse. However, Bernstein emphasised that his point of view was different from that of Foucault. While Bernstein attempted to totalise his form of analysis, Foucault avoided holistic and systematic forms of analysis. While Foucault's theoretical ensemble rested upon a historical (diachronic) view, Bernstein proceeded through synchronic analysis. Foucault described multiple devices of power; Bernstein was more interested in the semiotic grammar of power and its multiple realisations in social processes of interaction, communication, and reproduction. It was in the eighties that Foucault's

influence became deeper. For a study of the relations between Bernstein and Foucault, see Diaz (1984).

7. We can find in Foucault a basis for the generation of descriptive and analytic devices of power and control. What Foucault defines as "pastoral power" is an implicit allusion to the pedagogic device in education. *Discipline and Punish* (Foucault, 1977a) is another indirect reference to the pedagogisation of subjects through normalisation and individualisation. A last, informal reference made by Bernstein in a conversation with me, to the pedagogising of the subject through the pedagogising of human orifices, was very close to Foucault's embodiment of power in the subject: My only contact with the world is through the holes of my body. It is through them that myself is penetrated by the social norms of nature (Foucault, 1980).

8. Bernstein's development of this issue can be the object of misconceptions, leading us to the notion of the founding subject. I would argue that the subject's field in Bernstein (if we can think of subjectivity in terms of field or in terms of space) is neither original nor determined by the objective, originating experience of agents.

Bibliography

Bernstein, B. (1971). *Class, codes and control: Vol. I, Towards a sociology of language*. London: Routledge & Kegan Paul.

———. (1977). *Class, codes and control: Vol. III, Towards a theory of educational transmissions* (2nd ed.). London: Routledge & Kegan Paul.

———. (1981). Codes, modalities and the process of cultural reproduction: A model. *Anglo-American Studies*, *1* (1).

Castells, M. (1996). *The information age—Economy, society and culture: Vol. I, The rise of the network society*. Oxford: Blackwell.

———. (1997). *The information age—Economy, society and culture: Vol. II, The power of identity*. Oxford: Blackwell.

Derrida, J. (1972). *Marges de la philosophie*. Paris: Gallimard.

Diaz, M. (1984). *On pedagogic discourse. Bernstein and Foucault*. Unpublished manuscript: Institute of Education, University of London.

Foucault, M. (1977a). *Discipline and punish: The birth of the prison*. Harmondsworth, England: Penguin Books.

———. (1977b). *Language, counter-memory, practice*. New York: Ithaca.

———. (1980). *Power/knowledge: Selected interviews and other writings 1972–1977.* Brighton, England: Harvester Press. (Ed. by Colin Gordon).

Lacan, J. (1977). *Le seminaire: Livre II.* Paris: Seuil.

Olsson, G. (1991). *Lines of power/limits of language.* Minneapolis: University of Minnesota Press.

Chapter 4

Bernstein and Activity Theory

Harry Daniels

In this chapter I draw on two theoretical traditions: activity theory (Engestrom et al., 1999) and the work of Basil Bernstein (1981). The starting point in this discussion is the suggestion that in order to try and understand why people act in particular ways we should study thinking, feeling, and communication in the context of specific forms of institutional organisation and practice.

A central figure in the development of current theoretical accounts of the socio-genesis of individual consciousness is the Russian psychologist and semiotician L. S. Vygotsky. Wertsch (1985) suggests that Vygotsky's theoretical work can be understood in terms of reliance on a developmental method. Vygotsky claims that higher mental functioning in the individual has its origins in social life; that a full account of human mental functioning must be based on an understanding of the way in which psychological tools and signs act in the mediation of social factors. Here, psychological tools are those symbolic artefacts—signs, symbols, texts, formulae, graphic-symbolic devices—that help individuals master their own "natural" psychological functions such as perception, memory, and attention (after Kozulin, 1998).

Within this theoretical framework there is a requirement for a structural description of social settings which provides principles for distinguishing between social practices. Descriptions of this sort would be an important part of the apparatus required to carry out empirical investigation and analysis of the consequences of different forms of social organisation for individuals. However, description itself would not be enough. Vygotsky's writing on the way in which psychological tools and signs act in the mediation of social factors does not engage with a theoretical account of the appropriation and/or production of psychological tools within specific forms of activity within or across institutions.

The initial psychological studies of developing cognition tended to ignore the context or to provide an only very incomplete view of the relationship between context and cognition. The early cognitivist approach tended to exclude societal and cultural factors from its notion of context. The initial theorising in ecological psychology tended to focus on the description of settings and to ignore the relations between the persons acting and those settings (see Cole, 1996, for a discussion).

Recent times have witnessed a rapid growth in the number of approaches which attempt to investigate the development of cognition in context using non-deterministic, non-reductionist theories developed from the original Vygotskian thesis. Amongst these are cultural historical activity theory (Cole & Engestrom, 1993), socio-cultural approaches (Wertsch, 1991; Wertsch, Del Rio, & Alvarez, 1995), situated learning models (Lave, 1988), and distributed cognition approaches (Salomon, 1993). These all share the view that the theory developed by L. S. Vygotsky provides a valuable tool with which to interrogate and attempt to understand the processes of the social formation of mind (Daniels, 1996).

The essence of the developmental model advanced by Vygotsky is a dialectical conception of the relations between personal and social life. Specific social practices may be associated with modes of discourse and modes of personal thinking (Olson & Torrance, 1996). The key concept of "mediation" opens the way to a non-deterministic account in which "psychological tools" serve as the means by which the individual acts upon and is acted upon by social, cultural, and historical factors. Some approaches have tended to focus on semiotic means of mediation (Wertsch, 1991), whereas others have tended to focus more on activity itself (Engestrom et al., 1999).

In that the original theory and its subsequent developments seek to combine semiotic and activity-based accounts of the effects of the social on the individual, the potential for understanding cultural and social factors as they impact on individual understanding and learning is provided. However, a good deal of the post-Vygotskian research conducted in the West has focused exclusively on the effects of interaction at the interpersonal level, with insufficient attention paid to the form of collective social activity with specific forms of interpersonal communication interrelations between interpersonal and socio-cultural levels. "As a rule, the socio-institutional context of action is treated as a (largely unanalysed) dichotomised independent variable—or left to sociologists" (Cole, 1996, p. 340).

Davydov (1988) argues that Vygotsky saw the pathway of the formation of the individual consciousness as follows:

collective (social) activity taking
the form of interpersonal communication

I

culture

I

symbols

I

individual activity

I

individual consciousness

In his clarification of the distinction between collective aspects of activity and individual subjectivity, Davydov distinguishes between epistemological and psychological aspects of knowledge:

> in psychology one cannot talk about the determination of consciousness by activity and ignore the plane of the ideal (or the cultural) as a determinant of individual consciousness, one has to recall the super individuality of the ideal. (Davydov, 1995, p. 16)

Schooling constitutes a form of collective social activity with specific forms of interpersonal communication. Furthermore, within schools and between schools, there are differences in the content, structure, and function of interpersonal communication. In the most recent translation of chapter 6 of *Thinking and Speech* Vygotsky claims a particular function for speech in instruction within schooling:

> The instruction of the child in systems of scientific knowledge in school involves a unique form of communication in which the word assumes a function which is quite different from that characteristic of other forms of communication [...]
> (1) The child learns word meanings in certain forms of school instruction not as a means of communication but as part of a system of knowledge.
> (2) This learning occurs not through direct experience with things or phenomena but through other words. (Vygotsky, 1987, p. 27)

Participation in specific forms of social practice is linked in this way with the development of word meaning. In order to understand the development of word meaning, the characteristics of particular practices of communication must be understood. School effects may then be seen as the outcome of acts of cultural transmission. Lemke has applied this understanding to subject-specific practices within schooling:

> Social semiotics begins from a very simple principle: that all meaning is *made* by specific human social practices. When we say that the mastery of physics or literary criticism means being able to talk physics like a physicist or write analyses like a critic, we are talking about *making the meanings* of physics and literary criticism using the resources of spoken and written language. Talking physics and writing criticism are *social practices*. They are parts of larger social activities. They are learned socially, function socially, and are socially meaningful. Spoken and written language are social resources for making social meaning. And the specific *genres* and *semantic patterns* of physics, or of literary criticism, are institutionalised social formations, patterns of language *use*, and patterns of *deployment* of the social resources of language in particular communities and subcommittees. (Lemke, 1988, p. 82)

Wells (1993, 1994) has attempted to bring together theories of discourse with activity theory in the analysis of teaching and learning in the classroom. Bazerman (1988, 1994) extends the notion of "genre", beyond that of textual forms, to forms of life, ways of being, frames for social action in his attempt to theorise environments for learning and teaching. Both Bazerman and Wells provide extensions to the concept of genre as developed in Christie's (1985, 1993) formulation of curriculum genres. These studies contribute to the development of a theory of learning and discourse within the activity of schooling yet still do not provide a verifiable model of socio-institutional effects.

Researchers working from within both "situated learning" and "activity theory" approaches have expressed dissatisfaction with the lack of theoretical progress in this aspect of the field. Lave (1996) has suggested that "without a theoretical conception of the social world one cannot analyse activity *in situ*" (p. 7). Similarly, Axel has noted limitations within activity theory:

> Leonte'ev talks about an activity system not about social organisations and formations. His combination of social theory and psychology remains too abstract and is only rudimentarily and inconsistently developed. (Axel, 1997, p. 140)

These post-Vygotskian developments have not, as yet, realised some of the goals sketched in the original thesis.

Although he did not develop an appropriate methodology, Vygotsky attached the greatest importance to the school itself as an institution. His particular interest lay in the structuring of time and space and the related system of social relations between the pupils and the teacher, between the pupils themselves, between the school and its surroundings, and so on (Ivic, 1989). In their overview of current thinking that claims a Vygotskian root, Minick, Stone, and Forman (1993) argue that the culturally specific nature of schools demands close attention to the way in which they structure interactions between people and artefacts such as books. They also emphasise the need to focus on the ways that actors interact with one another in particular educational contexts:

> educationally significant human interactions do not involve abstract bearers of cognitive structures but real people who develop a variety of interpersonal relationships with one another in the course of their shared activity in a given institutional context. [...] modes of thinking evolve as integral systems of motives, goals, values, and beliefs that are closely tied to concrete forms of social practice. (Minick, Stone, & Forman, 1993, p. 6)

Their use of the term "in a given institutional context" implies that differences between institutional contexts may be of significance though this suggestion seems to be both under-theorised and under-investigated. For example, in a discussion of recontextualisation of everyday activities within schooling, Saljo and Wyndhamn state that

> institutions of formal learning have established themselves as yet another "system of activity" which to a certain extent has developed autonomous rules and traditions for communication and for the definition of phenomena such as learning and competence. (Saljo & Wyndhamn, 1996, p. 328)

They appear to suggest that schooling is a generic activity, as if it is a social institution which is uniform in its psychological effects. However, it is highly likely that within schools and between schools there are differences in the content, structure, and function of interpersonal communication. There is a need to articulate the different modalities of pedagogic practice within an activity theory framework and investigate the relation between these modalities and the forms of communicative competence that are regarded as appropriate.

Cole, Engestrom, and Vasquez (1997) develop Engestrom's suggestion that activity systems contain a variety of different viewpoints or "voices", as well as layers of historically accumulated artefacts, rules, and patterns of division of labour. They argue that the multivoiced and multilayered nature of activity systems is both a resource for collective achievement and a source of compartmentalisation and conflict. Contradictions are seen as the engine of change and development in an activity system as well as being seen as a source of conflict and stress. Thus, an analysis of power and control must be brought into an activity theory framework.

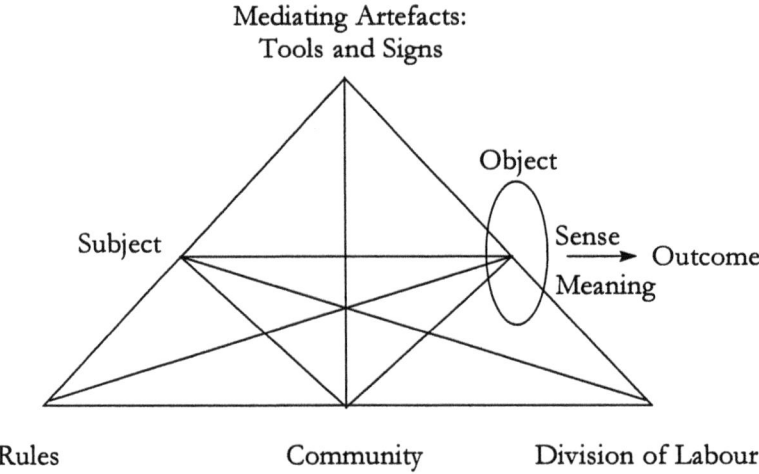

Figure 4.1—*The structure of a human activity system.*

Engestrom opens the way for such a development in his expansion of the basic Vygotskian mediational triangle (subject, tools, object → outcome) to include other people (community), social rules (rules), and the division of labour between the subject and others (Cole & Engestrom, 1993, p. 8).

In the model (Figure 4.1), the subject refers to the individual or sub-group whose agency is chosen as the point of view in the analysis. The object refers to the "raw material" or "problem space" at which the activity is directed and which is moulded and transformed into outcomes with the help of physical and symbolic, external and internal mediating instruments, including both tools and signs. The community comprises multiple individuals and/or sub-groups who share the same general object and who construct themselves as distinct from other communities. The division of labour refers to both the horizontal division of tasks between the members of the community and to the vertical division of power and status. Finally, the rules refer to the explicit and implicit regulations, norms, and conventions that constrain actions and interactions within the activity system.

Engestrom's work can be said to establish the need for a theory of activity which permits the structure of local discourses to be theorised in relation to rules, community, and division of labour. This is not explicitly stated as a developmental need within the theoretical framework. Tudge and Winterhoff argue that

> Meanings, tools and goals all necessarily relate the individual and the social world of which the individual is part, for they are all formed in socio-cultural context. Understanding the use of tools (psychological or physical) is jointly constructed by the developing child and by the culture in which the child is developing, with the assistance of those who are already more competent in the use of those tools and in culturally appropriate goals. These units of analysis therefore integrate the micro-social contexts of interaction with the broader social, cultural and historical contexts that encompass them. (Tudge & Winterhoff, 1993, p. 67).

Bernstein (1993, pp. xix–xx) seeks to link semiotic tools with the structure of material activity. Crucially, he draws attention to the processes which regulate the structure of the tool rather than just its function.

Once attention is given to the regulation of the structure of pedagogic discourse, the social relations of its production, and the various modes of its recontextualising as a practice, then perhaps we may be a little nearer to understanding the Vygotskian tool as a social and historical construction.

Bernstein also argues that much of the work that has followed in the wake of Vygotsky "does not include in its description how the discourse itself is constituted and recontextualised":

> The socio-historical level of the theory is, in fact, the history of the biases of the culture with respect to its production, reproduction, modes of acquisition and their social relations. (Bernstein, 1993, p. xviii)

In Engestrom's work, the production of the outcome is discussed but not the production and structure of the tool itself. The failure of activity theorists to identify the concrete social organisation of activity can be traced all the way back to Vygotsky and Luria. For all their stated emphasis on the socio-historical nature of psychology, Vygotsky and Luria did not consider the ways in which concrete social systems bear on psychological functions. They discussed the general importance of language and schooling for psychological functioning, but they failed to examine the real social systems in which these activities occur and are reflected (Ratner, 1997).

The most obvious source for this position is to be found in Vygotsky's "Experimental Study of Concept Formation". Here, Vygotsky argued that social life is important for the development of conceptual thinking in adolescence. However, instead of analysing the social demands and activities that occur during adolescence, he postulated that a new abstract use of words during adolescence generates concept formation:

> The feature that can be viewed as the proximal cause of the maturation of concepts, *is a specific way of using the word*, specifically the functional application of the sign as a means of forming concepts. (in Vygotsky, 1987, pp. 131, 160)

Vygotsky never indicated the social basis for this new use of words. His social analysis, thus, was reduced to a semiotic analysis which overlooked the real world of social praxis (Ratner, 1997).

While it is quite possible to interpret "a specific way of using the word" as an exhortation to analyse the activities in which the word is used and meaning is negotiated, this was not elaborated by Vygotsky himself. The analysis of the structure and function of semiotic psychological tools in specific activity contexts has not been undertaken within the activity theory approach.

Thus, the following issues may be regarded as points for development in contemporary post-Vygotskian theory and research:

1. insufficient empirical study of socio-institutional effects;

2. a tendency to under-theorise differences between schools in terms of institutional effects on the social formation of mind;

3. a tendency to focus either on the mediational function of semiotic means or on the activity;

4. the lack of a theory of the structure of psychological tools;

5. the lack of a theory of its own constitution and recontextualisation.

Bernstein's 1981 paper outlined a model for understanding the construction of pedagogic discourse. In this context, pedagogic discourse is a source of psychological tools:

> the basic idea was to view this [pedagogic] discourse as arising out of the action of a group of specialised agents operating in a specialised setting in terms of the interests, often competing interests of this setting. (Bernstein, 1981, p. 116)

This work was based on theoretical developments made in Bernstein's (1975) *Class, Codes and Control, Vol. III*, which focused on two levels: a structural level and an interactional level. The structural level was analysed in terms of the social division of labour it creates and the interactional in terms of the form of social relation it creates. The social division was analysed in terms of the strength of the boundary of its divisions, that is, with respect to the degree of specialisation. Thus the key concept at the structural level is the concept of boundary, and structures are distinguished in terms of their category relations. The interactional level of analysis focuses on the regulation of the transmission/acquisition relation between teacher and taught. It refers to the pedagogic context and the social relations of the classroom or its equivalent. The curriculum may then be analysed as an example of a social division of labour and pedagogic practice as its constituent social relations through which the specialisations of that social division (subjects, units of the curriculum) are transmitted and expected to be acquired. Power is manifested in category relations and control is the communicative realisation of these relations. Power is manifested in category relations which themselves generate recognition rules. Control is manifested in pedagogic communication governed by realisation rules:

> Recognition rules create the means of distinguishing between and so recognising the speciality that constitutes a context, and realisation rules regulate the creation and production of specialised relationships internal to that context. (Bernstein, 1981, pp. 328–329)

The distribution of power and principles of control differently specialise structural features and their pedagogic communicative relays.

Daniels (1989) utilised the distinction made by Bernstein (for a full discussion of which, see Bernstein, 1996) between instructional and regulative discourse. The former refers to the transmission of skills and their relation to each other and the latter refers to the principles of social order, relation, and identity. Whereas the principles and distinctive features of instructional discourse and its practice are relatively clear (the what and how of the specific skills/competences to be acquired and their relation to each other), the principles and distinctive features of the transmission of the regulative are less clear, as this discourse is transmitted through various media and may, indeed, be characterised as a diffuse transmission. Regulative discourse communicates the school's (or any institution's) public moral practice, values, beliefs, and attitudes, and principles of conduct, character, and manner. It also transmits features of the school's local history, local tradition, and community relations. Regulative discourse is transmitted essentially, but not wholly, through the following:

1. *symbolism and ritual*, for example, memorial plaques; ritual displays such as assemblies, entrance and exit practices; controls on movement and approaches to special places such as the head teacher's room, libraries, staff rooms, and so on;

2. *interaction*, for example, spoken or written communication concerned with establishing and maintaining principles and practices of expected conduct given usually by staff; and

3. *instruction*, for example, where regulative discourse has its own instructional discourse and its own specialist transmitters—special courses on social and life skills, sex education, and so on.

The form taken by instructional discourse in classroom practice itself contains important regulatory features. The more highly controlled the instructional discourse, the more likely it is that regulative discourse will be constituted by imperative and positional modes. Regulative discourse will be created through a more personal mode when learners have more control over instructional practice. The more implicit is the hierarchy, the more the control will inhere in interpersonal communication. Pedagogic discourse is a single discourse created by the embedding and interpenetration of instructional and regulative discourse. Both these aspects of pedagogic discourse may be described in terms of distribution of power and principles of control; a variety of pedagogic structures may be generated according to their organising principle, that is, in terms of their underlying code. The form of the code (its modality) contains principles for distinguishing between contexts (recognition rules) *and* for the creation and production of specialised communication within contexts (realisation rules). This model of pedagogic discourse provides a response to one of the many theoretical demands which have remained unmet in the post-Vygotskian framework. The rejection of the cognitive/affective dualism which Vygotsky announced was not followed by the construction of a model within which a unitary conception of thinking and feeling could be discussed and implemented in empirical research.

The language that Bernstein has developed allows researchers to take measures of school modality, that is, to describe and position the discursive, organisational, and interactional practice of the institution. The theory identifies measures of pupils' recognition and realisation rules which are themselves open to scrutiny. Research may then seek to investigate the connections between the rules the children use to make sense of their pedagogic world and the modality of that world.

In his last article, Bernstein (1999) moved his analysis to the internal principles of the construction and social base of pedagogic discourses. Having provided a theory of the construction of pedagogic discourse, he moved to an analysis of the discourses subject to pedagogic transformation. This move will be seen to be of particular significance when this body of theory and its language of description is brought to bear on the discussion of the relationship between everyday and scientific concepts as outlined in *Thinking and Speech*. The analysis outlined by Bernstein (1999) allows for greater differentiation within and between the forms identified by Vygotsky. The analytical power of the distinctions made between vertical and horizontal discourses and hierarchical and horizontal knowledge structures gives scholars an enhanced capacity to provide descriptions that capture the delicacy of the forms and their interrelation. This last article by Bernstein sets an important agenda for work in the future.

Bernstein provides an account of cultural transmission which is avowedly sociological in its conception. In turn, the psychological account that has developed in the wake of Vygotsky's writing offers a model of aspects of the social formation of mind which is underdeveloped in Bernstein's work. Taken together, these theoretical positions constitute important tools for research and theoretical development.

Bibliography

Axel, E. (1997). One developmental line in European activity theories. In M. Cole, Y. Engestrom, & O. Vasquez (Eds.), *Mind, culture and activity: Seminal papers from the laboratory of comparative human cognition*. Cambridge: Cambridge University Press.

Bazerman, C. (1988). *Shaping written knowledge: The genre and activity of the experimental article in science*. Madison: University of Wisconsin Press.

———. (1994). Systems of genres and the enactment of social intentions. In A. Freedman & P. Medway (Eds.), *Genre and the new rhetoric* (pp. 79–101). London: Taylor & Francis.

Bernstein, B. (1975). *Class, codes and control: Vol. III, Towards a theory of educational transmissions*. London: Routledge & Kegan Paul.

———. (1981). Codes, modalities and the process of cultural reproduction: A model. *Language and Society, 10,* 327–363.

———. (1993). Foreword. In H. Daniels (Ed.), *Charting the agenda: Educational activity after Vygotsky.* London: Routledge.

———. (1996). *Class, codes and control: Vol. V, Pedagogy, symbolic control and identity: Theory, research and critique*. London: Taylor & Francis.

———. (1999). Vertical and horizontal discourse: An essay. *British Journal of Sociology of Education, 20* (2), 157–173.

Christie, F. (1985). *Language education*. Geelong, Victoria, Australia: Deakin University Press.

———. (1993). Curriculum genres: Planning for effective teaching. In B. Cope & M. Kalantzi (Eds.), *The powers of literacy: A genre approach to teaching writing* (pp. 154–178). London: Falmer.

Cole, M. (1996). *Cultural psychology: A once and future discipline*. Cambridge, MA: Belknap Press of Harvard University Press.

Cole, M., & Engestrom, Y. (1993). A cultural-historical interpretation of distributed cognition. In G. Salomon (Ed.), *Distribute cognition: Psychological and educational considerations*. Cambridge: Cambridge University Press.

Cole, M., Engestrom, Y., & Vasquez, O. (1997). Introduction. In M. Cole, Y. Engestrom, & O. Vasquez (Eds.), *Mind, culture and activity: Seminal papers from the laboratory of comparative human cognition*. Cambridge: Cambridge University Press.

Daniels, H. (1989). Visual displays as tacit relays of the structure of pedagogic practice. *British Journal of Sociology of Education, 10* (2), 123–140.

———. (Ed.). (1996). *An introduction to Vygotsky*. London: Routledge.

Davydov, V. V. (1988). Problems of developmental teaching: The experience of theoretical and experimental psychological research. *Soviet Education, 30* (8), 3–87; (9), 3–56; (10), 2–42.

———. (1995). The influence of L. S. Vygotsky on education theory, research and practice. *Educational Researcher, 24* (3), 12–21.

Engestrom, Y., Meiettinen, R., & Punamaki, R. J. (1999). *Perspectives on activity theory.* Cambridge: Cambridge University Press.

Ivic, I. (1989). Profiles of educators: Lev S. Vygotsky (1896–1934). *Prospects, 19* (3).

Kozulin, A. (1998). *Psychological tools: A sociocultural approach to education.* London: Harvard University Press.

Lave, J. (1988). *Cognition in practice: Mind, mathematics and culture in everyday life.* Cambridge: Cambridge University Press.

―――. (1996). The practice of learning. In S. Chaiklin & J. Lave (Eds.), *Understanding practice: Perspectives on activity and practice.* Cambridge: Cambridge University Press.

Lemke, J. (1988). Genres, semantics and classroom education. *Linguistics and Education, 1*, 81–99.

Minick, N., Stone, C. A., & Forman, E. A. (1993). Introduction: Integration of individual, social and institutional processes in accounts of children's learning and development. In E.A. Forman, N. Minick, & C. A. Stone (Eds.), *Contexts for learning: Sociocultural dynamics in children's development.* Oxford: Oxford University Press.

Olson, D. R., & Torrance, N. (Eds.). (1996). *Modes of thought: Explorations in culture and cognition.* Cambridge: Cambridge University Press.

Ratner, C. (1997). *Cultural psychology and qualitative methodology: Theoretical and empirical considerations.* London: Plenum Press.

Saljo, R., & Wyndhamn, J. (1996). Solving everyday problems in the formal setting: An empirical study of the school as context for thought. In S. Chaiklin & J. Lave (Eds.), *Understanding practice: Perspectives on activity and context.* Cambridge: Cambridge University Press.

Salomon, G. (1993). *Distributed cognitions: Psychological and educational considerations.* Cambridge: Cambridge University Press.

Tudge, R. H., & Winterhoff, P. A. (1993). Vygotsky, Piaget and Bandura: Perspectives on the relations between the social world and cognitive development.. *Human Development, 36*, 61–81.

Vygotsky, L. S. (1987). *The collected works of L. S. Vygotsky: Vol. I, Problems of general psychology.* New York: Plenum Press.

Wells, G. (1993). Re-evaluating the IRF sequence: A proposal for the articulation of theories of activity and discourse for the analysis of teaching and learning in the classroom. *Linguistics and Education, 5*, 1–37.

———. (1994). The complementary contributions of Halliday and Vygotsky to a "language-based theory of learning". *Linguistics and Education, 6,* 41–90.

Wertsch, J. (1985). *Vygotsky and the social formation of mind.* Cambridge, MA: Harvard University Press.

———. (1991). *Voices of the mind: A socio-cultural approach to mediated action.* Cambridge, MA: Harvard University Press.

Wertsch, J. V., Del Rio, P., & Alvarez, A. (Eds.). (1995). *Socio-cultural studies of mind.* Cambridge: Cambridge University Press.

Chapter 5
The Teaching of Sociology: Towards a European Comparison of Curricula

Philippe Vitale

Introduction

Considerations of teaching content and academic courses, of their structure and modes of transmission, do not seem to provoke much interest among sociologists in French education. Such questions in this vein, initially raised by Durkheim's (1938/1969) *L'évolution Pédagogique en France*, tend to be identified with the British wave of the New Sociology of Education (NSE) which reached its apogee in the 1970s and seems to have finally vanished in 1988 with the publication of *Curriculum and Democracy* by M.F.D. Young, editor of its founding collection. Although I will not discuss here the merit of the critiques offered *a posteriori* by numerous sociologists regarding the fruitfulness of this movement, it would be unfortunate if I threw the baby out with the bath water by evading questions pertaining the types of knowledge being taught. In that spirit, this article asks a simple question: Why teach one thing in sociology rather than another?

It is a matter of irony that, while there is a sociology of the curriculum, there are few, if any, major studies of the curricula of sociology. While there are studies of changes in the orientation and organisation of knowledge, there are few, if any, major empirical sociological studies of the orientation or generating principles of the content of curricular knowledge. Following the line of research I initiated in my thesis (1999), I try to create a language which will enable recognition of the distinctive features of sociology as a teaching form, provide the means of comparing European sociological curricula, and explain their sources of difference.

Teaching Content and What Is at Stake

What could justify choosing sociology as the object of study rather than pursuing a comparison within economics, mathematics, or biology which would have avoided much of the classic empirical problem related to excessive closeness to one's study? In the beginning, my objective was to respond to one of Durkheim's (1895/1986) *Règles de la Méthode Sociologique*, which suggests that the most familiar universes are those in which we are most likely to hold preconceptions.[1] However, the choice was also related to other factors arising from both the historical and the geographic contexts within which the study is situated and from the particularity of the teaching structure of the discipline.

The 1990s, Europe, and sociology curricula

The decade of the 1990s was an eventful period in European education. In a climate of post-Maastricht European unity, we have witnessed growing instability in curricula and growing inquiry into the justification for what is taught and what is not. Such questioning, without being the object of real definition, has been regarded as indicating an education crisis. Nedelmann and Sztompka (1993) have contended that this may lead us towards a new golden age of sociology. While this may be presumptuous, we might well reflect upon the effects of the historical, geographical, and political contexts on sociology curricula.

Sociology instruction has not been spared this legitimating crisis, given the utilitarian discourse applied to education-employment relationships within the context of high unemployment. One can easily understand that sociology appears to be a suitable subject about which to generate heuristic questions on teaching content and the cultural stakes involved in different types of educational choices. What really deserves to be taught in sociology? Is it a question of making choices based on culture, politics, the views of ministers of education, and so on or, rather, a consequence of the micro-level singularities of each sociology department and professor?

These questions might seem superfluous in the light of the instrumentalism, the discourse of adaptation and temporary utility, that currently prevails. Nevertheless, according to Forquin, contemporary pedagogic thought cannot ignore examining the question of culture and the cultural stakes of different types of educational choices, without risking a fall into superficiality. [...] Shedding light today on the cultural foundations and implications of education, is without a doubt, a task that can only be approached in an indirect and fragmentary way, but which is, in any case, worth pursuing, since it has a justification of educational undertakings at stake. (Forquin, 1990, p. 8) [2]

Sociology instruction

While it is not my intention here to re-trace the history of sociology instruction, it is nevertheless important to remember that it entered the universities only relatively recently. In France, sociology courses are considered to have originated in 1887 in the Faculty of Arts of Bordeaux when the chair in Teaching and Social Science was awarded to Durkheim. The first master's degree in sociology was granted only in 1958.

The focus of this chapter is the current situation of sociology instruction in relation to the knowledge being imparted and the discipline's place in various European countries. The question is: How do we account for teaching choices in a sociology department? In answering, I shall demonstrate that a study of sociology curricula cannot go forward without an analysis of the discipline's teaching structure and language, the key characteristics of its organisation and knowledge selection.

The Structure of Sociology Instruction

In the eyes of many sociologists, the empirical output of the NSE suffered from theoretical and methodological deficiencies. For the purpose of this analysis, Bernstein's works appear to offer greater potential for the analysis of concrete curriculum studies, in particular those outlined below.

The two forms of knowledge and the curriculum

Bernstein distinguishes two types of knowledge associated with pedagogical discourse. The first form is horizontal discourse,

> The form of knowledge usually typified as everyday, oral or commonsense knowledge [which] has a group of features: local, segmental, context dependent, tacit,

multilayered, often contradictory across contexts but not within contexts. Today the objects of such knowledge are likely to be volatile and substitutable for each other. (Bernstein, 1996, pp. 170–171)

Bernstein contrasts this form of discourse with what he describes as vertical discourse, which

> takes the form of a coherent, explicit, systematically principled structure, hierarchically organised or it takes the form of a series of specialised languages with specialised modes of interrogation and specialised criteria for the production of texts. (Bernstein, 1996, p. 171)

This distinction between horizontal and vertical discourse bears the imprint of Durkheim's *L'évolution Pédagogique en France* (1938/1969) which refers to sacred and profane knowledge of the eighth-century monastic period.

Bernstein distinguishes two forms of vertical discourse. The first has a coherent, explicit character and a hierarchical, normative organisation of knowledge which approaches the model of the natural sciences. The second gives rise to a series of specialised languages, each possessing their own definitional criteria, such as are found in the social sciences and the humanities.

According to this distinction within vertical discourse, Bernstein distinguishes "hierarchical knowledge structures" and "horizontal knowledge structures". He takes the example of natural sciences and contrasts them with social sciences. One might question, at this point, the relevance of a natural sciences/social sciences contrast to a comparative study of sociology curricula. It is, however, through this contrast, which is comparable to the hard science/soft science relationship, that I attempt to mark out the characteristics of the structure of sociological instruction itself and carry out a concrete study of curricula on a European scale.

Instruction in natural sciences:
A type of hierarchical knowledge structure

The hierarchical knowledge structures that characterise the vertical discourse found in the natural sciences give rise, according to Bernstein, to teaching structures fundamentally tied to what he calls the integrated code. I will not elaborate on the natural sciences except to compare them with sociology. In science, hierarchical knowledge structures produce knowledge forms whose principle moves realisations towards more and more general propositions to generate knowledge both at a lower level and across an expanding range of apparently disparate phenomena. The natural sciences generate knowledge forms which aim to integrate a diverse range of apparently discrete phenomena in general propositions.

Horizontal structures of knowledge and serial codes: The sociology example

Horizontal knowledge structures are related to what Bernstein defines as *a serial code or collection code*.[3] They are particularly interesting in respect of the sociology curriculum. In searching for an ideal-type model, the sociology curriculum will initially be characterised fairly generally; subsequently, we will linger longer over the specific characteristics of this university discipline.

With very few exceptions, sociology as a form does not generate an integrated code but gives rise to a series or a collection of theories which are language specific. Each language possesses its own incomparable, descriptive principles which, nevertheless, often function by the "addition" of other languages. Passeron (1991) thinks it better to speak of "accumulation" than "cumulation" in the Mertonian sense. This problem of cumulation of languages does not present itself in the same way in some fields of sociology, such as electoral sociology or certain areas of the sociology of education.

Bernstein (1996) illustrates the concept of serial code with reference to sociology:

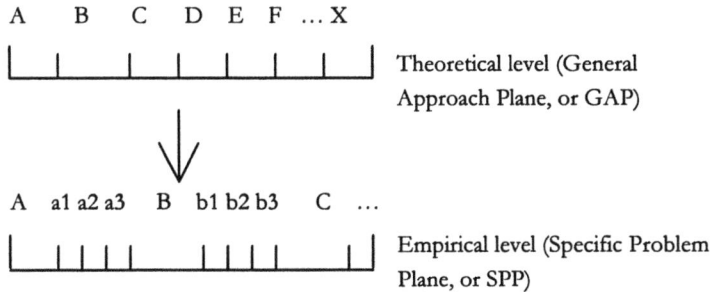

The letters A, B, C, D, and so on, refer to the different theoretical languages that are found in a sociology curriculum, such as ethnomethodology, structuralism, methodological individualism, and symbolic interactionism, and in general to their level of theoretical abstraction. This level consists of metalanguages which contain their own concepts and their own descriptive languages of the world, which legitimate the way in which a phenomenon must be understood, observed, and interpreted.

Bernstein refers to the second level as the Specific Problem Plane (SPP) consisting of empirical studies in a particular field of study, tied to the General Approach Plane (GAP). The GAP is segmented by different languages and the SPP by different problems and different languages. The important thing to specify is that Bernstein's classification concept marks the relational space between different categories. Indeed, the discourse series A, B, C, D, and so on, does not make sense except through the relationship of A to B, A to C, and so forth. From this perspective, one might ask what then justifies the strong classification and the isolation of different types of discourse and of different subjects. Bernstein suggests that the space between types of discourse creates their specialisation.

I hope not to misrepresent Bernstein in arguing that,

Sociology curriculum: $\{A = A \Leftrightarrow A \neq B, C, D \ldots X\}$

Where A is A (sociological discourse, a subject in a sociology curriculum), if, and only if, A cannot be related to B, C…(in relationship to other subjects) and if it can be different from B, C …

I must now make another distinction within the horizontal structure of knowledge itself which concerns what Bernstein calls the grammar of discourse, in specifying more delicately and subtly what constitutes the characteristics of sociology as a university discipline, in an attempt to describe an ideal-type curriculum.

The grammar of sociological discourse

The study of the grammar of discourse constitutes the most developed part of Bernstein's last works. Without getting into the details of Bernstein's analysis, classification, as we have already seen, refers to the "what" of transmission. While Bernstein's study of the communication of knowledge seems fundamental to me, I am only interested here in a minute part of this analysis which concerns the knowledge present in a curriculum at a given moment, the "what" rather than the "how" of the knowledge being taught in sociology, that is, classification, not framing.

In distinguishing between the different types of discourse presented in a horizontal structure of knowledge, Bernstein compares discourses endowed with a "strong grammar" to those with a "weak grammar". The terms "strong" and "weak" do not refer in Bernstein's work to any value judgement but to the degree of normativity of discourse that can be found in a curriculum. Bernstein defines discourse with a strong grammar as being explicit, endowed with a precise articulation of its concepts and procedures, such as can be found in linguistics or economics. Discourse with a weak grammar is characterised by rules with low levels of formalisation and explicit procedure, such as sociology and social anthropology. The distinction between strong grammar and weak grammar leads me to investigate the language of sociology and to consider the question raised by Ramognino (1998): *In which ways are the language structures borrowed by sociology different from those used in the hard sciences?*[4] Ramognino sees the question of "soft" and "hard" science, as being raised from the moment one describes theories. "Hard sciences", as a general rule, use a type of language that may be termed "formalisation": the construction of an object language which is not only supposed to be different from natural language but which, above all, serves as the vehicle of validation testing in vigorous and precise ways. Hard science, in fact, calls upon two types of language, in addition to experimental construction:

- a special language, in general formalised by mathematical propositions, with an internally defined standardised use which constitutes the object language of hard science disciplines. The object language can be called syntax within the framework of a logical system, a model, or can even be called a structure;

- a natural language that provides style to the formalisations and functions either as a metalanguage or as the object language.

According to Ramognino, what is striking at first glance in soft science, or at least in sociology, is that there is no clear-cut division between structure and style. One can use a specialised language or not—to take the place of the object language—but even in its texture, this "object language" is already a combination, different each time and in some ways random, of a formalised language or a "natural language", without any sort of clarification or any division between the two. The mixture of various types of concepts and natural languages means that neither vocabulary nor relevant ideas in arguments in sociology are precisely defined, and reading them remains a matter of interpretation and co-construction of their meaning. Ramognino takes the example of the term "influence" in the sociology literature and asks what are we talking about here, a causality relationship in the strictest sense, a relationship of complex structural causality, dependence or interdependence, juxtaposition or proximal relationship? This example and the specificities of sociological language lead us directly to a consideration of the issue of relativism.

Sociology curriculum and relativism

The contemporary situation in sociology seems to be marked by relativism. The problems that relativism may or may not pose in the abstract are beyond the scope of this investigation. I will confine my question to the effect of relativism on the knowledge being taught in sociology in present curricula.

A fundamental issue concerns the plurality of disciplines present both in the GAP and in the SPP that can be found in a sociology curriculum. Referring to Europe, Boudon speaks of "balkanised sociology":

> There are many indications pointing in this direction. One of them (which could itself lead to a long discussion) is the semantical anarchy[5] which characterises the use of many concepts in the sociological community. Even such a crucial concept as "theory", for instance, which in the natural sciences and in the CMP [Classical Mainstream Program] has a clear stable meaning, always more or less directly related to the basic notion of generative model, has an impressive number of heterogeneous meanings in sociology. The polysemy [...] is a precious indicator of the fact that contemporary European sociologists are socially well, but intellectually ill integrated. (Boudon, 1993, p. 43)

Again, the intention here is not to discuss how well-founded the heterogeneity of the field of sociology is, but to attempt to see the relationship between scientific relativism and the sociology curriculum. Does scientific relativism have a direct effect on the structure of the sociology curriculum and on the classification of different disciplines which are presented as specialities? Is there relativism in different curricula in European sociology?

The history of sociology has been marked by relativism from its beginning. This point, which I will not develop here, could lead to a consideration of the contemporary situation of sociology in geographic and cultural contexts, which I noted as having potential for this study. We speak commonly of French sociology, Anglo-Saxon sociology, and so on, to emphasise the cultural specificities which mark each type. Ramognino (1998) asks, *What about physics, chemistry, or biology, could we qualify them in the same way?* Similarly, Nedelmann and Sztompka ask themselves

> [if there's] any meaning to the notion of "European sociology"? Would it make sense to speak of "European mathematics", "European chemistry", or "European astronomy"? In the case of the natural sciences it would at most indicate the location of laboratories, the addresses, national origin, or researchers; it would be significant for correspondence, or forming national chapters of academies, and not much more. But in the case of social sciences it means a great deal more. Sociology is a form of reflective self-awareness of societies, and as such it mirrors their concrete, particular experiences, their unique history, specific culture, local tradition. (Nedelman & Sztompka, 1993, p. 2)

This geographic and cultural variation echoes Davies' (1994) thoughts, that "national styles" of "doing sociology" exist, all celebrating respective "founding fathers". My hypothesis is that these ways of doing sociology are fully realised in the teaching of the discipline at university.

I have briefly considered the specificity of sociology as a knowledge form. I now need to specify the effects of relativism on sociology instruction and any given sociology curriculum. It can be expected that knowledge being taught within a sociology curriculum will be plural and heterogeneous and tied to its geographic and cultural origins; this would be impossible without the acquiescence of the learned community.

Relativism is concretely materialised in a sociology curriculum in its plurality of languages or in Weber's (1922/1965) terms the existence, side by side, of incommensurable theories. In different societies and historical periods the knowledge considered necessary for sociology students to learn will vary. More concretely, the discipline and the knowledge present in a given sociology curriculum will depend on the value placed on them by the learned community of a given country in a given period. These different conditions will lead to the assimilation or the rejection in the curriculum of some knowledge, authors, and languages by agreement of the scientific community. However, this agreement is not necessarily self-evident for Ramognino:

> The contemporary situation in sociology seems to have added a second degree of relativism to the geographic and cultural origins; this has to do with their blossoming, which is itself related to the blossoming of the social practices and contempo-

rary territories which are their subjects. The divisions are no longer only cultural, as their internal divisions cross each other; thus the paradigms no longer have any borders but are also due to the development and blossoming of the discipline into a specialisation. (Ramognino, 1998, p. 22)[6]

This second level, pertaining to specialisation, directly asserts the problem of integrating knowledge and paradigms from one language into the other within a sociology curriculum.

Categorizing knowledge within the teaching of sociology

We have previously seen how Bernstein presents the form of knowledge in sociology and humanities as a horizontal knowledge structure marked by a serial code which joins two levels, the GAP and the SPP. The teaching contents of this type of curriculum are serial, non-comparable, and segmented. My hypothesis is that this particular form of knowledge has a direct effect on the structure of its relativist curriculum. I now examine how, within a sociology curriculum, the different paradigms "that know no more boundaries" are assimilated into a discipline or a given speciality.

The empirical study and conceptual base of an analysis of sociology curricula is inevitably complex. Any university curriculum can be said to take two forms; an external, official, or public one consisting of documents, guides, syllabus, bibliography, and rules of access and evaluation and an internal version of all of these that approximates what is actually transmitted and acquired. These two forms can be called the official curriculum and the curriculum as activity. Both are subject to internal regulation within the department and university and, depending on the institution's autonomy and status, to external regulation. Such regulation can affect the resources available to a department of sociology, the distribution of resources within it, its orientation, and the social composition of the students and staff.

The external influence on sociology is weak. We find that a number of hours are required in economics, demography and other subjects in official sociology curricula without any explanation of the reasons behind these choices. It could be hypothesised that, following Passeron (1991), the choice of fields in a sociology curriculum might come from a "Koïnè" or "sabir" which seems to come from a common culture among sociology instructors.[7] "Koïnè" comes from the Greek adjective "koinos" which means *common to several people.* "Koïnè" is from the Greek common language of the Hellenistic and Roman periods, "sabir" is from a slang mixture of several languages, mostly used in commerce. While the Koïnè does not produce identical operationalisations and thus cannot be assimilated into a unified language as found in the hard sciences, what I want to emphasise here is the possibility of a specific agreement among sociology instructors concerning their epistemological positions relative to a sociology curriculum. The Koïnè brings us back to the cultural level already defined: there are culturally different ways of doing sociology. Thus we can imagine a hypothesis according to which the different fields of study, as well as the different disciplines located within a sociology curriculum, would be a function of Koïnè, of the group of instructors in a sociology department in a given country, in a given period. The schema that I have previously suggested concerning the sociology curriculum, following Bernstein, would then take the following form:

$$C = \frac{\{A=A \Leftrightarrow A \neq B, C, D, X \ldots\}}{K}$$

C = Curriculum of sociology

A, B, C, = sociology course

{ } = the given group that homogenises the different courses: curriculum structure

―― = anything that is under the line "depends" on what is over the line; instruction is embedded in regulation

K = Koïnè for the group of instructors for courses A, B, and C in a given sociology department

Sociological discourses marked by relativism create curricula through the selection, division, and structuring of knowledge in strongly compartmentalised disciplines. Once instituted as specialities (Education and Culture, Gender Inequality, etc.) the different types of discourse will be legitimised through the power relationships that exist amongst various sociology instructors. Selective, arbitrary, and compartmentalised, the knowledge being taught becomes part of a curriculum marked by a Koïnè (K), a language common to sociology instructors with a common sociological meaning and a common epistemological space.

In Search of Koïnè(s)

I have attempted in this chapter to demonstrate the importance that curriculum structure assumes in sociology instruction. This has required an investigation of the languages of the discipline. A comparative investigation of European sociology curricula leads to mark out both the heterogeneity and the plurality of the discourses of the discipline and also the Koïnè of one (or more) sociology department(s) in a given country. My intention has not been to examine the epistemological assumptions of discourses, or the power relationships and strategies of agents and institutions, or the national or local contexts which shape concerns and lead to the specialisation of the sociological stance, but to examine the intrinsic features of the teaching discourse of sociology itself, its social morphology, its segmentation, and its possible underlying commonality in Koïnè. This focus is descriptive/analytic rather than diagnostic and has sought a variety of settings that maximise the possibility of studying a range of curricular types.

My empirical research involved a comparison of the official curriculum and the curriculum as activity, the internal curriculum, of three pairs of highly contrasting universities, in France, Belgium, and Britain. The data are derived from two sources: national and local documentation of the external, or official, curriculum and interviews with professors of sociology. It is important to underline the difficulties involved in the collection of these data. The sociology arena is especially hostile to sociological investigation.

The investigation showed that there is no single model that encompasses sociology curricula. These curricula vary according to countries, and the vagueness and/or absence of official directions opens the way to local university expression. The documents which present curricula are heterogeneous and plural. Some departments but not others offer syllabuses to students. Two logics underlie these syllabuses. The first is pedagogic and the second is a delimitation of sociological territory. Once the visible part of a Koïnè was located I pursued its roots, in interviews with professors of sociology. I finally constructed six Koïnès, showing that the teaching of sociology in the three countries functions more according to a federalist model than according to a unionist model. Each state is autonomous, each department develops its own research programs and curriculum. There is no European Union as regards sociology, though the traditional national sociologies are giving way to international recontextualisations of authors and methodologies. The genesis of the current curricula in sociology occurred at the end of the 1950s but it is difficult today to see the influence of the founders of departments, the mandarins, in today's pattern.

While my research highlighted the existence of six Koïnès, they are not the focus of this chapter. I wish, rather, to emphasise the heterogeneity of the teaching in each department which we questioned in the light of the hypothesis as to the existence of Koïnès. The fundamental underlying question is: If there are as many different Koïnès as departments of sociology, why did I not refer to Bernstein's hypothesis relating to the segmentation produced by the non-translatable specialised languages of sociology and their social implication? The plurality of curricula does not necessarily contradict the hypothesised existence of Koïnès. If one does not settle immediately for the relativist argument, understanding the circulation of sociology knowledge requires a shift in emphasis to the teaching of sociology. The hypothesis of a Koïnè opens a debate which goes beyond the arena of the sociology of the curricula and invites scholars, to read and reread the works of Bernstein in order to question the normativity of sociology.

Notes

* For their support and encouragement in preparing this chapter, I am grateful to Nicole Ramognino, Professor of Sociology, Département de Sociologie, Université de Provence.

1. See Durkheim, 1986, pp. 15–46.

2. My translation.

3. A code "is a regulative principle, tacitly acquired, which selects and integrates relevant meanings, the form of their realisation and evoking context" (Bernstein, 1996, p. 11).

4. My translation.

5. Emphasis mine.

6. My translation.

7. At the same time, the distinction Kuhn makes between "symbolic generalization" (an expression which is used without questioning or dissent by the members of the group and which easily takes on a logical form), "metaphysical paradigms" (collective adherence to certain beliefs), "values" (which give specialists in the natural sciences, as a whole, the feeling of belonging to a group), and "examples" (concrete solutions to the problems that students encounter, tacit knowledge), suggests that the disciplinary matrix cannot be applied to sociology.

Bibliography

Bernstein, B. (1971). *Class, codes and control: Vol. I, Theoretical studies towards a sociology of language.* London: Routledge & Kegan Paul.

———. (1973). *Class, codes and control: Vol. II, Applied studies towards a sociology of language.* London: Routledge & Kegan Paul.

———. (1975). *Class, codes and control: Vol. III, Towards a theory of educational transmissions.* London: Routledge & Kegan Paul.

———. (1990). *Class, codes and control: Vol. IV, The structuring of pedagogic discourse.* London: Routledge.

———. (1996). *Class, codes and control: Vol. V, Pedagogy, Symbolic Control and identity: Theory, research, critique.* London: Taylor & Francis.

Berthelot, J. M. (1990). *L'intelligence du social.* Paris: Puf.

———. (1996). *Les vertus de l'incertitude.* Paris: Puf.

Boudon, R. (1993). European sociology: The identity lost. In B. Nedelman & P. Sztompka (Eds.), *Sociology in Europe.* Berlin: De Gruyter.

Bourdieu, P., & Gros, F. (1989). *Principes pour une réflexion sur les contenus d'enseignement.* Paris: Ministère de l'Education Nationale.

Davies, B. (1994). Durkheim and the sociology of education in Britain. *British Journal of Sociology of Education, 15* (1), 3–25.

Durkheim, E. (1969). *L'evolution pédagogique en France.* Paris: Puf. (Originally published 1938).

———. (1986). *Les règles de la méthode sociologique.* Paris: Puf. (Originally published 1895).

———. (1991). *Les formes élémentaires de la vie religieuse.* Paris: Poche. (Originally published 1912).

Establet, R. (1990). Education, l'influence oblique de Durkheim. *Cahiers Français, 247,* 80–81.

Forquin, J. C. (1990). *Ecole et Culture.* Brussels: De Boeck-Wesmael.

Kuhn, T. (1982). *La structure des révolutions scientifiques:* Paris: Flammarion. (Originally published 1962).

Lepennies, W. (1990). *Les trois cultures.* Paris: Maison des Sciences de l'Homme.

Mauss, M. (1983). *Sociologie et anthropologie.* Paris: Puf. (Originally published 1950).

Nedelmann, B., & Sztompka P. (1993). *Sociology in Europe.* Berlin: De Gruyter.

Passeron, J. C. (1991). *Le raisonnement sociologique.* Paris: Nathan.

Ramognino, N. (1998). *L'observation dans les sciences-sociales.* Unpublished manuscript: Université de Provence.

———, & Houle, G. (1999). *Sociologie et normativité scientifique.* Toulouse: P.U.M.

Société Française de Sociologie (1983). *Enquête sur l'enseignement de la sociologie.* Paris: S.F.S.

Vitale, P. (1999). *L'enseignement de la sociologie: Vers une étude comparative des curricula européens.* Thèse de Doctorat de Sociologie, Université de Provence.

Weber, M. (1965). *Essais sur la théorie de la science.* Paris: Plon. (Originally published 1922).

Young, M. (1971). *Knowledge and control: New directions for the sociology of education.* London: Collier Macmillan.

———. (1988). *Curriculum and democracy: Lessons from a critique of the New Sociology of Education.* London: Institute of Education.

Chapter 6

Intimations of Boundlessness

Johan Muller

"Dérèglement"

Boundaries are the condition of intelligibility of ourselves and of our world.[1] This Kantian precept snakes its way through much of the social theory of the early twentieth century only to come up short against a trend of social thought that is evident everywhere as the century ends. It sometimes even seems as if the notion of boundary has become the quintessence of totalitarianism. To live a life beyond bounds and without boundaries is the dominant ethical ideal (Jardine, 1999); to enquire into facts and meanings that exceed epistemological boundaries is the primary research ideal (Lather, 1991); to teach children to cross boundaries wherever they may find them is the pedagogical ideal (Giroux & McLaren, 1994). To treat the world as a continuous network of interlinked intensities and flows beyond all divides and divisions is all there is and all there should be (Deleuze, 1995).

There is something disconcerting about this turn of events. Not that it is a completely novel view from nowhere. A version of it has been central to progressive, evolutionary, or revolutionary views since at least the Enlightenment, where change, whether driven by aesthetics, by science, or by politics, was considered to be a bounds-transcending event-series. What distinguishes the more recent constellation from the standard progressivism or romanticism of modernity, however, is a certain extremism—as if modernity were taken to a logical, but mad, conclusion. It seems as if, as in forms of paranoia, a certain organising centre is missing from an otherwise rational edifice.

Georg Simmel expresses a version of the earlier orthodoxy with representative elegance. Boundaries, or forms, are the precondition for meaningfulness. Without them, the immensity of the world would swamp life and render it a marsh of senselessness and uncertainty. "The boundary, above and below, is our means for finding direction in the infinite space of our worlds [...]" (Simmel, 1971, p. 353). This does not mean that life is defined only by forms and boundaries; life is also self-defining, and to that degree, boundary-transcending. Consequently, life and form, existence and boundary, are "partners of a dialectic" (Tester, 1993, p. 11): boundaries and forms create the conditions for meaningfulness and sense; life transcends those forms and boundaries in order to extend that sense. In other words, boundaries are the condition both for the constitution of sense and for the transcendence of boundaries. A mass of contemporary sociological theorising, perhaps most explicit in Giddens's successive versions of structuration theory, comes to mind here. A central nostrum of modernity also comes to mind: that there can be no progress or innovation, let alone violation, without boundaries; conversely, there can be no boundaries without their transgression. As Durkheim was wont to say, the episodic violation of a rule "serves to re-affirm the sanctity and authority of the rule" (quoted in Wrong, 1994, p. 57). Form and life are both logically and sociologically co-dependent. This much is standard to Freud as well as to most of the sociological greats, and is captured with stark economy in Borges's aphorism, "oppression is the mother of invention". It is also standard to attempts in the sociology of science to understand the social construction of truth: "[...] all distrust presupposes a system of takings-for-granted which make *this instance* of distrust possible. Distrust is something which takes place on the *margins* of trusting systems" (Shapin, 1994, p. 19).

Everything depends on the maintenance of a certain balance, a certain symmetrical dance between fluidity and fixity. Here is the rub. For a great many contemporary writers, this dialectic has become radically destabilised, and forms that were once merely constructively constraining have become reified and life-constricting. Simmel's two great examples are, of course, money and theory, both of which assert the precedence of form over life. The reified forms become prisons, naturalised cages that might once have been the product of creative genius but now stifle it. In the current cultural temper they are depicted as the radical other of genius, of freedom, of the life of the spirit, of the autonomous citizen of the globalised world.

In this generic approach, Great Divides abound: between the subject and the object; between culture and nature; between the solitary person and the collective; between the state/market/bureaucracy and the people; all these are versions of the life-form dialectic now polarised and fixed into implacable opposition. The definitional activity of forms, on the one hand, and self-definition, on the other, are irreconciled and irreconcilable. Between ourselves as self-definers and that "other" definer, a gulf of mistrust opens up in which civil social relations, civility as social cement in Shapin's (1994) terms, must wither. For the would-be explainer of social life, a certain principle of dynamism, modernity's dynamic principle of form-transcendence, goes by the board. It might not have been a particularly elegant or even adequate principle, and it has certainly been shot full of holes by successive waves of avant-garde social theory. But in one version or another, it formed the organising basis of every sustaining theoretical grand narrative of modern social science.

No more. Social theory collectively simply does not credit the form-transcendence account anymore, save for the odd stout soul. We seem trapped once more in one or other of Leibnitz's two labyrinths of reason, the labyrinth of liberty or the labyrinth of necessity (Turner, in Buci-Glucksman, 1994, p. 24). This is an aporia of the cruellest sort, for it forces social theory to one or other end of the Great Divide, or leaves it to scratch in the ruins for prefigurations of the next staging of an unforeseeable transcendence, for the messianic moment which can only come unannounced (Benjamin, 1969). The latter is the honourable or gallant thing to do, perhaps, but most writing flies with one or other wing of the dichotomy. This takes the form of either a melancholic (or tragic) response to the skeptical turn, or a joyous and celebratory one. Both of these deal with boundaries in an unmediated or dichotomising way. In the idiom of this paper, they either reaffirm the Great Divide or collapse it.

Central to the joyous response is an acceptance of the perspective of life unconcerned with the shaping power of form: Where boundaries are, freedom should be. This celebratory voluntarism, which deals with boundaries by using various discursive strategies of ontological disavowal, epistemological trivialisation, or conflation, is self-defeating. What matters for the present argument is that this kind of social analysis takes as its central premise the assumption that boundaries are always and by definition imprisoning, and should therefore be crossed, transgressed, combatted, and otherwise wished away wherever they appear to manifest themselves. Or, as Tester (1993) puts it, giving this trend one current appellation, "Post-modernity can be interpreted as the intimation of boundlessness [...]" (p. 28).

This chapter is a meditation on the fate of boundaries under conditions of skepticism or incredulity, when intimations of boundlessness abound. The specific domain-focus will be on the curious way in which "New Literacy Studies" have come to define literacy; and the empirical focus, albeit brief, will be on some practices of a non-literate worker on a wine farm outside Cape Town. But first, back to basics.

Sacred and Profane

Emile Durkheim is the exemplary sociologist of the boundary. Taking as his focus "primitive cultures", systems of classification in pre-modern society, Durkheim set out to construct a way of grasping the fundamentals of cultural classification—the why and the how of boundary-instantiation. In *The Elementary Forms of the Religious Life* he draws a famous distinction between two orders of existence which relate thought and practice in two fundamentally different ways. The first order is the everyday world of "sensual representations", the world of matter and sense, where meaning arises directly out of bodily encounters with the world, with other people, with reality. It is a world of flux and of particulars, and it is driven by the most practical and direct wisdom: proverbs, prudence, street lore, on-the-job knowledge, the rhythmic language and wisdom of the domestic community (cited in Lyotard, 1991, pp. 191–196). Schutz would characterise this as the world of the "natural attitude", Geertz as common sense as a cultural system. For Durkheim, this was the profane world.

The second order is the religious world, one of prescriptions and interdictions that are not pragmatically modifiable but "fixed and crystallised", "immutable" (Durkheim, 1915, p. 433). This sacred world is an order of verities not originating in bodily hexis, and therefore arbitrary, in Pierce's sense of unmotivated: Taboos, explains Durkheim, can be attached to any object. The religious world is thus a world of arbitrary conceptual relations, a symbolic order constructed by an accretion of "collective representations" (1915, p. 434), which are a collective accomplishment, the "work of the community", in contrast to the "sensual representations" of the everyday world that are the work of continually changing experiential particulars.

Religion is, then, for Durkheim the ur-cognitive classificatory scheme of the sacred, the ur-form of ordering social representations in non-empirical, formal ways. The force of the ordering comes from "outside of the object in which it resides" (quoted in Thompson, 1994, p. 125), not from the object itself. It is the result of a process of "examination and elaboration" (p. 126): It is the result of a cognitive process of idealisation.

Durkheim brings at least two meanings to this faculty of idealisation. The first is clearly the purely cognitive or speculative sense of being able "to connect things with each other, to establish internal relations between them, to classify them and to systematize them" (quoted in Thompson, 1994, p. 133). The second is that of forward projection towards an order and a world more desirable, more felicitous, more powerful—in a word, better—than the one we have in hand at any specific point in history.

Durkheim thus plays upon the double sense of ideal: ideal, first, as the faculty to manipulate objects and relations in non-empirical virtual space— in thought, as he says; ideal, second, as the projection into and towards that which is more desirable. Both together allow us to break with empirical facticity and to imagine an ordering of objects that is "logical" and "hierarchical" (quoted in Thompson, 1994, p. 137). This is a key feature of virtual connections, which allows, as Foucault (1981) says in a related idiom when discussing disciplinarity, "the possibility of formulating new propositions, ad infinitum" (p. 59), or as Hacking (1985) says when discussing styles of reasoning, to "generate new classes of possibilities" (p. 156).

The faculty of idealisation is thus Durkheim's motor-force for cultural change. With this, he is in a position to effect his startling reversal. Quite against the conventional progressivism of his Victorian contemporaries, including Frazer, Durkheim makes the argument, more strongly as the book progresses, that science, far from making a break with superstition and religion, is formally isomorphic with religious thought. Both are sacred modes of cognition. Indeed, "the fundamental categories of [...] science, are of religious origin" (Durkheim, 1915, p. 418). Given his second sense of "ideal", Durkheim is progressive enough to want some forward movement, so "scientific thought is only a more perfect form of religious thought" (quoted in Thompson, 1994, p. 133). But on the formal level they are equivalent.

Furthermore, science, like religion, arises from the collective, not from the individual: It is "at the school of collective life that the individual has learnt to idealise" (quoted in Thompson, 1994, p. 130). This too marks relatively a profound reversal from the "great cultural-historical tradition which assigned truth to individual disengagement and error or distortion to membership in the polity" (Shapin, 1994, p. 40). Truth is produced in social communities, not by solitary souls in isolated creative ferment, despite science's persistent self-presentation of the truth-making process as solitary.[2]

In other words, Durkheim's strong hypothesis might be stated as follows: The prototype of socially constructed social knowledge is the outcome of, and depends upon, a hard distinction between everyday, particular, sensory, individual "profane" knowledge, and esoteric, collective, generalisable, non-sensory "sacred" knowledge. Religion and science are both forms of the sacred, of the esoteric, and of the social.

The sacred is characterised by an "extraordinary contagiousness of character" (Durkheim, 1915, p. 318), a sort of spontaneous associational bent which must be curbed, because the principle of meaningful organisation of the everyday depends crucially on the "intrinsic attributes" (p. 323) of the objects found there, while that of the sacred depends on the idealised system of connections established by the communal canon. Allowing contagion free play would open the pragmatism of the everyday to arbitrary investitures of meaning, emotion, and moral sense. Or to put it another way, common sense must be protected from the power and proclivity of esoteric knowledge to remake commonsense in the self-image of esoteric knowledge. Apparent here is an early intimation of the concept of recontextualisation and translation.

Does this not make religion or the esoteric life irrational? Not at all, says Durkheim. They are merely non-empirical, not irrational, and certainly not unsystematic: these non-empirical connections are, furthermore, the engine of knowledge since they allow inquirers to break with the naturalising logic of the everyday, allowing them "to bind together things which sensation leaves apart from one another" (1915, p. 325).[3]

A position like Durkheim's is invariably in favour of disciplinary specialisation. Not only is such specialisation a defining instance of the division of labour, says Durkheim, but it cultivates social interdependence, which is a mark of advanced civility (see also Shapin, 1994). Durkheim's response to those who lament the fragmentation of knowledge and society is to assert that the generally educated man, the transdisciplinary epigone of globalisation theorists of the learning society, is bound to be an antisocial egoist, since his polymathy all too easily breeds a smug and false sense of self-sufficiency. Far better to cultivate a sense of mutual interdependence, to drive people, who might not otherwise do so willingly, to act with co-operative civic-minded virtue.[4] New sociologists of work echo Durkheim's emphasis upon co-operation and interdependence in the global workplace (see Elam, 1993). So too the sociologists of science: "The very power of science to hold knowledge as collective property *and* to focus doubt on bits of currently accepted knowledge is founded upon a degree and a quality of trust which are arguably unparalleled elsewhere in our culture" (Shapin, 1994, p. 417).

Part of Durkheim's distinctiveness lies in what Ringer (1993) calls his "hostility to interpretation" (p. 299). On the one hand, this means that his primary stress is upon the *differences* between profane and sacred logics. On the other hand, because interpretation as a problem is shifted to the background, the operation of "crossing-over", or the redescriptive process of idealisation itself, is left unexamined. Durkheim routinely supposed that intellectual "facts" were immediately and unproblematically intelligible. Does this mean, then, that such a position automatically leads to an undervaluation of interpretation and a proclivity to positivism?

Not necessarily. Shotter (1993), for instance, has shown that what holds together a wide range of interpretivist writers—including Vico, Wittgenstein, and Bakhtin—is a view remarkably close to Durkheim's. According to Vico, the "sensus communis" of everyday life is created by flows of activity, which in turn generate "sensory topics", which emerge as spaces, or habitats, of shared meanings and feelings in already shared circumstances. Webs of metaphor connect the shared topoi to the sensus communis and back to the transactions of the everyday, ensuring practical continuity. These connections, importantly, are tacit. Everyday metaphors thus do not explain but "show" participants a common quality of life that is neither rationally deducible nor reducible: "As such, it (the *sensus communis*) cannot be 'explained' [...] (either from within an academic discourse, or in any other way)" (Shotter, 1993, p. 470).

Shotter goes on to show how this view compels a distinction between common sense and esoteric discourse. First, the subject matter of common sense is determined by sensuous events and is thus wholly contingent on circumstance, whereas that of esoteric discourse is predetermined by the arbitrary systematics of the canon. Secondly, because of its systemic objectivisation, the subject matter of esoteric discourse can, as Wittgenstein has said, be "surveyed" in rational contemplation, while that of common sense not. Why? Because it is only a set of ordered statements that enables us to see how, within the subject matter of the discourse, things, as Rorty (1979) says, "hang together". Indeed, it is this ability of "surveying", of showing that we know how things "hang together", that we must be able to display in order to display competence.[5] Thus, as Shotter says, paraphrasing Foucault, esoteric discourses "form as systematic the objects of which they speak, *i.e.* form them as mental representations" (Shotter, 1993, p. 473).

The key point Shotter is extracting from the interpretivists he surveys is that the topic of common sense, because of its functional orientation to everyday problems, is very rarely arbitrary, while the object of esoteric discourse, and its relation to other objects in the discourse, often is. Once again, "arbitrary" in this context means non-iconic, or metonymical, rather than iconic or analogical. As we saw above, this is a key reversal that Durkheim effects, in his distinction between the sacred and the profane, a reversal not only of the conventionally accepted view of things, and of the view of nineteenth-century anthropology, but also of all those who define modernity, along with Habermas, as the passage from mythos to logos.

Amongst the many implications here, I comment on only one. When the constructivists emphasise the unfoundability of all accounts of the world in order to establish the equal unfoundability and hence radical equality of all forms of knowledge and domains of meaning, they make an epistemological point that does the *reverse* of what they intend it to do.

As McCarthy (1989) shows, using Rorty as his example, such an epistemological claim is utterly alien to common-sense thinking. Ordinary people in the everyday sensuous world believe in that world as a precondition for acting in it. We routinely treat, and hold our co-participants accountable for so treating, the reality and the objectivity of the world as invariant to discrepant reports, as Pollner (1975) would say. Objectivity and the invariance of the world is an idealising presupposition and precondition for all interaction and social practice in the everyday world. And scientists are not immune from this logic: "It is, as we know, an important part of going to the doctor, flying on a plane and, indeed, maintaining social order generally. Not only is it not wise for science-studies analysts to invest their life savings in palladium futures: to do so would be to ignore a crucial part of the story" (Simon, 1999, p. 74).

Durkheim, then, true to his exemplary modernism, constructs a series of binaries separated by a discontinuous, if permeable, interdictory boundary. It is a binary grid which reverses a number of the standard tropes of mainstream modernity:

sacred	profane
future-oriented	tradition-oriented
collective	individual
ideal	sensory
speculative	practical

Most dramatically, science is aligned with religion and against the everyday by defining the common roots of science and religion in idealisation, which is the condition for explicit and systematic classification, an operation that the pervasive allegoricity of the everyday is unable to perform.[6] More importantly perhaps, and undermining the Great Divide schema that aligns form with Nature and life with Culture, Durkheim's genius is to show that form and truth reside with, and spring from, Culture, while Nature's place is with the naturalising suppositions of the natural attitude. In doing this, Durkheim removes the production of truth from the domain of Nature and the solitary man or woman, and restores the sacred to collective life.

For all that, Durkheim's inversions are only partly helpful. In his desire to characterise both religion and science as non-sensory, and the everyday world as solely sensory, he ends up characterising two worlds of existence in exclusively epistemological terms. The problem here is that epistemological domains are not coterminous with sociological ones. No one lives only in the sacred or only in the profane. The problem also runs deeper: Neither the everyday world nor the world of science is epistemologically homogeneous. Indeed, argues Latour (1993), science has always comprised "hybrid monsters", productively mixing science and society. At least part of the burden of the constructivist challenge to science studies has been to show that the practice of science always partakes of the profane as well, contains profanely structured practices, and cannot therefore be adequately explained without reference to patterns of the profane—that is, to sociological patterns: "(was the sacred always hybrid?)" Knorr Cetina (1994, p. 18) asks in parentheses. The orthodox Durkheimian answer is no, and it is this answer that every periodic wave of protesting realists (see Atkins, 1995, for an example) has given to the hybridical persuasiveness of the constructivists, those new young Hegelians, as Fuller (1995) calls them.

In giving the answer in this strictly Durkheimian way, the new defenders, like the old, and like Durkheim himself, render themselves unable to acknowledge, let alone investigate, the profane practices nesting within the social institutions of religion and science; for that matter, they render themselves unable to investigate the sacred practices in everyday life, and it is this latter inability which is of interest in the present chapter. But this is not to agree with the constructivist hybridisers. To concede that the social institution of science has always been hybrid, or has always produced hybrids, is not to concede anything about the epistemological integrity of the sacred part of scientific practice. That being so, one is not forced into a tactic of defensive pluralisation which conceives of the domain of social action as radically plural and radically equal, as the "new literacy" theorists are inclined to do (see below) in order to shore up the integrity of profane practice, thereby losing any possible analytical edge from the concept of "literacy" by losing all sense of the sacred.

Only certain kinds of scientific practice are sacred, not the entire form of life. Once this reasonable point is established, then one can proceed to ask how, wherever we may find them, in whatever pure or hybrid form, are we to characterise the different forms of epistemological practice of sacred and profane? Or, "on what basis are we going to establish the comparison of collectives?" as Latour (1993, p. 127) asks, but sadly doesn't answer. For a start in this direction, we must turn to another exemplary neo-Durkheimian, Basil Bernstein.

Vertical and Horizontal

Constructivism deals with the Great Divide, the asymmetry of discourses, by collapsing the distinction between the sacred and the profane. Specialised knowledge ensembles are to be treated as in principle the same as everyday knowledge ensembles, and are to be discussed in terms of their continuity with the latter. This is a direct result of treating them all as sociocultural practices. Hereafter, all discursive ensembles are to be treated as arbitrary, since they are now solely products of cultural activity.[7]

Latour (1993) has pointed out one paradoxical effect of this one-way conflation. By construing everything in terms of social construction, the Social (or Cultural) becomes the pre-predicative and therefore "natural" real which all other things are henceforth judged in relation to: "Constructivist where Nature is concerned, it is realistic about society" (p. 94). This helps to explain why many constructivists, formally relativist, hold such strong, even dogmatic, views about the explanatory priority of social context.

Such a paradoxical realism about society leads to a singular occlusion. If all cultural content is arbitrary, then the analytical task must always be to expose the basis for its arbitrariness, which necessarily lies in the social field from which that arbitrary content issues: "It follows from this conceptualising that sociological analysis should be concerned more with the activity of the field, that is the procedures of its reproduction, than with any given content of the field, for any given content is arbitrary" (Bernstein, 1996, p. 169). The internal structure of the symbolic system is thereby prevented from having any structuring significance, and this, for Bernstein, is the great flaw in Bourdieu's analysis of culture: It is about the social field and its structures and activities, and has nothing to say about symbolic systems themselves. To put this another way, Bourdieu (1990), and other adherents of what Callon (1995) calls the "competition model", reduce all differences of cultural content to the play of power and interest. As a consequence,

Bourdieu has little to contribute to an investigation of the way that rules in knowledge forms and rules in social relations may be mutually implicated.

To start, then, a way of talking about forms of knowledge is required. In a way reminiscent of Durkheim's sacred and profane, Bernstein first distinguishes between *horizontal discourse*—local, segmental, context-dependent, tacit, multilayered; and *vertical discourse*—a coherent, explicit, systematically principled structure, that is either hierarchically organised or takes the form of a series of specialised languages.[8]

The difference between the two is clearest when considering acquisition. Horizontal discourse is acquired in segments where there are only loosely organised rules of distribution. It is context-dependent, and transfer across contexts can occur only on the basis of analogic extrapolation. Vertical discourse cannot be acquired segmentally, only via access to the explicitly assembled symbolic structure, which occurs via specific *principles of recontextualisation*, and access to which is regulated by explicit distributive rules (who can get what, when, and how).

So far, Bernstein has extended Durkheim's schema by collapsing the distinction between forms of mastery. Both horizontal and vertical discursive mastery can occur only through the manipulation of duly constituted objects of a discourse: The former is not "practical" and the latter "formal". Indeed, they are both "formal", but their forms differ, as do the distributive rules which govern them.

Bernstein (1999) now springs a Durkheimian reversal by distinguishing, within vertical discourse, between *hierarchical* and *horizontal knowledge structures*. Horizontal discourse does not and cannot have knowledge structures because it has no recontextualising principle, regulating distribution in terms of time, space, and actors, because it is by definition common to all who belong to the *domus*. Hierarchical and horizontal knowledge structures, as modes of vertical discourse, both do have knowledge structures. Hierarchical knowledge structure, the paradigm case being physics, is pyramidical in shape, and new knowledge is integrated into propositions that are as inclusive or general and as few in number as possible. Set aside for the moment the now commonplace modification that "knowledge is less cumulative than we thought" (Hacking, 1985, p. 148). Horizontal knowledge structure takes the form of an expanding series of non-translatable *specialised languages* with non-comparable principles of description. Growth of knowledge here occurs by the addition of specialised languages, only very rarely by their integration. Further, Bernstein distinguishes within horizontal knowledge structures between those with *strong* grammars of realisation (like economics) and those with *weak* grammars (like sociology and anthropology). These latter are not acquired by learning "procedures of investigation and instruments of observation and understanding of the theory" (Bernstein, 1999, p. 165). They are learnt by acquiring a "gaze", a particular mode or style of recognising and realising what counts as reality (1999).

Horizontal knowledge structures thus partake of the vertical in that they, like any knowledge structure in vertical discourse, are regulated by a more or less specific principle of recontextualisation. That is, competent members can give an explicit account of the way in which they have arrived at a specific position; they can re-trace their steps and show how they have made the recontextualised objects "hang together". This is essentially an elaboration of Durkheim's faculty of idealisation, and it is a defining feature of all examples of vertical discourse (see Entwhistle, 1998). On the other hand, a horizontal knowledge structure partakes of the horizontal in that its specialised languages relate to each other in the manner of segments of horizontal discourse: "both are serial, segmental, and have *potentially* volatile contents" (Bernstein, 1996, p. 178): That is, they are strongly insulated from each other, non-translatable and non-comparable.

The main point that Bernstein wishes to make with this argument, against the reductionism of Bourdieu, is that only after we have understood the internal structuring of symbolic systems, and the way in which that structuring creates rules of distribution which shape possibilities for positionality within that system, can we come to a complete understanding of social positionality in relation to cultural formations. "To privilege the particular features of the field and the habituses these select, sponsor, and legitimate, whilst excluding the features of knowledge, reduces the power and possibilities of analysis" (Bernstein, 1996, p. 180).

Bernstein has thus returned to Durkheim's binary schema, not simply to replicate it, but rather to pay Durkheim the ultimate compliment, to take a leaf out of his performative book and "do for science what Durkheim had done for religion" as Latour (1993, p. 54) describes the "Edinburgh daredevils" (the proponents of the "strong programme") as having done. That is, Bernstein has re-theorised the sacred by delineating invisible alignments in Durkheim's binary table: He has attempted to show that the distinction between sacred and profane is not quite the same as that between written and oral, formal and practical mastery, by showing the fundamental role of distributive rules in both, as well as in the social relations which optimise the discourse.

Prometheus Unbound, or What Does It Mean to Be Literate?

In this part of the chapter I examine New Literacy Studies (NLS) in terms of some lessons extracted from Durkheim and Bernstein. The intention here is not to present a comprehensive discussion of NLS. What follows hardly does justice to NLS, and is intended simply to display a non-Durkheimian approach to Great Divides, and to examine some of its consequences from a neo-Durkheimian perspective.

NLS comprises a cluster of approaches to the concept and practice of literacy that has recently rejuvenated the way that literacy is considered, especially cross-culturally.[9] A core precept of NLS, shared with much of contemporary ethnology, is that the Great Divide between oral and literate cultures, and between related binaries like concrete and abstract thought, is a self-serving one that should be collapsed forthwith. Formal reading and writing, or print literacy, should be seen as only one literacy amongst others; hence, literacies.

There are two ways in which this is typically taken forward in NLS. The first, following Heath (1983) and Street (1984, 1993), talks about a "literacy event", or "literacy practice", as an everyday occasion where print literacy is used, or referred to, or conceptualised, as part of a broader socio-ideological context of practice. In Street's view, this means that print literacy becomes part of a broader class of communicative practices (after Grillo, 1989). The second approach, following Gee (1990), likewise sees print literacy as a practice that belongs to a broader class of practices, this time "secondary discourse", "secondary" because acquired in formal, non-intimate contexts. By this definition, and true to NLS's founding precept, literacy is a practice like "oral literature".

The first definition, therefore, defines print literacy as a communicative practice that involves written language in some way or other; the second defines it in terms of competency in a secondary discourse. Both of these re-definitions collapse the Great Divide by nesting print literacy within profane practice (Durkheim) or horizontal discourse (Bernstein), in much the same way as did that other anthropologist, Bourdieu, and with much the same result: Namely, that the option of considering literacy as a structured symbolic practice *sui generis*, or as part of a broader category of symbolic practice different from profane everyday practices, is hereby surrendered. Of course, much can be said and has been said about the social, political, and ideological embeddedness of print literacy. But as we saw above in Bernstein's discussion of Bourdieu, once the boundary between the sacred and profane is collapsed, nothing further can be said about literacy as a discourse, because any investigation of the formal properties of discourse, the formal properties of the content of symbolic systems, is precluded by the conflationist strategy adopted by NLS with regard to the Great Divide.

This strategy is formally the same as, though the mirror opposite of, that adopted by Levi-Strauss, who addressed the Great Divide between "primitive" mentality and "scientific" mentality by making his "savages" look and think like "scientists". NLS, in an attempt to deal with the same problem, construes print literacy as primarily another kind of cultural accomplishment, and much of NLS scholarship endeavours to show that there is, after all, very little that can be accomplished by print literacy competency that cannot be quite satisfactorily accomplished by other, equally meritorious, cultural accomplishments (Prinsloo & Breier, 1996). One is ineluctably left with the question of "who then needs it?" In similar vein, the sociologists of science who debunk the pretensions of science to transcendental Truth see themselves not as refuting scientific truth claims but as unmasking their unwarranted metaphysical aspirations (Hacking, 1998). Whether or not the scientists appreciate this form of cognitive therapy or not is moot: There are certainly increasing signs that they don't, nor do they appreciate the subtle distinction between "refuting" and "unmasking" (see Sokal & Bricmont, 1998, for example). The consequences of such diminishment in the educational domain are different, and could be far-reaching. If print literacy has no cultural advantage over other literacies, and if analyses show that alternative literacies more than compensate for its absence, then this form of analysis ends up providing an alibi for a lack of access to formal education. Latour (1993) scathingly asks: "Is there a better way to finish off those one wants to save from condemnation?" (p. 98). The final part of this chapter briefly examines an example of how the optic produced by NLS creates a particular disabling blindness, by coding a certain practice by an illiterate worker as just another everyday cultural accomplishment.

Migiel Hendricks is a farmworker at a wine and fruit farm in the Breerivier Valley near Cape Town. He never went to school, although he did attend literacy classes for a while: He was under the impression that he needed to be literate to get his driver's licence, which is not the case in South Africa. He confesses: "I really did not learn anything. Only that the girls had nice legs" (Gibson, 1994, p. 35).[10] Hendricks is a tractor driver at the wine farm. He welds, lays out fertiliser and irrigation systems, and is a general vehicle repairman.

Singularly, he also builds wagons from scratch, which includes designing and constructing the frame, surface, and beam, all correctly positioned about the axle or axles. When asked how he made a particular wagon, he comments: "I just looked at an old wagon standing there at the top. Then I measured it and made a plan in my head how exactly I wanted to make this one" (Gibson, 1994, p. 36). Hendricks's modesty aside, his ability is not merely mimetic. He builds wagons from specifications given by the farmer, sometimes unlike any he has seen before:

> The boss said what kind of wagon he wanted. Then I went and sat down and thought about how I was going to build it. For this kind of wagon, with a shorter "bak" [enclosed boot] it costs less and makes it lighter if you use only one axle. But the axle must be in the correct place or the wagon will also tip over. It depends on where you attach the jack, how long and heavy the jack is. (Gibson, 1994, p. 37)

Hendricks goes on to explain, in graphic detail, using a wheelbarrow and using his arm and wrist to display articulation, what is at stake in calculating this. "You have to use your common sense," he says.

Hendricks is clearly performing some kind of abstract calculation here, a calculation of the sort which is precisely not common-sensical. It is a process of extrapolation that he describes as follows: "I may not be able to read or write, but I use something I have learnt in one case and adapt it" (Gibson, 1994, p. 38). This goes for the construction of plans and the estimation of materials: "By the second wagon I almost always ordered the correct amount of material" (Gibson, 1994, p. 38).

How would one go about understanding what Hendricks is doing here? If we follow a Heath/Street definition, we will probably not identify this as a literacy "practice" or "event": neither reading nor writing is involved, and although Hendricks is able to reconstruct his mental steps and communicate them to the interviewer, it is clear from what he says that his wagon-building is by and large a solitary activity. Gee may well identify it as an example of secondary discourse, although apart from a short course in welding, we might be hard put to identify the context of acquisition of this undoubted skill, formal or otherwise. NLS has, in fact, very little to say about it at all.

Hendricks can, in his own words, make a plan in his head, and he is able to extrapolate—"pas dit aan", or "pass on the metre". Durkheim would identify it as an example of the faculty of idealisation, a case of "examination and elaboration". He is clearly able to manipulate objects in virtual space, even if only analogically. Hendricks is able to redescribe the features of a wagon into the formal measurements, dimensions, and quantities that make up a plan, and he is able to translate the plan into a wagon. He is deploying some principle of transcontextualization here, and because of it, he can generate new forms and combinations: He can build a wagon he has never seen before. Hendricks, in the terms developed in this paper, displays elements of an under-elaborated faculty of verticality. This takes the form of a germinal horizontal knowledge structure, admittedly with a highly simple grammar. It is, in other words, a rather sacred form of common sense, a style of reasoning evolved all by himself, but a style of reasoning for all that.

This style of cognition is surprisingly similar in form to the one Entwhistle (1998) found amongst his Edinburgh undergraduates reviewing for their exams. Some of the most successful students did not try to memorise every fact *seriatim*, but constructed summary nodes, or what Entwhistle calls "knowledge objects". Such a "knowledge object" is more than merely a mental image: "It can pull into awareness currently unfocused knowledge, almost in the way that hypertext in computing uses certain emphasised words to indicate the existence of additional information" (Entwhistle, 1998, p. 96). The understanding thus produced translates into a distinct "feeling of confidence that an understanding can be reconstructed at will from sets of interlinked ideas and information" (Entwhistle, 1998, p. 96). This "pull-down" competence, in a vastly different time and place, is, I suggest, what Migiel Hendricks exhibits when he builds his wagons. One student describes it in uncannily similar terms:

> I clear my mind and something comes [...] it was almost as though I could see it all fitting into an overall picture [...] it pulls in pictures and facts as it needs them and suddenly you know where you are going next. (Entwhistle, 1998, p. 96)

Is it far-fetched to say that Hendricks has acquired, and can realise, a related (meta)cognitive skill usually associated with advanced literacy? Is Hendricks's cognitive skill communicable? The neo-Durkheimian approach is not to look for whether it occurs in a communicative context or not, as Gee would, but to examine first the communicative entailments of different "orders of discourse". Hacking (1985, 1992) shows, for example, that our empirical knowledge, those "observation sentences" which we know because they correspond to encounters with sensuous reality, are easily understood across contexts, cultures, even languages. They are relatively easily translatable. As long as one has been in that situation, one will know what the person is talking about. Not so the sentences within a style of reasoning. These are generated as intelligible and interesting only from within that style of reasoning; And to understand them—to be a communicative recipient—requires first sharing that style of reasoning, which in Bernstein's language means having been inducted into the relevant principle of recontextualisation.

Communication thus figures differently whether we are within horizontal or vertical discourse. In the first, communication depends upon having had the same sort of experiences, having been exposed to similar sensuous particulars as your co-communicator. In the second, communication depends upon sharing a style of reasoning, or "discourse", which means in turn having accessed the same recontextualising principle. No such principle is necessary for communication within horizontal discourse.

Hendricks's "explanation", or reconstruction, of his operations is at least partly understandable to the interviewer, and my citing it here presumes some understanding by the reader. But how understandable would Hendricks be to his fellow workers on the farm? Could Hendricks explain to a non-initiate fellow-worker how to build a wagon? This is at least a testable question, but I doubt that such an explanation could be easily given. Why? Because most of the non-literate workers on the farm are unpracticed in the skill of recontextualisation since they have not had exposure to a sustained process of induction into recontextualisation—that is, literacy. For what, after all, can literacy be but the generic context for induction into principles of recontextualisation? And what reason might we have for not regarding this faculty of Hendricks's as a kind of "writing within speech" (Derrida, 1978, p. 197), a proto-literacy in all but name, and one moreover that can only be invisible to the old and the new literacy studies alike?[11]

Hendricks has evolved his protean capacity with, as far as we know, little more assistance than the farmer's encouragement. The really interesting question would be how he stumbled, uninducted as it were, into the realm of the sacred, into vertical discourse. One would have to identify the vertical or proto-vertical discourses that inhabit Hendricks's habitat and that have helped to construct the habitus of this singular puissant subject. There are literate people on the farm, to be sure, the farmer probably foremost amongst them. Then there are television, the church and the Bible, unsuccessful literacy classes, and communal readings of the newspaper on Sunday. These do not exhaust the possibilities, nor even suggest anything plausible. Recall, too, that Hendricks lives in a rural enclave, within a neo-feudal set of relations between worker and farmer, where occupational mobility is low and career advancement limited, and anyway not in terms of occupational categories that might have literacy requirements. NLS might conclude with some justification that Hendricks really does not need literacy, and I am quite sure this is the answer he himself would give if asked. But from a neo-Durkheimian perspective the question is how, and under what conditions, can vertical discourse be accessed outside of formal contexts of transmission? A thorough-going answer may well contribute to a rethinking of the role of formal educational institutions given the cognitive demands and requisites of late modernity (see Young, 1999). And it would certainly also help to explicate how sacred practices lie nested, often unremarked, within the routines of the everyday. Above all, however, it would question whether we advance our understanding of knowledge practices in any way if we merely regard literacy as another mundane kind of social accomplishment, as NLS does.

Does this conclusion not also consign Hendricks to perpetual illiteracy and merely recapitulate Latour's dereliction by another route? The neo-Durkheimian answer is no, since idealisation and vertical discourse are here distinguished from horizontal discourse, and valued as a distinct form of symbol system with a distinct social role. Social differentiation depends upon knowledge differentiation for Durkheimians, and systematic idealisation is the only way to project benign possible futures. Without it, no concept of social change is possible, and no revolution (an idea borrowed by politics from science, after all [Latour, 1993, p. 70]). How will this conclusion help Hendricks? It probably won't, but then, for Durkheimians, the task is to understand the conditions for social development, not the development of individuals, in the first instance. The really interesting task, then, is to understand the role of vertical discourse in social change and the ways in which access to it is or is not, can or cannot be, advanced by education. Hendricks's story is a pinprick of light in this dark firmament, but it burns brightly for all that.

Notes

1. Dérèglement is "Abandonment to the absence of boundaries" (Blanchot, 1988, p. 3).

2. "[...] perhaps, to repeat a myth, Thales did singlehandedly open up the continent of mathematics. The typical case, however, is a large number of people approaching the same subject matter with related styles of argumentation. This must necessarily be the case. For a style of reason opens up a new field of discourse, with new positive propositions to assert or deny. Such a new field is a relatively large-scale social phenomenon. A body of discourse needs quite a lot of speakers" (Hacking, 1985, p. 149).

3. It is for this reason that Foucault's (1977, pp. xv–xx) laughter at Borges's Chinese encyclopaedia is so oddly misplaced. What Foucault takes to be an impossible or heterotopic order is merely a non-empirical invisible or arbitrary one—that is to say, a sacred one. It belongs to the common realm of the scientific rather than being opposed to it. Although Foucault's larger point is certainly profound, it is odd that he has to make the point in this way.

4. "This *culture générale*, formerly lavishly praised, now appears to us a loose and flabby discipline [...] We disapprove of those men whose unique care is to organise and develop all their faculties [...] as if each man were sufficient unto himself, and constituted an independent world. It seems to us that this state of detachment and indeterminism has something antisocial about it. The praiseworthy man of former times is only a dilettante to us [...] The categorical imperative of the moral conscience is assuming the following form: *Make yourself usefully fulfil a determinate function*" (Durkheim, 1964, pp. 42–43).

5. "The examination is nothing but the [...] official recognition of the transubstantiation of profane knowledge into sacred knowledge" (Marx, quoted in Bourdieu & Passeron, 1990, p. 141).

6. "If anything can mean anything else, as allegory tends to believe, then it is both enriched and impoverished" (Eagleton, 1998).

7. Li Puma (1993) illuminatingly distinguishes between a formal and a substantive notion of arbitrariness. A formal notion, shared by most anthropologists and Durkheim, holds that social valuations of cultural forms are arbitrary; a substantive notion, held by Bourdieu, holds that cultural contents are historically arbitrary, and that any symbol could, in principle, have been replaced by any other.

8. It is possible to align this discussion with trends in contemporary psychology. Luria (1976), for example, distinguishes between situational and abstract thinking, in ways that resonate with Bernstein's horizontal and vertical discourse. Luria also goes on to associate the capacity for abstract thinking with literacy and the higher capacities of language. I have avoided making this connection here. It tends to essentialise the subject (Larochelle, 1994) by suggesting that we can speak of situational or abstract thinkers. The position taken here is that these are discourses which subjects access or are positioned in some of the time. A psychological framework is also difficult to use to discuss conditions under which sacred tendencies interrupt profane contexts and vice versa (see also Dowling, 1994).

9. The discussion draws on a helpful paper by Breier (1995).

10. This excerpt and all subsequent ones come from the excellent ethnography by Diana Gibson (1994). Page numbering refers to the draft copy of the report.

11. Gibson (1994, p. 41) tentatively proposes this idea but does not elaborate.

Bibliography

Atkins, P. (1995). Science as truth. *History of the Human Sciences, 8,* 97–102.

Benjamin, W. (1969). *Illuminations.* New York: Schocken Books.

Bernstein, B. (1996). *Class, codes and control: Vol. V, Pedagogy, symbolic control and identity: Theory, research, critique.* London: Taylor & Francis.

———. (1999). Vertical and horizontal discourse: An essay. *British Journal of Sociology of Education, 20* (2), 157–173.

Blanchot, M. (1988). *The unavowable community.* New York: Station Hill Press.

Bourdieu, P., & Passeron, J. C. (1990). *Reproduction in education, society and culture.* London: Sage Publications.

Breier, M. (1995). *Defining literacy.* Unpublished manuscript, University of the Western Cape, South Africa.

Buci-Glucksman, C. (1994). *Baroque reason: The aesthetics of modernity.* London: Sage Publications.

Callon, M. (1995). Four models for the dynamics of science. In S. Jasanoff, G. E. Markle, J. C. Petersen, & T. Pinch (Eds.), *Handbook of science and technology studies.* London: Sage Publications.

Deleuze, G. (1995). *Negotiations: 1972–1990.* New York: Columbia University Press.

Derrida, J. (1978). *Writing and difference.* London: Routledge & Kegan Paul.

Dowling, P. C. (1994). Discursive saturation and school mathematics texts: A strand from a language of description. In P. Ernest (Ed.), *Mathematics, education and philosophy: An international perspective.* London: Falmer Press.

Durkheim, E. (1915). *The elementary forms of the religious life: A study in religious sociology* (J. W. Swain, Trans.). London: George Allen & Unwin.

———. (1964). *The division of labour in society* (G. Simpson, Trans.). Glencoe, IL: Free Press.

Eagleton, T. (1998). Newsreel history. *London Review of Books Online, 20* (22) [Online]. Available at: http://www.lrb.co.uk/v20/n22/eagl2022.htm.

Elam, M. (1993). Markets, morals and powers of innovation. *Economy and Society, 22,* 1–41.

Entwhistle, N. (1998). Approaches to learning and forms of understanding. In B. Dart & G.

Boulton–Lewis (Eds.), *Teaching and learning in higher education*. Melbourne: Acer Press.

Foucault, M. (1977). *The order of things: An archaeology of the human sciences*. London: Tavistock.

———. (1981). The order of discourse. In R. Young (Ed.), *Untying the text: A poststructuralist reader* (pp. 48–78). London: Routledge & Kegan Paul.

Fuller, S. (1995). On the motives for the new sociology of science. *History of the Human Sciences, 8*, 117–124.

Gee, J. (1990). *Social linguistics and literacies: Ideology in discourses*. London: Falmer Press.

Gibson, D. (1994). *Farm workers, literacy and literacy practices in the Breerivier Valley. The social uses of literacy research project*. Unpublished manuscript, University of the Western Cape, South Africa.

Giroux, H., & McLaren, P. (Eds.). (1994). *Between borders: Pedagogy and the politics of cultural studies*. New York: Routledge.

Grillo, R. D. (1989). *Dominant languages*. Cambridge: Cambridge University Press.

Hacking, I. (1985). Styles of scientific reasoning. In J. Rajchman & C. West (Eds.), *Post-analytic philosophy*. New York: Columbia University Press.

———. (1992). *The taming of chance*. Cambridge: Cambridge University Press.

———. (1998). On being more literal about construction. In I. Velody & R. Williams (Eds.), *The politics of constructionism*. London: Sage Publications.

Heath, S. B. (1983). *Ways with words*. Cambridge: Cambridge University Press.

Jardine, D. W. (1999). *To dwell with a boundless heart: Essays in curriculum theory, hermeneutics, and the ecological imagination*. New York: Peter Lang.

Knorr Cetina, K. (1994). Primitive classification and postmodernity: Towards a sociological notion of fiction. *Theory, culture and society, 11*, 1–22.

Larochelle, M. (1994). *Radical constructivism: Notes on the implications for education and for educators*. Unpublished manuscript, Université Laval, Québec.

Lather, P. (1991). *Getting smart: Feminist research and pedagogy with/in the postmodern*. London: Routledge & Kegan Paul.

Latour, B. (1993). *We have never been modern*. Hemel Hempstead, England: Harvester Wheatsheaf.

Li Puma, E. (1993). Culture and the concept of culture in a theory of practice. In C. Calhoun, E. Li Puma, & M. Postone (Eds.), *Bourdieu: Critical perspectives*. Cambridge: Polity Press.

Luria, A. R. (1976). *Cognitive development: Its cultural and social foundations*. Cambridge, MA: Harvard University Press.

Lyotard, J.-F. (1991). *The inhuman: Reflections on time*. Cambridge: Polity Press.

McCarthy, T. (1989). Philosophy and social practice: Avoiding the ethnocentric predicament. In A. Honneth, T. Mccarthy, C. Offe, & A. Wellmer (Eds.), *Zwischenbetrachtungen im prozes der aufklärung*. Frankfurt am Main: Suhrkamp Verlag.

Patton, P. (Ed.). (1996). *Deleuze: A critical reader*. Oxford: Blackwell.

Pollner, M. (1975). Mundane reasoning. *Philosophy of the social sciences, 4*, 35–54.

Prinsloo, M., & Breier, M. (Eds.). (1996). *The social uses of literacy: Case studies from South Africa*. Cape Town: Maskew Miller Longman.

Ringer, F. (1993). *Fields of knowledge. French academic culture in comparative perspective, 1890–1900*. Cambridge: Cambridge University Press.

Rorty, R. (1979). *Philosophy and the mirror of nature*. Princeton, NJ: Princeton University Press.

Shapin, S. (1994). *A social history of truth: Civility and science in seventeenth century England*. Chicago: University of Chicago Press.

Shotter, J. (1993). Harre, Vygotsky, Bakhtin, Vico, Wittgenstein: Academic discourses and conversational realities. *Journal for the Theory of Social Behaviour, 23*, 459–482.

Simmel, G. (1971). *On individuality and social forms*. Chicago: University of Chicago Press.

Simon, B. (1999). Undead science: Making sense of cold fusion after the (arti)fact. *Social Studies of Science, 29*, 61–85.

Sokal, A., & Bricmont, J. (1998). *Fashionable nonsense: Postmodern intellectuals' abuse of science*. New York: St. Martin's Press.

Street, B. V. (1984). *Literacy in theory and practice*. Cambridge: Cambridge University Press.

———. (1993). *Cross-cultural approaches to literacy*. Cambridge: Cambridge University Press.

Tester, K. (1993). *The life and times of postmodernity*. London: Routledge & Kegan Paul.

Thompson, K. (Ed.). (1994). *Readings from Emile Durkheim*. London: Routledge & Kegan Paul.

Wrong, D. H. (1994). *The problem of order: What unites and divides society.* New York: Free Press.

Young, M. (February, 1999). *Knowledge, learning and the curriculum of the future?* Inaugural Lecture, Institute of Education, University of London.

Chapter 7

Founding the Sociology of Knowledge: Basil Bernstein, Intellectual Fields, and the Epistemic Device

Rob Moore
Karl Maton

> Observation is always selective. It needs a chosen object, a definite task, an interest, a point of view, a problem.
>
> [Karl Popper, 1963, p. 27]

Introduction

The starting point for this chapter is a paradox in the sociology of knowledge, namely, that it cannot see its ostensible object of study: *knowledge*. Although the early 1970s "New Sociology of Education" (NSE) in Britain proposed a rejuvenated sociology of knowledge (e.g., Young, 1971), "this programme, whatever else it produced, did not produce what it called for" (Bernstein, 1990, p. 166). It focused on what Bernstein (1990, pp. 165–180) describes as "relations to" (such as relations of class, race, gender *to* knowledge) rather than "relations within" (the structuring of knowledge itself), and thus developed a sociology without a theory of knowledge (Moore, 1996a, 2000). Our original (and ongoing) intention was (and is) to analyse Anglophone sociology of education to highlight and account for this development. This task, however, poses a "Catch 22" dilemma. Not only does this endeavour involve producing knowledge about the production of knowledge, it does so both within the context and through the study of a field which, we have been arguing, cannot *see* knowledge as an object of study in its own right. If the sociology of knowledge has such a blindspot, then the analytical tools at our disposal would re-create the very phenomenon we wished to explain, by permitting only a partial (sociologically reductionist) account of its development. Moreover, describing what is obscured by a blindspot is extremely difficult, for what you are trying to point to simply cannot be seen through the current lens. One must, therefore, first establish what it is one is actually looking at and the means for doing so—a new lens.[1]

Here one may turn to Basil Bernstein's recent work on knowledge structures and "grammars", concepts which offer a means of systematically describing differences between intellectual fields in terms of the organising principles of their knowledge formations. However, as we point out, these concepts take us only part of the way. What is still required is a means for describing what produces these structures of knowledge, their underlying generative principles. In a recent paper, Bernstein states that the term pedagogy "has restrictive references", one of which is that it does not "point to the phenomena to be described". One of these phenomena, and our focus here, concerns the production of knowledge. We argue that, in order to address these areas, we need to move Bernstein's framework forward, as he puts it, "from pedagogies to knowledges". This is to say that, though Bernstein provides a sophisticated theory of the construction of *pedagogic* discourse, studying the *production* of knowledge brings to light a new issue: the basis of knowledge claims.

It is worth emphasising that this is *not* an oversight in Bernstein's work but rather what his approach highlights as the next stage in the analysis of intellectual fields. The organisation of existing knowledge and the procedures for creating new knowledge have long been a central concern in the work of Bernstein, and movement in this direction into the future can be illustrated by considering the development of his ideas (see Table 7.1). In a recent article, Bernstein outlines the trajectory taken by his work over the past 30 years in terms of what can be described *inter alia* as a movement from the analysis of pedagogic transmission/acquisition of existing knowledge within educational contexts, through a theory of the construction of this pedagogic discourse, to analyses of the knowledge subject to such pedagogic transformation (1999, p. 157). In a series of seminal papers during the 1970s, he developed distinctions between, for example, "collection" and "integrated" codes in the classification and framing of school knowledge (1975, pp. 85–115) and between "visible" and "invisible" pedagogies (1975, pp. 116–145). Such distinctions formed the basis for addressing a wide range of issues relating to how the organisation of educational knowledge regulates consciousness or forms pedagogic identities, regulates the relationship between the "inner" and the "outer", and influences the socialisation of individuals into fields of knowledge. During the 1980s, Bernstein focused on developing a theory of the construction of this pedagogic discourse, analysing the principles and social bases of its distribution, recontextualisation, and evaluation in terms of the "pedagogic device" (1990, pp. 165–218). More recently, this work has been built upon to analyse the knowledge structures from which pedagogic discourse is selected and recontextualised (1996, pp. 169–181; 1999). This trajectory thus traces a cumulative and progressive movement through analyses of the reproduction, recontextualisation, and production of knowledge (Table 7.1).

Table 7.1: *A trajectory through Bernstein's analysis of the construction of knowledge*

Principal focus of theoretical development	Main decade of circulation of theory	Principal publication (Class, Codes and Control)
Transmission/acquisition of pedagogic discourse	1970s	Volume 3 (1975)
↓		
Structuring of pedagogic discourse	1980s	Volume 4 (1990)
↓		
Knowledge structures from which pedagogic discourse is recontextualised	1990s	Volume 5 (1996, 2000)
↓		
Production of knowledge structures	2000s	Future development

Bernstein has also addressed the question of relations between theory and research (e.g. 1996, pp. 91–144). For Bernstein, there is a dynamic interplay between the theoretical construction of and empirical research into objects of inquiry. Throughout his work, theoretical development has made visible new objects of study for empirical research, which in turn have evoked and necessitated the development of theory, which raises further issues for research, and so on. In this chapter, we aim to contribute to the ongoing development of the trajectory by building upon Bernstein's recent work to further examine intellectual fields of knowledge production. Specifically, we intend to begin moving to the next step in this trajectory, by analysing the ways in which knowledge structures are themselves produced. As Bernstein suggests, this focus brings to light a new object for inquiry. Indeed, developing Bernstein's approach, we shall outline the necessary foundation and fundamental theoretical object for the sociology of *knowledge*, that is, its defining object of inquiry. In a manner deliberately analogous to Bernstein's concept of the pedagogic device, we refer to this object as the *epistemic device*. In brief, this device regulates how knowledge comes to be viewed as legitimate by altering relations between the arbitrary and non-arbitrary in knowledge; that is, whether knowledge claims are legitimated on the basis of external relations of power or by principles intrinsic to knowledge itself. To put it another way, central to the realisations of the device (and so to the form taken by intellectual fields) is whether knowledge is addressed in terms of "relations to" or "relations within". Thus, an analysis of the workings of the epistemic device will also begin to shed light on the development of the sociology of knowledge itself.

The chapter comprises three main interrelated parts. First, we set our analysis in context by briefly outlining Bernstein's recent conceptualisation of knowledge structures and grammars, and establish the necessity of theoretical development by highlighting the specificities of fields of intellectual production. Secondly, we describe the nature of our object of inquiry (the epistemic device) through an illustration of its effects when intellectual fields are described as undergoing changes of paradigm (such as occurred at the birth of the NSE). This provides a way into outlining the basic conceptual building blocks for analysing realisations of the device. Thirdly, we focus in more depth on two contrastive examples of intellectual fields with (horizontal) knowledge structures similar to these of sociology of education, but with differing strengths of grammar: literary criticism and mathematics. We explore the ways in which the different "settings" of the epistemic device dominant within each intellectual field shape their parameters and possibilities, both sociologically and epistemologically. In conclusion, we clarify the nature and status of the epistemic device, its relationship to Bernstein's "pedagogic device", and the ramifications of our analyses for the sociology of knowledge.

Conceptualising Intellectual Fields

Reviewing dominant approaches within the sociology of education, Bernstein argues that despite surface differences they overwhelmingly share both a common focus and a common blindspot (1990, pp. 165–180). The shared focus is on analysing the ways in which pedagogic discourses work to reproduce external social relations of power, such as class, race, and gender; the shared blindspot is the analysis of pedagogic discourse itself, its "intrinsic features". "It is as if", Bernstein writes, "pedagogic discourse is itself no more than a relay for power relations external to itself; a relay whose form has no consequences for what is relayed" (1990, p. 166). The sociology of education has, in other words, focused on relations *to*, and neglected relations *within* (educational) knowledge. Bernstein is describing here not simply alternative objects of study but also different sociologies of education with differing principles of organisation and thereby differing possibilities and parameters for producing new knowledge. The organisation of knowledge within an intellectual field is not simply the way in which previously produced knowledge is arranged into some kind of order (although this itself is a feature of interest). It is characterised by a *principle* that also regulates the manner in which new knowledge is produced and its form. As this principle differs, so will the organisation and, crucially here, the *mode of production* of knowledge within the field. In other words, any specific intellectual field is organised in such a way as to make certain things visible and potential objects for knowledge, and other things invisible within its current field of vision.

We, therefore, suggest that the two sociologies Bernstein describes ("relations to" and "relations within") are sociologies operating under different principles of production, and through different modes of production. The difference between them is thus a difference of *principle* and not just of focus or perspective. It is not that the sociology of education has failed to address the intrinsic features of knowledge through neglect or misplaced priorities, but rather that it cannot *see* an object of this *kind* as an object of study in its own right because of the way in which the intellectual field itself has been constituted and located. It is a matter not so much of intention and commitment as of effect and consequence (Maton, 2000c). The following questions thus arise: What is the nature of this principle? How can we conceptualise this principle? And what are the main forms its realisations take? Here, one may turn to Bernstein's recent work for answers.

Hierarchical and horizontal knowledge structures

Bernstein has recently developed distinctions between the forms taken by differing structures of knowledge within intellectual fields (1996, 1999). These he defines as hierarchical and horizontal knowledge structures with weak and strong grammars, which we briefly outline in turn. Bernstein defines a hierarchical knowledge structure, exemplified by the natural sciences,[2] as characterised by

> attempts to create very general propositions and theories, which integrate knowledge at lower levels, and in this way shows underlying uniformities across an expanding range of apparently different phenomena. Hierarchical knowledge structures appear, by their users, to be motivated towards greater and greater integrating propositions, operating at more and more abstract levels. (Bernstein, 1999, p. 162)

In contrast, horizontal knowledge structures, exemplified by the humanities and social sciences, "consist of a series of specialised languages with specialised modes of interrogation and criteria for the construction and circulation of texts" (Bernstein, 1999, p. 162). They comprise a series of segmented languages or approaches, which Bernstein visually represents as

$$L^1 \ L^2 \ L^3 \ L^4 \ L^5 \ L^6 \ L^7 \ldots L^n$$

He illustrates this by referring to the specialised languages of criticism in English literature, and, for example, to functionalism, post-structuralism, post-modernism, and Marxism, in the case of sociology. A crucial distinction between the two forms of knowledge structure is the form taken by their development. While hierarchical knowledge structures are based on integrating codes, horizontal knowledge structures are based on collection or serial codes. Development in the former takes the form of the greater generality and integrative potential of new theory, whereas, in the latter, development proceeds by the addition of a new language, an additional segment: "integration of language in one case and accumulation of languages in the other" (Bernstein, 1999, p. 163).

Weak and strong grammars

Bernstein makes a further distinction between *horizontal* knowledge structures with relatively "strong" and "weak" grammars, in order to distinguish those whose languages have an explicit conceptual syntax capable of "relatively" precise empirical descriptions and/or of generating formal modelling of empirical relations, from those languages where these powers are much weaker. (Bernstein, 1999, p. 164)

Examples of horizontal knowledge structures with strong grammars include mathematics, logic, and economics; examples of those with weak grammars include social anthropology, cultural studies, and (crucially for our focus here) sociology.

Analysing intellectual production: Principles, modes, and devices. What Bernstein provides here is a means of systematically describing differences between intellectual fields in terms of their organising principles, rather than simply their outcomes or empirical characteristics. What is now required is a means of conceptualising the practices which generate these; that is, the underlying generative principles which give rise to these knowledge structures and grammars and enable change between them (i.e., the aforementioned "principle"). For reasons we have already introduced, this necessitates conceptual development.[3]

Crucial to this necessity is a significant difference between considering the *production* of knowledge and considering its recontextualisation and reproduction. As Bernstein makes apparent with his concept of recontextualisation, fields of knowledge production are irreducible to fields of reproduction. As one cannot read off the form taken by the teaching of physics from the research practices of physicists, so the converse holds true; these two fields of practice have their own specificities. Similarly, what may be tacit in fields of recontextualisation and reproduction may be more evident in fields of production—analysing the latter may open up new concerns for analysis. In the case of reproduction (especially at the level of the school) a crucial role is played by the "pedagogic device" which regulates the distribution, recontextualisation, and evaluation of pedagogic discourse (Bernstein 1990, pp. 165–218). This device is the key to understanding how knowledge generated by intellectual fields of production comes to be transformed into *pedagogic* discourse (see Beck, 1999). However, as the trajectory of Bernstein's analysis has led to development of the theory, which in turn brings new concerns to light, so the analysis of fields of intellectual production brings to light new issues, which necessitate development of the theory.

One such issue which knowledge *production* highlights is the basis of knowledge claims, and specifically relations between the arbitrary and non-arbitrary in knowledge. By "arbitrary", we mean the way in which knowledge may be shown to be related to historically situated social relations of power; by "non-arbitrary" we mean that dimension of knowledge which is irreducible to such social relations of power. In effect, the arbitrary and the non-arbitrary could be said to refer to the traditional foci of the sociology of knowledge and epistemology, respectively. The question of the significance of these two interrelated but analytically distinguishable dimensions of knowledge is not, we suggest, of *primary* significance in arenas of recontextualisation and reproduction. Here, the principal questions concern the articulation of extant knowledge—the processes whereby *pedagogic* discourse is socially constructed. In production, however, knowledge is specialised, in different ways, by irreducible principles intrinsic to itself—the non-arbitrary. Whether knowledge claims deny this non-arbitrary dimension (e.g., forms of relativism and idealism) or rely exclusively upon notions of their own non-arbitrariness (e.g., positivism), they highlight and refer to this dimension. In arenas of knowledge production, the question of the basis of knowledge claims is thus less subdued—it touches upon the very *raison d'être* and conditions of existence of such fields—and the question is centrally focused on relations between the arbitrary *and* the non-arbitrary.

The question becomes: What lies behind the ongoing reproduction, transformation, and change of intellectual fields as sites of knowledge *production*? What is required is a means of conceptualising their generating principles; that is, an analogue of the pedagogic device, but focused on the question of the basis of claims to new knowledge, a question which addresses this crucial issue of (non)arbitrariness. The first task is to conceptualise intellectual fields in terms of knowledge production. Here we turn to the conceptual framework developed by Maton (1998, 1999, 2000b, 2000d), which argues that relations between these two dimensions of knowledge—the arbitrary and the non-arbitrary—proclaimed by actors within fields of intellectual production represent *principles of legitimation*. Different settings of the relations between these two dimensions are conceptualised as forming the basis of differing *modes of legitimation*, which have ramifications for the form taken by knowledge production and its social contexts. This conceptual framework provides a means of systematically describing differences between intellectual fields in terms of the organising principles of the *production* of knowledge. If Bernstein provides the lens to see knowledge as an object of study, this brings the question of its production into focus.

The second task is to conceptualise the generative principles which give rise to these modes of knowledge production. We argue that the principles of legitimation active in an intellectual field are, in turn, regulated by what we term the *epistemic device*. The concept of principles of legitimation describes relations between the arbitrary and non-arbitrary in the distribution, recontextualisation, and evaluation of legitimacy within intellectual fields (see Maton, 1998, 2000b, 2000d). The epistemic device is the means whereby actors, groups of actors, or institutions may alter these relations. In other words, control of the device is access to a ruler and distributor of legitimate claims to new knowledge, legitimate membership of the field (professional identity), legitimate practices, and so forth. The epistemic device is thus the *precondition* of knowledge production; without the epistemic device, there is no means of establishing the basis of knowledge claims. As we show, the epistemic device is also the means, through its realisation in differing modes of legitimation, whereby the knowledge structures and grammars of intellectual fields are maintained, reproduced, transformed, and changed. Whoever owns or controls the epistemic device possesses the means to set the structure and grammar of the field. This is also to say that the device is the object, the means, and the stakes of struggles within intellectual fields. To control the device is to establish specific modes of legitimation as dominant within a field, and so revalorise different forms of capital active within it, restructuring relations between positions. In other words, the epistemic device is the key to symbolic domination.[4]

Such conceptualisations, however, require illustration, as confusion is likely to arise over their ontological status. Bernstein, for example, has had to repeatedly emphasise the distinction between educational knowledge codes and the distributive, recontextualising, and evaluative "rules" regulated by the pedagogic device (which are the *resources* for codes). Such confusions reflect an empiricist tendency to substantialism, that is, to asking *where* the device may be seen, rather than *when*. Crucially, such postulated generative principles are realised not in space, but in time. One sees, as it were, the *effects* of the device, rather than the device itself. To both clarify this point and introduce these concepts, we now provide an illustration of the kinds of things and events we have been referring to. Given our focus on the sociology of education—which Bernstein characterises as a horizontal knowledge structure—our focus is on explicating the notion of differing strengths of grammar rather than differences between forms of knowledge structure.

Illustrating the Switch Event: From "Perspectives" to "Paradigms"

There was a widespread tendency in the early 1970s to employ Kuhn's (e.g., 1962) ideas about paradigm "crisis", "revolution", and "change" in the natural sciences as a way of describing and accounting for differences between theoretical perspectives in sociology and moves between them within its sub-disciplines. (What came to be known as the "New Sociology of Education" is a prime example of this.) Such changes were often described, using Kuhnian terminology, as shifts between incommensurable "paradigms". The introduction of a new self-description of an intellectual field in this manner goes to the heart of our analysis, providing an illustration of the effects of the epistemic device. Bearing all this in mind, imagine the following scenario whereby an intellectual field is redescribed by its members; from a field of "perspectives" to one of "paradigms".

Imagine, first, an intellectual field comprising a range of languages, constituted by schools of theory, methodological approaches, definitions of problems and interests, established bodies of knowledge, and so forth. Within this field, some members are primarily interested in, say, macro-level structural concerns, tend to work with large data sets, and use quantitative forms of analysis. Elsewhere in this field there might be another group of members whose interests are at the micro level and who employ ethnographic methods to investigate in-depth processes, perceptions, and social interactions. These "Macros" and "Micros" see their field as comprising a range of *perspectives*. They come together at conferences and exchange ideas and information. They come from different cultures spanning the globe, encompass all stages of the academic career, and include researchers of different genders, sexualities, social backgrounds, and so on. In these gatherings they seek ways to integrate their knowledge and attempt to develop a conceptual language that moves between the macro and the micro. So, though the approaches, substantive topics, and methods of this kaleidoscope of people differ, they are able to speak to each other, to discuss and contest issues and ideas. Debates, arguments, disputes may rage at various moments, but within an atmosphere of mutual understanding. They have, in other words, established criteria and procedures sufficiently explicit for collective decisions to emerge as to which particular perspective most adequately accounts for what is agreed to be the case. This field of "perspectives" is a field of *specialisms* but one which employs (or aspires to) a language of mediation between levels and between approaches. "Macros" and "Micros" speak to each other through a particular kind of *grammar* (more or less explicit or systematic) that enables them as a community to retain a sense of inclusiveness that transcends their specialist intellectual differences and so to engage in the task of theoretical and substantive integration.

Now, imagine what happens if a group emerges which declares that this is not, in fact, a field of perspectives, but rather a field of competing *paradigms*. This portrayal, crucially, attempts to change the relationship between the array of perspectives and the possibilities of what members of the field can say to each other: Differences between "Macro" and "Micro" are now claimed to be differences of exclusiveness and incommensurability. Criteria and procedures for establishing significant questions and provisional solutions are no longer the subject of debate and negotiation but are viewed as entirely dependent on incommensurable differences of worldview. This new portrayal thus posits a different understanding of the organisation and production of knowledge within the field. When "perspectives" are changed into "paradigms", adherents to various perspectives can no longer talk to each other—there is very little to say beyond "Who are you? One of us or one of them, friend or foe?" This is no longer a field of *specialists* speaking a language of complementary knowledge integration, but one of exclusively *specialised* knowers (Maton, 2000b, 2000d), each speaking in its own distinctive and incommensurable language or "voice" (Moore & Muller, 1999). The grammar of the field has undergone a fundamental transformation.

The nature of the event

Now, what sort of thing has occurred? What we have described is a move from a horizontal knowledge structure with a (relatively) strong grammar to one with a weaker grammar. Both states of the field represent horizontal knowledge structures (comprise a series of different languages), but the "paradigms" field possesses a relatively weak grammar as its languages have a comparatively low level of integrative power. Essentially, what has changed is the strength of classification between the perspectives (or languages L^1, L^2, L^3 ... L^n) within the field. The introduction of Kuhn's terminology to redescribe the field thus attempts to "switch" the strength of grammar of the field.

If this describes the underlying differences between the two states of the field, what, then, is generating these different knowledge formations and, in particular, enabling the process of change from one to another? This question can be addressed by emphasising that "paradigms" is only one *possible* description of the field. It is likely that other actors would contest this view and argue against the imposition of the particular "epistemology" (or, more precisely, anti-epistemology) that advocates of the paradigm model propose. A conflict would then follow between those who support "perspectives" and those who support "paradigms" as the way of understanding the field. In this situation a new *kind* of struggle would emerge: one related to how the field itself is understood rather than to rival knowledge claims between competing perspectives. Hence the introduction of a language of "paradigms" in self-representations is not simply the introduction of one more perspective; it is the emergence of an attempt to fundamentally restructure the nature of the field by weakening its grammar. It is a struggle between explicit *languages of legitimation*: claims about the nature of what is to count as knowledge and the procedures and criteria that members of the field can legitimately employ in its production (Maton, 2000b, 2000d).

Languages, principles, and modes of legitimation. This raises questions concerned with what it is that actors engaged in such conflicts are struggling over and how. Actors struggle for the right to define the field and its practices, but what is the mechanism, the "switching device", by which this may be achieved? What we are suggesting is that such struggles are for control of the epistemic device—the generative means whereby the parameters and possibilities of the field, its structure and grammar, are established—and that such struggles comprise the proclamation, in languages of legitimation, of differing *principles* of legitimation.[5] These principles of legitimation set out ways of conceiving of the field and its practices and thus propose a ruler for participation within the struggles and criteria by which achievement within the field (including success in these struggles) should be measured (Maton, 2000b, 2000d). This is to say that languages of legitimation, such as those of "perspectives" and "paradigms", posit a principle, a specific articulation between the arbitrary and the non-arbitrary, as *the* basis for legitimacy within the field. Different principles of legitimation proclaim different answers to the question of whether knowledge and its production is to be understood as sociologically and historically contingent, or as ontologically necessary, or as particular configurations of both.

The configurations comprising principles of legitimation can be conceptualised by conceiving of the arbitrary/non-arbitrary in terms of what

Maton (1998, 1999, 2000b, 2000d) defines as the "epistemic relation" and the "social relation" of knowledge. These refer to two analytically distinctive but empirically interrelated dimensions of knowledge and practice within intellectual fields of production. In short, they conceptualise the ways in which claims to knowledge are both *by authors in social-historical contexts* and *about the world*, that is, that knowledge claims are *by somebody* and *about something*. The epistemic relation is the relation between knowledge and that part of the world of which knowledge is claimed (its proclaimed object of study). The social relation is between knowledge and its author, the subject making the claim to knowledge. Languages of legitimation are conceptualised in terms of the strength of boundaries around (classification) and control over (framing) *what* knowledge may be claimed and *how* (epistemic relation), and *who* may claim knowledge (social relation). Crucially, the forms these relations take within languages of legitimation may vary independently of each other; each may be strongly or weakly classified (C) and framed (F).

In these terms, languages of legitimation can be rewritten as expressing particular configurations of strong/weak C and F for these two relations: as specific *principles* of legitimation (Maton, 2000b, 2000d). These specialise knowledge in particular ways. In the above example, the field was portrayed as first a series of specialisms ("perspectives") and then as specialised knowers ("paradigms"). The perspectives field exhibits strong C and F of the epistemic relation (emphasising the significance of specialised procedures), but weak C and F of the social relation (knowers are not the issue). The paradigms field *reverses* these strengths, specialising and privileging positions within the field on the basis of *who* is making the claim to knowledge, regardless of the procedures used and the objects studied. In other words, attempts to redescribe the field from comprising "perspectives" to comprising "paradigms" are also attempts to "switch" the ways in which knowledge is specialised to and within the field: in this case, from a *knowledge mode* of legitimation to a *knower mode*.[6] As such, these attempts aim to control the epistemic device, for whoever controls the device controls the generator of status hierarchies in the field; they are able to set the switch in their favour, so to speak, by establishing particular modalities of legitimation as dominant within the field, and so structuring relations between its constituent elements ($L^1, L^2 \ldots L^n$) in different ways.

We develop the substantive analysis further in the next section of the chapter. Before doing so, we need to address a potential misreading concerning the dichotomous resonances of "switch". Our discussion of different strengths of grammars and two modes of legitimation, alongside the (heuristically intended) "switch" metaphor, may suggest dichotomies: strong/weak grammar; knowledge/knower modes. In terms of the theory, these are not the case, but for differing reasons. When discussing grammars, Bernstein emphasises their *relative* strengths; the grammar of a field of "perspectives" may be stronger than that of a field of "paradigms", but nonetheless remains weaker than that of logic or mathematics. (We focus on the example of mathematics below.) Thus our description of attempts to *weaken* (or strengthen) grammar—a process of change rather than movements between polar states. In the case of modes of legitimation, knowledge and knower modes are those forms most often encountered when analysing such intellectual fields as contemporary sociology. (Varying C/F for epistemic and social relations independently gives *four* possible modes; see Maton, 2000d.) Furthermore, neither grammars nor modes of legitimation represent ideal types, which remain at the level of the empirical; rather, they represent real principles whose empirical realisations are dependent on the enabling context (Bernstein, 1999; Maton, 2000b). As we show, the fact that these grammars are typically conceived as absolute states and modes of legitimation, portrayed as an either/or choice, itself reveals something of the nature of these fields, namely, their tendency to construct false dichotomies of complete rupture. The "switch" is held to have only two settings, and changes between them are described as totalising.

Grammars, Modes, and Communities: The Cases of Literary Criticism and Mathematics

We now deepen and expand the analysis to explore the ramifications of differing strengths of grammar and modes of legitimation for the form taken by fields of intellectual production. Here we apply the conceptual framework outlined above to examine two contrastive examples: one where the dominance of a knower mode of legitimation results in recurrent attempts to "switch" the grammar of the field to a weaker form (literary criticism); and one where a knowledge mode underpins a relatively strong grammar (mathematics). We focus in particular on the two dimensions highlighted by the epistemic and social relations: the form taken by the epistemological and sociological features proclaimed as defining and legitimating the fields.

We should first emphasise that within certain epistemological parameters (given by the ontology of a field's domain), the strength of grammar current at any moment in time (its capacity to produce knowledge and in what form) is contingent upon the *condition* of the field in terms of its location within the broader structural dynamic of the education system. This will be strongly influenced by factors such as educational expansion, state policies regarding funding, and the degree of external regulation of institutions. These issues are not the focus of analysis here. The necessarily partial nature of the following accounts is intended to illustrate the effects of differing realisations or "settings" of the epistemic device in shaping intellectual fields, rather than to represent attempts to fully account for these fields. Our intention is *not* to displace the focus of conventional sociologies of knowledge but rather to highlight the structuring effects of a generative mechanism hitherto absent from their analyses.

The paradigmatic episode: The case of literary criticism

The schismatic phenomenon represented by the move to weaken grammar, though never before systematically theorised, has been recognised in a number of ways for a long time. Perhaps its most oft-noted form is that of a generational conflict (e.g., Hoggart, 1995; Moore, 1996b). Senior members of an intellectual field bemoan junior members' lack of originality and proclaim with a jaundiced eye: "We've heard this all before!" Conversely, younger members of the field bemoan the inability of their elders to break free of their outdated ideas, recognise their obsolescence, and allow the birth of the "new". The senior members despair at the lack of understanding of the history of their discipline; the junior members view this as just so much dead weight. The young are said to be living as if the past never happened; the old to be living in the past.

One could analyse this as simply a "conflict of the generations", a battle between the established and the newcomers, the conservative old guard and the Young Turks.[7] There is, however, more to it than that. Such events take the form of *schism*, the proclamation of a radical break, typically either *serially* as a break in time or *segmentally* as a break in space between contemporaneous "standpoints". The 1960s, for example, witnessed a large crop of notices of births and deaths: the death of God, the traditional family, élite higher education, the classics; the arrival of the "new student", "new sociology of education", "new universities" (indeed, Christopher Booker [1969] christened the decade the "age of the neophiliacs").

Examples of the present-day form of segmental "breaks" are provided by forms of "standpoint" theory and "voice" discourse (Moore & Muller, 1999). Whichever form the schism takes, it announces a language unique to itself and incommensurable either with the past or with the "normal" paradigm or dominant standpoint. Furthermore, this "paradigm" event has a paradigmatic form. Within sociology it appears that Kuhn's "revolutionary science" is normal, and a period of "normal science" would be revolutionary.

In literary criticism during the early 1960s a event similar to our "paradigms" example occurred, when proclamations of the "new" and claims for rebirth became the focus of much debate, including a series of lectures by Frank Kermode entitled *The Sense of an Ending*:

> When we survive, we make little images of the moments which have seemed like ends; we thrive on epochs. Fowler observes austerely that if we were always quite serious in speaking of "the end of an epoch" we should live in ceaseless transition; recently Mr. Harold Rosenberg has been quite seriously saying that we do. *Scholars are devoted to the epoch.* (Kermode, 1967, p. 7, emphasis added)

Kermode's discussion highlights two points we explore here, namely, that such claims are based on an apocalyptic ontology and that they represent what can be described as "creative fictions". We discuss these points in turn.

Apocalyptic ontology. Such arguments for "crises" and "breaks" in intellectual fields often proclaim an apocalyptic event in the world; they are, Kermode suggests, secular versions of apocalyptic cosmology. A rupture or radical break with the past is proclaimed: from the modern to the postmodern novel (world, condition, subject, etc.). This change in the object of study is held to require new ideas, rendering all existing work obsolete. Thus, with the addition of each new language, the object of study is said to have radically changed. Although one should remember that this new portrayal of the field is likely to be (and indeed was) contested, if it did become the dominant way of seeing the field, the effects of these kinds of claims about "the new" would be to restrict the epistemic community and intellectual focus of literary criticism to the here and now. First, it sets the present adrift from the past, which indeed becomes a "foreign country"—in fact, an incommensurably different culture. The old and the young (in this example, though we could also base our example on class, gender, race, religion, and so on) are held to literally inhabit different worlds, and authors from before the proclaimed break are said to have little to say about now.

Second, this way of representing the field makes location in time or social space the basis of knowledge claims. To draw the line between "the past" and "the modern" (or "post-modern") in this manner not only sets the present adrift from the past, it also specialises the present (or at least those who proclaim themselves its representatives). For, although a new world is proclaimed, the basis of access to legitimate knowledge of this world does not reside in procedures specialised by this new world but in the ability of the knower to *see* this new world at all—it is the new *knower* and not the new world which forms the basis of new knowledge. So, each new knower, with a gaze specialised by time and place, brings along a new and different language and object of study. In other words, each generation (paradigm or standpoint) rewrites the world in its own image. Crucial here is the emphasis placed on the social and temporal co-ordinates of the specialised knower: *Who* you are is more important than *what* you are discussing or *how*—a knower mode of legitimation.

This knower mode problematises communication between different groups of knowers within the field (in this case between past and present members) resulting in a restricted epistemic community. Although each segment or language of the knowledge structure is cohered by shared socio-cultural dispositions (values, aspirations, beliefs), cohesion and communication between segments is at best uncertain and fragile (and often merely tactical, as in defence of the entire field from external attack). Here, knowledge is always *somebody's* knowledge and nothing but. In terms of the conceptual framework, the social relations of the field are strongly classified and strongly framed—each segment represents an epistemic community restricted in time and space. "Knowers" are located within a tightly bounded set of co-ordinates specified by membership criteria, separated from the past (the past is that of the dominant other or before the crucial break) or segregated from contemporaries who do not share membership criteria. The privileged epistemic community, in other words, exhibits space-time compression.

This compression is, moreover, a dynamic process which may fragment the field, as the criteria for legitimate knower membership are inherently unstable. A characteristic of this form of intellectual field is its tendency towards proliferation and fragmentation into ever-smaller knower communities. Indeed, Kermode's starting point was Harold Rosenberg's (1962) description of *The Tradition of the New*—reports of the field's rebirth were occurring so often that it had become a tradition. With each new break proclaimed, the new epistemic community of privileged knowers becomes smaller, as each new knower brings a new object of study, with knower membership defined by increasingly hyphenated descriptions of identity and membership—to paraphrase Michael Ignatieff, a narcissism of ever smaller differences. Thus the move to weaken grammar tends to recur episodically, breaking the knowledge structure down into its constituent parts (see Maton, 2000b).

Creative fictions. The second point Kermode highlights is that claims of a major change in the object of the study are presented as descriptions of the world. However, as Kermode suggests, they are best understood as representing changes in the conditions of some members of the intellectual field (the new knowers), rather than changes in the condition of the world (compare Singh, 2000). A recent example is that of various "post" theories which argue that society is undergoing space-time compression. The analysis presented here suggests that such experiences reflect the situation of members of specific intellectual fields rather than the world at large. As Proust remarked, the one thing that does not change is that at any and every time it appears that there have been "great changes". Yet, as Kermode puts it, "if we were always quite serious in speaking of 'the end of an epoch' we should live in ceaseless transition" (Kermode, 1967, p. 7). In other words, they are at best creative fictions, heuristic devices which highlight specific developments, and should be approached with what Kermode calls "clerkly scepticism". Representing these claims as facts about the larger world is commiting what Bourdieu (2000) calls the "scholastic fallacy".

It is, however, extremely difficult in intellectual fields undergoing such attempted redescription to make this argument. The proclaimed change is not itself the object of study; it is announced rather than hypothesised and represents an article of faith, the doxa of the new knowers. The epistemic relations between the language and the object of inquiry are weakly classified and framed—it is not the object which regulates the new language, but the knower's "gaze", specialised by the "break", which constructs the object. This sensibility, the ability to see the new world, not only specialises those who possess it, but also privileges their point of view. To question the break is to be assigned to the other side of the divide and thus have no access to legitimate knowledge of the post-apocalyptic world. Those who cannot see what the new knowers see (and only the elect can) have by definition nothing to say about it. All past languages are therefore redundant, and so past work is displaced rather than integrated. One either "gets it" or one doesn't: "The times they are a-changing" combines with "something is happening and you don't know what it is, do you, Mr. Jones?"

Strong grammars and the knowledge mode: The case of mathematics.

We now compare this intellectual field with one where proclamations of "ruptures", "breaks", and the birth of the "new" are relatively rare: mathematics. If literary criticism represents a "paradigms" example, mathematics represents the "perspectives" field. Bernstein cites mathematics as an example of a horizontal knowledge structure ("a set of discrete languages, for particular problems") with a relatively *strong* grammar (1999, p. 164). Again, our focus is on analysing the generative principles underlying this grammar and its ramifications for the field. To illustrate the different form taken by mathematics, consider the following potted version of Hoffman's (1998, pp. 183–201) story of Fermat's Last Theorem:

- In 1637 in France, Pierre de Fermat (born 1601) is reading a treatise on number theory by Diophantus.

- Diophantus lived in Alexandria, possibly sometime between the first and third century A.D. In his treatise, *Arithmetica*, he discusses at length the "Pythagorean theorem", observing that "there are an infinite number of Pythagorean triplets, whole numbers x, y and z that solved the equation $x^2 + y^2 = z^2$".

- Pythagoras lived in the sixth century B.C.

- The Babylonians had known about these triplets a thousand years earlier.

- Back in seventeenth-century France, Fermat formulates his famous "Last Theorem" in response to a problem he has derived from Diophantus. He notes that he has "a truly marvellous demonstration" of this theorem that is too big to write in the margin of the *Arithmetica*. Fermat dies in 1665, but the "demonstration" is never found.

- To cut a long and fascinating story short, each subsequent century sees further work on the theorem by scores of mathematicians (male and female, from a variety of countries) until…

- In 1993, Andrew Wiles, concluding his lectures at a mathematics conference in Cambridge, writes one last statement on the blackboard and says, softly, "This proves Fermat's Last Theorem. I think I'll stop here". However, by December he has to admit to an *inconsistency* in his proof.

- By September 1994, with the help of a colleague, "the hole is patched" and the Last Theorem is considered officially proved.

What is so striking about this story is its sheer *scale* in historical time and in geographical and cultural space. It tells a story of a mathematician in late-twentieth-century England effectively communicating with a French judge at the court of Louis XIV, and through him with Babylonians from three millennia ago.[8] It represents an epistemic community with an *extended* existence in time and space, a community where the past is present, one in which the living members interact with the dead to produce contributions which, when living members die, will be in turn the living concern of future members—"a partnership not only between those who are living, but between those who are living, those who are dead, and those who are to be born" (Burke, 1989, p. 147).

What enables this extended epistemic community becomes clearer when one compares the ways in which literary criticism and mathematics are legitimated. In the case of a "paradigms" portrayal of an intellectual field, legitimacy within the field is measured by focusing on the knower. This knower mode of legitimation may be summarily represented as

$$\text{Knower} \longrightarrow \text{Language} \longrightarrow \text{Object}$$
$$(\text{"gaze"})$$

where the arrows indicate the direction of specialisation and regulation. The legitimate language is held to be specialised to the knower, and in turn is said to specialise the object of study; only the privileged knower's "gaze" may access the object of study. In other words, it is possession of the specialised sensibility, typically restricted to a social-temporal category of knower, which is the purported criterion for membership of the field—the means of socialisation into its principles of organisation is social rather than epistemic. In contrast, the "perspectives" portrayal of a field illustrated by mathematics reverses the direction of the arrows: the object (or problem) is held to specialise the language (procedures) required to access knowledge of the object, and this in turn is held to specialise knowers; that is, it is possession of the specialist language which is the purported criterion for membership of the field and the means of inculcation into its principles of organisation. This knowledge mode of legitimation may be represented as

$$\text{Object} \longrightarrow \text{Language} \longrightarrow \text{Knower}$$
$$\text{(procedures)}$$

where, as before, the arrows indicate the direction of specialisation and regulation. This highlights two fundamental differences, to which we now turn, based on the different roles played here by the epistemic relation and social relation: the status of mathematicians' creative fictions and of the mathematical knower.

Invented worlds. As in literary criticism, mathematicians create fictions. They have the freedom to invent problem-situations, where different imagined mathematical worlds may exhibit different qualities (for example, in some geometries, parallel lines converge at infinity, whilst in others they do not) and may be designed precisely for that purpose. As the mathematician Ronald Graham explains,

> In so many areas of mathematics it seems natural or appropriate to create your own mathematical world. You have a lot of choices. I want to consider structures that have thus-and-such properties. I want this structure and not that one. (quoted in Hoffman, 1998, p. 265)

The specialised languages of mathematics are specialised to these different problem-worlds, the nature of each problem regulating the form taken by its procedures. However, mathematicians cannot explore these worlds just as they like. Once a problem is established, the parameters of the problem and the criteria of its solution remain relatively constant: a strong grammar. A "fiction" (problem or theoretical postulate) is constructed whose nature and criteria of solution are held to be intransitive. Furthermore, certain kinds of procedures, values, and principles (such as consistency) will hold constant whatever the nature of the problem. If a theorem (in whichever problem "world" of maths) is demonstrated to be inconsistent, then it just *is*; its author cannot legitimately make *ad hoc* claims. Andrew Wiles, for example, could not claim that although his first attempt at solving Fermat's Last Theorem was inconsistent in Cambridge it was consistent in Oxford, or that though inconsistent in 1993 it would be consistent if Manchester United lost their next game. Mathematics has explicit criteria whereby particular claims can, at the end of the day, be demonstrably shown to be true or false, right or wrong, legitimate or illegitimate, to transcend specific worlds and endure over time. In terms of legitimation, the epistemic relation is thus strongly classified and strongly framed.

Mathematical knowers. These explicit criteria are said to transcend differences in the social and temporal co-ordinates of actors. Thus, discoveries by men and women of genius in the intellectual field, once they are established, can be used by people of no genius at all in a semi-mechanical manner in order to obtain legitimate results (cf. Berlin, 2000, p. 25). In such a field, problem-situations may persist over centuries and span the globe, previous work may be built upon and developed regardless of context, and answers may be adjudicated and progress judged by anyone sufficiently trained in the field's specialised procedures. One's claims to be a specialised knower (one's professional identity as a mathematician, a Fermat's theorem expert, etc.), one's use of antecedent knowledge, and one's decisions as to the legitimacy of one's own and others' claims to new knowledge—are all held to be motivated by purely "intellectual" (or mathematical) considerations, themselves regulated by the specific problem or object of inquiry. They thus focus on knowledge of specialised procedures, which anyone may use, regardless of location in time and space: The social relation of knowledge is one of relatively weak classification and framing. Paradoxically, it is this, so to speak, partial negation of history by the knowledge mode of legitimation that enables the history of the discipline to remain alive. Rather than specific knowers being locked into their socio-historical contexts, they remain active contributors to the field's current production—the past may be a foreign country, but it is not an incommensurably different culture. The fact that Fermat, for example, is one more Dead White European Male is deemed to be irrelevant to the *form* in which his Last Theorem remained active within the problem field of the discipline.[9] In other words, questions of who is a specialist knower are said to be the domain of the epistemic relation rather than of the social relation of knowledge.

This way of understanding an intellectual field thus generates a strong grammar which enables both cumulative development of work over time within each (problem-specialised) language and also communication between different languages. It is said, for example, that very few mathematicians actually understand Wiles's solution and so remain unable to personally judge whether he has indeed solved Fermat's Last Theorem (Hoffman, 1998, p. 198). However, though working in other problem-worlds, they trust those who work in this particular area to use the explicit criteria. There is thus a connection with the past and with other knowers in the present in an extended epistemic community.

Summary. Both literary criticism and mathematics are examples of intellectual fields with horizontal knowledge, but they differ in their relative (weak and strong) strengths of grammar. Bernstein's concepts thus enable us to describe similarities and differences between fields beyond their empirical and substantive characteristics. Our focus here has been on the principles underlying and generating these differing strengths of grammar and their ramifications for the form taken by intellectual fields. Our examples illustrate two settings for the epistemic device, realised in two different modes of legitimation, which give rise to these different grammars. The "tradition of the new" in literary criticism is an example of an explicit attempt to seize control of the epistemic device in order to impose a particular configuration of the arbitrary and non-arbitrary as the dominant mode of legitimation in the intellectual field. In this case, the mode emphasises the social and historical arbitrary as central to legitimacy, focusing on the *relations to* knowledge of the knower, resulting in a weak grammar and restricted epistemic community. Once established as dominant within a field, such a *principle* is particularly difficult to change (though the empirical realisations of the principle may be subject to ceaseless change), for emphasis is increasingly placed on *who* owns the epistemic device, giving rise to a succession of new knowers. In contrast, the knowledge mode of legitimation exemplified by mathematics emphasises the non-arbitrary relation of procedures to their objects of study, focusing on epistemic relations *within* knowledge, and giving rise to a strong grammar and extended community. Here, who owns the device is not a matter of explicit contention; it is, so to speak, the social property of the field itself. Thus, paradoxically, those fields often thought of as socially oriented, such as sociology, may be grounded in individualism, and vice versa. In both examples one sees the workings of the epistemic device in terms of its *effects*, which are realised through mode of legitimation and strengths of grammar. The epistemic device's settings shape, for example, the manner in which the past, as when it is embodied in a literary canon, is available as an intellectual resource and as a continuing repository of problems and material to be transformed within the current production of knowledge. With a knower mode and weak grammar, the past of the field is more a mass of debris to be cleared away to enable the building of fresh knowledge. For extended epistemic communities, the past remains a basic source of material to incorporate within current production.

Our analysis should not, however, be understood as diminishing the significance of social and institutional factors in the *enacted* practices of intellectual fields, as would be argued by conventional sociologies of knowledge. Rather, our intention has been to illustrate the force and effects of (more or less tacit or explicit) self-representations of a field's operations. The distinction between extended and restricted epistemic communities, for example, refers to the ways *members* of a field define it at any particular time, rather than to the structures of fields *in themselves* (see Popper, 1972). Differing languages of legitimation, similarly, represent not perspectives *within* a field but perspectives *towards* the field, and they affect the relationship of the *community* to the field—it is the community of practitioners (or groups within it) that is "extended" or "restricted", rather than the field itself. To reiterate, our aim is to contribute to the integration of the insights of existing approaches to knowledge, rather than to displace them. As we have illustrated, the epistemic shape of an intellectual field has ramifications for its social form. Thus, paradoxically, an exclusive focus on the *sociology* of knowledge underestimates the significance of the sociological nature of *knowledge*.

Conclusion: Devices and the Sociology of Knowledge

What we have termed the "epistemic device" is an analogue of the "pedagogic device". Here we briefly consider the relations between these two devices to clarify the nature of the epistemic device and open up the issue of realising a sociology of knowledge which does more than analyse "relations to".

As we have outlined, the epistemic device is the generative principle for the construction of knowledge, or more precisely, for the distribution, recontextualisation, and evaluation of *legitimacy* in intellectual fields of knowledge production. That is, the epistemic device regulates who can produce legitimate knowledge, the ways in which antecedent knowledge is selected and transformed in the course of producing new knowledge, and the criteria for adjudicating claims to new knowledge. This is achieved through the form taken by principles of legitimation, that is, their modalities (e.g., knowledge and knower modes).

To introduce this concept alongside the pedagogic device is to imply neither that the latter is inapplicable to fields of intellectual production, nor that there are two devices at work within arenas of knowledge *production* but only one within those of recontextualisation and reproduction. Both devices form the basis of all three arenas. We suggest, however, that whilst the epistemic device is not absent from the latter two, in their practices it is secondary to a wide range of other, primary *pedagogic* concerns. The specificities of intellectual fields, and specifically their concern with the basis of knowledge claims, bring this device to our attention. So, we can state both that all new knowledge is recontextualised knowledge—knowledge is socially produced by means of antecedent knowledge—and also that, conversely, all educational knowledge is subject to the epistemic device. For example, a child in a history lesson who declares, "I don't know what happened, Miss, I wasn't alive three hundred years ago", is positing settings for the epistemic device by proclaiming a knower mode of legitimation. One of the achievements of Bernstein's work has been to widen the question of the pedagogical nature of social relations well beyond the school classroom. Here we are arguing that the epistemological nature of social relations is similarly universal and ubiquitous—if it were not, we would not be able to function on a day-to-day basis. In short, the epistemic device moves the focus from the sociological to encompass also the epistemological. It moves us from thinking about pedagogies to also thinking about knowledges as well.

The contrast we are making between these two devices is thus *not* one between a social principle (pedagogic) and a *logically formal* epistemological principle (as was sought by positivist attempts to reconstruct the logic of scientific discovery in terms of formal logic). As realist philosophy of science has long recognised, the logic of discovery and its associational forms is *intrinsically* social in character, but it is social in a very particular and specialised way (though there is no complete agreement as to its form: see Moore, 2000). It is what Luntley (1995) terms that "simple truth" about our relationship to the world that makes *any* form of effective action possible. Hence, the epistemic device is *social* in character, and, though most of its realisations are most systematically developed in university disciplines (especially within the natural sciences), *necessarily* ubiquitous and universal. It is the precondition of knowledge. The question this raises is the nature of relations between the pedagogic and epistemic devices. At this stage, we suggest that they represent two parts of a bigger picture, dimensions of an overarching knowledge device. This represents, we believe, a crucial next step for empirical and conceptual enquiry.

Similarly, though principles of legitimation are most immediately and clearly expressed in the kind of languages of legitimation illustrated by the literary criticism example, this is not to say they are absent elsewhere. Often they are realised in and simply accepted as the routine activities of actors—what could be termed *tacit* languages of legitimation (as illustrated here by mathematics). In other words, whilst struggles over ownership of the epistemic device are constant and ongoing, they often bubble under the surface until such times as the field turns in upon itself. At such moments of open conflict, they assume the form of intellectually developed positions and become a major focus of interest and work within the field in their own right, signalling a rearticulation (or at least sustained reappraisal) of the principles of legitimation underlying the field. This opens up for examination the question of why intellectual fields bubble over at specific periods.

Finally, this analysis indicates some intrinsic reasons for the lack of a theory of knowledge which has characterised the NSE's proclaimed sociology of knowledge. Where grammar is strong, knowledge claims are in effect being detached from their authors—*who* is speaking makes no difference to whether or not what is being said is true (Gellner, 1974). It was precisely the insistence upon this that enabled Western universities to free themselves from control by religious and political authorities, and enabled the massive advance of secular critical rationalism at the beginning of the modern period. In a peculiarly contradictory move, those positions within horizontal knowledge structures with the weakest grammars (voice and standpoint theories, etc.) seek to reverse this and return to a new form of the pre-modern (though relabelled "*post*-modern") position where *who* knows is what counts, not *what* is known or *how* (Maton, 2000c). When an intellectual field is characterised by a very weak grammar and a knower mode of legitimation, then the focus for its languages of legitimation becomes the voices relayed by the epistemic device, rather than the nature of the relay itself (cf. Bernstein, 1990, pp. 165–180). Knowledge is held to be nothing but arbitrary; the non-arbitrary is erased. One reason why the "intrinsic features" of knowledge have not been analysed within the sociology of education is, thus, that they cannot be made visible within the current condition of the field; given a knower mode of legitimation, weak grammars cannot *see* the epistemic device. However, to adapt a passage from Bernstein (1990, p. 190), any sociology of knowledge should have a theory of the epistemic device. Indeed such a theory could well be its necessary foundation and provide the fundamental theoretical object of the discipline.

It is the realisation of this necessity which Bernstein's approach enables and which his and, in a more modest fashion, our own work furthers.

Notes

* The authors wish to thank John Beck and Peter Huckstep for their enlightening comments.

1. As will become apparent, for actors in fields such as sociology, producing new knowledge is a less enticing task (and a less enjoyable read) than critiquing existing knowledge. One could suggest that this chapter is "out of step" with the current condition of its contextual field; its reception within that field may substantiate the analysis.

2. See Bernstein (1996, p. 172). Compare Albert Einstein: "The grand aim of all science is to cover the greatest number of empirical facts by logical deduction from the smallest number of hypotheses or axioms" (quoted in *Life Magazine*, January 9, 1970).

3. Within an intellectual field characterised by a horizontal knowledge structure with a weak grammar, as is the case with sociology, our emphasis on explicating the ontological necessity for conceptual development may appear unduly cautious, if not anxious. Such a sociologically reductive response would reinforce our analysis, which itself aspires towards a (strong grammar) knowledge mode of legitimation.

4. Space precludes discussion here of how this conceptual framework complements and develops the approach of Pierre Bourdieu to the analysis of intellectual fields (see Bernstein 1996, pp. 169–181; Maton, 1999, 2000a, 2000d). In future publications, we shall elaborate the role of the epistemic device in symbolic domination.

5. The term "legitimation" was chosen to embrace the insights of both sociological and epistemological approaches to knowledge (see Maton, 2000b). It is preferred to "epistemology", as not all "epistemologies" are epistemological in nature (Popper, 1972); some are *sociologies* of knowledge. Epistemology embraces only the epistemic relation of knowledge—the nature of relations to the non-arbitrary—whereas (as we show) many so-called "epistemologies" base knowledge claims on the social relation of knowledge.

6. Maton (2000d, p. 88) emphasises that "Both these modes of legitimation involve a relation to a proclaimed object of study (knowledge of something) and a relation to a proclaimed subject of study (someone who knows it). The distinction between them refers to which relation is emphasised within the language of legitimation; in other

words, whether the field is said to be specialised by procedures related to its object of study (the epistemic relation) or by the unique insight of the author (the social relation). For each mode it is, therefore, the relation which is *strongly* classified and framed which comprises the basis of knowledge claims".

7. This is a typical explanation offered by sociological studies of knowledge, such as that of Bourdieu. Interestingly, the present chapter is collaboratively authored by a senior and a junior member of an intellectual field.

8. It might be argued that the fact that Andrew Wiles worked in isolation for 8 years to solve the theorem contradicts the argument made here, at least in terms of communication with other living mathematicians. This would be mistaken on at least three counts. First, such an individualised mode of working is relatively rare in modern mathematics (see Hoffman, 1998, pp. 183–184). Second, this mode of discovery does not negate the extended epistemic community engaged in the mode of demonstration; Wiles may have worked alone, but the legitimation of his proof was social. Third, and most importantly, actors need not be in contact with one another (or even alive) to be fellow members of a field's active epistemic community. An epistemic community is thus, in Benedict Anderson's phrase, an "imagined community" (1983).

9. We are not suggesting that sociological factors play no part in access to and positioning within intellectual fields. The focus here is on the ways in which these fields *describe themselves*, their *modes of legitimation*, and their effects on intellectual fields, rather than the working of fields as arenas of social practice.

Bibliography

Anderson, B. (1983). *Imagined communities: Reflections on the origins and spread of nationalism.* London: Routledge & Kegan Paul.

Beck, J. (1999). Makeover or takeover: The strange death of educational autonomy in neo-liberal England. *British Journal of Sociology of Education, 20* (2), 223–238.

Berlin, I. (2000). *The power of ideas.* London: Chatto & Windus.

Bernstein, B. (1975). *Class, codes and control: Vol. III, Towards a theory of educational transmissions.* London: Routledge & Kegan Paul.

———. (1990). *Class, codes and control: Vol. IV, The structuring of pedagogic discourse.* London: Routledge.

———. (1996). *Class, codes and control: Vol. V, Pedagogy, symbolic control and identity: Theory, research, critique.* London: Taylor & Francis.

——. (1999). Vertical and horizontal discourse: An essay. *British Journal of Sociology of Education, 20* (2), 157–173.

——. (2000). *Class, codes and control: Vol. V, Pedagogy, symbolic control and identity: Theory, research, critique.* (Rev. ed.). Oxford: Rowman & Littlefield.

Booker, C. (1969). *The neophiliacs: A study of the revolution in English life in the fifties and sixties.* London: Collins.

Bourdieu, P. (2000). *Pascalian meditations.* Cambridge: Polity.

Burke, E. (1989). Reflections on the revolution in France. In L. G. Mitchell (Ed.), *The French revolution.* Oxford: Oxford University Press.

Gellner, E. (1974). *Legitimation of belief.* Cambridge: Cambridge University Press.

Hoffman, P. (1998). *The man who loved only numbers.* London: Fourth Estate.

Hoggart, R. (1995). *The way we live now.* London: Pimlico.

Kermode, F. (1967). *The sense of an ending.* New York: Oxford University Press.

Kuhn (1962). *The structure of scientific revolutions.* Chicago: Chicago University Press.

Luntley, M. (1995). *Reason, truth and self: The postmodern reconditioned.* London: Routledge.

Maton, K. (1998). *Basil Bernstein and trajectories of taught academic subjects.* Paper presented at Knowledge, Identity and Pedagogy Conference, University of Southampton, England.

——. (1999). Extra curricular activity required: Pierre Bourdieu and the sociology of educational knowledge. In M. Grenfell & M. Kelly (Eds.), *Pierre Bourdieu: Language, culture and education—Theory into practice.* Bern: Peter Lang.

——. (2000a). *For reflexivity, against narcissism: Pierre Bourdieu and the social and intellectual conditions of social scientific knowledge.* Paper presented at Conference on "Bourdieu in the 21st Century", University of East London, England.

——. (2000b). Languages of legitimation: The structuring significance for intellectual fields of strategic knowledge claims. *British Journal of Sociology of Education, 21* (2), 147–167.

——. (2000c). *Popes, kings and cultural studies: Placing the commitment to non-disciplinarity in historical context.* Paper presented at Conference on "Cultural Studies & Interdisciplinarity: Difference, Otherness, Dialogue, Translation", University of Leeds, England.

——. (2000d). Recovering pedagogic discourse: A Bernsteinian approach to the sociology of educational knowledge. *Linguistics and Education, 11* (1), 79–99.

Moore, R. (1996a). Back to the future: The problem of change and the possibilities of advance in the sociology of education. *British Journal of Sociology of Education, 17* (2), 145–161.

———. (1996b). Extended review: "The way we live now". *British Journal of Sociology of Education, 17* (4), 521–530.

———. (2000). For knowledge: Tradition, progressivism and progress in education—reconstructing the curriculum debate. *Cambridge Journal of Education, 30* (1), 17–36.

Moore, R., & Muller, J. (1999). The discourse of "voice" and the problem of knowledge and identity in the sociology of education. *British Journal of Sociology of Education, 20* (2), 189–206.

Popper, K. (1963). *Conjectures and refutations: The growth of scientific knowledge.* London: Routledge & Kegan Paul.

———. (1972). *Epistemology without a knowing subject.* Oxford: Oxford University Press.

Rosenberg, H. (1962). *The tradition of the new.* London: Thames & Hudson.

Singh, P. (2000). Local and official forms of symbolic control: An Australian case study of the pedagogic work of para-educational personnel. *International Journal of Inclusive Education, 4* (1), 3–21.

Young, M. (Ed.). (1971). *Knowledge and control: New directions for the sociology of education.* London: Collier Macmillan.

PART 3

Classroom Contexts and Pedagogic Practices

Chapter 8
Pedagogic Social Contexts: Studies for a Sociology of Learning

Ana Morais
Isabel Neves

Introduction

The late seventies and early eighties were marked by a crisis in science education, which gave rise to research around the world aiming at finding out why children did not learn the science we wanted them to learn. The research was mostly based on psychological and epistemological theories, which, after 20 years, more sensitive science educators feel are being overtaken by the State crisis again silently imposed on us.

The eighties saw the beginning of a quite different approach, which, based on sociological assumptions, has tried to put together social constructivism, on the one side, and symbolic interactionism and structuralism, on the other. This approach has considered Vygotsky's (1978, 1992) ideas of active learning in social contexts and teachers as the creators of these contexts. Bernstein's theory of pedagogic discourse (1990, 1996) has provided us with the concepts to define those contexts and the interactions which occur in them, and to analyse the influence they may have on children's learning. The same concepts have also been used to study teachers' training contexts and the interactions which occur in them, as well as family contexts and their relations with school contexts. Studies completed so far cover distinct levels of schooling, scientific areas, and micro-contexts within the context of science classrooms. They also cover regulative contexts within these and other learning contexts.

The central objective of the research has been analysis of the influence of family-school and teacher-children interaction in the achievement of socially differentiated learners. We have sought to discover which pedagogic practices improve the learning of children, especially among disadvantaged social groups, without decreasing the level of conceptual demand made upon them. At the same time we have worked at understanding the relationships between specific characteristics of the pedagogic contexts of school, family, and teachers' education and the acquisition by children of the recognition and realisation rules needed in the production of texts required in specific instructional and regulative contexts of school learning. Our work is within the sociology of learning and we have aimed at making a contribution to a sociological theory of instruction and learning. Overall, our research has been directed at examining the extent to which

1. specific power and control relations that characterise school pedagogic practices lead to differential access to recognition and realisation rules which regulate their learning contexts;

2. children's specific coding orientations (recognition and realisation rules) act as mediating sociological factors in the relation between family and school discourses and practices;

3. specific power and control relations that characterise trainer-teacher interaction lead to differential access to recognition and realisation rules which regulate teachers' learning contexts; and

4. teachers' specific coding orientations (recognition and realisation rules) act as mediating sociological factors in the relation between family and school discourses and practices.

School has been the centre of our intervention and analysis, in the context of family-school-teachers' training relations. In our research methodology, rejecting both analysis of the empirical without an underlying theoretical basis and uses of theory which do not allow for its transformation on the basis of the empirical, we have used an external language of description derived from the internal language of description, as advocated by Bernstein (1996), whereby the theoretical and empirical are viewed dialectically. Theoretical propositions, the language of description, and empirical analysis interact transformatively to produce depth and precision. Our specific language of description clearly indicates our approach as being sociological, focusing on the social relations that constitute pedagogic activity. We point to the importance of calling for order in research within the field of educational sociology. We believe that its "disorder" has been partially responsible for the rejection of sociological approaches by many educators, including science educators.

Unlike Dowling (2000), we clearly acknowledge our commitment to using a Bernsteinian internal language of description. This language allows us to use the same concepts in contexts as distinct as families, schools, and teachers' education, and across both monologic and dialogic texts (textbooks, syllabuses,[1] classroom practices, family practices, teachers' training practices). Bernstein's theory has also provided our research with a conceptual structure that is diagnostic, predictive, descriptive, explanatory, and transferable, broadening the relationships studied and permitting conceptualisation at a higher level, without losing a dialectical relation between the empirical and the theoretical (Figure 8.1).

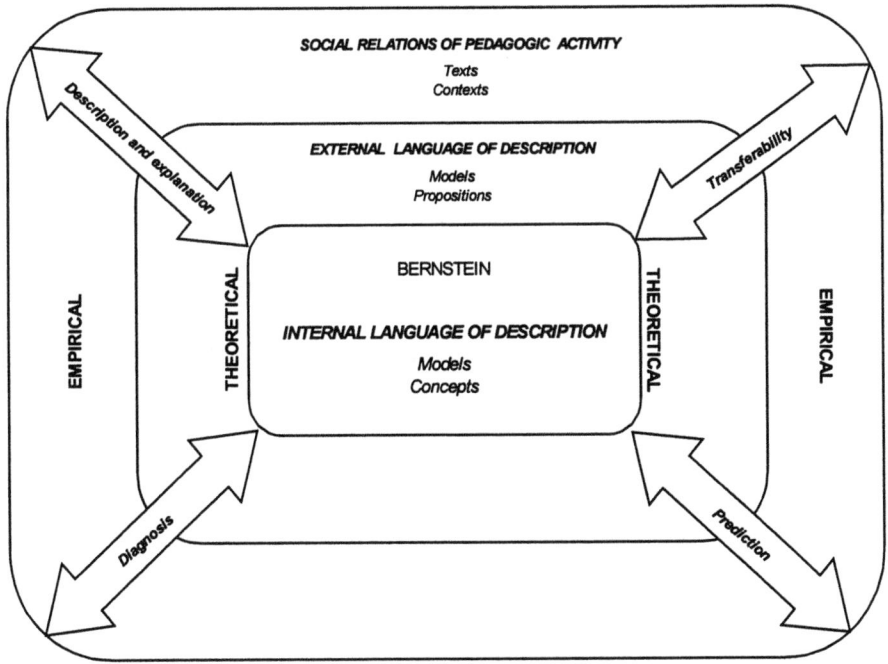

Figure 8.1—*A sociological research model of methodology, after Bernstein (1996).*

In this chapter we give particular importance to the research method used in distinct pedagogic social intervention and analytic contexts, showing how we have developed an external language of description which provides textual indicators of the specific characteristics of the contexts under study.

We start by referring to these pedagogic social contexts, then we describe some of the models and instruments we constructed for use in the contexts. We give examples of the relationships contained in those models/instruments and refer to empirical cases. Our conclusions attempt to synthesise the main results of several of our studies.

Pedagogic Social Contexts

Pedagogic social contexts are defined by specific power and control relations between subjects, discourses, and agencies/spaces. The interactional dimension of a context is given by relationships between its subjects, the organizational by those between discourses and spaces. Bernstein used classification and framing to analyse pedagogic contexts, whether in the school or at home. Classification (C) refers to the degree of maintenance between categories (subjects, spaces/agencies, discourses), and framing (F) to the communicative outcomes of the relations between categories in the context of the pedagogic relation (Figure 8.2). Framing between subjects refers to the control they have over selection, sequence, pacing, and evaluation criteria, that is, the discursive rules which regulate instructional pedagogic practice. It also refers to the hierarchical rules which regulate norms of social conduct, or regulative pedagogic practice.

Classification and framing refer either to relations within a given agency (internal C and F) or to relations between agencies (external C and F) and can vary according to different degrees of power and control in the relations between categories. Variations in classification and framing at various levels and in the coding orientation itself determine specific modalities of code. These modalities of code regulate specific pedagogic practices, either in the school or in the family. Classificational values in a pedagogic practice create specific recognition rules whereby students recognise the specificity of a particular context. If classificational values change from strong to weak, so do their contexts and recognition rules.

Framing values shape the form of pedagogic communication and context management. Different framing values transmit different rules for the creation of texts, whether these texts are instructional or regulative. Just as different classificatory values produce and expect different recognition rules on the part of the student, so different framing values produced by teachers or schools entail different realisation rules to be acquired by the student.

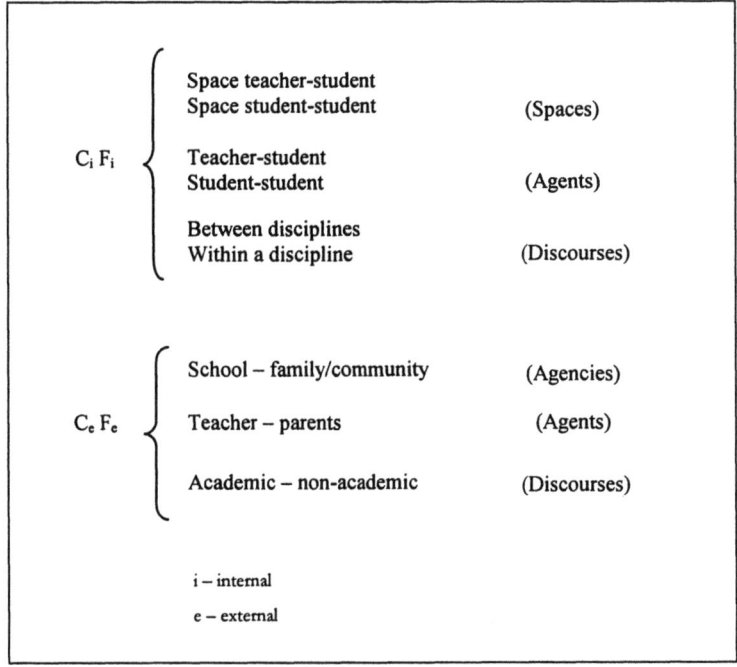

Figure 8.2—*Classification and framing relations.*

The classification and framing relations in school contexts presented in Figure 8.2 apply equally well to family contexts, provided we change teacher to mother/father, student to child, and disciplines to family knowledges. They also apply to teacher education contexts, exchanging teacher for trainer, student for teacher, parents for other agents, school-family/community for teachers' educational agencies/external agencies, and non-academic knowledge for teachers' practical knowledge.

Figure 8.3 presents pedagogic social contexts which have been the objects of our intervention and analyses. They have been mainly centred on school learning in general contexts and on science classrooms (Morais et al., 1992, 1993, 1996; Morais, Neves, & Pires, 2001; Morais, Neves, et al., 2000; Antunes, 1998), particularly in specific instructional and regulative contexts. The specific instructional contexts studied were problem solving (Morais, Fontinhas, & Neves, 1992; Ferreira & Morais, 1998, 2000), concept understanding (Afonso & Neves, 2000; Câmara & Morais, 1998), experimental work (Matos, 2000), and assessment (Morais & Miranda, 1996). Outside the school, in informal education we have studied interactive museums (Botelho, 2000). The specific regulative contexts studied concerned social development through the learning of socio-affective competences (Morais & Antunes, 1994; Morais & Rocha, 2000). We have also developed a study to investigate the extent to which children were able to distinguish power and control relations in the classroom (Antunes & Morais, 1998).

Figure 8.3—*Pedagogic social contexts: Intervention and analysis.*

Our studies of teacher training contexts were focused on both initial and in-service education. Analyses and intervention at the level of in-service education have always been closely linked with learning within action-research[2] projects (Morais et al., 1993, 1996; Morais, Neves, & Afonso, 2001; Rocha & Morais, 2000). Initial teacher training in science methods has been the object of continuous analysis and intervention at the level of the disciplines that we teach in the university. We are aware that, in this case, the results may be challenged on the grounds that, as researchers, we were also the objects of research.

Both passive and active family learning contexts have always been analysed in relation with school contexts (Morais et al., 1992, 1993; Morais & Neves, 1993; Neves & Morais, 1996; Pires & Morais, 1997a, 1997b; Afonso & Neves, 1998; Câmara & Morais, 2000).

Research Methodology: Developing an External Language of Description

School learning contexts

Pedagogic practices—Planning and characterization. Our planning for research on school learning contexts has always been carried out within action-research studies because we have wanted to analyse the implementation of pedagogic practices with given characteristics, in a process of interaction between theoretical propositions and empirical evidence. Pedagogic practices have also been studied where there has been no intervention, both in general and specific school and classroom contexts.

We constructed instruments to refer to both instructional and regulative dimensions of learning, containing indicators for each relation between spaces, discourses, and subjects. A scale of classification and framing described power and control relations for each indicator. The instruments were always the result of previous observation and of our guiding theory modified by further observation. These changes included the introduction of new indicators whenever the text under analysis required more precision or revealed unexpected features. The number and type of indicators for each relation varied according to the context under analysis. We exemplify the analysis by presenting extracts from the instrument used for the planning of pedagogic practices in the general context of science learning at the primary school (Morais, Neves, et al., 2000; Morais, Neves, & Pires, 2001). The first (Table 8.1) refers to discursive rule evaluation criteria and the second (Table 8.2) to hierarchical rules. Each contains only one of the indicators used in the analysis of those rules. Each is followed by excerpts from classroom interactions where we indicate, within a 4 point scale of framing (F^{++}–F^{--}), their values.

Table 8.1: *Discursive rule—Evaluation criteria: Instrument of analysis*

INDICATOR	F^{++}	F^{+}	F^{-}	F^{--}
IN GROUP WORK PRESENTATION	The teacher systematically points out what is incorrect and indicates in a clear and detailed way what is missing in text production.	The teacher points out, in general, what is incorrect and indicates in a generic way what is missing in text production.	The teacher points out what is incorrect but does not clarify what is missing in text production.	The teacher accepts children's productions. Her questions are intended only to clarify those productions.

Examples

F_i^+ The teacher reads the answer of one of the groups about its members observation of water condensation and adds:

     Teacher – Attention, you should *explain*... how do you explain the results obtained?

     The children say that the results are a consequence "of heat", or "the temperature", or "the cooling".

     Teacher – Yes, the lid cooled off... yes, go on... and then?... Attention, I want you to explain why the lid sometimes became dry and sometimes became humid... why?

     Child – Because the temperature changed.

     Teacher – Well, but explain that... because of temperature changes, but explain that (teacher finishes the discussion of this group's work).

F_i^- Children in groups attempt to answer a problem about how to handle a syringe so that liquid for injection may enter it. A child reads a group answer to the whole class:

     Child – So that all the air comes out.

     Teacher – Here it *says* "explain why". Only "so that the air comes out?!" But there we had to say something else (passing immediately to listen to another group's answer).

Table 8.2: *Hierarchical rules: Instrument of analysis*

INDICATOR	F ++	F +	F -	F --
WHEN STUDENTS ASK QUESTIONS	The teacher ignores questions.	The teacher answers the student directly.	The teacher answers, asking questions and giving some information to help the student find the answer.	The teacher answers by promoting discussion between students and teacher in order to arrive at a conclusion.

Examples

F_i^{++} Children and teacher are correcting a question from a test.

     Joana – May I give my answer?

     The teacher ignores her question and asks Daniela:

     Teacher – Daniela, why was there higher evaporation of the river's water?

     Daniela – Because it was very hot.

     Joana tries again. Since the teacher does not answer, she says:

     Joana – I answered between 2 and 4 pm...

     Teacher – The river's water heated and evaporated [...] (ignoring Joana's intervention).

F_i^- *Nelson* – [...] I have one [doubt] [...] but here with the syringe did not work [for the water to reach the outlet], I made it a while ago... it did not work to fill with the water because of the air inside [...] but if we have a glass it works, with water?

Teacher – When you fill a glass up with water... doesn't the air come out when you fill it up with water?

Nelson – Yes, it comes out, but over there [in the syringe] a while ago it did not come out, why?

The teacher demonstrates with a syringe so that all children can see what happens when one tries to put water in a glass and in a syringe and says:

Teacher – Let us all pay attention to this, Nelson's question, let us see who is able to answer it.

All children participate in the discussion, giving explanations. But the question remains unanswered:

Nelson – Nelson's doubt is: Why can I introduce water in the glass [...] and if I put it like this (demonstrates with the syringe) [the water] does not go into the syringe, does it? Why?

The children get involved again in the discussion and finally they get the right answer.

The same methodological procedure was used for planning and characterizing pedagogic practices in the specific regulative context of social competences. We held that learning specific regulative discourse is regulated by instructional practice and can be analysed in terms of discursive rules or selection, sequence, pacing, and evaluation criteria. The following extracts show part of the instrument used in the planning and characterising of pedagogic practice which guided the learning of given social competences of co-operation, respect, responsibility, and autonomy at the primary school level (Morais & Rocha, 2000) (Tables 8.3 and 8.4). The extracts refer to selection and evaluation criteria and contain only one indicator for each rule. Each extract is followed by examples of distinct degrees of framing (on a 4 point scale) in observed teacher-student interaction.

Table 8.3: *Discursive rule—Selection: Instrument of analysis*

	COMPETENCE AND INDICATOR	F ++	F +	F -	F --
Responsibility	TAKING CARE OF CLASSROOM JOBS	The teacher arbitrarily chooses the children to carry out tasks.	The teacher looks at the task board and indicates every day who is going to do each task.	Some children remind others that they should look at the task board, so that each one of them does what he/she should.	Children look at the task board and do what they are supposed to do.

Examples

F_i^{++} When entering the classroom, Fábio and Vítor go to look at the task board.
Teacher – Hey, hey, kids! What are you doing ?!... Sit down!... I'll tell you who is going to do what!

F_i^- When entering the classroom Elsa, Fernão, and Joaquim go to the task board.
  Elsa – Today is my turn to hand out the notebooks!... And Alberto is going to water the plants!
  Fernão – I take care of the weather!
  Joaquim – It is not my turn to do anything!

Table 8.4: *Discursive rule—Evaluation criteria: Instrument of analysis*

INDICATOR	F ++	F +	F -	F --
IN POINTING OUT THE LEGITIMATE TEXT	The teacher decides what the legitimate text of the specific regulative discourse is and tells children what it is.	The teacher refers to the agreed legitimate text which constitutes the standard according to which children will be evaluated.	The teacher, and children recall the legitimate text which constitutes the standard according to which children will be evaluated.	The teacher does not make any reference to the form and parameters according to which children will be evaluated

Examples

F_i^{++} Before starting group work, the teacher reminds the children:
  – You should help each other, respect others' work and each one of you should do his/her part.

F_i^- The teacher indicates the task and asks the children:
  – How do you think you are going to do it? How are you going to behave yourselves?
  The class is silent. The teacher insists:
  – Have you already forgotten?!
  The class stays silent. The teacher says:
  – You should do what I have told you.

Using these methods, it was possible to describe in great operational and theoretical detail the various sociological relationships which characterise the instructional and regulative dimensions of the pedagogic practice which occur in general and specific contexts of learning. Figure 8.4 shows an example of the results of the analysis of the relationships characterizing the instructional context of two modalities of pedagogic practice implemented in science classrooms in the 5th and 6th years of schooling (ages

10⁻–12⁺) (Morais et al., 1996).

Figure 8.5 shows an example of the relationships suggested by the analysis of the regulative context of three modalities of pedagogic practice implemented in years 1 and 2 (ages 6–8) of primary school, for learning social competences (Morais & Rocha, 2000).

The studies which led to the characterization of the pedagogic practices referred to in Figures 8.4 and 8.5 were developed within action-research projects. They involved conceiving theoretical profiles of the pedagogic practices to be implemented; planning and organizing classroom activities and tasks accordingly; and observing using audio and video taping. Theoretical profiles were elaborated through a dialectical relationship between the empirical and the theoretical, where classroom observation to find appropriate relationships, indicators, and behaviours was carried out and profiles were changed as necessary. Such procedures at the level of classroom context contributed to the development of a model which both distinguishes and characterises the various relationships which define a given pedagogic practice.

Text production in specific instructional and regulative contexts. To study the instructional and regulative texts produced by children in specific contexts of learning we constructed a model (Figure 8.6) which shows the relations between specific coding orientations and socio-affective dispositions in text production. The interrelation shown in the model between specific coding orientation and socio-affective disposition is intended to highlight their mutual influence. Although constituting different realities within the subject, the possession of a specific coding orientation may be limited by socio-affective dispositions, which are in turn limited by coding orientation.

According to Bernstein (1990), text production in a given context depends on the possession of the specific coding orientation to that context. This means that subjects must have both the recognition rules, that is, be able to recognise the context, and the realisation rules, that is, be able to produce a text adequate to that context. Realisation rules concern both the selection and the production of meanings. Subjects must select adequate meanings and produce texts according to them, in this way showing correct performance in context, demonstrating possession of both recognition and realisation rules.

PEDAGOGIC PRACTICES	RELATION BETWEEN SUBJECTS TEACHER-STUDENT (Ci Fi)					RELATION BETWEEN DISCOURSES (Cie Fe)	
	POWER RELATIONS (Ci)	CONTROL RELATIONS (Fi)				Academic-non-academic knowledge (Ce Fe)	Knowledges within the discipline (Ci)
		Selection	Sequence	Discursive rules SIP Pacing	Criteria		
P1	Ci ++	Fi +	Fi +	Fi --	Fi ++	Ce ++ Fe -	Ci -
P2	Ci +++	Fi ++	Fi ++	Fi +	Fi +	Ce ++ Fe +	Ci -

i – internal
e – external

Figure 8.4—*Power and control relations in the instructional context of two pedagogic practices (5th and 6th years of schooling).*

PEDAGOGIC SOCIAL CONTEXTS   197

PEDAGOGIC PRACTICES AND TEACHERS	RELATION BETWEEN SUBJECTS TEACHER-STUDENT (Gi Fi)						RELATION BETWEEN SPACES (Gi)
	POWER RELATIONS (Gi)	CONTROL RELATIONS (Fi)					
		Discursive rules SIP				Hierarchical rules SRP	Teacher-student spaces
		Selection	Sequence	Pacing	Criteria		
P1 YV	Gi⁺	Fi⁻	Fi⁻⁻	Fi⁻⁻	Fi⁺⁺	Fi⁻⁻	Gi⁻⁻
P2 XZ	Gi⁺	Fi⁺	Fi⁻⁻	Fi⁻⁻	Fi⁺	Fi⁻	Gi⁻
P3 T	Gi⁺⁺	Fi⁺⁺	Fi⁻⁻	Fi⁻⁻	Fi⁻	Fi⁺⁺	Gi⁺

i – internal
T, V, X, Y, Z – Teachers

Figure 8.5—*Power and control relations in the regulative context of three pedagogic practices (1st and 2nd years of schooling).*

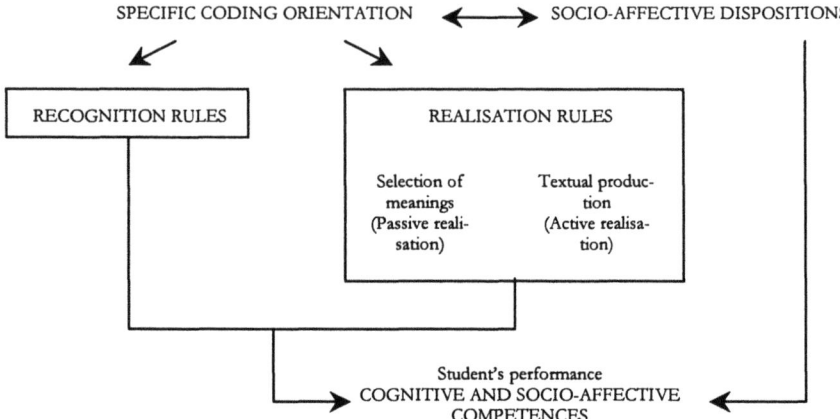

Figure 8.6—*Cognitive and socio-affective competences as given by coding orientation and socio-affective dispositions specific to the context.*

Failure to show performance may indicate lack of recognition or realisation rules or both. As to realisation rules, subjects may not be able to select meanings or produce them or both. If they are able to select meanings but are incapable of producing the text, we say that they have a passive realisation. If the text is produced, they exhibit active realisation. However, for text production to be accomplished, subjects must also possess socio-affective dispositions specific to the context, that is, they must have the appropriate aspirations, motivations, and values. According to Bernstein, recognition rules regulate realisation rules. Both principles and the requisite socio-affective dispositions are socially acquired and become part of the subjects' internal structures.

Exemplifying these relations among the cognitive competences required in specific classroom contexts, we would say that students receiving a pedagogic practice which requires, for instance, problem solving competence succeed by (a) recognising the specificity of the micro-context of problem solving within their practice (recognition rules); (b) selecting meanings adequate to that micro-context, that is, knowing how to proceed to solve problems correctly (passive realisation); (c) producing the text, that is, presenting a correct solution to the problem (active realisation); and (d) possessing socio-affective dispositions favourable to that realisation (motivations, aspirations, values). In the case of socio-affective competences, students receiving a pedagogic practice which requires, for instance, the competence of co-operation succeed if they (a) recognise the specificity of the micro context of co-operation within the regulative context of their practice (recognition rules); (b) select meanings appropriate to that context, that is, know what should be done to achieve co-operation (passive realisation); (c) produce the text, that is, co-operate according to the rules of the classroom (active realisation); and (d) have socio-affective dispositions towards that realisation (motivations, aspirations, values).

In these terms, a relation of continuity is established between family and school whenever an elaborated orientation is present in the former and both practices are convergent in terms of the classification and framing relations present in their socialisation processes. However, a relation of discontinuity is not a necessary condition of children's school failure, that is, it is not a condition of non-recognition and non-realisation in the school-specific contexts in which students are evaluated. Specific characteristics of school pedagogic practices can be favourable for the acquisition of the recognition and realisation rules underlying the development of cognitive and socio-affective competences, such as those required in the science classroom (Morais, Fontinhas, & Neves, 1992; Morais & Câmara, 1997; Morais & Rocha, 2000).

We studied the acquisition of recognition and realisation rules in science classrooms in the specific contexts of problem solving, concept understanding, assessment, and experimental work, as well as in informal education and at the level of specific regulative context. We wanted to find out whether students possessed the specific coding orientation needed to produce texts adequate to given micro-contexts of scientific and social learning. For these analyses we developed instruments conceived in terms of the specificity of the micro-context under analysis and of the text to be produced. The instruments took the form of open and/or closed questionnaires and were administered to children at interviews. Children were asked to group objects (pictures, sentences, etc.), to choose between several answers, or to produce free answers. Through these various methods we obtained the degree of children's specific coding orientation.

To illustrate the methodology followed in analysing students' recognition and realisation rules, we present examples from science learning of instruments constructed for problem solving, concept understanding and assessing. The first refers to the 6th year of schooling (ages 11^- –12^+), the second to kindergarten (age 5), and the third to the 5th year of schooling (ages 10^- –11^+). In the examples which follow, we refer to the instruments'

200   TOWARDS A SOCIOLOGY OF PEDAGOGY

general structure and we indicate the correspondence we have established between the type of questions they contained and their meaning in terms of recognition and passive and active realisation rules. We also give examples of the empirical analysis which showed that correspondence.

Problem solving. The instruments constructed to analyse the specific coding orientation in the micro-context of problem solving followed the same general pattern; they contained problematic situations whose solution required the use of scientific knowledge previously acquired. For each question, there was a free answer and a multiple choice question. In some studies (Morais, Fontinhas, & Neves, 1992), the instruments allowed only analysis of the possession of recognition and realisation (passive and active). Further studies (Ferreira & Morais, 1998, 2000; Morais, Neves et al., 2000) also permitted discrimination of recognition in terms of the scientific knowledges and competences involved in the micro-context of problem solving.

The example which follows refers to one of these more recent instruments, which took the form of a questionnaire (Ferreira & Morais, 1998, 2000). The free question was intended to find out whether children possessed active realisation (RLa), the multiple choice question to find out if children who did not produce the correct text in the free answer were capable of passive realisation (RLp) or not and, in this case, if they possessed recognition either of scientific knowledge (RCk) or of the competence (RCc) involved in the problematic situation. Scientific knowledge might be only partially recognised (RCk -).

Questionnaire

Problematic situation:
You have noticed that to remove the mist of the car windows we only have to switch on the heating system for a while.

Free question: Explain this situation on the basis of the knowledge acquired in your science classes (RLa).

Multiple choice question: Mark with an X the answer you think most adequately explains the situation:
    A. The surrounding water vapour loses energy when it is in contact with the glass and passes to the liquid state and this makes it become misty (RCc).
    B. Vapourisation is the change of a body from the liquid state to the gaseous state when it gains energy by heating (RCk).
    C. The window's mist gets away because it is hot and this makes the water

that is on the windows disappear (RCk ⁻, RCc).

D. The drops of water, which make the windows become misted, gain energy when heated and pass to the gaseous state so that the windows become demisted (RCk, RCc, RLp).

Children are shown to possess active realisation (RLa) when they give a text of option D type in answer to the free question.

To determine students' specific orientation to problem solving, we followed a complex methodology which cannot be explained in the space available here. All the texts produced by students were analysed according to a system of categories we created for both recognition and realisation rules. Numeric scales were attached to these categories.

Concept understanding. Our example (Morais & Câmara, 1997) was inspired by Holland's study (1981), designed to analyse text produced about understanding the concept of *insect*, explicated in terms of the principle "number of legs". The instrument contained four questions based on three sets of six pictures each concerning insects, arachnidae and miriapodae. The first question established whether or not children had recognition (RC) and active realisation (RLa). In the second question, the context was given and children were probed for passive realisation (RLp). If they were not able to achieve passive realisation, the context was orally identified and they were taught how it should be done, in order to change their specific coding orientation by giving them the appropriate recognition and realisation rules. The third question sought active realisation (RLa), while the fourth was similar to the first question, seeking to find out if the children already recognised the context (RC) and could actively realise legitimate text (RLa).

Interview

1. The interviewer gives six pictures of 6 animals[3] to the child.
   Interviewer – Look carefully at these animals. Make groups with these animals, placing them in the boxes. Make the groups you wish. There are many boxes, use those you wish. Why did you group (place) the animals in this way? (RC; RLa)

2. The interviewer takes out the same pictures and makes three groups herself, using the principle, "number of legs". (If the child has already used this principle in the first question the interview proceeds to question 2.2.).

   2.1 *Interviewer* – Look carefully at the groups I made. Find out why these animals are grouped in this way. *(RLp)*

If the child answers correctly, the interview proceeds. If not, the interviewer explains the reason for the grouping, using reception learning.

    2.2. The interviewer gives the child six pictures of six other animals with the same characteristics[4] as those in question 1.

Interviewer – Look carefully at these six animals. Place each one of them in one of these groups I made. Explain as you go along. *(RLa)*

The pictures are then removed.

    3. The interviewer gives the child six pictures of six other animals with the same characteristics as those used in questions 1 and 2.

Interviewer – Look carefully at these six animals. You are now going to make groups again in these boxes as you wish. *(RC; RLa)*

On this basis we obtained a relative value for each child with respect to the acquisition of recognition rules, realisation rules, and specific coding orientation. These values represented a measure of scientific achievement with respect to the concept of *insect*. We constructed a 4 point scale which measured increasing degrees of the specific coding orientation for the micro-context of concept understanding.

Assessing. The instrument we constructed to analyse recognition and realisation rules in the assessing context (Morais & Miranda, 1996) took the form of a semi-structured interview. In the first part of the interview, we sought to analyse recognition rules (RC). We wanted to see if students could recognise the basic principle in marking (grading) test answers, distinguishing between *correct* and *incorrect*. In the second part, we sought to elicit their realisation rules (RL). Did students reproduce their teacher's text when correcting and marking? The questions asked related to tests which had already been given to children; one of these tests assessed factual knowledge, a second assessed concept understanding, and a third assessed the use of knowledge in new situations. Answers to each, covering the widest possible range of teachers' marks, were considered.

Interview

First stage (RC)

1. The student is given the first question and a set of 10 answers to it.
   Interviewer – Here is a question from the test made by your teacher and 10 answers given by some of your classmates to that question. Please group the answers as you wish.

2. Students are asked to indicate the answers in each of their groupings (through the notation $A_1, A_2...$) and to explain the reason for each grouping.

3. The second and third questions and sets of answers are presented, and for each question, procedures 1 and 2 are repeated.

Second stage (RL)

4. Students are again given the first question, the "correct answer" and mark value, and a set of 5 answers.
   Interviewer – You have here the first question you were given before, and this is a correct answer. You are going to take on the role of your science teacher, correcting and marking the tests. These cards are for you only, so you can write whatever you wish on them.

5. Students are then asked to justify the mark they gave for each answer and to explain the meaning of the notations they have made.

6. The second and third questions and their values are given, and for each one, procedures 4 and 5 are again followed.

In order to analyse recognition rules, we organised the texts produced by students in the first stage of the interview according to categories, based on previous analysis of their text to the "why" of answers group formation, distinguishing acquisition and non-acquisition. The following examples show the meanings and categories assigned to students' texts when explaining group formation. We show, for two students, the groups they made and the reasons they gave:

> *Category:* The student groups according to the degree of similarity of the answers.
> DOES NOT POSSESS RECOGNITION RULES

Student's text
First group: A_1 and A_6 because they are similar.
Second group: A_2 and A_{10} because they are equal.
Third group: A_4, A_7 and A_8 because they tell the same thing.

Category: The student groups according to the correct/incorrect criterion, with intermediate degrees.
POSSESSES RECOGNITION RULES

Student's text
First group: A_1, A_3, A_4 and A_9 because I think these are the ones which are right.
Second group: A_2 and A_6. These are also right, but for me the most right are these four (the answers of the first group).
Third group: A_5, A_7, A_8 and A_{10}. These are what I think is not right.

In analysing realisation rules, categories were similarly constructed, on the basis of a previous analysis of students' answers, the mark value given, and teachers' notations to answers, again distinguishing acquisition and non-acquisition.

Category: Student values an answer (or part of it) which is out of context.
DOES NOT POSSESS REALISATION RULES

Student text
Does not answer the question, but is appropriate to another question.

Category: Students give the same mark as teacher's.
POSSESSES REALISATION RULES

Student text
For correct answers: It means the same as the answer provided in different words.
For incorrect answers: It does not make sense.
For partially correct answers: The answer is not finished, it does not tell... (student explains).

We determined the degree of acquisition of recognition and realisation rules by numeric scaling of categories. We then determined the specific coding orientation of each student, for the micro-context of assessing, through a composite index from recognition and realisation.

Teacher training contexts

We used the same kind of conceptualisation for teachers' educational contexts (Morais, Neves, & Afonso, 2001; Rocha & Morais, 2000) as for school learning contexts. We present extracts from the instrument used to plan and characterise researcher-teacher relationships in one of our action-research studies (Morais, Neves, & Afonso, 2001) (Tables 8.5 and 8.6).

They correspond to the same rules that we gave for teacher-children relations (see above). Each extract is followed by examples of researcher-teacher interactions where degree of framing is measured on a 4 point scale.

Table 8.5: *Discursive rule—Evaluation criteria: Instrument of analysis*

INDICATOR	F ++	F +	F −	F −−
TASKS TO BE CARRIED OUT	During the discussion, the researcher makes clear not only the objective of the task but knowledges and also the paths to be used.	During the discussion, the researcher makes clear the objective of the task, without detailing knowledges and paths to be used.	During the discussion, the researcher raises questions about ways of dealing with the task and about its solution.	During the discussion, the researcher accepts any form of dealing with the task and also accepts multiple solutions.

Examples

$F_i{+}$ Teachers are planning an experiment to test the hypothesis of the relationship between the amount of lichen covering trees and the distance of those trees from the town. Some teachers propose experiments whose procedures and results are not in accordance with the hypothesis. The researcher recalls it and discusses, in general terms, whether the procedure is appropriate to obtain the information needed.

$F_i{-}$ Teachers give several examples of successful and unsuccessful experiences they have had with their children. They speak about possible causes and diverse strategies which they have used to solve problems. The researcher listens to the various reports and poses some questions which aim at better understanding of the situations reported.

Table 8.6: *Hierarchical rules: Instrument of analysis*

INDICATOR	F ++	F +	F −	F −−
IN THE RELATION OF COMMUNICATION	The researcher privileges a vertical and unidirectional relation of communication.	The researcher promotes a vertical and unidirectional relation of communication, with occasional intervention of teachers.	The researcher promotes researcher-teacher communication but the vertical relation is also frequent.	The researcher privileges a permanent communication between researcher and teachers.

Examples

$F_i{++}$ Teachers and researcher analyse the problem of school success/lack of success. The researcher shows a transparency with three graphs. She starts by describing the data given in the first graph. She goes on to describe the data in the second graph. Finally she describes the data in the third graph. The teachers follow attentively.

F_i · All teachers group the leaves of various plants according to their own personal criteria and compare them with those of their colleagues. They verify that they have used similar criteria (colour, texture, size). They refer to their use of leaves in various activities (in the study of the seasons of the year, in arts…). Afterwards, a dychotomic key is given. The teachers engage in a lively discussion when they find out that their criteria do not coincide with scientific criteria. They discuss why this happens: Some teachers do not accept that colour is not an important criterion for classifying, while others find justifications for the fact that the criteria they used are not valued in the scientific context.

Family learning contexts

The studies directly centred on the family (Morais & Neves, 1993; Neves & Morais, 1996; Pires & Morais, 1997a, 1997b) have followed a model (Figure 8.7) which, starting from Bernstein's concept of pedagogic code, sought to illuminate relationships between the discourses and practices of family and school.

In this model the pedagogic code of the family is analysed at two levels which, although interlinked, are taken as separate components of realisation code at discursive and transmission levels. Analysis of the discursive level, which refers to both family instructional discourse (FID) and family regulative discourse (FRD), is focused on knowledges/activities and norms of social conduct present in the family. Through an indirect pedagogic practice (IPP), children, as spectators of the discursive universes of the families, learn (in a non-evaluative context) to value the meanings transmitted by parents' instructional and regulative discourses. Analysis of the transmission level, which refers to the realisation of families' pedagogic discourses, that is, to the instructional and regulative practices of families, focuses on the process of transmission-acquisition developed by parents in pedagogic interaction with their children. Through a direct pedagogic practice (DPP), children as active participants in the learning process acquire (in an evaluative context) specific skills and norms of social conduct, in social roles which determine how they behave in other contexts of learning. The contextual realisation of meanings is established by using the values of classification and framing which define the pedagogic code. The model also considers coding orientation (elaborated or restricted), the meanings which are present in the family's discourses and practices. At the level of the contextual realisation of meanings, it directly considers the communicational dimension of the pedagogic code and also, indirectly, its organisational dimension.

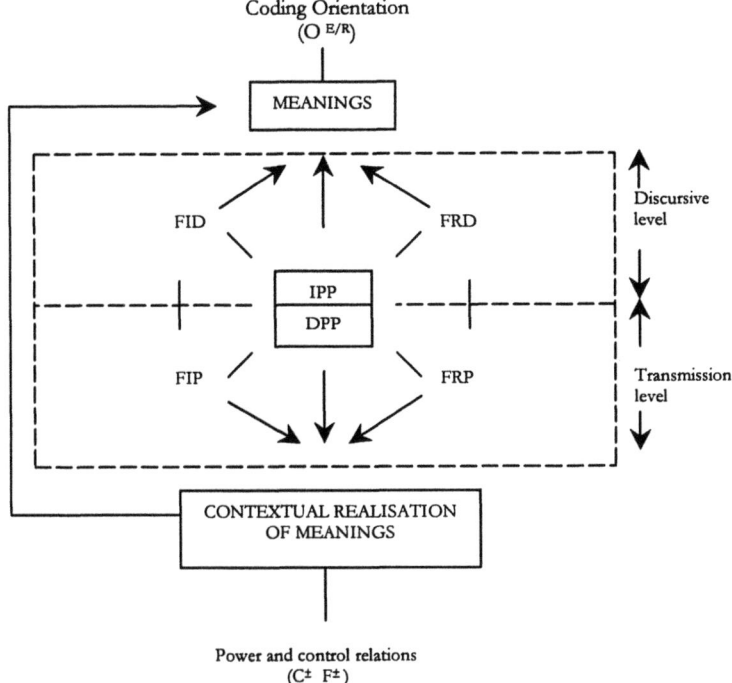

Figure 8.7—*Theoretical model of family's pedagogic code.*

On the basis of the concept of pedagogic practice defined in the model (Figure 8.7), it was possible to derive the following dimensions of empirical analysis:

1. the knowledge/activities and norms of social conduct which are present in families' everyday lives;

2. the principles adduced by parents as underlying the knowledge/activities and norms of social conduct which they value;

3. the form used by parents to transmit their knowledge and norms

of social conduct and to explain tasks to children;

4. the modality of social control used by parents in their communicative relations with children;

5. the form in which pedagogic spaces and materials are organised at home; and

6. the principles adduced by parents as underlying the ways they teach their children.

Dimension 1 refers to the discursive universe of the family and provides data both about the relative importance given at home to manual and non-manual tasks and to academic-non-academic knowledges (instructional discourse) and also about the positional/interpersonal nature of the relations of social conduct according to age, gender, and parental status (regulative discourse). Dimensions 2 and 6 give the coding orientation of the family, providing data about the particularistic and universalistic nature of the meanings underlying its general form of communication (dimension 2) and the meanings underlying the form according to which parents teach their children (dimension 6). Dimension 3 refers to the theory of instruction valued by the family, providing data about the discursive rules (selection, sequence, pacing, evaluation criteria) which regulate the process of transmission-acquisition in the family instructional context. Dimension 4 refers to the form of communication privileged by parents in their social relations with children, providing data about the hierarchical rules which regulate the modality of control in the family regulative context. Finally, dimension 5 refers to the organizational dimension of the pedagogic code, providing data about the characteristics of the local pedagogic space.

To analyse pedagogic practice in the family context, we took the text produced by parents in an interview situation. The instrument guiding the interview contained a set of propositions and research questions refined in pilot interviews. Classification and framing scales used in the characterization of family's pedagogic practice were similarly constructed. An interview guide was constructed, to be administered to parents, and the results of the interview gave answers to research questions.

In order to show the form taken by the analysis, we present the part of the instrument (propositions and research questions) which referred to the characterisation of discursive rules selection and evaluation criteria and hierarchical rules (Neves & Morais, 1996), with illustrative extracts, indicating the degree of framing on a scale of F^{+++} to F^{---}.

Discursive rule—Selection

> *Proposition:* At home one may only say/do given things or one may say/do anything one wants.
>
> *Research question:* Do children only say/do what is established by parents, or do they say/do what they want?
>
> *Examples:*
> F_i^{+++} [...] he likes painting (the house walls) very much but cannot be allowed to do so... I don't let him (the son) paint.
>
> F_i^{---} He [the son] tried to make an omelette his way ... we even thought it was good he had initiative... because I think he should also take initiatives [...]

Discursive rule—Evaluation criteria

> *Proposition:* At home there may be established or free ways to say/do various things.
>
> *Research question:* Do children say/do things in the way that parents establish is correct or do they say/do things in the way they themselves think is correct?
>
> *Examples:*
> F_i^{+++} I taught him... the fork should be placed on this side, the knife on this, the napkin on this side outside the plate, the bread is placed in the saucer... It must be laid in this way according to hotel service standards.
>
> F_i^{---} [...] The way she [the daughter] tidies up [the toys] for me is not important... The way she tidies up is something personal...

Hierarchical rules

> *Proposition:* For controlling what children can say/do and how they say/do it, parents use control modalities which can be based on their authority or on each child's attributes.
>
> *Research question:* How do parents tell their children that they should only say/do things already accorded and how do parents tell their children the way they think it is correct to say/do things? By explaining the reasons why they should or should not say/do given things

and explaining the reasons why they should say/do things in a given way? Or simply telling them that they cannot say/do given things in the way they want and that they must say/do things in the way parents consider as correct?

Examples:
F_i^{+++} I beat her up and say she must pay more attention... if I am not to beat her up again.

F_i^{--} [...] For I tell him that I... daddy likes the fact that he has passed the year and has good results, that is good for him and I am pleased.

Synthesis

These examples of models, instruments, and interactions show how we have operationalised the concept of pedagogic practice and, particularly, the concepts of framing and discursive and hierarchical rules. These concepts are part of Bernstein's internal language of description. The models/instruments and the dimensions they contain, as well as the indicators and their descriptions in terms of various framing degrees, are the external language of description for a specific context. The examples of interactions are the empirical data. In constructing the models and instruments, we held empirical evidence and theoretical principles in dialectical relation. Transcripts were analysed on the basis of previous theory and models/instruments constructed and successfully transformed on the basis of empirical data. Through this process, the internal language of description underwent changes as a result of the empirical analysis.

The following are examples of this active methodological process related to classroom analysis. When everyday knowledge enters the classroom it could be considered as a weak framing of the selection. However, our empirical evidence showed that everyday knowledge can be brought in not only by children but also by teachers. In the first case framing of the selection would be weak and in the second strong. However, in both cases, classification and framing are weakened between academic and non-academic knowledges. That methodological process is also exemplified when, in correcting and marking a test, a teacher makes clear to each child what is missing in child's text. While this is rightly viewed as strong framing of evaluation criteria, there is in this case a simultaneous weakening of framing at the level of hierarchical rules as reasons are explained to students through a personal mode of communication. To give another example, when the teacher conducts a discussion in the classroom in order to lead children to a given concept, the selection is strongly framed at least at the macro level but framing is weak at the level of hierarchical rules in the relations between teacher-student and student-student.

A further example from classroom analysis also highlights how articulations between the theoretical and the empirical permitted the development of an external language of description which gave a higher degree of applicability to the internal language of description. We held that there is a specific regulative discourse for which there is an instructional pedagogic practice regulated by discursive rules of selection, sequence, pacing, and evaluation criteria, so that we characterised the transmission-acquisition of social competences in the same way as cognitive competences and processes. This definition of indicators was aimed at allowing the theoretical propositions which guided the characterisation of distinct modalities of pedagogic practice to come into relation with initial empirical data.

The fact that the instrument for guiding the analysis of families' practices and discourses was conceived on the basis of a model equally applicable to schools made possible the characterisation of families' practices and discourses in terms of their relationship with the school pedagogic context. In similar manner, trainer-teacher relations were characterised and also related to the modality of pedagogic practice privileged by teachers in their relations with children. Both sets of relations also show how the development of an external language of description contributed to the development and transformation of the internal language of description, and make evident the explanatory diagnostic and transferability power of the theory which guided the research.

The concepts of recognition and realisation rules provided by the theory have achieved a more extensive and broader meaning on the basis of empirical evidence and application in distinct contexts of textual production. The development of an external language of description has allowed a deepening of analysis at the level of textual production in both general instructional and regulative contexts and in specific micro-contexts of scientific and social learning. Good examples of this have been seen in the analysis of textual production in distinct learning contexts; in the definition of indicators to differentiate between the two components of realisation (passive and active); and in the instructional micro-context of problem solving, not only in the recognition of content (knowledge) but in the recognition of competence. While enriching and broadening the conceptual language, the research carried out at this level has also revealed the importance of an external language of description for activating the internal.

Examination of the relation between discourses encompassed distinct disciplines (interdisciplinarity), school and family-community knowledges (academic/non-academic), and between knowledges within a given discipline (intradisciplinarity). This last relation is not taken into account or worked out in common discourse relation analyses. Weak classification at the level of intradisciplinary knowledges means a close relation between those knowledges, that is, a relation between concepts of distinct specificities and orders in the direction of higher levels of conceptualisation and consequently more meaningful scientific learning. The consideration of the classification between concepts of a given discipline also means an extension of the internal language of description.

Final Considerations

An important aspect of our research concerns the models constructed in various studies to analyse pedagogic contexts and texts. These models made possible analyses at distinct levels and in many situations of learning and interaction. The models also revealed their potential to guide the planning of pedagogic practices and interactions and to evaluate their outcomes. This was made possible by the strong conceptual structure and explanatory power of the theory on which the research is based. The explanatory power of Bernstein's internal language of description has allowed us to use the same concepts in contexts as diverse as family, school, and teacher education to broaden the relationships studied and conceptualise the results at a higher level. However, much is still to be done in terms of operationalisation, in terms of greater precision of the indicators of each aspect of pedagogic interaction and its outcomes, and at the level of concrete and specific directions for teachers' and trainers' practices.

Through the development of a constructive external language of description, based on the relationship between Bernstein's concepts and the data suggested by empirical analyses, we followed a research methodology which made evident the diagnostic, predictive, descriptive, explanatory, and transferability potential of the theory. It has been possible, on the basis of the concepts and relations suggested by the theory, to make a *diagnosis* of the kinds of experimental work done by teachers in their classrooms and the kinds of family modalities of control; *predict* situations of school success or failure both on the basis of continuity or discontinuity of relationships between family and school discourses and practices and also on the basis of the relationship between the characteristics of teachers' pedagogic practice and the acquisition of the recognition and realisation rules needed for the production of the instructional and regulative texts required by the school; *describe* pedagogic practices in family and school and in teacher training; and *explain* reasons associated with families and schools for the success or failure of children from the same and different social groups and variations in the family's coding orientation within lower social groups. It has also been possible to explore the *transferability* of the theory, for example, when we apply to the analysis of family learning and teacher training contexts the concepts and relations used in the analysis of school learning contexts. The transferability power of the theory is also evident when we develop the analysis of transmission-acquisition of specific regulative discourse by applying concepts associated with instructional practice of specific instructional discourse, as well as in the characterisation of family pedagogic practices and teacher training processes by using the model developed for characterising school pedagogic practices. The external language of description we have developed has contributed to the activation of Bernstein's internal language.

Our research *as a whole* has shown how specific power and control relations in classrooms and in schools lead to differential access to recognition and realisation rules which regulate the multiple contexts of pedagogic interaction. These relations also lead to differences in socio-affective dispositions. Children's success in school, in scientific and social learning, requires the acquisition of recognition rules which permit them to distinguish the specificity of the multiple micro-contexts where that learning takes place and of realisation rules which enable the selection of legitimate meanings for each micro-context and the production of text appropriate to it. Studies developed outside specific learning contexts and focused on more general school contexts and curriculum organization (Daniels, 1989; Holland, 1981; Whitty, Rowe, & Aggleton, 1994) have also shown the importance of these processes. When family codes and practices are in continuity with school pedagogic codes and practices, acquisition of the recognition and realisation rules appropriate to school contexts is facilitated by the elaborated orientation brought in by children. Similar power and control relations in the family and the school permit more efficient access to recognition and realisation rules in school contexts. This immediately gives an advantage to children whose processes of primary socialisation are regulated by pedagogic codes similar to school codes. In general, these children tend to come from higher social or dominant ethnic groups.[5] However, this situation can be altered by school pedagogic practices whose characteristics permit access to the school coding orientation. Teachers' acquisition of the recognition and realisation rules and socio-affective dispositions appropriate to the implementation of such pedagogic practices is crucial for such change.

The aspect which is revealed to be most crucial in the research we have carried out is the explication of evaluation criteria, that is, the presence of a strong framing at the level of this discursive rule. Such explicitness, which in our studies was achieved by making clear to children the specificity of a given context and what needed to be added to their textual production for it to be correct in both transmission and evaluation contexts, seemed to help them in acquiring both recognition and realisation rules. However, for evaluation criteria to be explicated by the teacher, time is necessary, that is, a *weak framing of pacing* is needed. At the same level, a correct textual production requires not only the possession of recognition and realisation rules but also positive socio-affective dispositions, motivations, and values towards the text to be produced. Weak framing at the level of hierarchical rules, that is, personal control in an open relationship with children, where reasons for contents, competences, and procedures are explained and discussed, tended to produce acceptance and enjoyment by children of the contents, competences, and procedures developed in their classes. Such relationships tended, when the text was constructed with students, in turn, to influence the acquisition of recognition and realisation rules in which children developed a greater degree of involvement. Such acquisition was also influenced where weakening of the classification and framing between academic and non-academic contexts occurred. When teachers introduce examples of everyday situations and these are explained on the basis of school knowledge, they provide simultaneous access to both contexts and, implicitly, introduce the principles which permit distinction between those contexts. Continuous access to both is likely to enable students to construct recognition rules. When teachers accept and integrate examples brought by children (weakening of framing in selection), such construction is also greatly facilitated. This, of course, can only occur if the criteria are clearly explicated, for to weaken the strong classification and framing present in the socialisation of disadvantaged children between academic and non-academic contexts constitutes a considerable step, not always easy for those children. What we did, in fact, was to make clear the strong classification between the two contexts and their specificity. It should be noted that the weakening of framing, at the level of micro-level selection and, even more, at the level of hierarchical rules, carries with it the raising of children's position or status, which is also a condition for success at school.[6] Only a pedagogic practice which takes into account *all* children can contribute to a higher status for disadvantaged children.

Explaining evaluation criteria, together with the weakening of framing at the level of hierarchical rules, either in the context of transmission or in the context of evaluation, constitutes, from a sociological perspective, an innovative strategy. To give children access to the principles which direct all of teachers' actions, to make visible an usually invisible message, means to give them the possibility of challenging teacher-student power relations. And if this message is more invisible for disadvantaged children, a pedagogic change in that direction is a considerable change, for it leads to forms of equality in school and society.

Contrary to what is argued by many progressive educationalists (e.g., Montessori and Klein, cited in Bernstein, 1977, p. 131), as to the potentialities of a totally invisible pedagogy characterised by weak classifications and framings (as in the case of the open school), our studies so far show that while these weak classifications and framings are an essential condition for learning at the level of pacing, hierarchical rules, knowledge relations (interdisciplinary, intradisciplinary, academic-non-academic), and relations between spaces, they are less so at the level of selection (at least at the macro level) and, certainly, at the level of evaluation criteria. This conclusion does not support either a return to the traditional education of strong classifications and framings or a total acceptance of progressivism. Rather, it suggests a *mixed pedagogy*, a prospect suggested by the language of description derived from Bernstein's theory enabling distinction between specific aspects of classroom social contexts, going well beyond the dichotomies of open/closed school, visible/invisible pedagogies, and discovery learning/reception learning, introducing a dimension of great rigour into research on teachers' pedagogic practices.

In defence of some educators committed to a pedagogic code characterised by weak classifications and framings, it is possible that a fundamental confusion exists between regulative and instructional contexts, particularly between the hierarchical and discursive rules which regulate the regulative and the instructional practices in the classroom. If a weakening of framing at the level of hierarchical rules and a weakening of classification at the level of the relations between spaces seem to be clearly favourable to students' learning (to have access and have the opportunity to discuss teachers' reasons and to acquire a high status), the weakening of the framing of evaluation criteria and even of selection leaves children who entered school in disadvantage more disadvantaged—there is a text legitimised and valued by school and by society to be learned and *all* students should have access to that text. Only by explicating evaluation criteria and having control over selection (at least at the macro level) can teachers lead children to understand what is required from them.

The conclusions reached in our studies focused on scientific learning are complemented by research which highlights the importance of learning social competences, pointing to the need to start such undervalued processes in the first years of schooling. The importance of promoting children's personal and social development in school, in order to prepare them for contexts related to citizenship, mutual respect, co-operation, and freedom, renders serious reflection and a grounded intervention indispensable in the hope that differential pedagogic practices may enhance development. As with scientific learning, the pedagogic practices more favourable to the social learning of disadvantaged children do not point to generally weak classifications and framings. Such practices leave the text legitimised by the school and society invisible, increasing the differences marking children of distinct social and cultural backgrounds on entering school. Pedagogic practices can be changed in order to obtain better school results, particularly with children of disadvantaged social groups; without such educational innovation, schools institutionalise inequalities in the acquisition of the discourses of power and in access to the power of the discourse.

Our research also contributes to a better understanding of family factors which explain the general failure of socially disadvantaged children. The studies make clear that there are fundamental differences within the working class which are reflected in children's primary socialisation and which, in turn, reflect on their actions at school. The studies can lead schools and teachers to understand how some children succeed and others fail. We believe that teachers' knowledge of primary socialising discourses and practices may give them a clearer vision of the causes of success and failure of children from lower social backgrounds and enable teachers to act in a more explicit and efficient way in classroom contexts to improve such children's learning. Our reading of our results and conclusions does not allow us to condone schools' inaction. On the contrary, our reading impels us to think about *how* and *where* the school should intervene. We believe that there is an urgent need for more studies of primary socialising processes, to improve thinking about school-family relations and to enable us to act more successfully at the level of secondary socialisation, particularly in the early years of schooling.

Pedagogic innovation is possible whenever teachers undergo a process of professional development where they have access to an education which promotes the acquisition of recognition and realisation rules and socio-affective dispositions appropriate to implementing such acquisition. Pedagogic change may result from joint work between teachers and researchers, provided we manage to transmit to teachers the idea that they have more power and competences than they currently believe they do. They have, in many respects, "a considerable space available for the *how* of school learning, that is, for pedagogic practice and its realisation. It is possible that the how of the acquisition is more important than the what; in fact it may even model the what" (Morais et al., 1993, p. 519).

Finally, we want to make clear that although we consider that the studies we have carried out and the research methodology we have used have important potential in the field of educational research, pedagogic intervention, and teacher education, we are aware of their limits. It is work to be continued.

Notes

1   The work we have been developing also includes analyses of textbooks and syllabuses (see chapter 9 in this volume).

2   The concept of action-research that we have used in our studies differs in many aspects from perspectives which consider it as a weak classification and framing researcher-teacher relation. We consider action-research as a process of teacher training where the researcher intends to pass new knowledges and competences to teachers while taking into account the level of teachers' practical knowledge.

3   Ant, mosquito, housefly, spider, centipede, "milpés".

4   Animals belonging to the same taxonomic groups.

5   Various studies (e.g., Morais et al., 1993; Morais, Neves, et al., 2000) have shown that families at lower social levels can create primary socialising contexts similar to school contexts, depending on particular conditions, such as their access to agencies of challenge, resistance, or opposition (e.g., trade unions, political parties) or even to agencies of cultural reproduction (e.g., dominant religious institutions, sports associations).

6   The studies that we have carried out have developed ways to analyse children's positioning in family and school and to implement strategies towards its change in the

school (e.g. Morais et al., 1993; Morais, Neves, et al., 2000). We believe that, together with coding orientation, positioning is crucial for children's success. Space limitations do not allow us to elaborate in this chapter.

Transcription conventions

[...]   = Text omitted
...   = Pause

Bibliography

Afonso, M., & Neves, I. P. (1998). Socialização primária e concepções das crianças em ciências. *Revista de Educação*, VII (1) 107–119.

———. (2000). Influência da prática pedagógica na mudança conceptual em ciências: Um estudo sociológico. In A. M. Morais, I. P. Neves et al., *Estudos para uma sociologia da aprendizagem* (chap. 6). Lisbon: Institute for Educational Innovation and Centre for Educational Research (SSUL).

Antunes, H. (1998). *Contexto regulador e ensino das ciências: Um estudo com crianças dos estratos sociais mais baixos*. Unpublished doctoral thesis, School of Science, University of Lisbon.

Antunes, H., & Morais, A. M. (September, 1998). *What are we going to do with them? A study with children at risk*. Paper presented at the European Conference on Educational Research 98, School of Pedagogy, Ljubljana, Slovenia.

Bernstein, B. (1977). *Class, codes and control: Vol. III, Towards a theory of educational transmissions* (2nd ed.). London: Routledge & Kegan Paul.

———. (1990). *Class, codes and control: Vol. IV, The structuring of pedagogic discourse*. London: Routledge.

———. (1996). *Class, codes and control: Vol. V, Pedagogy, symbolic control and identity: Theory, research, critique*. London: Taylor & Francis.

Botelho, A. (2000). *Museus interactivos e desenvolvimento científico—Estudo sociológico de desempenhos e aprendizagens dos alunos*. Unpublished master's thesis, School of Science, University of Lisbon (in preparation).

Câmara, M. J., & Morais, A. M. (1998). O desenvolvimento científico no jardim de infância: Influência de práticas pedagógicas. *Revista de Educação*, VII (2), 179–199.

———. (2000). A aprendizagem das Ciências da Natureza no jardim de infância: Processos de socialização primária. In A. M. Morais, I. P. Neves, et al. *Estudos para uma sociologia da aprendizagem* (chap. 8). Lisbon: Institute for Educational Innovation and Centre for Educational Research (SSUL).

Daniels, H. (1989). Visual displays as tacit relays of the structure of pedagogic practice. *British Journal of Sociology of Education, 10* (2), 123–140.

Domingos, A. M. (now Morais), Barradas, H., Rainha, H., & Neves, I. P. (1986). *A teoria de Bernstein em sociologia da educação.* Lisbon: Gulbenkian Foundation.

Dowling, P. (2000). *Basil Bernstein in frame: "Oh dear, is this a structuralist analysis?"* Unpublished manuscript, Institute of Education, University of London.

Ferreira, L., & Morais, A. M. (1998). Os problemas na aula de ciências: Estudo de aprendizagens individuais e em grupo. *Revista de Educação, VII* (1), 91–105.

———. (2000). A resolução de problemas em ciências e as modalidades de prática pedagógica. In A. M. Morais, I. P. Neves, et al., *Estudos para uma sociologia da aprendizagem* (chap. 3). Lisbon: Institute for Educational Innovation and Centre for Educational Research (SSUL).

Holland, J. (1981). Social class and changes in orientation to meanings. *Sociology, 15* (1), 1–18.

Matos, M. (2000). *Trabalho experimental na aula de Físico-Química do 3° ciclo do ensino básico—Teorias e práticas dos professores.* Master's thesis, School of Science, University of Lisbon (in preparation).

Morais, A. M., & Antunes, H. (1994). Students' differential text production in the regulative context of the classroom. *British Journal of Sociology of Education, 15* (2), 243–263.

Morais, A. M., & Câmara, M. J. (1997, September). *Science in kindergarten—The sociology of learning in the classroom.* Paper given at the First Conference of ESERA—European Science Education Research Association, University of Rome Tre, Rome, Italy.

Morais, A. M., Fontinhas, F., & Neves, I. P. (1992). Recognition and realisation rules in acquiring school science: The contribution of pedagogy and social background of students. *British Journal of Sociology of Education, 13* (2), 247–270.

Morais, A. M., & Miranda, C. (1996). Understanding teachers' evaluation criteria: A condition for success in science classes. *Journal of Research in Science Teaching, 33* (6), 601–624.

Morais, A. M., & Neves, I. P. (1993). Práticas pedagógicas e teorias de instrução no contexto de socialização familiar: Um modelo de análise. In A. M. Morais et al., *Socialização primária e prática pedagógica: Vol. 2, Análise de aprendizagens na família e na escola* (chap. 14). Lisbon: Gulbenkian Foundation.

Morais, A. M., Neves, I. P., & Afonso, M. (2001). *Os professores e a educação científica no 1° ciclo do ensino básico—Desenvolvimento de processos de formação.* School of Science, University of Lisbon. (ongoing project).

Morais, A. M., Neves, I. P., Antunes, H., Fontinhas, F., Medeiros, A., Peneda, D., & Reis, E. (1996). Práticas pedagógicas e aprendizagem científica: Um estudo sociológico. *Revista de Educação, V* (2), 69–93.

Morais, A. M., Neves, I. P., Medeiros, A., Peneda, D. Fontinhas, F., & Antunes, H. (1993). *Socialização primária e prática pedagógica: Vol 2, Análise de aprendizagens na família e na escola.* Lisbon: Gulbenkian Foundation.

Morais, A. M., Neves, I. P., & Pires, D. (2001). *Práticas pedagógicas inovadoras em educação científica—Estudo no 1° ciclo do ensino básico.* School of Science, University of Lisbon. (ongoing project).

Morais, A. M., Neves, I. P., et al. (2000). *Estudos para uma sociologia da aprendizagem.* Lisbon: Institute for Educational Research and Centre for Educational Research (SSUL).

Morais, A. M., Peneda, D., Neves, I. P., & Cardoso, L. (1992). *Socialização primária e prática pedagógica: Vol 1.* Lisbon: Gulbenkian Foundation.

Morais, A. M., & Rocha, C. (2000). Development of social competences in the primary school: Study of specific pedagogic practices. *British Educational Research Journal, 26* (1), 91–119.

Neves, I. P., & Morais, A. M. (1996). Teorias de instrução na família e aproveitamento escolar. *Sociologia, 19,* 127–164.

Pires, D., & Morais, A. M. (1997a). Aprendizagem científica e contextos de socialização familiar: Um estudo com crianças dos estratos sociais mais baixos. *Revista de Educação, VI* (2), 57–73.

———. (1997b). Contextos familiares e aproveitamento na aula de ciências: Estudo de características específicas dos processos e socialização primária. *Análise Social, XXXII* (1), 143–186.

Rocha, C., & Morais, A. M. (2000). A relação investigador-professor nos processos de investigação-acção: Uma abordagem sociológica. In A. M. Morais, I. P. Neves et al., *Estudos para uma sociologia da aprendizagem* (chap. 17). Lisbon: Institute for Educational Innovation and Centre for Educational Research (SSUL).

Vygotsky, L. (1978). *Mind in society: The development of higher psychological processes.* Ed. M. Cole, V. John-Steiner, S. Scribner, & E. Souberman. Cambridge, MA: Harvard University Press.

———. (1992). *Educational psychology.* Winter Park, FL: PMD Publications.

Whitty, G., Rowe, G., & Aggleton, P. (1994). *Subjects and themes in the secondary school curriculum.* Research Papers in Education. London: Institute of Education, University of London.

Chapter 9

Texts and Contexts in Educational Systems: Studies of Recontextualising Spaces

Isabel Neves
Ana Morais

Introduction

Educational researchers have studied curriculum organization and development at both the macro and micro levels using epistemological, psychological, and sociological approaches. However, in science education there is no widely accepted curriculum paradigm which directs either broad or systematic research. Without undervaluing other perspectives, we want to highlight the importance of a sociological approach for the development of such a curriculum paradigm.

We consider that Bernstein's model of pedagogic discourse (Bernstein, 1990, 1996) permits a comprehensive sociological analysis of the processes and relationships which characterise curriculum development at the macro and micro levels. It also allows an exploration of the autonomy which is given to teachers and textbook authors within the educational system. We think that both teachers and authors ought to be aware that the potentialities and limits of their pedagogic intervention, in terms of innovation, depend on the recontextualisations which can occur at the various levels of the educational system. Teachers are not necessarily only reproducers of the curriculum; they can be curriculum constructors. However, if they are to innovate, they must recognise the context and the possible influences to be taken into account in their activity, critically reflecting on the multiple paths open to them.

On the basis of the conceptualisation provided by Bernstein's model of pedagogic discourse, we have conducted extensive research centred on current Portuguese science education reform at the compulsory schooling level (ages 10–15). Here we have sought to study the sociological meaning of changes that have been introduced and to analyse the degree and direction of the recontextualising which has taken place at the various levels of the pedagogic device. Our research includes a comparative study in which, for each level, we compare texts from the present period of science education reform (dating from 1991) with texts from the science education reform of the late 1960s and early 1970s. We aimed to study *the extent to which the texts of a science education reform contain a message of change or a message of continuity with regard to the sociological principles which characterise the multiple relationships present in educational action*. We aimed also to explore the *contextualising and recontextualising processes which can occur at the various levels of educational intervention in terms of the socio-political context in which reform takes place*.

It is important to grasp something of the character of the Portuguese socio-political situation. Portugal was a dictatorship for more than 40 years, becoming a democracy only in 1974. Due to both overt international pressure and the influence of educational changes in the USA, a reform of the educational system began in the late 1960s. This reform started at the level of the 5th and 6th years of schooling (ages 10^-–12^+) and was known as the *Veiga Simão reform* after the minister of education of the time. New syllabuses were developed in science education. The pedagogic principles underlying these syllabuses departed in many crucial aspects from the principles established in the 1933 Constitution, which governed the country during the whole dictatorship period, and in the educational basic law of the time. External and internal pressures, together with the death of the dictator Salazar in 1970, created the conditions for the weakening of the regime. A new educational basic law was approved in 1973, containing some principles of a more open society which were not in accordance with the 1933 Constitution which was still in effect. The revolution which took place in 1974 found the educational system in a state of considerable incoherence. At this time, syllabuses for the 5th and 6th years, together with isolated educational experiences in middle and high school, were based on new content and quite open relations. In the unstable post-revolutionary year of 1975, and before a new constitution and educational basic law could be developed and approved, the reform had moved into the 7th year of schooling.

The present reform (1991) followed trends similar to those of the reforms in other countries such as the United Kingdom and Spain and was set in a well established democratic system, within a new constitution (1976) and a new educational basic law (1986). We wanted to see the extent to which it introduced changes from the reform of the late 1960s and early 1970s. While the present reform has taken place in a stabilised society where constitution, educational basic law, and syllabuses followed each other in time and where contextualising and recontextualising can be coherently analysed, the earlier reform developed in a non-linear sequence, where change in the educational basic law came after the development of the 5th and 6th year syllabuses, under a dictatorial regime, and before the new 7th year syllabuses that were part of the same reform but were developed later, within a democratic system.

In this chapter, we start by presenting the theoretical framework which has guided our research. We refer briefly to the various levels and relations present in the production and reproduction of pedagogic discourse officially institutionalised as the pedagogic text to be used by teachers and textbook authors. We then proceed to the presentation and discussion of the study we have developed and undertaken on the basis of the model. Finally we offer a synthesis of the results suggested by our research, with particular emphasis on the potentialities offered by the model for a methodology which simultaneously operationalises that model and broadens its applications.

Theoretical Framework

Focusing on the distinctive characteristics which constitute and distinguish the specialised form of communication which is realised by pedagogic discourse, Bernstein (1990) constructs a model which seeks to show the multiple and complex relations which intervene in the production and reproduction of such discourse. In the model, the production of official pedagogic discourse is seen as the result of relations which are established at the generative and recontextualising levels of general regulative discourse. General regulative discourse contains the dominant principles of society and is generated as a result of the relations and influences between the State field and the fields of production (physical resources) and symbolic control (discursive resources). It is also, to a lesser or greater extent, under international influence. The State functions at the generative level to legitimise the principles of distribution of social power and control which are incorporated in official pedagogic discourse. However, official pedagogic discourse is not the mechanical result of the dominant principles of society because these principles undergo a recontextualising process. In this recontextualising process, two fields intervene directly—the official recontextualising field, which is directly controlled by the State, and the pedagogic recontextualising field. They are both influenced by the fields of production and symbolic control and their main activity is the definition of the *what* and the *how* of pedagogic discourse. When pedagogic discourses produced at the level of the official and pedagogic recontextualising fields are inserted at the transmission level, they can still undergo a recontextualising process dependent on the specific context of each school and the pedagogic practice of each teacher. In this way, discourse reproduced in schools and classrooms is influenced by the relationships which characterise its specific transmission contexts. It can also be influenced by relations between schools and family and community contexts.

The model suggests that the production and reproduction of pedagogic discourse involve extremely dynamic processes. On the one hand, the dominant principles which are conveyed by general regulative discourse reflect positions of conflict rather than stable relationships. On the other hand, there are always potential and real sources of conflict, resistance, and inertia among the political and administrative agents of the official recontextualising field, among the various agents of the pedagogic recontextualising field, and between the primary context of the acquirer and the principles and practices of the school. Furthermore, teachers and textbook authors may feel unable or reluctant to reproduce the educational transmission code underlying official pedagogic discourse. It is this dynamism which enables change to take place. According to Bernstein, a pedagogic device which offers greater recontextualising possibilities through a greater number of fields and contexts involved, and/or a society characterised by a pluralistic political regime, can lead to a higher degree of recontextualising and, therefore, to greater space for change.

In Portugal, the syllabus of a given discipline embodies the official pedagogic discourse produced by the Ministry of Education, the official recontextualising field agent. This official text carries messages containing the principles and norms which constitute the general regulative discourse that characterises a given socio-political context. However, as a pedagogic text it also carries messages which reflect a set of options, considered adequate to a given educational context, which are influenced by various fields. The textbooks for a given syllabus express this discourse produced in the pedagogic recontextualising field. Although translating the principles legitimised by the syllabus, they also reflect options which depend on the multiple relations between different pedagogic fields.

Pedagogic discourse embeds instructional and regulative discourse, in such a way that the latter incorporates and dominates the former. A specific instructional discourse refers to knowledges and cognitive competences, and a specific regulative discourse refers to values, attitudes, and socio-affective competences which establish order, relation, and identity in the teaching-learning context.

The conceptualisation and the empirical properties of the model enable analysis of the sociological messages present in a given pedagogic text (syllabus, textbook, teacher's practice) with respect to the multiple relations which characterise the teaching-learning process. This analysis involves considering the messages in terms of the *what* and the *how* of pedagogic discourse, that is, in terms of what is to be transmitted and how it is to be transmitted. The model also makes possible analysis of the sociological messages presented to teachers in a given syllabus by the Ministry of Education. We have considered the messages in terms of the control used by the Ministry of Education to make teachers and textbook authors conform to its values as to the *what* and the *how*.

In such an analysis, it is important to characterise the *what* of pedagogic discourse not only as the values given to instructional and regulative discourses but also as the emphasis, within these discourses, given to cognitive and socio-affective competences of distinct levels of complexity. In the characterisation of the *how* of pedagogic discourse and of Ministry of Education-teacher relations, the sociological relations between categories (subjects, discourses, spaces) become areas of analytical interest. These relations entail power and control relations which are characterised in terms of classification and framing. The research we have been carrying out is centred on the production of the pedagogic discourse at the generative and recontextualising levels, analysing the sociological messages contained in texts produced in two distinct periods in terms of socio-political context and curriculum development.

Application of the Pedagogic Discourse Model in the Analysis of Science Curriculum Reforms: Exemplar Research Studies

In our study we started from the assumption that the analysis of changes introduced by a given educational reform is deepened if those changes are compared with previous reforms and explored in terms of the socio-political context in which they took place. For that reason, our study compared the sociological messages contained in the syllabuses of our present reform period with the messages contained in syllabuses of the previous reform period. We also studied the recontextualising which occurs between the principles of general and educational policies present in constitutions and basic laws and the pedagogic guidelines given by syllabuses and between the syllabuses and the textbooks (Figure 9.1).

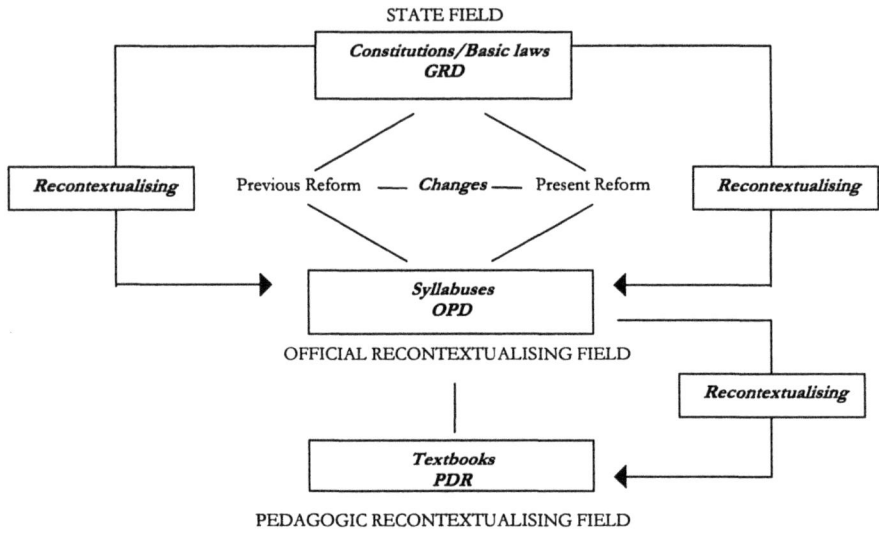

GRD – General Regulative Discourse
OPD – Official Pedagogic Discourse
PDR – Pedagogic Discourse of Reproduction

Figure 9.1—*General diagram of relations analysed.*

The focus was on analysing science syllabuses and textbooks in use in various years of compulsory schooling. Space restrictions permit us to describe only the studies centred on natural science syllabuses. However, brief reference will be made to studies of other disciplines and textbooks.

Relations underlying the teaching-learning process

The studies carried out by Morais, Neves, and Fontinhas (1999), Morais and Neves (1999), Neves and Morais (1997), and Neves, Morais, Medeiros, and Peneda (1999) addressed the following research question: *What is the extent to which the present science education reform changes the text of syllabuses, in terms of the relations underlying the teaching-learning process?*

These studies focused on the natural science syllabuses in use in the 5th/6th, and 7th years of schooling (ages 10⁻ –13⁺)[1] and were centred on two aspects of the teaching-learning process: (a) the value given to different discourses and competences; and (b) the value given to various teaching-learning relations (Figure 9.2).

We used a qualitative approach based on an interpretative model. Our unit of analysis[2] was the sentence.[3] The analysis not only focused on syllabus sections which contained the guidelines specifically related to the discipline but also on sections which referred to general aspects of the whole curriculum and which might also contain guidelines related to the discipline.

To characterise the sociological messages contained in the syllabus texts, we defined indicators for each one of the relations under analysis. At the empirical level, that definition followed the criteria for the nature of those relations and the specificity of distinct syllabus sections. In order to compare the various syllabuses at the level of their global message and at the level of the message contained in distinct syllabus sections, sentences were grouped in five categories. Two categories referred to the curricular dimension and three to the disciplinary dimension. We classified all the sentences contained in the syllabuses and calculated their percentage distribution in terms of the indicators selected by the whole syllabus and by each of its dimensions (curricular and disciplinary).

Analysis of the value given to different discourses and competences was based on sentences which referred to "contents" related to general regulative discourse (GRD), specific instructional and regulative discourses (SID, SRD), and simple and complex cognitive and socio-affective competences (SC, CC, SSA, CSA). According to the theoretical framework of analysis and taking into account the limitations inherent in analysis applied to a syllabus, the criteria for identifying sentences were as follows:

a. when the sentence referred only to the educational macro level, expressing intentions and general principles about knowledges, values, and attitudes to be considered in the general educational context, it was classified as transmitting the GRD;

b. when the sentence referred to the micro level of the classroom, expressing knowledges and competences to be developed in the teaching-learning process, it was classified as transmitting the specific discourse (SID if the sentence was focused on cognitive

230 TOWARDS A SOCIOLOGY OF PEDAGOGY

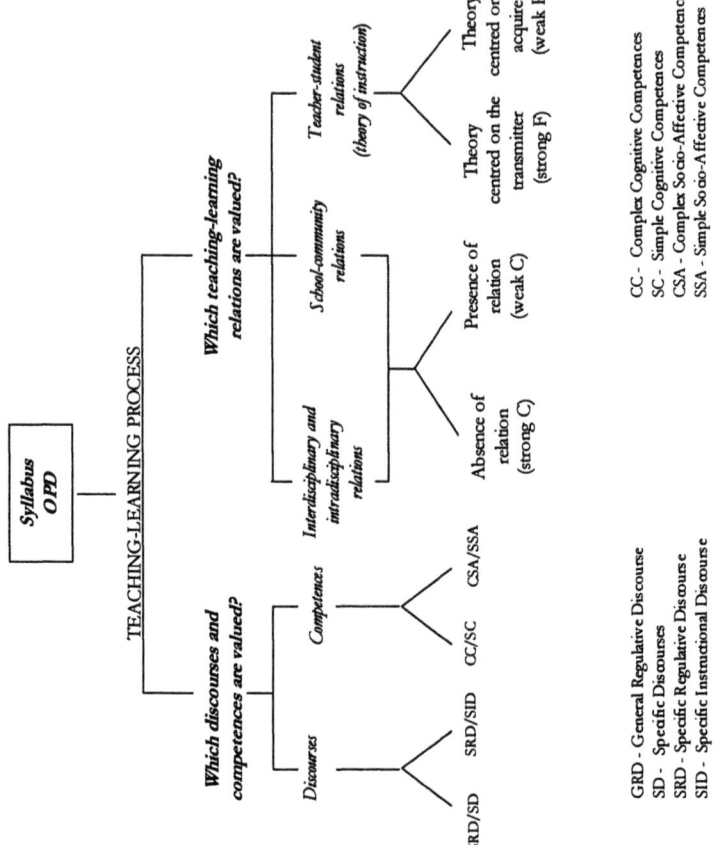

Figure 9.2—*Diagram of the relations underlying the teaching-framing process.*

knowledges and competences and SRD if the sentence was focused on attitudes and socio-affective competences);

c. sentences containing SID were classified as valuing CC whenever they referred to concepts at a high level of abstraction or expressed complex cognitive competences even if factual knowledge or concepts at a low level of abstraction were their referents[4] and they were classified as valuing SC whenever both knowledges and competences were of a low cognitive level;

d. sentences containing SRD were classified as valuing CSA whenever they referred to values or expressed attitudes at a complex level and they were classified as valuing SSA whenever competences valued were of a simple level;[5]

e. although complex competences presuppose simple competences, if the sentence expressed only complex competences, these were the only ones considered; only when the sentence clearly expressed the two types of competences were both considered.[6]

The indicator of the value given to different discourses and competences was the percentage distribution of sentences containing the following comparative elements: (a) general regulative discourse in relation to specific instructional and regulative discourses; (b) specific instructional discourse in relation to specific regulative discourse; (c) within specific instructional discourse, complex cognitive competences in relation to simple competences; within specific regulative discourse, complex socio-affective competences in relation to simple competences. We also analysed the kind of values and the kind of competences of higher levels of complexity which are emphasised in syllabuses.

Analysis of the value given to various teaching-learning relations was centred on interdisciplinary and intradisciplinary relations, school-community relations, and teacher-student relations. This analysis was made on the basis of the percentage distribution of sentences which indicated a distinct degree of relation between the categories under study. To characterise the degree of relation of each sentence we used a 3 point scale for classification (C^{++}, C^{+}, C^{-}) or framing (F^{++}, F^{+}, F^{-}) relations. According to these scales, the highest value (C^{++} or F^{++}) means absence of relation and the lowest value (C^{-} or F^{-}) means presence of relation; the intermediate values

(C⁺ or F⁺) mean little explicit relation. The values of these scales were established on the basis of criteria derived from a previous analysis of all sentences. That analysis allowed an identification of the empirical indicators that were more adequate to the type of relations under study and to the particular nature of the various parts of the text under analysis. For example, the scale we constructed to analyse interdisciplinary relations contained three degrees of classification defined according to the following criteria:

a. C⁺⁺ – the sentence omitted knowledge of other disciplines and referred exclusively to knowledge of the discipline under analysis;

b. C⁺ – the sentence contained references to other curricular disciplines, although those references were vague or implicit;

c. C⁻ – the sentence contained references to other curricular disciplines, pointing explicitly to relations between their knowledge and the knowledge of the discipline under analysis.[7]

The scale we constructed to analyse the teacher-student relation and its implied theory of instruction contained three degrees of framing defined according to the following criteria:

a. F⁺⁺ – the sentence contained statements which gave a clear emphasis to the directive role of the teacher in the teaching-learning process (for example, the teacher "tells", "informs", "explains") or the sentence referred to cognitive and/or socio-affective competences which suggest little intervention by the student and indicate that the syllabus values a theory of instruction more or less exclusively centred on the transmitter;

b. F⁺ – the sentence contained statements which emphasised the orientating role of the teacher in the teaching-learning process (for example, the teacher "guides", "accompanies", "appeals to the student's participation") or when the sentence referred to cognitive and/or socio-affective competences which suggest some participation of the student and indicate that the syllabus values a theory of instruction which, although centred on the transmitter, also considers student intervention;

c. F- – the sentence contained statements which emphasised a higher degree of intervention of the student in the teaching-learning process (for example, the student engages in "free activities", "independent tasks", or "project work") or when the sentence referred to cognitive and/or socio-affective competences which suggest a higher degree of student autonomy indicating that the syllabus values a theory of instruction mainly centred on the acquirer.[8]

The studies revealed that current science syllabuses contain a global message which

a. gives more value to the regulative dimension of learning;

b. reinforces the importance given to the competences of higher levels of complexity (especially socio-affective competences);

c. gives greater emphasis to interdisciplinary and intradisciplinary relations and to school-community relations; and

d. gives less control to the acquirer in teacher-student relations (i.e., legitimises a theory of instruction less centred on the acquirer).

Changes were more evident (and sometimes only present) in the 7th year of schooling. The studies also revealed that in present science syllabuses the values and kinds of cognitive and socio-affective competences of higher levels of complexity are intended to reflect principles seen to be oriented to a democratic society (e.g., freedom, solidarity, responsibility, cooperation) and competences related to functional scientific literacy (e.g., scientific inquiry competences, metacognitive competences) and to higher personal and social development (e.g., self-confidence, persistence, justice, truth). These kind of values and competences were already present in the previous reform but they are now more diverse and clearly specified. Indeed, the studies suggest that change has gone mostly in the direction of reinforcing these principles.

In spite of these changes, our present science syllabuses contain a global sociological message which does not substantially alter the principles which characterised earlier syllabus relations. In fact, the change is not as great as we might expect in face of the social principles which characterise our present, democratic society. However, when the curricular and disciplinary dimensions of the syllabuses are analysed separately, we see that there are some differences in the sociological messages they contain. It is in the curricular dimension of the syllabuses that the regulative dimension of learning is more apparent, the cognitive and socio-affective competences of higher levels of complexity and interdisciplinary and school-community relations more valued, and a theory of instruction more centred on the student legitimised. These differences suggest the recontextualising which can occur, within the same syllabus, when passing from curricular intentions to guidelines specifically directed to a discipline. As a consequence of this recontextualising, the curricular innovations which are introduced in a reform may be submersed in the syllabuses' global message.

The recontextualising which is evident in the syllabuses of the two reforms (although it is greater in the previous reform than in the present reform) leads to a reflection on what should be done when syllabuses are changed. If the educational principles expressed in the general intentions of the curriculum are not effectively present in the specific guidelines for a discipline, change intentions will be in jeopardy. It can be argued that, provided innovation is present in curricular guidelines, teachers can, in an autonomous and flexible way, manage the disciplinary components of the syllabus. However, since teachers' actions depend on their pedagogic education and ideology, teachers may not use the space for intervention that they possess. For that reason, change intentions should assume an explicit form in the specific guidelines of a discipline. Although this would constitute reduction of teachers' control in relation to officially legitimised principles, it could be argued that it is important and justifiable when teachers have not received an education which permits reflection on the meaning of the sociological messages contained at various syllabus levels.

In order to widen and deepen our analyses of the sociological meaning of changes introduced in the present science education reform, in terms of the relations underlying the teaching-learning process, we developed further studies centred on physics and chemistry syllabuses for the 8th and 9th years of schooling[9] (Lopes, 1998; Nascimento, 1998) and textbooks for natural science in the 7th year of schooling (Lourenço, 1997; Lourenço & Neves, 1998). Analyses of the physics and chemistry syllabuses reflect the trends in natural science syllabuses discussed above, reinforcing the idea that innovations intended in the general curriculum are neither fully nor clearly present in the specific discipline guidelines. Recontextualising within syllabus, from the curricular to the disciplinary level, approximates the sociological messages contained in the discipline guidelines in both these cases.

Our study of natural science textbooks for the 7th year revealed differences between the sociological messages contained in them, generally according to the relationship under analysis and the syllabus. In general, their messages were less innovative than those expressed by the whole syllabus. Our study suggested a different degree of recontextualising between the pedagogic discourse of textbooks and the two dimensions of the syllabus, the curricular and disciplinary levels. There is more recontextualising in relation to the general curricular principles and less recontextualising in relation to the specific guidelines for the discipline.

Overall, current science education reform reveals potential changes in the curricular directions of syllabuses but these are blurred in specific discipline guidelines and in textbooks. This raises important questions about processes and relations in effective implementation of an educational reform. The importance of the pedagogic education and ideology of teachers and textbook authors to curriculum development appears as a crucial aspect to be considered when innovation is intended.

Ministry of Education-teacher relations:
Potentialities and limits of teacher intervention

The study carried out by Morais and Neves (1999) addressed the following research question: *What are the changes introduced by the present science education reform syllabuses with regard to Ministry of Education-teacher relations?* The study was centred on the natural science syllabuses of the 5th/6th, and 7th years of schooling, and we followed a methodology similar to that already described.

We started from the assumption that the Ministry of Education-teacher relation was one of transmitter (Ministry of Education) and acquirer (teacher, textbook author) in which the official pedagogic discourse contained in the syllabus constituted a text to be transmitted-acquired. Ministry of Education-teacher relations were analysed in terms of the control exerted by the Ministry on teachers and textbook authors in its directions about official pedagogic discourse. Two aspects of the Ministry of Education's control were considered. The first was its degree with regard to the pedagogic text to be "acquired" (implemented) by teachers and textbook authors, and the second was the form of communication used by the Ministry in conveying its intentions. For the first, we used the degree of content explicitness of the syllabus as an indicator; for the second, the presence or absence of the reasons given by the Ministry of Education about syllabus construction and implementation (Figure 9.3).

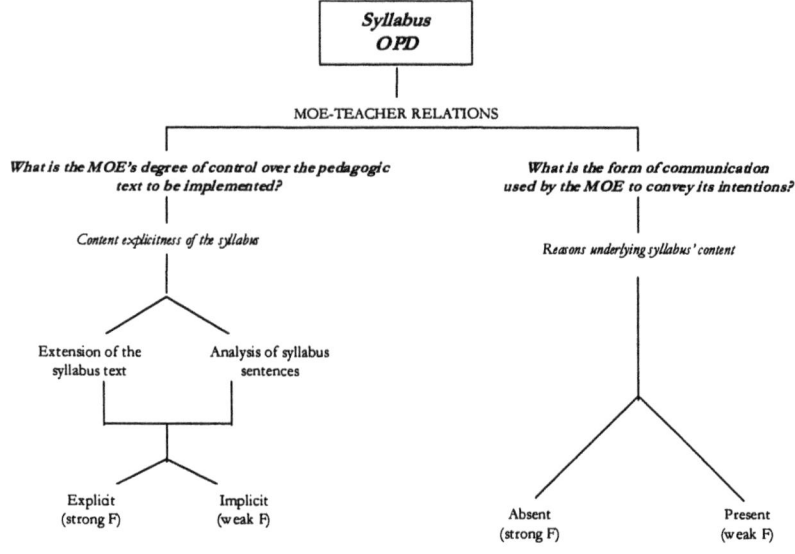

Figure 9.3—*Diagram of Ministry of Education (MOE)-teacher relations.*

The degree of content explicitness of the syllabus was measured by considering its extent and the framing value of each sentence. The extent of the syllabus text was measured by the number of sentences contained in it as a whole and the percentage devoted to each syllabus dimension. We assumed that more text means greater explicitness. Sentence analysis was done using a 3 point scale for framing, where the highest value expresses a higher degree of content explicitness and the lowest value expressed less explicitness. In the analysis we used the following criteria: F^{++}—the sentence expressed in a detailed and/or "directive" way what the Ministry of Education intended, making the syllabus content very explicit; F^{+}—the sentence expressed in a relatively specific and/or slightly "directive" way what the Ministry of Education intended, making the syllabus content less explicit; F^{-} —the sentence expressed in a vague and/or "flexible" way what the Ministry of Education intended, making the syllabus content mostly implicit. The indicators used for classifying the sentences took into account the specific nature of syllabus topics.

For example, at the level of curricular aims, when a sentence referred to an objective expressed in a very clear and precise way we gave it the value F^{++}, when the sentence referred to an objective expressed in a not very precise way we gave it the value F^+, and when the sentence referred to an objective expressed in a very vague way we gave it the value F^-. At the disciplinary level, the sentences which contained expressions such as "should be done" or "it is intended that" were classified as F^{++} because they transmit the idea of a relatively directive attitude from the Ministry of Education, leaving teachers no space for freedom of action in whatever direction; the sentences which contained expressions like "the teacher can", "we suggest that" were classified as F^+ because, in this case, the idea of a more permissive attitude on the part of the Ministry of Education is transmitted, leaving the teacher some freedom of action; and the sentences which contained expressions like "the teacher has autonomy", "according to his/her experience", "the teacher can change" were classified as F^-, expressing a fairly open attitude on the part of the Ministry of Education, leaving teachers a greater degree of freedom of action.[10]

When the Ministry gives teachers reasons for its directions, the Ministry is using an interpersonal form of control (weak framing). When reasons are not given, the Ministry is using a positional form of control (strong framing).[11]

The study revealed differences between the two reforms, present and past, with regard to the degree of explicitness of the Ministry of Education's intentions and to the form of communication used by the Ministry in expressing its intentions. In our present science syllabuses, directions are more explicit about the text to be transmitted in the teaching-learning context and these directions are given through a more interpersonal form of communication. This suggests a higher degree of control over the pedagogic text to be implemented and, at the same time, a more open form of communication by the Ministry of Education in telling teachers and textbook authors of its intentions. This seems to reveal a preoccupation by the Ministry of Education with passing on the "new" message of the syllabuses in such a way as to give teachers access to the principles which guided their creation. Such access may guarantee more effective accomplishment of the Ministry's intentions.

The study also revealed that the Ministry of Education's control is now different with respect to the curricular and disciplinary dimensions of the syllabuses. In the curricular dimension there is, in general, a greater explicitness in syllabus content in the present reform in comparison with the earlier change. The Ministry of Education's control over the pedagogic text to be implemented tends to be greater in the present reform than in the previous one. In contrast, the explicitness of the disciplinary dimension was similar or even greater in the previous reform in comparison with the present one, so that at the level of specific disciplinary guidelines there now tends to be less control. However, it is at the level of the syllabuses' curricular dimension that the Ministry of Education's intentions are made explicit, in both reforms though now through a more interpersonal form of communication.

It is also interesting to note that whereas change towards greater explicitness is more evident in the 5th/6th years, change towards a more interpersonal form of communication is more evident in the 7th year. Comparing these results with our earlier findings, we may now note that the syllabus which in the present reform revealed less change in the pedagogic text (5th/6th years) is the syllabus where there was greater explicitness with regard to pedagogic text by the Ministry of Education. The 7th year syllabus, where change in the pedagogic text was more evident, shows less explicitness. It seems, that, whereas at the lower level of schooling the main intention is to reinforce the pedagogic text legitimised in the previous reform, at the higher level of schooling the main intention is to introduce changes in the pedagogic text itself.

The dominant principles of society and curricular reform: The influence of the socio-political context

The studies carried out by Fontes, Morais, and Neves (1996a, 1996b) and Neves and Morais (1999, 2000) analysed the dominant principles of society and their relation to the pedagogic principles established in syllabuses including the natural science syllabuses of the 5th/6th, and 7th years. Analyses focused on official general policy and educational policy texts including political constitutions and basic laws[12] asking: *What is the extent to which science syllabuses embody a recontextualising of the dominant principles of society and to what extent does the socio-political context influence the degree and direction of that recontextualising?* Once more, we used an approach similar to that described above, qualitatively analysing the principles contained in the political constitutions and basic laws associated with each reform period.

TEXTS AND CONTEXTS IN EDUCATIONAL SYSTEMS

The general regulative discourse present in general policy (constitutions) and in educational policy (basic laws) was analysed in terms of the *hierarchical structure of society* and a set of norms/values which express *principles of order and social identity* (Figure 9.4). Although interrelated, these dimensions correspond analytically to the nature of power relations between categories (agencies, agents, discourses) which represent various sectors of society and the nature of norms/values which direct social conduct.

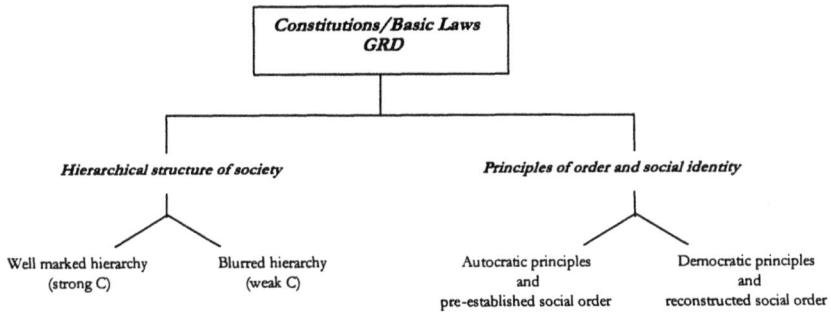

Figure 9.4—*Diagram indicating the sociological principles underlying the constitutions/basic laws.*

To characterise the power relations between the categories under study we used a 4 point scale of classification (C^{++}, C^{+}, C^{-}, C^{--}), where the highest value (C^{++}) suggests a well marked hierarchy and the lowest value (C^{--}) a blurred hierarchy. We then attributed to each sentence a given classification value.[13] The classification relations expressed in the texts under study gave us a general trend relative to the *hierarchical structure of society*. For the characterisation of the norms/values which express the *principles of order and social identity*, we considered the cognitive competences, knowledges, and values/attitudes legitimised in the texts under study. We analysed the various sentences and we grouped them according to the indicators referred to above. From an overall or global appreciation of the norms/values[14] present in each set of sentences, we synthesised them in two sets of principles—autocratic principles/pre-established social order and democratic principles/reconstructed social order.

The studies showed that there are differences between the two periods, revealing the specificity of the socio-political context in which the two curriculum reforms were carried out. The Constitution of 1933 and its revision in 1971 privileged a very strong classification between categories representing the various sectors of society, suggesting a strongly hierarchical structure of society dominated by dictatorial principles in which the social order is pre-established. The constitution of the period of the present reform (1976, revised 1982) reveals a weakening in classification, which suggests a less hierarchical structure of society and the legitimising of democratic principles as the social order is reconstructed. Differences found between the basic laws of the two periods reflect differences in political constitutions with regard to classification relations. With respect to the principles of order and social identity, the analysis revealed that the democratic principles contained in the present basic law (1986) already existed to some extent in the law of 1973 when they co-existed with dictatorial principles, displaying contradictions with regard to the values expressed.

The studies also showed that there is not a total correspondence between the sociological messages expressed in the constitutions and basic laws of either of the two periods and that this is more marked in the former period than in the present one. This suggests that there is some recontextualising of the dominant principles of general political discourse (constitutions) to the guiding principles of the educational political discourse (basic laws) and also that this recontextualising tended to be greater in the former period of reform.

When we considered the relation between the syllabuses' overall message and the dominant principles of society, it appeared that syllabus changes have not been as great as might be expected in light of the democratic principles which characterise present Portuguese society. However, the difference between general regulative discourse and official pedagogic discourse does not mean that the message of the latter subverts the former. Rather, it means that the dominant principles of society became diluted, weakening the message they contain. It was also interesting to note that the differences between the curricular and disciplinary dimensions of syllabuses suggest a closer relation between general regulative discourse and official pedagogic discourse at the level of curricular directions than at the level of disciplinary guidelines. When we considered the socio-political context in which reforms were implemented, a greater recontextualising of the dominant principles of society was evident in earlier reform syllabuses than in present syllabuses, representing a change from autocratic to democratic principles in the former, whereas, in the present period, recontextualising produces only a small change in the direction of less democratic principles than those expressed in the constitution.

We are led to some conclusions about the processes which interfere in the production of the educational discourse. Our findings seem to contradict the idea that recontextualising tends to increase within socio-political conditions which offer greater space of change, for we found greater differences between constitutions and basic laws and general regulative discourse and official pedagogic discourse in the earlier period. Since we were, in the period of that reform, in the presence of an autocratic regime, we would anticipate less recontextualising space. However, a deeper analysis of the socio-political context reveals data which show the contradiction to be more apparent than real. When the former reform started to be implemented, it was a time of some social instability in which political and economic change reflected, to some extent, the increasing influence of the fields of production and of symbolic control. It is in this period that the Parliament brought together some groups opposing the regime, whose presence led to the creation of opposition, conflict, and resistance. It was also in this period that the hybrid 1973 Basic Law was passed and compulsory schooling was extended. The messages of the 1973 Basic Law and of the syllabuses of the same period were influenced not only by ongoing socio-political changes but by educational theories of the field of symbolic control which, at the international level, were valued as better than indigenous beliefs, particularly at the level of compulsory schooling.

Final Considerations

The dominant principles of society are contextualised and recontextualised in the sociological messages transmitted by reformed educational syllabuses influenced in degree and direction by their socio-political context. Syllabus guidelines are contextualised and recontextualised in textbook guidelines.

Our studies centred on science syllabuses suggest that the present curricular reform introduced slight overall changes in teaching-learning relations but quite marked changes in Ministry of Education-teacher relations. The overall relations valued in the present reform express, to a greater or lesser extent, the principles of a democratic society and were already in part valued in previous reform syllabuses. The Ministry of Education-teacher relations reflected in the present reform carry a message of greater explicitness in the pedagogic text embedded in a more interpersonal form of communication. This may suggest that the Ministry of Education is telling teachers to do more efficiently what they have always done. This may lead students to learn the same things they were supposed to learn in the past.

Our studies also suggest that changes introduced by the present reform are more evident at the level of the general intentions of the curriculum than at the level of specific discipline guidelines, and that the general intention express a message closer to the principles established in the constitution/basic law. There is evidence that textbooks covering the same syllabus transmit different messages and that these are closer to the discipline guidelines than to the curricular principles of the syllabus. This suggests recontextualising processes. These processes are important to an understanding of the real meaning of changes. In any reform, the official pedagogic discourse reflects a recontextualising of the general regulative discourse. Our work shows that the recontextualising was greater in the earlier reform than in the present one. This might seem contradictory because the previous reform began to be implemented under a dictatorial regime while the present reform has been implemented in a stabilised democratic regime. However, this evidence reinforces the explanatory potentialities offered by the model at the empirical level, where we see that although State official texts legitimised strong hierarchical relations and autocratic principles in which social order was imposed, conditions already existed in the pre-revolutionary period for innovative curricula.

Our research reveals the multiplicity of factors involved in the implementation of reform and also shows how, at the level of the pedagogic device, there are reproduction and recontextualising processes which are decisive in giving more or less relative autonomy to education. It is possible to say that changes in the dominant principles of society give rise, in general, to changes in the sociological messages transmitted by the pedagogic discourse of syllabuses and textbooks. The contextualising of the general regulative discourse of society in its pedagogic discourse reveals the processes of reproduction of its dominant principles and the relation of dependence of education to those principles. The neutrality which is often attributed to education is, in fact, more apparent than real. Education has autonomy, which is relative, and the relations to which we have referred illustrate that relativity precisely. However, it is also the case that the sociological messages of syllabuses and textbooks do not totally reproduce the dominant principles of society. There are differences which express distinct changes of direction and degree according to the period in which the reform is made, embodied in the recontextualising of general regulative discourse in pedagogic discourse. The autonomous character of education will be greater if the socio-political context of the time leaves greater space open to recontextualising. A factor which plays an important part in this process is the character of the agents and their ideologies which are located in the various recontextualising fields and within the same field. For example, our research showed that curriculum guidelines and discipline guidelines were produced by different groups of educators, who were hired by the Ministry of Education to construct the syllabuses within the official recontextualising field. The discipline guidelines were constructed by science teachers, whereas the curriculum guidelines were constructed by general educators. This was certainly one reason for recontextualising within the same field.

The application of the model in the analyses we carried out required an operationalisation of its concepts, through a language of description which was adequate to each of the relations under analysis and which made possible their comparison at various levels. This methodological aspect constitutes, in terms of the model's application, a fundamental (if not the most fundamental) dimension of the research, given the potentialities revealed in the analysis and interpretation of the results obtained at the various levels of application. The methodology has revealed not only the complexity of the relations and processes which underlie the implementation of an educational reform but also the great explanatory power of the theoretical model used in the analysis of those relations. It shows how crucial, in educational research, is the use of methods of analysis which have the potential to be applied to various levels of the pedagogic device and in the context of distinct disciplines.

It is important to point out that our research did not explore either real teachers' practices or the real control of the Ministry of Education over the implementation of syllabuses at the level of teachers' practices. According to the classification of Robitaille et al. (1993), we can say that we have explored the "intentional curriculum" and not the "implemented curriculum" or the "attained curriculum". For this reason, the messages expressed by the texts analysed should be taken as representing intentions only and not as representing indicators of what is effectively transmitted or practiced, let alone acquired. The degree of correspondence between the transmitted and the acquired depends on the degree of centralised control the Ministry of Education exerts over the evaluation system. Compulsory schooling in Portugal is centralised at the transmission level but not at the acquisition level, with reduced control by the Ministry of Education over evaluation. To reflect upon a real change brought by the present educational reform at this level would require analysis of the messages contained in the text as they were really implemented by teachers.[15]

The studies conducted involved texts produced at various levels of the educational system, and they focused on syllabuses and textbooks of various science disciplines in various schooling years. Further studies of other syllabuses and textbooks that include analyses centred on real teachers' practices and are conducted in the context of other educational systems are indispensable if the proposed methodology is to open up new paths in educational research at the level of science curriculum development. We believe that the research already carried out makes some contribution in this direction.

Notes

* The authors acknowledge the help of the Institute for Educational Innovation in financing the research.

1. See SEEBS (1975a, 1975b) and DGEBS (1991a, 1991b, 1991c, 1991d). Syllabuses for the 5th and 6th years were analysed together because they are part of the same cycle of studies. Thus, we use "5th/6th" in the text.

2. The analysis involved a dialectic relation between theoretical and empirical components. An external language of description was developed on the basis of the theory of the internal language of description underlying the study. In other words, we did not follow an orthodox content analysis, which is often concerned with apparently self-announcing contents (Bernstein, 1996, p. 136). Instead, we used principles of description for constructing what are to count as empirical relations and for translating those relations into conceptual relations as described in chapter 8 of the present volume.

3. The "sentence" is not taken here in a grammatical sense; it corresponds to a portion of the text containing one or more sentences which, as a whole, have a given semantic meaning.

4. For example, problem solving requires high level cognitive competences even when the concept(s) involved are of a low level of abstraction.

5. The distinction between simple and complex socio-affective competences depends on the idea that students' conduct may embody only dispositions to accept/follow/receive given norms or to respond/react to those norms. It can also embody attitudes which reveal that the student has interiorised a set of specific values, and is starting to construct his/her own system of values and to act according to that system. From this point of view, fulfilling previously given orders and revealing obedience are examples of

simple competences. Revealing responsibility or co-operation in group activities gives examples of complex competences. In a way, simple competences reveal attitudes which, from the point of view of social relations, are positional (students' conduct is directed by pre-established norms); complex competences reveal more interpersonal attitudes (students' conduct is directed by negotiated norms/principles).

6. The following sentences illustrate this classification:
General regulative discourse
From this follows the need for promoting the child's awareness of his/her surroundings so that a sense of responsibility for the environment, society, and culture is inculcated.
Specific instructional discourse
Simple cognitive competences
Learn the location of distinct lithological formations [...].
Complex cognitive competences
Understand that materials' circulation in a food chain corresponds to energy transferences.
Specific regulative discourse
Simple socio-affective competences
Respect general norms [...].
Complex socio-affective competences
Promote the recognition of the social value of labour in all of its forms and promote a sense of help and co-operation.

7. Examples of such sentences indicating *Interdisciplinary relations* were:
C^{++} – Understand that materials' circulation in a food chain corresponds to energy transferences.
C^{+} – [...] it was considered important to take into account the economic aspects of fauna and flora.
C^{-} – [...] Develop interdisciplinary projects which lead to actions in recovery of areas of damaged spaces [...].

8. Examples of sentences portraying *Teacher-student relations (theory of instruction)* were:
F^{++} – Among the sedimentary formations with an organic origin, refer to coals and oils [...].
F^{+} – The teacher should find general processes to intervene in the orientation of students' work [...].
F^{-} – Collect [the students'] information about environmental conditions.

9. See DGEBS (1991b, 1995).

10. Examples of sentences on MOE control of curriculum were:
F^{++} – When developing the learning process, it is intended to organise information in terms of fundamental concepts.
F^{+} – The suggestions which follow should be taken as examples which can be used by the teacher as a starting point for the development of each one of the syllabuses'

themes.

F⁻ – The study of each one of the human body systems may be carried out following the sequence indicated or teachers may change it according to their experience or students' requests.

11. Examples of sentences underlying the *Presence of reasons* (interpersonal control—weak framing) were:
    Use a prudent approach when teaching this theme [life transmission] by taking into account ethical and affective aspects, as sexuality is a global multifaceted reality [...].
    Recycling the same notion several times does not mean repetition, as there are varying degrees of conceptualisation according to different developmental levels.

12. See Assembleia Nacional (1933, 1971, 1973), Assembleia da República (1976, 1982), and Ministry of Education (1986).

13. Examples of sentences relating to the dominant principles of society were:
    Relations between subjects
    C⁻⁻ – All Portuguese have the right to education and culture.
    Relations between agencies
    C⁺⁺ – Education provided by the State [...] will obey the principles established in the Constitution [...].
    Relations between discourses
    C⁻⁻ – The State does not have the right to programme education and culture according to any philosophical, aesthetic, political, ideological, or religious directions. (1976 Constitution)
    C⁺⁺ – Arts and sciences will be supported and protected in their development, education [...] provided the Constitution, the hierarchy, and the State coordination action are respected. (1933 Constitution)

14. Some examples of overall principles expressed in the constitutions/basic laws were:
    Intellectual education, mental discipline, scientific mind, nationalism, authoritarism, hierarchy, willingness, responsibility. (1933 Constitution/1973 Basic Law)
    Humanistic, artistic, physical, scientific, and technological education. Critical and creative thinking. Responsibility, autonomy, solidarity, co-operation, liberty, equality. (1976 Constitution/1986 Basic Law)

15. Other studies have focused on the analysis of teachers' pedagogic practices (Morais et al., 1992, 1993, 2000).

Bibliography

Assembleia Nacional. (1933). Decreto de aprovação da Constituição de 1933. *Diário do Governo*, I série – no. 83.

———. (1971). Lei no. 3/71. *Diário do Governo,* I série – no. 192, Suplemento.

———. (1973). Lei no. 5/73. *Diário do Governo,* I série – no. 173.

Assembleia da República. (1976). Decreto de aprovação da Constituição de 1976. *Diário da República,* I série – no. 86.

———. (1982). Lei constitucional no. 1/82. *Diário da República,* I série – no. 227.

Bernstein, B. (1990). *Class, codes and control: Vol. IV, The structuring of pedagogic discourse.* London: Routledge.

———. (1996). *Class, codes and control: Vol. V, Pedagogy, symbolic control and identity: Theory, research, critique.* London: Taylor & Francis.

DGEBS. (1991a). *Organização curricular e programas: Vol. I, 2° ciclo do ensino básico.* Lisbon: Ministry of Education.

———. (1991b). *Organização curricular e programas: Vol. I, 3° ciclo do ensino básico.* Lisbon: Ministry of Education.

———. (1991c). *Programa de ciências da natureza—Plano de organização do ensino-aprendizagem: Vol. II, 2° ciclo do Ensino Básico.* Lisbon: Ministry of Education.

———. (1991d). *Programa de ciências naturais—Plano de organização do ensino-aprendizagem: Vol. II, 3° ciclo do Ensino Básico.* Lisbon: Ministry of Education.

———. (1995). *Programa de ciências físico-químicas—Programa e organização curricular: 3° ciclo do ensino básico.* Lisbon: Ministry of Education.

Domingos, A. M. (now Morais), Barradas, H., Rainha, H., & Neves, I. P. (1986). *A teoria de Bernstein em sociologia da educação.* Lisbon: Gulbenkian Foundation.

Fontes, A., Morais, A. M., & Neves, I. P. (1996a, September). *A política educativa da actual reforma: Um estudo comparativo das leis de bases de 1986 e 1973.* Paper presented at the Second Algarve Congress of Education, University of Algarve, Faro, Portugal.

———. (1996b). *Os princípios dominantes da sociedade e as reformas curriculares de 1975 e 1991: Estudo comparativo das leis de bases e das constituições.* Unpublished manuscript, ESSA, School of Science, University of Lisbon.

Lopes, A. (1998). *O programa de ciências físico-químicas do 8° ano de escolaridade e a sua recontextualização pelos professores: Uma análise sociológica.* Unpublished master's dissertation in education, School of Science, University of Lisbon.

Lourenço, A. (1997). *O discurso pedagógico em manuais escolares: Uma análise sociológica centrada nas ciências naturais do 7° ano de escolaridade*. Unpublished master's dissertation in education, School of Science, University of Lisbon.

Lourenço, A., & Neves, I. P. (1998, September). *Syllabuses and textbooks: Recontextualising the official pedagogic discourse*. Paper presented at the European Conference on Educational Research 98, School of Pedagogy, Ljubljana, Slovenia.

Ministry of Education. (1986). Lei no. 46/86—Lei de Bases do sistema educativo. *Diário da República*, I série – no. 237.

Morais, A. M., & Neves, I. P. (1999, September). *What did science educational reforms change? A comparative analysis of what is told to teachers and how*. Paper presented at the Second International Conference of the European Science Education Research Association, Kiel, Germany.

Morais, A. M., Neves, I. P., & Fontinhas, F. (1999). Is there any change in science educational reforms? A sociological study of theories of instruction. *British Journal of Sociology of Education, 20* (1), 37–53.

Morais, A. M., Neves, I. P., Medeiros, A., Peneda, D., Fontinhas, F., & Antunes, H. (1993). *Socialização primária e prática pedagógica: Vol. 2, Análise de aprendizagens na família e na escola*. Lisbon: Gulbenkian Foundation.

Morais, A. M., Neves, I. P., et al. (2000). *Estudos para uma sociologia da aprendizagem*. Lisbon: Institute for Educational Innovation and Centre for Educational Research, School of Science, University of Lisbon.

Morais, A. M., Peneda, D., Neves, I. P., & Cardoso, L. (1992). *Socialização primária e prática pedagógica: Vol. 1*. Lisbon: Gulbenkian Foundation.

Nascimento, T. (1998). *Programas e sua recontextualização pelos professores: Uma análise sociológica no âmbito da disciplina de físico-química do 9° ano de escolaridade*. Unpublished master's dissertation in education, School of Science, University of Lisbon.

Neves, I. P., & Morais, A. M. (1997, September). *The relation between school and family/community. Is there any change in present education reforms?* Paper presented at the First Conference of the European Science Education Research Association, Rome, Italy.

———. (1999, August). *What is in syllabuses that is in the constitutions? Study of recontextualising in two educational reforms*. Paper presented at the Eighth Conference for Research on Learning and Instruction, Gotenborg, Sweden.

———. (2000). Política educativa e orientações programáticas: Análise da educação científica em dois períodos socio-políticos. *Revista de Educação, IX* (1) 93–109.

———. (in press). Teacher's space for change in educational reforms: A model for analysis applied to a recent reform in Portugal. *Journal of Curriculum Studies.*

———. (in press). Knowledges and values in science syllabuses: A sociological study of educational reforms. *British Journal of Sociology of Education.*

Neves, I. P., Morais, A. M., Medeiros, A., & Peneda, D. (1999). Relação entre conhecimentos nos currículos de ciências: Estudo comparativo de duas reformas. *Revista de Educação, VIII* (2), 63–76.

Robitaille, D., et al. (1993). *Curriculum frameworks for mathematics and science.* TIMSS monograph, no. 1. Vancouver: Pacific Educational Press.

SEEBS. (1975a). *Programas do ensino preparatório.* Lisbon: Ministry of Education and Scientific Research.

———. (1975b). *Programas do 7º ano de escolaridade.* Lisbon: Ministry of Education and Scientific Research.

Chapter 10
Pedagogic Discourses and Student Resistance in Australian Secondary Schools

Parlo Singh

Introduction

Since the early 1980s, radical pedagogues have produced a considerable body of literature naming and describing pedagogies designed to contest educational disadvantage. This literature spans a wide field and encompasses socially critical pedagogies, pedagogies of hope, feminist pedagogies, post-structural pedagogies, pedagogies of whiteness, and pedagogies of positionality (see, for example, Giroux & McClaren, 1986; Kenway et al., 1994; Maher & Thompson Tetreault, 1997). The aforementioned diversity of radical pedagogic models attests to the positions, tensions, conflicts, and struggles within this field of research literature. For example, tensions exist over the conception of "empowerment" and what it means to give voice to members of disadvantaged groups within schooling (see, for example, Ellsworth, 1989). Critical pedagogues advocate that students from oppressed groups should be given opportunities to have their voices heard in rational classroom dialogue. However, one group of post-structural or post-critical feminist educational researchers has argued that the injustices of racialised, classed, and gendered power relations distort communication in the classroom. Consequently, these researchers have suggested that it is important to examine the social conditions which construct positions of speech and silence within the classroom and thereby inhibit the social construction of the ideal speech community—the conditions for rational dialogue advocated by critical pedagogues (see Luke & Gore, 1992). In addition, post-structural shifts in the research field have produced studies that do not focus solely on marginality. Rather, post-structural pedagogies focus on relational positions of dominance and marginality, such as the power relations of "whiteness" and "blackness" and/or "masculinity" and "femininity" (Maher & Thompson Tetreault, 1997).

Within this field of research, advancement of knowledge is measured by the addition of new pedagogies which "give voice to" or "attend to" the politics of difference in "new times". This has produced an abundance of pedagogies to accommodate social category membership (i.e., gender, race, class, disability, and so forth) and/or power relations within and between these social categories. Common to the radical pedagogies literature is a critique of the ability of existing pedagogies to represent each new "voice"—the voice of the working class, women, people of colour, the disabled, and so forth. Legitimation of different pedagogies is based upon the personal experience of a knower. As a new pedagogy is constructed to celebrate each new "voice", the category of the privileged knower becomes smaller (Maton, 2000; Moore & Muller, 1999). For example, critical pedagogy (Giroux & McClaren, 1986) has been challenged by post-structural feminist pedagogies (Luke & Gore, 1992), which in turn have been challenged by post-colonial pedagogies (Crowley, 1998; Matthews, 1998; Hickling-Hudson, 1998), and so forth. Within this field of literature "[k]nowledge forms and knowledge relations are [often] translated as social standpoints and power relations between groups" (Moore & Muller, 1999, p. 190). Consequently, many radical pedagogues focus on the sociology of "knowers and their relationships" (Moore & Muller, 1999, p. 190), at the expense of analysing the internal structuring of the specialised forms of knowledge transmitted through schooling.

This chapter aims to contribute to the literature on pedagogies and educational inequality. It does so by drawing on concepts from Bernstein's "sociology for the transmission of knowledges" (see Epilogue, in this volume) to critically analyse the internal structuring of English curricular knowledge and forms of teacher-student interaction in two secondary school classrooms in Queensland, Australia. Thus, the next section delineates a Bernsteinian theoretical framework.

Theoretical Framework:
Analysis of the Structure of Pedagogic Discourse

In his last paper, "From Pedagogies to Knowledges", Bernstein (in this volume) argued that "today in the United Kingdom there is growing evidence of the developments of the totally pedagogised society" (TPS). As evidence of developments towards a TPS, Bernstein referred to the proliferation of discourses celebrating education, trainability, and life-long learning as "a condition for the effective informational society". Moreover, he suggested that the current period constitutes the "second totally pedagogised society; the first being that of the medieval period initiated by Religion". However, Bernstein contended that despite this propagation of discourses relating to education, there remains a "triumphant silence" about the rules or principles generating modes of curricular knowledge and the forms of specialised interactions constituted to transmit knowledge.

Over four decades of research, Bernstein wrote about the rules/principles generating the transmission (i.e., selection, organisation, and evaluation) of knowledge through schooling. He proposed that formal institutions for the transmission of knowledge, such as schools, "evolved to apprentice children into decontextualised ways of meaning thus enabling them to develop an orientation to meaning that is abstracted from familiar local contexts" (quoted in Rose, 1999, p. 224). Moreover, the institution of the modern school, Bernstein proposed, was designed to transmit forms of moral training, that is, particular compartments of the person. Bernstein (1990, 1996) suggested that these two modes of knowledge (knowledge pertaining to abstract concepts/skills and knowledge pertaining to moral conduct) are transmitted principally via a specialised discourse, that is, pedagogic discourse. This discourse, however, comprises both an instructional and a regulative component. Recontextualising agents, such as syllabus writers and classroom teachers, select, from contexts outside of schooling institutions, two types of discourses, instructional discourse (ID) and regulative discourse (RD), to produce a specific discourse (pedagogic discourse) represented thus: ID/RD. The solidus indicates the incorporation or embedding of the instructional discourse in the regulative discourse, such that the latter dominates the former. Instructional discourse is the knowledge that is selected, organised, and defined in evaluative criteria, for the purposes of teaching and learning. Regulative discourse establishes the order within the instructional discourse. It generates principles of selection, organisation, pacing and criteria of skills, concepts, and information (i.e., the arbitrary internal ordering of school knowledge). It also mobilises theories of instruction, and thus contains within itself "a model of the learner and of the teacher and of the relation" between teacher-learner (Bernstein, 1996, p. 49). Thus the specialised modes of social interaction or communication between teacher and student, including whole class teacher monologue, triadic dialogue (teacher question-student response-teacher evaluation), and seatwork activities, are constituted by the regulative discourses. Bernstein refers to these forms of classroom communication as specialised interaction practices. However, the model of the learner, teacher, and teacher-student communication "is never wholly utilitarian; it contains ideological elements" (Bernstein, 1996, p. 49). Thus, regulative discourses perform a crucial ideological function because they conceal the relations of power and control generating the arbitrary internal ordering of school knowledge.

Power relations refer to the strength of the insulation of the boundaries between categories of agents, pedagogic discourses, and institutional contexts. Through relations of power, the categories of persons who interact in pedagogic communication, the categories of pedagogic discourses transmitted in these interactions, and the categories of institutional contexts are constituted. In other words, "power relations […] create boundaries, legitimise boundaries, reproduce boundaries, between different categories of groups, gender, class, race, different categories of discourse, different categories of agents. Thus power always operates to produce dislocations, to produce punctuations in social space" (Bernstein, 1996, p. 19). In this way, power relations establish legitimate relations of social order.

Relations of symbolic control refer to the legitimate relations of communication appropriate to the different categories of agents (i.e., teacher-student, different categories of students), discourses (different categories of knowledge), and contexts (i.e., spaces within the school). Principles of control therefore carry the boundary relations of power and socialise individuals into these relations. However, the principles of control carry both the power of reproduction and the potential for its change. Thus, principles of control carry power relations *within* the school (amongst teachers, teacher-aides, different groups of students). Principles of control also carry power relations *between* institutions, for example, the flow of pedagogic discourses between the home/church and the school via community members, parents, and students.

Bernstein (1975, 1996) proposed that regulative discourses constitute the moral order of schooling, and are thus the major mechanism of social consensus. Moreover, under certain conditions, regulative discourses are prone to re/produce extensive forms of ritualisation within schooling institutions (Bernstein (1975, p. 55). The two main types of rituals in school, consensual and differentiating, are major mechanisms for the internalising and revivifying of social order. Consensual rituals refer to school uniforms, assemblies, school mottoes, emblems, and so forth. Differentiating rituals mark off groups within the school from each other, usually in terms of age, gender, sporting ability, academic attainment, and cultural/ethnic identity. Thus, differentiating rituals such as school multicultural celebration "deepen local attachment behaviour to, and detachment behaviour from, specific groups; they also deepen respect behaviour to those in various positions of authority, and create order in time" (Bernstein, 1975, p. 56). These two main types of ritual function to "buttress the formal authority relations and evoke respect through the ritualisation of difference and similarity of function; they create continuity in individual and social time and relate the value system and its derived norms to an approved external order" (Bernstein, 1975, p. 56). Thus, regulative discourses (and instructional discourses) operate not only at the level of general school objectives and rationales, but also, and principally, through disciplinary practices and administrative procedures, as well as through the organisation of space and time (see also Hunter, 1994).

The task of the school, Bernstein (1975) proposed, is to encourage all students to adopt a subject position committed to both the instructional and the regulative discourses of schooling. He suggested that these discourses may constitute a variety of subject positions for teachers and students, modes of teacher and student relationships, and students' friendship and pressure groups. Moreover, these discourses may set up contradictory and conflicting subject positions. These subject positions have been described as commitment, detachment, deferment, estrangement, and alienation.[1] Bernstein (1975) argued that this scheme for analysing student behaviour directed attention to the culture of the school, as constituted by specific pedagogic discourses, rather than to the culture of the local community or family in terms of analysing educational disadvantage.

The remainder of this chapter is focused on empirical data analyses. First, a critical analysis is undertaken of interview data collected from Samoan students attending one of the "disadvantaged"[2] secondary schools participating in the research study, and Samoan community members working in the para-educational networks[3] around these schools. The aim of this section is to identify salient features of pedagogy that may address the educational disadvantage experienced by Samoan students in such schools. In the next section, the focus of the data analyses is on pedagogic practices in two different Year 10 English classrooms.[4] Some of the Samoan students interviewed for the study were participants in these Year 10 English lessons. Moreover, some of the Samoan community members worked in a para-educational capacity with the teachers and students participating in these lessons. Thus the analyses of classroom data are informed by the interview data produced by the Samoan community members and students interviewed for the study.

Interview Data: Samoan Members of Para-Educational Networks and Students

The Samoan students at the centre of the study were members of a community formed during the 1990s, mainly by immigrants from New Zealand—the most established of the Samoan diasporic communities (Franco, 1997). From the literature it is clear that the educational achievement of Samoan children in New Zealand, as in diasporic communities in the USA, is generally low (Graves, Graves, Vineta, Sam, & Sam, 1982; Jones, 1991; Luce, 1985; Mara, Foliaki, & Coxon, 1994; Mau, 1995). As similar findings began to emerge in the newly established diasporic community in Queensland,[5] the study reported in this chapter was conducted, with the support of school and community personnel, in order to develop new ways of theorising and analysing the educational disadvantage of Samoan students.

Interviews[6] were conducted with 36 Samoan students (15 males and 21 females) who attended the schools participating in this study. These students were between the ages of 15 and 17 and had attained varying levels of educational success. All of the students interviewed for the study indicated that Samoan was spoken at home, while 42% stated that the language of the home was exclusively Samoan. Nobody suggested that English was the only language spoken at home. All of the students indicated that they attended church services regularly, but they were members of different religious organisations such as the Assemblies of God and the Mormon, Seventh Day Adventist, Methodist, and Uniting churches. Interviews[7] were also conducted with 35 Samoan community members who worked in the para-educational networks around the schools that provided the classroom data analysed in this chapter (Sanunder and Bluehills), and neighbouring schools (Fullner and Newell).

All of the Samoan interviewees described communication practices in the pedagogic contexts of the local government secondary schools and in church institutions servicing the Samoan community in the local area, as well as in their respective homes and extended family institutions. Moreover, all of the interviewees provided a variety of explanations for the educational disadvantage of Samoan students (see Singh, 2000; Singh & Sinclair, 2001). Of particular interest to this study were explanations that involved the pedagogic relation of teacher and student. Two variants of this explanation are illustrated in Extracts 1 and 2.

The first extract was excerpted from an interview with the Reverend Josia Lepa (who taught religious education[8] in the case-study schools) and

Mrs. Ana Lepa (the minister's wife). Reverend Lepa noted that the school his children attended was regularly described as "really rough" "with quite a lot of bullying around", and "problems with drugs" and "smoking and drinking". Moreover, "quite a lot of students had been expelled from the school for selling marijuana and other stuff". Through a series of questions, the researcher encouraged Reverend and Mrs. Lepa to elaborate on what they perceived to be their children's concerns about their schooling experience.

Extract 1 [9]

1   *R:* So your children were concerned about things that were happening not so much in the classroom but outside of the classroom?

2   *Mrs. Ana Lepa:* They weren't worried about the curriculum. It was the relationships.

3   *R:* Right ... so the relationship amongst the students in the classroom as well?

4   *Mrs. Ana Lepa:* In and out of the classroom.

5   *R:* Oh, okay, what was happening in the classroom that they were worried about? Was it just the relationships between the students, or the teacher and the students as well?

6   *Reverend Josia Lepa:* I think the relationship not only of students to students but the teachers too.

7   *R:* Right, can you explain?

8   *Reverend Josia Lepa:* Ah, this freedom ((given to students at school)) gets them. Some students don't care what the teacher said. Sometimes the students swear to the teachers. And of course, that type of bad language is another thing because in our own family our children don't do that ... Coming back to this ((point about)) children living in a, perhaps in a home with ((a Pacific Islander)) life and cultural background and all of a sudden they get into this open thing ((at school)) where everything goes. It's really not for them.

9   *R:* You said it wasn't part of the curriculum but it was part of the relationships, but that's part of the curriculum too, isn't it?

10   *Mrs. Ana Lepa:* Well I suppose to some extent, but what I'm saying here it's not the teaching of the subjects, but it's the relationship of the children and the relationship of the children and the teacher, teacher-child relationship.
((A number of turns are omitted because another topic is introduced and discussed))

11   *Reverend Josia Lepa:* ... sometimes I question the value of the education system in Australia, where they really take away from the teacher any power to do some discipline at school. Because they ((the teachers)), they're really frightened to touch any child ... Now that's a different thing with school back home ((in Samoa)) you know. Your parents said, "You go to school and the teacher is your boss." And if you can't stand that, then the parents will have to help the teacher.

12   *R:* Mmm, mmm, so that would be the difference, between the Samoan

schooling system and the Australian schooling system, about respect for teachers?
13 *Reverend Josia Lepa:* Discipline is lacking.
14 Mrs. *Ana Lepa:* (Respect is) important ((in Samoan pedagogy)). If you talk to a kid, a child, they'll never answer back, they'll do what you tell them to do. They'll never answer back.

Reverend and Mrs. Lepa focused their criticism on the general regulative discourses constituting the moral order of the local secondary school. Principally, they argued that the moral order of schooling did not incorporate the values of the Samoan community and consequently did not evoke respect between teacher-student and student-student. They suggested that some students in the local secondary school did not heed teacher directives, and at times were known to "swear to the teachers". Pedagogic relations were described as lacking in discipline and characterised by excessive student "freedom" and use of "bad language". By contrast, pedagogic relations in Samoan contexts were described as respectful and characterised by the following student behaviours: "they'll never answer back" and "they'll do what you tell them to do".

The concerns about the disadvantaging effects of the general regulative discourses instituted in local secondary schools were produced in response to a question about a moral category that was often invoked by the Samoan interviewees, namely "respect". This value was mentioned an average of 5 times per interview by 18 of the 35 Samoan community members who worked in the para-educational networks in and around the secondary schools participating in this study. It was also invoked by 17 of the 36 students interviewed for the study. Importantly, those students who did not explicitly mention the Samoan value of respect spoke about "Samoan discipline" and "strict rules" in the course of the interviews. Thus, 27 of the 36 students interviewed for the study spoke about one or more of the following consensual and differentiating rituals of the moral order of Samoan contexts:

- showing "respect" to elders and parents through appropriate use of language and modes of conduct such as serving visitors and doing chores;

- "strict rules" relating to brother-sister interactions, elder child-younger child interactions, appropriate clothing, and attendance at church services, Bible classes, and religious choir classes.

The discrepancies noted by the interviewees between the general regulative discourses of the school and the Samoan home/community context may result in subject positions of detachment, deferment, or alienation for Samoan students in the context of the case-study secondary schools. Students who adopt a detachment subject position may participate in acquiring the specific instructional discourses of classroom lessons, but be "cool or negative towards the [specific moral] order" (Bernstein, 1975, p. 45). Those who adopt a deferment subject position may defer their commitment to or involvement in both the instructional and regulative discourses of specific classroom practices. Moreover, students who take up an alienated subject position often do not understand and therefore reject both the instructional and the regulative discourses of specific classroom activities.

Samoan novelists have also described differences in the moral order regulating *palagi*[10] and Samoan institutions. For example, in her novel about an adolescent girl's experiences of growing up in Samoa, Figiel (1998) suggested that the values imbued in progressive modes of pedagogy might be antithetical to values transmitted via home and church contexts in Samoa and the Samoan diaspora. Indeed, Samoan parents who did not effectively inculcate the values of respect and obedience/servitude through overt disciplinary measures might be considered to be "unloving" parents (see also Tiatia, 1998; Wendt, 1987).

The second extract was taken from an interview with two Year 12 students, Leaula S. (female) and Vinni T. (male). Both students had ambitions of studying at an institute of technical and further education.[11] Both students were very proud of identifying as Samoan. On this point, Vinni suggested that "though I was brought up and raised in New Zealand ... I was brought up in the Samoan way of life." Similarly, Leaula suggested that "it's the way that you're brought up that makes you what you are." During the interview, both students suggested that the strategies used by teachers to select and organise curricular knowledge in the classroom, as well as the mode of teacher-student relations, affected learning outcomes. The researcher asked a series of questions to encourage elaboration on these points.

Extract 2

1   *R:* What about modern history? Would you learn, would you enjoy modern history taught in Samoan?

2   *Vinni:* I think I probably would have learnt more, if it was taught the Samoan way because the teachers are real strict and like and I know about the strap, and ((hitting across)) the fingers ((knuckles)). So I would have sat there and listened

and listened. And like, it would be interesting, learning it in the Samoan language. Because for me it would have been like there, there would be like no differences like in the class and with the way we learn. Like in our class there were sort of different levels of knowledge between us. Like a girl (Catherine) she's like way up here and I don't know who's second to her, probably (Sarah) or someone. And ... like when the teacher speaks, the Samoans, people like us, find it hard to understand, and she'll ((Catherine)) be like "oh yeah I understand" and like, she'll ((Catherine)) be like "good one."

3 *R:* Earlier when you were talking about maths, and saying that they teach it differently, did you mean Samoan teachers or back in New Zealand?

4 *Vinni:* Oh, Samoan teachers.

5 *Leaula:* Yeah, Yeah. Like, just their way, their methods, like the way my mother, if I can't understand something that I take home like maths, she'll teach it to me in a completely different way. And I'll show it to my teacher here how I did it, and she wouldn't understand what I was going on about.

6 *Vinni:* Although you'd arrived at the same answer.

7 *Leaula:* Yeah although I'd get the same answer I'd just go through a different way of getting that answer to the kids, that you know, get the same answer here.

8 *R:* So which, which do you think would be better for you, the Samoan way or the Australian way of teaching?

9 *Vinni:* I think, if the teachers or the Australian teachers, if they were as strict as the Samoan teachers that would be good for a lot of the students just as long as they don't use the Samoan punishment.
((numerous people laughing))

10 *Leaula:* It would be good for the other students, the Australian students, because it would show, because like with the Samoan teachers and students, the students show a certain respect for the teacher. And that respect is kept for a whole entire school year. And like that makes it easier for the Samoan student to understand *his* place in the class or her place in the class. And when you come here ((Australian secondary school)), its sort of like, it's funny because the teacher is not only a teacher but like sometimes she can be your friend kind of thing and she'll be easy on you. And you think, "oh, it wasn't like this before". And you think, "maybe I can get away with this".

Vinni and Leaula made two crucial points in this conversation. First, they suggested that teacher-student relations in Samoan pedagogies were imbued with Samoan values of respect and thus were more likely to be regulated by positional modes of social control and discipline. In the positional control system, the expectations for student behaviour are related to explicit social rules (Bernstein, 1975, 1996). These may be rules concerned with status (e.g., position in social division of labour, age, status),[12] an evoking context (home, church,[13] school), or culturally invariant rules (e.g., particular modes of showing respect to elders in the Samoan culture).[14] With positional rules, power relations are visible. They can be seen in the explicit power differentials which position students to "show a certain respect for the teacher" which is "kept for a whole entire year". According to Vinni and Leaula these attributes of Samoan pedagogies made it easier for students to understand their social position in the classroom in relation to the teacher. The students contrasted Samoan modes of pedagogy with pedagogical relations in the local secondary school. The latter context was characterised by teachers who not only conducted themselves as "teacher" but also sometimes as "friend". Leaula suggested that these modes of teacher-student relations caused some confusion for the Samoan students who were accustomed to "real strict" teachers. In the personal control system, implicit forms of social control are used to discipline students. In this form of control, power relations are masked, disguised, or hidden; that is, the hierarchical form of the teacher-student relation is implicit. In the personal control system, much more of the student is subject to evaluation (Bernstein, 1975, 1996).

The second point made by the students was related to the disadvantaging effects of the strategies used by some teachers to select and organise the instructional discourses of schooling. Specifically, Vinni suggested that students entered the classroom context with different instructional and regulative discourses, and therefore were differentially positioned in relation to the acquisition of pedagogic discourse. He alluded to a hierarchy of student groups in the classroom differentiated by "levels of knowledge". Those students who were positioned at the top of the hierarchy could readily engage with the instructional discourses selected and organised by the teacher, while those at the bottom of the hierarchy, "the Samoans, people like us", had difficulty engaging with the arbitrary organisation of school knowledge, and thus acquiring this knowledge.

The points made by both categories of interviewees in relation to the disadvantaging effects of pedagogic discourses and practices institutionalised in the case-study secondary schools have also been made in the research literature. Research studies in the area of effective pedagogies for Pacific Islander students attribute weak educational outcomes to differences in the modes of pedagogy operative in the institutions of school, home, and church. For example, in their study of patterns of classroom interaction, Jordan, Au, and Joesting (1981) noted that Pacific Islander children "must not only learn academic content, but a new set of communicative conventions at the same time" (p. 1). They suggested that the task of the teacher must be to ensure that Pacific Islander children participate in classroom speech rather than withdrawing into silence. This could be achieved by building on children's existing communicative strengths by "allowing them to teach and learn from peers". In addition, pedagogies should be "designed to elicit from the children increased attention to the direct instruction provided by the adult teacher" (Jordan et al., 1981, p. 20). Cazden (1988) summarised the main findings of the anthropological work undertaken by Cathie Jordan and Kathyrn Hu-pei Au on the KEEP project, which was designed to improve the educational outcomes of children of Polynesian descent, members of Hawaii's Indigenous community. According to Cazden (1988), the anthropologists found that the same group of children performed better on several proximal indices[15] with an experienced teacher "who held the children to academic topics but gave them more freedom to choose when to speak, even if it meant overlapping another child's talk" (p. 72). Moreover, Cazden (1988) stressed the importance of making curricula relevant by "finding ways to make connections between children's worlds, and their meanings and the meanings of the school" (p. 72). Jones' (1991) study of the secondary school experiences of a cohort of working class Pacific Islander girls in New Zealand produced similar findings. Jones argued that a particular type of talk was essential to receiving information through schools. Working class Pacific Islander girls were not inducted into these forms of talk or communication in contexts outside of the school. Moreover, many of the teachers were not familiar with the content and form of communication strategies used by the working class Pacific Islander girls. According to Jones (1991), teachers should analyse the skills, information, and forms of communication that students bring to a task, as well as the instructional content and interactions that they need to engage with in order to acquire school knowledge.

In the interview data extracts, two explanations were given for the educational disadvantage experienced by Samoan students attending the secondary schools in this study. One of these explanations was concerned with the form of teacher-student relations (see Extract 1, Turns 8, 10, 11 and Extract 2, Turn 10), and the selection and organisation of school discourses (Extract 2, Turn 2) in the local secondary schools. The other explanation was concerned with disjunctures between pedagogic relations in the institutions of the home, church, and school in the local community, and differences between schooling in Australia and Samoa (see Extract 1, Turn 11, and Extract 2, Turns 5, 9). As the data set examined in the next session consists of lessons taught in secondary schools in Australia only, the former explanation is used as an orienting hypothesis in terms of the analyses of classroom lesson data in this chapter.

Classroom Data:
Analyses of Pedagogic Discourses in English Classroom Lessons

In this section of the chapter, Year 10 English classroom lesson data collected from Sanunder and Bluehills State High Schools in Queensland, Australia, are analysed. These schools were located in urban areas that were statistically ranked in the lowest 5% of local areas in the State of Queensland with respect to median household income. In addition, the youth and adult unemployment levels of 31.4% and 21.7%, respectively, were substantially higher than the city averages of 14.1% and 9.9% (Australian Bureau of Statistics, 1998). A State Electoral Commission profile indicated that the electorates centred on Sanunder and Bluehills had the highest percentage of overseas-born residents in Queensland (33.67% compared to a state average of 17.41%). This document also revealed that the aforementioned urban areas had the highest percentage of residents speaking languages other than English at home (26.77% compared to a state average of 7.16%) (Electoral Commission Queensland, 1998).

At the time of this study, approximately 14% of the students at Sanunder and Bluehills secondary schools identified themselves as Pacific Islanders (most of these students also identified themselves as Samoan). Substantial cohorts of Vietnamese, Indigenous, and white working class students were also enrolled at these schools. This meant that out of a total of 20 to 30 students participating in a Year 10 English classroom lesson, an average of only 2 to 4 students identified themselves as Pacific Islanders.

In what follows, classroom lesson data collected from the case-study secondary schools are analysed[16] in terms of "the what" and "the how" of knowledge transmission in seatwork activities. During seatwork activities, students are required to listen to the teacher's preparatory spoken discourse, and then independently undertake a written task (Lemke, 1990). In addition, seatwork activities in lessons conducted at Sanunder and Bluehills were contrasted to identify differences in the way the teachers controlled the selection, organisation, and criteria of knowledge. One of these activities took place in a classroom where extended conflicts between teacher and students occurred regularly (Classroom A, Bluehills State High School). The other activity took place in a classroom where the disrespectful behaviours described by the Samoan community members and students were not only relatively rare, but also downplayed by the teacher (Classroom B, Sanunder State High School). Seatwork was of interest to this research study because preliminary observations of classroom lesson data indicated that the teacher-student relations questioned by the Samoan community members and students frequently occurred during the transition to this specialised interactional practice.

In addition, interview data produced by the teachers[17] who conducted the Year 10 English classroom lessons are analysed in this section of the chapter. The analyses focus on the relation between teachers' articulation of knowledge about Samoan students and inclusive literacy curricula, and the pedagogic discourses constituting the English classroom lessons. Following Anstey (cited in Anstey & Bull, 1996, p. 96), it is proposed that the different knowledge accessed by teachers and their beliefs about literacy teaching which arise from this knowledge are likely to produce different classroom practices, and therefore different learning outcomes for students.

Classroom A: Bluehills State High School

Ms. Jameson, the teacher in Classroom A, was in her fifth year of teaching service. Since graduating from university with a major in history, she had taught English and Studies in Society and Environment at Bluehills State High School. Throughout the interview, Ms. Jameson stated that her understanding of the local community and students attending Bluehills High was limited. Specifically, she claimed to have "never lived amongst another, um Aboriginal people, you know. I haven't had Samoans next door to me, you know". When talking about pedagogic relations in the school, Ms. Jameson invoked the moral category of respect. It will be recalled that Samoan community members and students also invoked the category of respect when describing differences in modes of pedagogic relations between Samoan institutions and the local secondary school. In response to a question pertaining to "the most significant educational issues for Samoan students", Ms. Jameson responded thus:

> ... I have great difficulties with Samoan boys in particular, and some Samoan girls, in getting them to accept that um, I am the teacher and I am here to be respected, in the way that I set up, and, you are here to learn. They seem to, I think there's behavioural things that get in their way. I think there's attitudes that come in that, um, particularly from the boys to female teachers, that get in the way of them accepting that all right, we're at school, this is a lesson, let's get down and do the work, you know? Um, and I've had troubles that way, with Samoan boys, and girls.

Specifically, Ms. Jameson attributed behavioural problems in the classroom to aspects of Samoan culture. She claimed that Samoan students, particularly boys, did not take up subject positions committed to the regulative discourse of English classroom lessons, that is, to the rules of classroom conduct and teacher-student relations. Ms. Jameson acknowledged that Samoan parents "would be aghast" if they knew their children were "being naughty or not getting down and doing the job". However, she suggested that perhaps there was "something else in the [Samoan] culture that like contradicts that in the way they act or what they do." Specifically, Ms. Jameson constructed Samoan interpretations of Christianity as problematic:

> ... I think that their Christianity doesn't, in the way that I understand a good Christian, doesn't influence them at all. They know their Bible and certainly the singing and stuff is strong, but I don't think it crosses over into behaviour. I don't think it's something that's useful. In fact it's the other way.

Thus, according to Ms. Jameson the problem of educational disadvantage for Samoan students rested squarely on specific elements of Samoan home and church culture. Furthermore, she described the local community as a "fringe area" with "dubious numbers of parents employed". In addition, she dismissed the career aspirations of students attending Bluehills High as a "fantasy reality ... the more hungry you are, the more you want, sort of". In particular, her response to the aspirations of Samoan boys to become policemen was to "keep telling them oh well, you might manage to be a bouncer [laughter]."

At no stage of the interview did Ms. Jameson critically question how her own classroom practices might have produced disadvantaging educational effects. As a recontextualising agent, Ms. Jameson was responsible for selecting the instructional (content and skills) and regulative (conduct, character and manner) discourses that constituted the pedagogic practices of English lessons. Moreover, she did not consider how the selection and organisation of pedagogic discourses might have produced student subject positions of alienation, detachment, and/or estrangement (see also Stone, 1981). For example, in response to a question about the challenges to teaching presented by a diverse student clientele, Ms. Jameson responded thus:

> I think that, OK, staff room terms that we use, like spoon-feeding kids and um, idiots [laughing] you know? Just, I think that, I can tell from the way that we talk about the kids and our frustration that there's, there's a change, particularly when

you're doing English, I think, and people think that English is easy. I mean what's there to do? We use the language every day. I mean what's so difficult about it? Whereas it's a really complex set of, you know, context and purpose and things like that.

Again, educational difficulties were attributed to students who were described as "idiots", and not to the content and organisation of the pedagogic discourses of English lessons.

The lesson represented in Extract 3 (a–c) focused on the reading habits of the class. However, the objective of the lesson was not made clear to students until the final activity. Only after a student request for clarification about assessment requirements did Ms. Jameson make evaluative criteria explicitly available to all students. Specifically, she stated that students were expected to write a 400-word journal entry on a novel of their choice and complete an oral book review for this particular unit of work.[18] The first two lessons of the unit of work comprised specialised interactional practices designed to elicit information about the reading world of the students. The relation between the instructional and regulative discourses of these interactional practices and the final assessment criteria for the unit of work was not delineated.

Three Samoan students participated in this lesson. According to Ms. Jameson, the two male Samoan students (Tali P. and Robert M.) were low achievers in English, while Lisa K. (a female Samoan student) was achieving average grades. Both male students, Tali and Robert, took up disruptive subject positions during the course of the lesson. Lisa engaged in off-task discussions with her peer group, and rarely participated in whole class discussion activities.

The 40-minute lesson was composed of two main instructional topics. The first topic related to students' reading practices during the previous day. Students were expected to participate in a number of specialised interactional practices, including whole class triadic dialogue and individual seatwork (completing a worksheet on reading habits), in order to acquire and display knowledge of pedagogic discourses. The second topic related to students' recollections of their pre-reading, early childhood, and primary school reading experiences. The specialised interactional practices used to develop this topic included whole class triadic dialogue, a reading aloud activity, and individual seatwork (writing a journal entry). In other words, for the first topic, the teacher used the specialised interactional practice of triadic dialogue (teacher question; student response; teacher evaluation) to elicit information from students about what they had read or recollections of early reading experiences. The function of this triadic dialogue was to transmit information that would enable students to complete the seatwork activity. For both topics, the teacher drew on her personal experiences to model appropriate literacy practices and what would count as legitimate criteria for the worksheet or journal entry. However, Ms. Jameson's attempts to create a common world of reading were constantly challenged by the students (see also Edwards & Westgate, 1994; Mercer, 1995). Forms of student resistance included the following:

- delaying tactics (e.g., "I didn't read nothing"; "Miss, I'm prejudiced against reading");

- introducing taboo content (e.g., "Read a cigarette packet in the school toilets"; "Read pornos Miss"); and

- direct confrontation with the teacher (e.g., "That ((question)) is so stupid"; "She ((my mother's)) not that stupid").

In developing the instructional discourses for the first topic, Ms. Jameson drew on examples of reading from the local community, such as reading traffic lights and the menu at the local Vietnamese bakery, to evoke a shared world of reading experience with the students. Early in the lesson Ms. Jameson had indicated that the focus was on "what sort of reader you are, how you read, how you respond to reading, what you like, what you don't like". Within the turn, however, she had emphasised that "you [students]" were actually part of a common world of readers to which she also belonged: "So, today and tomorrow, we're doing lots of little exercises to try and work out what sort of reader we are, and what we like reading, and what the difficulties are that we have".

In the data extract below, students resisted the discourses selected by the teacher to describe her own reading habits. Specifically, the teacher attempted to display her liberal Anglo middle class cultural style, for example, in revealing to the students predilection for "wonderful" ["little"] ethnic eateries and purveyors of exotic foodstuffs.

Extract 3 (a) [* denotes Samoan students]
1   Ms. Jameson: Oh and on my way here, I forgot to have breakfast, so I went to the lovely Vietnamese bakery ( ), and I had to read a list. What was it about? It was about the prices. Has everyone, anyone been to that bakery?
2   Students: No.

3   *Students:* Yes.
4   *Steven:* [Yes] and the cream is off.
5   *Ms. Jameson:* Well I don't [have the cream]
6   **Robert:* [Stale bread] and all that.
7   *Ms. Jameson:* Oooh no, the croissants, it's beau-, they're beautiful.
8   *Student:* Is that just in one morning?
9   *Ms. Jameson:* So I wanted a croissant.
10 **Robert:* They got stale bread.

In the dialogue represented in Extract 3 (a), the students explicitly challenged the common world of reading that the teacher tried to establish. This common world was designed to produce discursive resources from which the students could legitimately select content for completing the seatwork activity, which entailed recording their reading practices on a worksheet. Ms. Jameson then continued to clarify the criteria for completing the worksheet by initiating triadic dialogue on the topic of students' own reading from the previous day.

Extract 3 (b)
1   *Ms. Jameson:* Now, there's a whole list of things ((I read)). ((pause)) I want you to think of one thing you read yesterday, I want you to think about it now, and then I'm going to ask you about it. ((Pause)) Simone, what did you read yesterday?
2   *Simone:* When I was at home, I read *Dolly* magazine.
3   *Ms. Jameson:* Good, read your *Dolly* magazine. Gilbert, what did you read yesterday?
4   *Gilbert:* Nothing.
5   *Ms. Jameson:* Did you read the computer screen while Jason was playing Sin City?
6   *Gilbert:* Yeah.
7   *Ms. Jameson:* Right, well, so what did you read?
8   *Gilbert:* Information, the computer, data.
9   *Ms. Jameson:* John, what did you read?
10 *John:* TV pages.
11 *Ms. Jameson:* TV pages, good.
    ((Six turns of similar interaction omitted))
12 *Ms. Jameson:* And Michael B., what did you read, you did lots of reading yesterday?
13 **Robert:* He read (gay magazines)
14 *Mark:* My work.
15 **Tali:* Snakes.
16 *Michael:* Yeah, I read about snakes.
17 *Ms. Jameson:* Yeah, good. Now can you think, see how I've got a balance between things at school and at home. Jason would you have a balance of

things you read at school and at home?
18 *Jason:* Nah.
19 *Ms. Jameson:* Where do you do most of your reading?
20 **Robert:* At school.
21 *Mark:* At home.
22 *Jason:* Aaarh, in my room.
23 *Ms. Jameson:* What sort of things do you read in your room?
24 *Jason: Penthouse* magazine.
25 **Tali: Playboy* magazine.
26 *Students:* ((laugh))
27 *Ms. Jameson:* Aarh, so you do read, Jason?
28 *Jason:* Yeah.
29 *Ms. Jameson:* Right. Don't forget, like I said to Gilbert before, don't forget that computer screens, when you read information on computer screens, that's just as much reading.

As she worked through the questions listed on the overhead transparency (a replica of the worksheet to be completed by the students during seatwork), Ms. Jameson attempted to establish rules for recognising experience from which content for the reading logs could be legitimately selected. The reading of magazines, computer screens, the TV pages, and schoolwork all received Ms. Jameson's approval. Teacher control of the specialised interactional practice through which these discursive criteria were established was strong. For example, when Gilbert indicated that he had not read the day before (Turn 4), Ms. Jameson proceeded to set up a weighted choice (Turns 5–7) that pressured him into stating that he had, in fact, read. In Turn 29, the teacher held the class accountable for the criteria refined in this dialogue with Gilbert. Specifically, she reminded the whole class that working on the computer constitutes reading.

Jason's response to the teacher's question about what the students had read the day before seems to have been an attempt at student control of the pedagogic discourses of schooling. In introducing the issue of sexuality (Turn 24), he broached a subject that is more or less taboo in pedagogic discourse. Hence, his response could be interpreted as a contestation of the teacher's strong control over the selection of content for this lesson and hence her imposition of her social reality (the middle class reading world of an English teacher). This interpretation has credence because the teacher had directly asked Jason if there was a balance between his reading practices at home and at school, using the example of her own reading habits as a model. This contestation was negotiated by the teacher via a retroactive definition of Jason's response as a legitimate answer to her question: "Aarh, so you do read, Jason?" The weighted choice offered Jason in this agreement elicitation represented very strong teacher control of the pedagogic discourse. It can be interpreted as an effort to turn the student challenge into a contribution to the common world of reading from which meaning could be legitimately selected for the reading log. As Extract 3 (c) indicates, however, this strategy was a risky one because it set up conditions for further student contestation of the pedagogic discourses which constituted the reading lesson. The extract opens with the transition to seatwork.

Extract 3 (c)
1   Ms. Jameson: I've got one of those recording sheets for you now. Using the list of things down the bottom, I want you to tell me everything that you read yesterday and I want you to write it down.
2   *Robert:* The whole day?
3   *Tali:* I didn't read nothing.
4   Ms. Jameson: The whole day!
5   *Tali:* Oooh no.
6   Michael: I read *Penthouse* last night.
7   Ms. Jameson: Michael, you would not know what to do if you read a *Penthouse*.
8   Michael: Ooh-ooh, wouldn't I?
9   Students: ((laugh))
10 Mark: He wouldn't be too busy reading them, Miss, he'd be doing something else.
11 Ms. Jameson: They're pretty tame though really, aren't they?
12 Students: ( )
13 Ms. Jameson: Have you got access to black label,[19] Michael, then?
14 Michael: Your story, Miss.
15 Mark: Too busy with your pants down, hey Michael?
16 John: Yeah, and you watching, hey?

In Turn 1, Ms. Jameson explicitly marked the transition to independent seatwork. One student seemed to seek clarification of the criteria for the task: "The whole day?" However, this response could also be interpreted as a delaying tactic in terms of completing the written work task. Others overtly engaged in resistance by claiming to have read nothing (Turn 3) or read *Penthouse* (Turn 6). These claims entailed resistance to both the specialised interactional practice (regulative discourse) and the instructional texts of the lesson. Two students did not comply with the teacher's injunction to "write it down". By contrast, Michael complied with the criteria that established magazine reading as a legitimate source of material for the reading log. Specifically, he picked up on the latitude apparently offered by the teacher earlier by loudly proclaiming that he had read *Penthouse*. However, because he did not engage in the written task, Michael's claim about his magazine reading experience could be considered as a form of student resistance. The teacher met Michael's challenge by getting personal and embarrassing him: "Michael, you would not know what to do if you read a *Penthouse*". Michael's subsequent defiance ("Ooh-ooh, wouldn't I?") was followed by what seemed to be a conspicuously nonchalant display of worldliness on the part of the teacher enacted through a strongly controlled agreement elicitation that might have[20] brought the challenge to a close: "They're pretty tame though really, aren't they?" However, the start of the independent seatwork for this cohort of male students was further delayed. From the transcript it is not clear whether all the other students in the class were listening to the dialogue between the teacher and the cohort of male students or were engaged with the seatwork activity. In either case, the dialogue is typical of the "mucking-up", "back-chatting", and "answering-back" that the Samoan students and community members identified as a key source of educational disadvantage.

Classroom B: Sanunder State High School

The lessons organised and implemented by the teacher in Classroom B were remarkable for the absence of the type of disruption described in Classroom A. Ms. Byrce was in her second year of teaching at Sanunder State High School. Prior to requesting a transfer to Sanunder, she had taught for three years at a school that she described as "authoritarian" and "rigid". Her transfer request was specifically linked to the behaviour management problems she experienced when attempting to implement what she described as the authoritarian modes of pedagogy sanctioned by the administration at her previous place of work. By contrast, at Sanunder High, particularly in the Year 10 classroom lessons, Ms. Byrce claimed that she spent "a negligible amount of time on behaviour management":

> Like sometimes, there might be one particular student who's not doing much, and I might need to sort of sit with them and encourage them a bit, but it wouldn't be actually taking time out of what I'd already set for the other people to do. I don't ever have to stand and wait for them. Wait ages for them to be quiet or anything like that.

Ms. Byrce lived in the suburb adjacent to Sanunder and cycled to work each day. She stated that she had "always liked the idea of ... living in the community where [she] worked", and while she was not in "exactly the same suburb", she was in the area described as the "support centre network" of Sanunder. Like Ms. Jameson and the cohort of Samoan community members and students interviewed for this study, Ms. Byrce evoked the moral category of respect when describing pedagogic relations. Specifically, she stated that

> ... you get respect, if you show them [the students] respect, then you get respect in return and that's the sort of teaching I really, really like. I don't like to have to go in and assert authority because that's what is expected of me. I like to be able to go in and um, by earning the respect myself get the respect as well and um, and really enjoy working with the students and have a friendly relationship with them.

Ms. Byrce stated that there were only two Pacific Islander students in her Year 10 English class. She did not attribute the academic performance of these students to the "fact that they're from the Pacific Islands." Rather, she professed that "the most talented student that I have is, um, her parents are from Samoa. Beth is obviously very talented, um, Mia is really keen but struggles a little bit". In response to a question about specific educational difficulties experienced by Samoan or Pacific Islander students, Ms. Byrce suggested that "in some cases ... there is a problem with English being a second language". She elaborated on this point by providing anecdotal evidence about a Samoan student who was wrongly assigned to a remedial English class, and other Samoan students who were denied access to specialist English language tuition because of cutbacks in government funding. In addition, Ms. Byrce indicated that attempts to make schooling relevant and inclusive for Samoan students at Sanunder were limited to singing, music, and sporting activities. Little effort had been invested in modifying pedagogic discourses to meet the needs of the diverse clientele of students at the school.

The lesson discussed below was extracted from a 6-week media unit of work on the genre of stories. Ms. Byrce declared that the unit of work aimed to "look at the concept of stories. I've got short stories or folktales. Like a story way of telling stories and a newspaper report way of telling stories and the TV news report way of telling stories". For the unit assessment, students were expected to write a story utilising one of the following genres: newspaper report, TV news, folktale or short story. Moreover, they were expected to transpose one story format or genre to another. Ms. Byrce explained: "so they'll take a TV news, and make it into a newspaper report or they'll take a news report and make it into a short story". Her decision to use the folktale of the *Three Little Pigs* in this unit of work was based on the assumption that all students in the class would have heard about the story. Ms. Byrce claimed that she did not adopt a "really critical approach" in her English lessons. However, she did encourage students to think about how the selection and organisation of content in a TV news program, for example, was geared to providing entertainment rather than strict reportage of objective facts.

The data extracted below was taken from a lesson in the third week of the media unit. Ms. Byrce specified the objectives of this particular lesson:

> ... in this lesson ... I want to emphasise that in a newspaper report, you put the most important information right at the top whereas in a short story you're building up to that gradually. So I want them to be able to shuffle it [newsworthy information extracted from the folk tale, *Three Little Pigs*] around and end up with the newspaper report structure for this story.

Thus the 40-minute lesson comprised three main instructional topics. The first topic related to identifying relevant sections in a folktale that could be considered newsworthy information for a newspaper report or story. This topic had been covered in a previous lesson, and students were expected to finish underlining newsworthy sections on a worksheet (on the folktale, the *Three Little Pigs*) for homework. The specialised interactional practice of whole class triadic dialogue (going over homework and revising the previous day's work) was used to elicit students' knowledge of this topic. Moreover, Ms. Byrce elaborated on responses elicited from the students by using the specialised interactional practice of teacher monologue to review the literacy skills and information that had been introduced in the previous lesson. The following data extract (4 a) taken from the lesson illustrates this point.

> *Extract 4 (a)*
> *Ms. Byrce:* Okay, so all you need, the thing that I'm trying to emphasise with this, is you only need to pick out little, little bits out of what's happening. You only need to know who's doing the action, what happened to them, and what the outcome of that was. Okay? And it happens three times in this story which is probably not what would actually happen in the newspaper report. It normally, there'd be one person with one thing happening to them and some sort of outcome ... Okay?

The students were expected to practice the literacy skills of identifying newsworthy information by underlining, or checking that they had already underlined, relevant information on the worksheet, and then producing summary notes on this information. Moreover, Ms. Byrce emphasised the cognitive aspects of this literacy task, and demonstrated in practice how to complete it (see also Anstey & Bull, 1996). In other words, she explained her thinking processes (regulative discourse) while she enacted the literacy skill/task (instructional discourse). The following data extract illustrates this point.

> *Extract 4 (b)*
> *Ms. Byrce:* ... So we're down to one, two, three, four, five, six, seven. Paragraph 7. The big bad wolf watched from behind the trees. Okay, so we've got first little pig, straw, big bad wolf watched from behind the trees. So *think* about the way that we've been going through this, and the way that I'm only picking out really little bits. It doesn't matter if you feel like you're leaving most of the story out. You're just trying to get the basic facts. So *think* about that for the next paragraph. The little pig worked and worked until the sun went down. By this time the house of straw was finished. So we probably don't need to know about him working and working until the sun went down. What do you *think* is the next, next most important bit?

The second topic of the lesson was related to the "inverted pyramid structure" of the newspaper report. Ms. Byrce used the specialised interactional practice of teacher monologue to talk about the content and organisation of newspaper reports, utilising an article that the class had discussed in a previous lesson. Students were expected to practice the skills taught in this review activity by marking their worksheet (newspaper report) with numbers corresponding to items listed on an overhead projector transparency sheet. In other words, students were expected to identify the content or main ideas covered in each of the paragraphs of a newspaper report activity sheet, namely,

1. location and context;

2. explanation of the event;

3. order of occurrences;

4. relation to the circumstance;

5. reinforcement of interesting point (direct speech used to show it really happened); and

6. rounding-off piece of information.

The third and final topic of the lesson entailed transposing the relevant pieces of information extracted from the folktale into the structure of a newspaper report. This was the only new topic introduced during the lesson. The preparatory phase of the seatwork activity is represented in the following data extract (4 c). This phase was conducted in whole class spoken discourse. It was followed by a phase of independent work during which students were permitted to consult with peers, while the teacher circulated around the room, assisting students and occasionally addressing the whole class. The transition to the independent phase was free of the extended conflicts between teacher and student that were observed in Classroom A during Ms. Jameson's lesson. The extract opens at the beginning of the preparatory phase with the teacher checking that all the students had a copy of the newspaper article on which they had previously marked the generic features of news reports or stories.

> Extract 4 (c) [italics denote modal items]
> 1   *Ms. Byrce:* Okay, has everyone got those, the things it's marked on? Okay. Now, what I want you to use that for is to see the sort of information groupings that you *could* make with your "Three Little Pigs", so you *could* do the same sort of thing. Divide it up, even, into six sections, and make your news, and note that your news report was going to be, say about this length, and you *could* start off with a headline, the lead which is the most interesting thing but doesn't contain a lot of details, and then tell me the details in order, a bit of direct speech, something else interesting that happened and a final, a final thing to round it off with.
> ((student-teacher questioning about the final assignment of the unit omitted))
> 2   *Ms. Byrce:* So, we've only got 5 or so minutes left, but what I'd like you to start to do, while you've got people here to talk to and the person next to you to ask about, just turn up the page of your book, put up your heading, Newspaper Report for "Three Little Pigs". So this can be your heading. And before we got that information there, start to put down what order, or start to think about the order that you're going to write your report in. And you *might* like to do just a summary of the things that you've got to put in each of these. ... Or *would you prefer* just to go straight into writing about them in that order as a report? Have you got any thoughts? Okay, straight into the writing. Kelly? What would you (reckon)? Straight into the writing or do a summary first? Okay, anyone got any other thoughts?
> 3   **Beth:* What, Miss?
> 4   *Ms. Byrce:* What I'm wondering is *whether you wanted* to summarise the events that you're going to do in that order first or *whether you want* to just write the report straight out as a rough draft in that order.
> 5   **Beth:* Can we do, like headlines and ( )?
> 6   *Ms. Byrce:* Yeah, so you want to start off with the proper headline and the

```
         proper report?
7   *Beth: Yeah.
8    Ms. Byrce: Yep? All right. If as long as you feel confident to start straight,
         straight into the report.
```

Potential confusion and disruption was addressed by the way in which Ms. Byrce prepared the students for both "the what" and "the how" of the independent phase of the seatwork activity. Specifically, students were told that they were to produce a written display of newsworthy information organised under six themes while interacting with peers. The six themes (Extract 4 c, Turn 1) had been modelled repeatedly in previous lessons and revised during the second topic of the current lesson. The thematic structure was repeated here to make explicit the evaluative criteria for selecting and sequencing content (newsworthy information from the folktale) for the production of a news report or story. Ms. Byrce's pedagogic mode was thus oriented to the performance expected of the students.

Interpersonally, a great deal of effort on Ms. Byrce's part went into establishing working relations with the students. In the preceding data extract, the modality is very marked in the teacher's discourse. Her means of establishing control in the class were often indirect. In the words of Fran Christie,

> [t]his probably reflects, in part, the fact that she [...] recognises that she will be more successful if she seeks their [students'] co-operation rather than overtly orders them to do their work. In addition, it reflects her concern to set up a congenial working relationship, one on which a great deal of what is to be taught and learned will be negotiated. At issue is her very strong expectation and requirement that the students co-operate. A value is at work here, to do both with establishing respect for the teacher and with the values of the students respecting each other and learning to work together harmoniously. Such a value is constantly affirmed through the regulative [discourse]. It has consequences for the building of the pedagogic subject... (Christie, 1995, p. 231)

Discussion

The small-scale case-study reported in this chapter examined the discourses of educational disadvantage produced by Samoan community members, Samoan students, and two secondary school English teachers. All of these participants talked about the moral category of "respect" in terms of the pedagogic relation between teacher-student and student-student (regulative discourse). Specifically, the Samoan community members and students invoked the category of respect when talking about differences between pedagogic relations in the local secondary school and in the home and church institutions of the Samoan community. They suggested that institutions such as the church and the home in the Samoan community were regulated by positional modes of control. For example, transmitters within institutions of the Samoan diaspora were depicted as using overt and explicit relations of social control in their interactions with acquirers. In these contexts, Samoan children were characterised as unlikely to take up disruptive and disrespectful subject positions, and thus to engage in behaviours such as "answering back" and "not doing what they were told". By contrast, teachers at the local secondary school were portrayed as more likely to use personal modes of social control. In addition, interview participants stated that Samoan students might be confused or disoriented by the differences between the modes of social control regulating the institutions of the local secondary schools, and those regulating the home and church in the Samoan community. In turn, this confusion could cause some Samoan students to take up defiant and disrespectful subject positions in some classrooms within the local secondary school. Moreover, the students interviewed for the study claimed that they might be disadvantaged by some of the strategies deployed by classroom teachers to select and organise curricular content. In other words, these students alleged that the power and control relations generating pedagogic discourse (i.e., ideological bias) might position Samoan students in a disadvantaged relation to the acquisition of school knowledge.

Pedagogic relations between teacher-student and student-student in one of the classrooms (Classroom A—Bluehills High) portrayed in this chapter were characterised by frequent displays of the disrespectful student behaviours described by the Samoan interview participants. Ms. Jameson suggested that students from the local community did not know how to conduct themselves in secondary school classrooms. She demanded respect from the students, but made few attempts to negotiate respectful pedagogic relations in the classroom. Thus, aspects of Samoan culture, low socio-economic circumstances, and the diversity of the student population were all blamed for producing difficult teacher-student pedagogic relations. The pedagogic discourses constructed by Ms. Jameson in Classroom A focused on inculcating the students into a social world of white, English-speaking, middle class cultural habits. The school curriculum was not academically challenging, and did not transmit valued informational resources. Many of the students in Classroom A resisted the pedagogic discourses or common world of knowledge constructed by the classroom teacher. This resistance took the form of delaying tactics, the introduction of taboo content, and direct confrontation with the teacher.

By contrast, Classroom B was characterised by a lack of the disruptive and disrespectful student behaviours described by the Samoan interview participants as educationally disadvantaging. Ms. Byrce, the teacher in Classroom B, worked hard to build respectful teacher-student and student-student pedagogic relations. The pedagogic mode in Classroom B was oriented to the achievement of academically challenging literacy performance outcomes. Explicit instruction was provided in terms of "the what" (instructional discourse) and "the how" (regulative discourse) of English literacy. Moreover, Ms. Byrce modelled her own literacy practices by explaining her thinking processes while she demonstrated specific skills in practice. Interpersonally, Ms. Byrce exercised strong control over the specialised interactional practices (regulative discourse) of the classroom. However, she did not overtly order students to complete tasks. The regulative discourses constituting teacher-student pedagogic relations (i.e., conduct, character, and manner) in this classroom established the value of working together harmoniously. In turn, this had implications for the subject positions taken up by students within the pedagogic discourses of the classroom.

Although this case-study was limited by the number of participants, schools, and classroom lessons, it is suggested that the social constructions of the dis/advantaging effects of pedagogic discourses revealed by the detailed analyses hold true in environments far larger than that of the designated disadvantaged Australian secondary school.

Notes

* This study was part of a larger research project funded by the Australian Research Council.

1. Table 10.1: *Types of involvement in the role of pupil (adapted from Bernstein, 1975, 1996)*

Student Subject Positions		Instructional Order		Moral Order	
		Means	Ends	Means	Ends
1	Commitment	+	+	+	+
2	Detachment	+	+	+	–
3	Deferment	.....	.....	.....	.....
4	Estrangement	–	+	+	+
5	Alienation	–	–	–	–

Means: *understands* the means (+/–: Yes/ No)
Ends: *accepts* the ends (+/–: High/ Low involvement)

2. The term "disadvantaged" was used by the State department of education to develop meaningful comparisons across Queensland schools in relation to the allocation of re-

sources and setting up of operational performance targets. The following criteria were used to categorize schools as "disadvantaged": school size, socio-economic status, and the proportion of the population that was of Aboriginal or Torres Strait Islander background.

3. Hunter (1994) uses the term para-educational networks to refer to the parentals, professional and voluntary agencies, community liaison officers and parents' associations, community welfare experts and self-help groups, curriculum experts, and curriculum consultation committees that form a hybrid network to situate schools in their communities.

4. In Queensland, Australia, students obtain a junior certificate after completion of the compulsory years of schooling (Years 1–10).

5. Literacy tests (reading and viewing, and writing) and numeracy tests (relating to number, measurement, and space) administered in 1997 to 46,762 Year 6 students revealed that the performance of those who indicated that a Pacific Island language was spoken at home was *extremely below* the performance of the whole cohort of students on all literacy and numeracy indicators (Queensland School Curriculum Council, 1998).

6. Semi-structured interviews with students were guided by a set of questions designed to elicit information about the following:
   - Australian-Samoan identity formation in school and community institutions;
   - Similarities and differences between forms of social control in schooling and in local Samoan community institutions (i.e., home, church, sports clubs);
   - Similarities and differences between school practices in Australia, New Zealand, and Samoa;
   - Relations between teachers and Samoan students in Australian schools;
   - Relations of Samoan students to the school curriculum;
   - Pedagogic work that might improve educational outcomes for Samoan students.

7. The interviews were semi-structured, guided by a set of questions with the aim of eliciting information about the following:
   - The appointment criteria for work in para-educational networks;
   - The actual duties within these networks;
   - The socialization of para-educational personnel into their duties;
   - The social relations between the para-educational personnel, Samoan students, school teachers, and administrators;
   - Similarities and differences between forms of social control in schooling and local community institutions;
   - The representation of Samoan identity and forms of social control in school forums;
   - Pedagogic practices that improved educational outcomes for Samoan students;
   - Tensions between taking up the role of para-educational worker and being a member of the local Samoan community.

8. In Queensland state schools, religious education is a non-compulsory subject taught by volunteers from various Christian denominations.

9. For reasons of confidentiality, all names of people and places used in this chapter are pseudonyms. The following transcription conventions are used in the data extracts:

[	overlap or interruption
italics	emphasis
?	interrogative or upward intonation
(talk)	uncertain transcription
( )	untranscribable
((laugh))	lexical vocalisation
(( ))	text inserted for clarification purposes
...	talk omitted
45	interview turn number
R	Interviewer/Researcher

10. This is a Samoan word denoting European practices as distinct from Samoan practices.

11. An educational organisation akin to a United Kingdom college of further education and a North American community college.

12. According to Lawson (1996) and Freeman (1996), within the highly stratified Samoan society, rank is assessed in terms of political title (e.g., chief, orator, and positions within each of these statuses), church title (e.g., pastor, deacon), age, and generation, among other variables. The titled have higher rank than the untitled, and older persons of higher generations have higher rank than the young.

13. Christianity was not simply imposed on Samoans, but absorbed, adapted, and given a uniquely Samoan expression by the *faifeau* or pastor and his council of lay deacons. The *feagaiga* (the idealised principles of social order in Samoan society) drew a line between sacred and secular spheres of authority (see Mara et al., 1994; Schoeffel, 1995).

14. Ochs (1988) distinguished between two registers or ways of speaking Samoan, namely *tautala lelei* ("good speech") and *tautala leaga* ("bad speech"). These descriptions refer to contextually specific registers of Samoan language, rather than invariably good or bad qualities of speech. "Good speech" is characteristic of church services, church conferences, pastors' schools, and village public schools, and is the language of the Bible and all literacy materials. "Bad speech" is used outside these contexts by almost all members of the community, and is understood by everyone. In addition, "bad speech" and "good speech" are associated with different social relationships. "Good speech" tends to be used in more distant social relationships, while "bad speech" is used in closer relationships. In addition to "good" and "bad" speech, the Samoan language has a respect vocabulary. This specialised lexicon is used in both "good speech" and "bad speech" in interactions with persons of higher status, especially the titled (Ochs, 1988).

15. These indices are the "amount of academically engaged time, number of reading-related and correct responses, and number of idea units and logical inferences" (Cazden, 1988, p. 72).

16. *Preliminary Data Coding:*
A lesson is defined as the instructional unit located within a period of approximately 40 minutes and comprises a number of phases, namely, pre-lesson activities, getting-started activities, preliminary activities, diagnostic activity, main lesson activity, and interpolated activities. A phase is thus a segment of a lesson distinguished by the type of knowledge presented, topic covered, or form of specialised interaction.
Stage 1: The specialised interactional practices (SIP) and topics covered in each lesson were coded. The predominant specialised interactional practices in these lessons included teacher monologue, triadic dialogue (teacher question, student response, teacher evaluation), seatwork, and use of an external text.
Stage 2: Pedagogical strategies used to construct meanings within a topic and between topics were noted. In particular, strategies such as eliciting student responses, echoing student phrases, probing students to elaborate on responses, demonstrating knowledge, and giving positive and negative evaluations were coded.
Stage 3: Student disruptions or challenges to both the specialised interactional practices and the topics were coded at the level of the exchange and pedagogic move. An exchange was defined as a form of initiation in terms of information being presented and/or questions asked, a response and some sort of evaluation of this response being given, feedback being given or follow up being assigned.
Stage 4: Pedagogic moves were coded in terms of the instructional and regulative components of lessons. These were difficult to analyse separately as they often occurred simultaneously. However, the coders focused on talk explicitly pertaining to the transmission of skills and concepts (the formal instruction), and talk relating to the moral order of the classroom, that is, inducting students explicitly into particular forms of conduct, character, and manner.
Stage 5: The following questions were asked: How many disruptions are there per lesson? Which lessons are likely to have disruptions? Where are these disruptions likely to occur— phase, exchange, and pedagogic move? What strategies do teachers use to negotiate conflict or disruption in the classroom? Which strategies appear to work and why?

17. All of the teacher interviews were semi-structured, guided by a set of questions with the aim of eliciting information about the following:
    - Understandings of inclusive curriculum and social justice policies;
    - Challenges associated with teaching a diverse student clientele;
    - Curricular planning: knowledge selection and organisation in order to meet student needs;
    - Knowledge of local cultures/communities and how it influenced classroom/school practices;
    - Educational difficulties experienced by students in general, and Samoan students specifically;
    - English literacy difficulties experienced by students in general, and Samoan students specifically;

- Teacher-student relations at the school in general, and in terms of Samoan students specifically;
- Relationship with Samoan parents specifically, and the Samoan community more generally.

18. A unit of work involves approximately 12 lessons over the course of 4 weeks.

19. Black label magazines are sexually explicit magazines designed for the male adult market.

20. The teacher may have unintentionally disadvantaged the students.

Bibliography

Anstey, M., & Bull, G. (1996). Re-examining pedagogical knowledge and classroom practice. In G. Bull & M. Anstey (Eds.), *The literacy lexicon* (89–106). Sydney: Prentice Hall Australia.

Australian Bureau of Statistics. (1998). *1996 Census of population and housing: Selected family and labour force characteristics for statistical local areas, Queensland.* Canberra: Commonwealth of Australia.

Bernstein, B. (1975). *Class, codes and control: Vol. III, Towards a theory of educational transmissions.* London: Routledge & Kegan Paul.

———. (1990). *Class, codes and control: Vol. IV, The structuring of pedagogic discourse.* London: Routledge.

———. (1996). *Class, codes and control: Vol. V, Pedagogy, symbolic control and identity: Theory, research, critique.* London: Taylor & Francis.

———. (2001). From pedagogies to knowledge. (Epilogue). New York: Peter Lang.

Cazden, C. (1988). *Classroom discourse: The language of teaching and learning.* Portsmouth, NH: Heinemann.

Christie, F. (1995). Pedagogic discourse in the primary school. *Linguistics and Education, 7,* 221–242.

Crowley, V. (1998). Reading in the Antipodes: Postcolonialism, pedagogy and racism. *Discourse, 19* (3), 291–293.

Education Queensland. (2000). The framework for students at educational risk: Building success together. *Education Views* [Online]. [September 29, 10–11]. Available: *http://education.qld.gov.au.*

Edwards, A. D., & Westgate, D.P.G. (1994). *Investigating classroom talk* (2nd ed.). London: Falmer Press.

Electoral Commission Queensland. (1998). *Statistical profiles: Queensland state electoral districts*. Research Report 1/1998 Brisbane: Queensland Government.

Ellsworth, E. (1989). Why doesn't this feel empowering? Working through the repressive myths of critical pedagogy. *Harvard Educational Review, 59* (3), 297–324.

Figiel, S. (1998). *Where we once belonged*. Ringwood, Victoria, Australia: Viking.

Franco, R. W. (1997). The kingly-populist divergence in Tongan and Western Samoan chiefly systems. In G. M. White & L. Lindstrom (Eds.), *Chiefs today: Traditional Pacific leadership and the postcolonial state*. Stanford, CA: Stanford University Press.

Freeman, D. (1996). *Margaret Mead and the heretic. The making and unmaking of an anthropological myth*. Ringwood, Victoria, Australia: Penguin.

Giroux, H., & McClaren, P. (1986). Teacher education and the politics of engagement: The case of democratic schooling. *Harvard Educational Review, 56* (3), 213–227.

Graves, T. D., Graves, N. D., Vineta, N. A., Sam, S., & Sam, I. A. (1982). The price of ethnic identity: Maintaining kin ties among Pacific Islands immigrants to New Zealand. Research Report No. 22. ERIC Document No. ED 229 489.

Hickling-Hudson, A. (1998). When Marxist and post-modern theories won't do: The potential of postcolonial theory for educational analysis. *Discourse, 19* (3), 327–339.

Hunter, I. (1994). *Rethinking the school: Subjectivity, bureaucracy, criticism*. Sydney: Allen & Unwin.

Jones, A. (1991). *"At school I've got a chance." Culture/privilege: Pacific Islands and Pakeha girls at schools*. Palmerston North, New Zealand: Dunmore Press.

Jordan, C., Au, K. H., & Joesting, A. K. (1981). *Patterns of classroom interaction with Pacific Islands children: The importance of cultural differences*. Professional paper, National Centre for Bilingual Research, Los Alamitos, California. ERIC Document No. ED 221 632.

Kenway, J., Willis, S., Blackmore, J., & Rennie, L. (1994). Making "hope practical" rather than "despair convincing": Feminist post-structuralism, gender reform and educational change. *British Journal of Sociology of Education, 15* (2), 187–210.

Lawson, S. (1996). *Tradition versus democracy in the South Pacific*. Melbourne: Cambridge University Press.

Lemke, J. L. (1990). *Talking science: Language, learning and values*. Norwood, NJ: Ablex Publishing Corporation.

Luce, P. (1985). *The educational needs of American Samoan students.* ERIC Document Number ED 257 886.

Luke, C., & Gore, J. (1992). *Feminisms and critical pedagogy.* New York: Routledge.

Maher, F. A., & Thompson Tetreault, M. K. (1997). Learning in the dark: How assumptions of whiteness shape classroom knowledge. *Harvard Educational Review, 67* (2), 321–349.

Mara, D., Foliaki, L., & Coxon, E. (1994). Pacific Islands education. In E. Coxon, K. Jenkins, J. Marshall, & L. Massey (Eds.), *The Politics of learning and teaching in Aotearoa—New Zealand.* Palmerston North: Dunmore Press.

Maton, K. (2000). Languages of legitimation: The structuring significance for intellectual fields of strategic knowledge claims. *British Journal of Sociology of Education, 21* (2), 147–167.

Matthews, J. M. (1998). Hybrid muses and other sorts of romances: Feminism working out of postcolonial theory. *Discourse, 19* (3), 315–325.

Mau, R. Y. (1995). Barriers to higher education for Asian/Pacific-American females. In D. T. Nakanishi & T. Y. Nishida (Eds.), *The Asian American educational experience: A sourcebook for teachers.* New York: Routledge.

Mercer, N. (1995). *The guided construction of knowledge. Talk amongst teachers and learners.* Adelaide: Multilingual Matters.

Moore, R., & Muller, J. (1999). The discourse of "voice" and the problem of knowledge and identity in the sociology of education. *British Journal of Sociology of Education, 20* (2), 189–206.

Ochs, E. (1988). *Culture and language development: Language acquisition and language socialisation in a Samoan village.* Melbourne: Cambridge University Press.

Queensland School Curriculum Council. (1998). *Statewide performance of students in aspects of literacy and numeracy.* Report to the Minister of Education. Brisbane: Queensland Government.

Rose, D. (1999). Culture, competence and schooling: Approaches to literacy teaching in indigenous school education. In F. Christie (Ed.), *Pedagogy and the shaping of consciousness.* London: Continuum.

Schoeffel, P. (1995). The Samoan concept of feagaiga and its transformation. In J. Huntsman (Ed.), *Tonga and Samoa. Images of gender and polity* (pp. 85–105). Canterbury, New Zealand: MacMillan Brown Centre for Pacific Studies, University of Canterbury.

Singh, P. (2000). Local and official forms of symbolic control: An Australian case study of the pedagogic work of para-educational personnel. *International Journal of Inclusive Education, 4* (1), 3–22.

Singh, P., & Sinclair, M. (2001, March). Diversity, disadvantage and differential outcomes: An analysis of Samoan students' narratives of schooling. *Asia Pacific Journal of Teacher Education.*

Stone, M. (1981). *The education of the black child in Britain: The myth of multiracial education.* Glasgow: Fontana Paperbacks.

Tiatia, J. (1998). *Caught between cultures: A New Zealand-born Pacific Islander perspective.* Auckland, New Zealand: Christian Research Association.

Wendt, A. (1987). *Pouliuli.* Ringwood, Victoria, Australia: Penguin Books.

Chapter 11
Educational Evaluation: The Social Production of Texts and Practices

Joseph Solomon
Anna Tsatsaroni

Introduction

From October 1997 to June 1999, a pilot project entitled "Internal Evaluation and Planning at the School Unit" (IEP) was undertaken by a group of academic researchers and teachers *qua* education researchers seconded to the Evaluation Department of the Pedagogical Institute (the advisory organization of the Hellenic Ministry of Education) in collaboration with a number of schools and their teachers.[1] The project was designed to try out a model and a set of practices of school self-evaluation constructed by the researchers as part of the Evaluation Department's research and counselling initiatives.

An evaluation study was designed to assess the implementation of the project. In this chapter we outline and discuss the theoretical and methodological aspects of this evaluation study including the model of IEP and the material on which it was based. Basil Bernstein's ideas are used to produce a sociological description and understanding of this project, particularly its discourse, the form of practice instituted, and the positioning of teachers as subjects of self-evaluation.

Adopting a sociological perspective on the basis of broadly conceived action research principles makes this study distinctive in the area of evaluation research. Adopting Bernstein's sociological perspective to analyse discourse, positioning, and practices aims to strengthen sociological analysis in educational research where, under the impact of discourse theories, the concept of the social has been rewritten by non-sociologists, with considerable effects on research, policy, and practice (Bernstein, 2000).

In what follows we present, in turn,

- in the second section, the model of the IEP project, preceded by a brief analysis of the contexts in which it was created;

- in the third section, Bernstein's theoretical model, as it bears upon the current study;

- in the fourth section, the general methodological orientation, the research questions, and the means by which these questions are explored in our ongoing study;

- in the fifth section, an initial analysis of what in the study is called the transmitters' text, providing an illustration of the kind of approach the study adopts in the analysis of discourse focusing on the modality of practice, the mode of regulation, and the positioning of teachers; and

- in the final section, in focusing on important gains achieved by the theoretical and methodological choices of this study and revealing the social presuppositions of this modality of practice, we argue for the relevance of this approach to educational evaluation research.

The IEP Project and Its Contexts

Before presenting the actual model, it is important to explore briefly the context in which the IEP was created. Describing the context(s) of the model's creation may assist in understanding the conditions affecting the selection and formation of the practices and relations comprising the project (and their reception), as well as of the practices and relationships comprising the evaluation study. In particular, we aim at locating the difficulty in defining the study's object and delimiting its identity, in defining the framework for setting our main research questions, and, finally, in defining the methodology of data production and analysis.

Education policy and trends

To start with, reference must be made to the broader education policy context in Greece. Since 1995, several piecemeal reform attempts have aimed at the modernization of the centralised education system by focusing on the secondary school curriculum and, particularly, on student testing/assessment and tertiary education entrance examinations.

The issue of partial school or regional autonomy over curriculum regulation and textbook selection has been set aside by the Ministry of Education, while the issue of teachers' appointments has been totally excluded from the discussion of decentralisation. Autonomy over administration and financial management is reluctantly promoted at the institutional level and fiercely opposed by the central state bureaucracy and the civil servants. A strongly controlled hierarchical structure through which resources and a homogeneous curriculum are distributed remains dominant. Teacher and school culture are constituted accordingly and exhibit strong resistance to restructuring tendencies (Tyler, 1995).

Funds and guidelines for the restructuring of education, originating primarily from European sources and formulated in large programmes, allowed forces in the academic-research field to become involved and to strengthen their position in the Official Pedagogic Recontextualising Field (ORF) (Bernstein, 1990, 1996). In this context, schools were invited or allowed by the Ministry or its ORF agencies, such as the Pedagogical Institute, to participate in innovative, optional education projects in which members of the academic-research community often hold leading positions.

The programme entitled "Schools for the Implementation of Experimental Education Projects" (SIEP), of which the IEP project was a part, was, *par excellence*, one of the "umbrellas" under which such projects were financed and realised. Some of the innovational features of these projects were their interdisciplinary and thematic orientation; and their emphasis on the local, on group work and experience-based learning, on spatial rearrangement of the classroom, and on reorganisation of relationships within and between schools, as well as between schools and community. In this context, teachers and schools were given a limited degree of autonomy over administration and, to an even more limited extent, curriculum and pedagogy.

However, such innovative moves are met with distrust by traditionally dominant groups in the ORF and treated as marginal and temporary. Given the indisputably centralised character of decisions concerning key issues of educational provision, their impact on such decisions, as well as on school pedagogic practices and culture, needs empirical investigation.

Evaluation policy and the IEP project

Since 1997, the evaluation policy of the Ministry of Education, drawing upon a discourse of public control and accountability, has been centred on the introduction of a system focusing on the assessment more of teachers and less of schools by a body of permanent inspectors. Newly introduced standardised student tests and examination results in secondary education have only latterly been conceived as means for the evaluation of teachers, and of school performance and ranking, a job previously left to the media.

School self-evaluation was included in legislation passed in 1997 but only as a first step in a predominantly *external* and *hierarchical* evaluation chain. The 1998 decree on evaluation prescribed procedures for arriving at a school self-evaluation report.[2] This policy decision, as well as all other proposals involving external evaluation of teachers that have appeared since 1981 when the old inspectorate system was abolished by the socialist government, was met with strong reactions from teachers' associations and has not so far been implemented.

The model of the IEP project, with its emphasis on *internal* evaluation practices, stands in contrast to this decree, as will become apparent in a later section. In fact, while its development and evaluation have still been in progress, it has been used freely as a resource both by the central authorities and by teachers' associations and other interest bodies, the former in producing the decree on teachers' evaluation and the latter in their attempt to form their oppositional strategies. The partial and selective recontextualisation of its elements is, therefore, one of its distinguishing features.

The agency in which the IEP model was produced

The Pedagogical Institute is the leading agency of the ORF in Greece, charged with primary and secondary education curriculum production and control, as well as with providing counselling to the minister concerning several aspects of education policy, including evaluation. The creation of the SIEP framework and fund created the conditions for the IEP model to be formulated and approved, despite the fact that the model was clearly incompatible with the evaluation policy privileged by the Ministry of Education.

In its initial form, the model was strongly contested by the various forces in the Pedagogical Institute, mainly for not dealing explicitly with teachers' assessment and for being too close to the positions of the teachers' associations. Gradually it gained some mild support or, rather, tolerance, from some Pedagogical Institute officials, particularly after the Evaluation Department of the Pedagogical Institute organised a European-funded workshop in Athens during December 1997, where trends and issues of self-evaluation were discussed and the model's approach was endowed with some authority and status "from abroad". However, it was generally ignored by most Pedagogical Institute members and ministry officials as just another low-status experimental project promoted by the Evaluation Department. Further difficulties arose when its initiator resigned as president of the Evaluation Department, and returned to his academic job, while continuing as the director of IEP.

The IEP project appeared to be a product of the unrealistic ideas and whimsical activities of academic researchers who *occasionally* find themselves operating in positions within the ORF. At the same time, located in a field of multiple forces and incompatible interests, it had become part of an ongoing debate over the production of the dominant discourse of evaluation in Greece. The project was interrupted due to lack of funds so that its third year of implementation did not materialise. The lack of funds has affected the evaluation study, whose development and realisation have been reduced in scale and left purely to the will of a few motivated researchers.

The IEP model in brief

The publication of *Internal Evaluation and Planning at the School Unit* (Pedagogical Institute, 1999; henceforth referred to as PI, 1999; "the book"; "the manual"; or the "written transmitters' text") was mainly the work of teachers seconded to the Evaluation Department of the Pedagogical Institute operating as researchers. We were involved in both its conceptualisation and its writing.

The IEP model interrelated three sub-activities: data collection on school conditions; self-evaluation; and the planning and monitoring carried out by school personnel. The framework given in the appendix to this chapter underpinned them. It contains 20 thematic categories or Quality Indicators (QIs), distributed in seven Thematic Areas (TAs) comprising all those interdependent aspects of the school's complex and contingent "reality" that may be significant for the "quality" of the school and the education provided there.

The thematic categories are not arranged in a hierarchy of importance or value. They cover the following:

- student socio-cultural features and the socio-cultural context of the school (area 0);

- what is provided by the State to the school (areas 1–3);

- what happens in the school (areas 4–6);

- effects on students (area 7).

In relation to various models and experiences of self-evaluation and development, most of which are embedded in dominant school effectiveness and/or improvement research paradigms (e.g., MacBeath, Meuret, & Schratz, 1997), this model includes as objects of investigation aspects of school "reality" conceived as "input" or "context" usually ignored as issues or indicators for self-evaluation. Centrally provided and distributed material resources, curricula and syllabi, textbooks and teaching guidelines, and staff are suggested as important objects of investigation. Our model openly invites school agents to scrutinise elements of central state provision, and the information produced can, in turn, aid teachers in their formulation of demands or their justification of the need to improve the school as well as their own situation. (See, e.g., PI, 1999, p. 31.)

The importance of aspects of the social context of the school is underlined by the fact that these are neither ignored, nor reduced to an independent parameter, as when teaching practices are regarded, perhaps, as a drawback, or something to be aware of when teaching trying to obtain order in the classroom, or as just another quality indicator. Symbolically, as theme "0", they are presumed to interact with the full array of quality indicators (PI, 1999, p. 32). This is additionally made evident in our description of the QIs and in the methodological suggestions (PI, 1999, pp. 57–127). A sociological approach is also evident in the selection, structure, and description of the QIs, concerning more "internal" aspects of school function and teaching and learning practices and outcomes.

Multiple relations or dependencies between the thematic categories are noted as marked by educational research in different cultural and educational contexts but while emphasising the importance of context, the model denies the general validity of such relationships, and encourages teachers to investigate them anew. (See, e.g., PI, 1999, pp. 31–32.)

Each QI in each TA is briefly described, some possible means for its investigation by participants are presented, and a set of indicative criteria is given. An indicative framework for the organisation of processes of self-evaluation in the school unit is given: "diagnostic" (where the whole set of QIs is briefly reviewed by the school); and "exploratory" (where the QIs selected by the school are more thoroughly examined). Suggestions are made about which school agents apart from teachers (e.g., students, parents, counsellors) can participate in an IEP project. Suggestions are also made as to appropriate modes of grouping and guidelines for arriving at and composing reports on the phases of self-evaluation and for constructing, conducting, and monitoring an action plan, along with information about data collection instruments and a set of tables and a suitable software program for compiling data ("School Data") to assist the school in the self-evaluation process. Through the "Network for Educational Information", schools can communicate electronically with the Scientific Support Group of teachers-researchers based at the Pedagogical Institute and with other schools in the project, exchanging school data and other information. The Scientific Support Group provides distance (e-mail, fax, mail, and phone) and on-site training and assistance, intentionally restricted to clarifying procedures and suggesting ways of improving investigation instruments and steps. Other agents may, however, be selected by a school to provide further on-site assistance. In addition, according to the model, a set of abstracts from selected publications, which may assist the schools in their IEP work and in rethinking the school's context and practices, is also distributed through the network.

The IEP is, in certain respects, a researcher-led model. Two main features distinguish it from other related models of evaluation. First, although it starts with the view, favoured at least among some academic researchers today, that evaluation policy should adopt a model of internal evaluation of the school unit, it creates and proposes a specific frame of action for the school agents, claiming that school evaluation is the responsibility, concern, or action space not only of school-located agents but also of researchers. Secondly, although it utilises methodological procedures from the action research tradition (Patton, 1994; Cousins & Earl, 1995; Hopkins, Jackson, West, & Terrell, 1997; Worthen, Sanders, & Fitzpatrick, 1997) and encourages teachers to use findings from educational research studies, it is permeated by sociological concerns and modes of description. This is reflected in the attempt to inscribe a variety of discursive resources within a general sociological framework, and to create a particular "gaze" for teachers to view their school activity and practice.

It is these features of the model, as well as the assumption stated earlier that even as an experimental, low-status project and oppositional voice, the IEP participates in the production of the dominant discourse of evaluation, which constitute the study's claim to importance. These features have also informed our decisions regarding the theoretical and methodological issues.

Theoretical Considerations

Bernstein's theory of modes of pedagogic practice and their consequences for cultural production, reproduction, and change have strongly influenced the conception and design of the IEP project and the choice of theory for the evaluation study. To begin with, the IEP is essentially a pedagogical intervention aimed at teachers. The researchers' aim was to produce a model of internal evaluation and planning at the level of the school unit and to distribute it to teachers differently, not through courses but through the explication of a text, almost entirely inside the school, that is not theory oriented and decontextualised but directly relevant to the school's context and practices.

Bernstein's notion of recontextualisation is of extreme importance to this project. The model of internal evaluation developed in the context of the project is by no means original. On the one hand, it is a product of recontextualisation of evaluation discourse and particularly of recontextualisation of several other models or experiences of school self-evaluation developed for other contexts[3] but also varied, in some important respects.

On the other hand, it is a product of recontextualisation of a sociological discourse concerning processes of transmission and acquisition of educational knowledge, power, and control relations and conditions of change, aiming to make it directly relevant to teachers and school contexts, practices, and products.

Thus, the model is the product of recontextualisation of a multiplicity of more or less specialised discursive resources, including other models of evaluation, themselves the objects of recontextualisation of other discourses and practices, sociological theory and research discursive resources and practices. Agents operating within the ORF ("we" as developers of the model) performed a series of transformations (selection, simplification, condensation, repositioning, and refocusing) (Bernstein, 1990) on these multiple resources, in order to produce a new discourse to operate in a context that is different from their substantive contexts.

What does this new discourse do? It suggests and indicates ways for teachers to investigate their "ordinary" school contexts, activities, products, and possibilities. In other words, this discourse suggests a "gaze" for the school and aims at transmitting it to teachers (Foucault, 1963; Dowling, 1998; Bernstein, 1999b). In this sense, it is a pedagogic and pedagogising discourse for which Bernstein's theoretical model is an indispensable frame in analysis: It points to the need to identify the principle(s) of the recontextualising of the multiple resources that are used and the modality of pedagogic practice that the discourse constitutes, as well as the need to assess its consequences in the formation of teachers' identities.

In particular, the pedagogic discourse that was constructed in PI (1999) creates a specific modality of classification and framing of the specialised knowledge to be transmitted and acquired (Bernstein, 1996). According to Bernstein, in endeavours such as the pedagogising of specialised discourses, the acquirer rarely has access to the transmitter's recontextualising principle. More commonly, this principle is "tacitly transmitted and is invisibly active in the acquirer as his/her 'gaze' which enables the acquirer metaphorically to look at (recognise) and regard, and evaluate (realise) the phenomena of legitimate concern" (Bernstein, 1999a, p. 172). Of major sociological concern is whether the acquirer does, in fact, acquire recognition and realisation rules (Bernstein, 1990; Morais & Antunes, 1994; Davies, 1995; Morais, Fontinhas, & Neves, 1992; Morais & Miranda, 1996; Morais, Neves, & Fontinhas, 1999; Daniels, 1989; Cooper & Dunne, 2000; Ensor, 1999). In our study, this question is explored through a systematic analysis of both the transmitters' text and the acquirers' texts.

Bernstein's theoretical model provides us with specific concepts to explore pedagogical discourse in which instructional discourse is embedded in regulative discourse (ID/RD) (Bernstein, 1990, 1996). What our study aims to explore is the nature of this embedding, by subjecting its classification and framing values to systematic analysis. More specifically, our analysis considers the framing values of its instructional discourse and attempts to assess the extent to which these values allow acquirers to recognise and realise the discourse being recontextualised. At the same time, the analysis of the framing values of the instructional discourse helps us to specify these values' regulative consequences and to see whether the pedagogising discourse, as realised in the manual, constitutes an explicit regulative discourse. According to the theoretical model, the "message" regulating pedagogical relations, or the embedding of ID to RD, is a function of which elements of ID and RD are made explicit and which remain implicit. By identifying the nature of the embedding, this study aims to uncover the social basis of the form of pedagogical practice, as constituted in the discourse to be transmitted, and to locate the social presuppositions underlying the criteria of evaluation of the IEP model.

Bernstein always stresses that it is crucial to distinguish between (and analyse the relationship between) the two transformations of a specialised discourse when it becomes subject to recontextualisation processes for pedagogic purposes. The first is the transformation of the discourse within the recontextualising field and the construction of transmitters' discourse. The second is its transformation, in turn, as it becomes active in the process of the reproduction of acquirers. In the study in progress, we analyse both kinds of transformation. In his more recent writings, Bernstein distinguished between vertical and horizontal discourses and between a reservoir and a repertoire (Bernstein, 1996, 1999b). Transmitters' discourse, by recontextualising resources from vertical discourses, can be seen to constitute a privileged and privileging repertoire in that it incorporates a partial selection of contents and resources and their arrangement for the activities, which it constitutes into sequences (Bernstein, 1990; Ensor, forthcoming). The transmission and acquisition of its privileged repertoire would imply that acquirers are able to reproduce it discursively and realise it in constructing and deploying their own individual or school-specific repertoires. In addition to the concepts of recognition and realisation rules in the analysis of the acquirers' products, the notion of repertoire provides ways of exploring the conditions of recontextualisation in specific schools. For example, it helps one to examine how the existence of different repertoires of resources and practices in schools might affect the recontextualisation of the IEP model and the construction of individual teachers' repertoires (Domingos, 1989; Ensor, 1999).

Research Questions and Methodology

Within the context of the evaluation study, the IEP model is seen as the pedagogising of more or less specialised discourses *and* as a pedagogic intervention by researchers attempting to establish a pedagogical relationship with the participating teachers, who are, potentially, their peers. The main research questions sought to characterise the privileged repertoire in this pedagogical discourse, how it was distributed, how it positioned subjects, and what message it (re)produced.

It became apparent that the IEP comprised a set of activities engaging a complex of agencies, agents, and social relationships, among which three distinct social activities were important for the evaluation study:

a. those in which the IEP model was produced;

b. those in which it was recontextualised in schools; and

c. those in which the evaluation study was designed and executed.

As far as the third kind of activity is concerned, the studies of constructivist epistemologies provide several reasons to justify its treatment as a distinct activity.[4] The first two activities differ in one crucial respect. In the first, a group of researchers selects elements of specialised knowledge and skills and recontextualises them for the purposes of transmission, the decision of the researchers affecting the message and its distribution and evaluation, specialising voices, and distributing practices through the production of texts which we shall call the *transmitters' texts* (Bernstein, 1990; cf. Dowling, 1998; Ensor, 1999). Our study uses the written transmitters' text(s) as the source for the production of data on this activity. In the second kind of activity, groups of teachers participating in the IEP recontextualise the model in their specific school sites by carrying out the tasks suggested, reproducing the speciality of their voice and message, through the creation of *acquirers' texts* (Bernstein, 1990; Ensor, 1999), for data on which our study uses the reports which the teachers have compiled.

The first and second category of texts must be distinguished from the research study for which they are objects of investigation. In addition, a set of texts related to the objectives of the study is scheduled to be produced to satisfy the criteria of good research practice. For example, in order to investigate whether and how the privileged repertoire constructed in the transmitters' text relates to the repertoires which are deployed by teachers in carrying out tasks and which become part of their ordinary school activities, we interview them and others.

These distinctions direct analysis towards investigating how subjects are positioned in these activities and how they serve to (re)produce or change given social relationships. At the same time, these distinctions do not dictate how the texts, as empirical data, are to be treated in the analysis. For example, in analysing teachers' reports, we are not limited to the question of whether teachers have acquired and realised the privileged repertoire but we ask, like Brown (1999), what information teachers relay in their reports and how they relay it. We explore not only the question of whether the researchers' vision of productive change, a privileged repertoire, has any real effects on teachers' actual everyday school practice but also the rather different question of teachers' positioning in the discourse, in and through the production of their own texts and through the ways in which they relay information to the researchers and, possibly, others. While we oriented our investigation towards the texts of acquirers, as both learners and actors, the concerns that will inform the analysis of a particular text are left to the empirical data to dictate.[5]

The Analysis of Transmitters' Texts

The object of this analysis is the text regulating *assisting* learning and its social relations. The "investigation" concerns the school's context, activity, and product and the subjects are primarily teachers and other school agents (students and parents). Changes that this pedagogic activity may bring to teachers' identities, practices, and relations, as well as to the school, will also be considered.

The transmitters' text and voice constitution

In order to understand the particular form of pedagogic relationship standing at the basis of this activity (assisting learning to investigate the school's context, activity, and product), let us first consider matters of insulation/classification and voice constitution.[6] We must ask if a voice is constituted, how distinct it is, and what kind of voice it is. What is the transmitters' agency and frame of reference? What is the position of the actual agents (the authors-as-transmitters and the Scientific Support Group as support providers) in or in relation to this agency and in relation to other agencies in the Pedagogic Recontextualising Field (PRF)?

The transmitters' written text (PI, 1999), a manual composed for the regulation of the IEP activity, is published under the auspices of the dominant ORF agency as material for purposes of experimentation on innovational school practices, not as an official policy document. It is a well-structured book, each chapter/material supported by a substantial bibliography designed to convince the reader/user of its "scientific" nature. As such, it claims a position of authority within the field of educational evaluation, one not particularly rich or well cultivated in Greece, and a dominant position in the particular new domain of self-evaluation. However, the text is declared to be unfinished and open to reformulation, not least because its contents are to be tested in the context of the experimental project. Other members of the research/education community are invited to contribute to the text's next edition, though only in ways that will be controlled by the authors. The book includes specific forms on which "outsiders" can submit their comments and suggestions. No barriers are set up against its use and reformulation in other contexts and by other agents. An indication of this is its circulation on the Internet. Its authors-as-transmitters are presented as an occasional group of academic researchers and teachers'-education researchers temporarily employed by the agency.[7]

The text is the outcome of the recontextualisation of a multiplicity of discourses, not all originating in the field of educational evaluation. Discursive elements from the sociology of school and classrooms, cultural studies, psychology, curriculum studies, and so on are selectively used and recontextualised to suit the purposes of the IEP model, to embed an Instructional Discourse (ID) in a Regulative Discourse (RD) where its ID draws from and recontextualises mainly resources of educational research discourses and its RD draws from and recontextualises a variety of resources, including the therapeutic, instrumental, and managerial (Bernstein, 1996, 1999a).

The "voice" of this text is constituted rather weakly; its insulation from other agencies and discourses is recognisable but relatively weak. Its relations with other discourses *as resources* (recontextualisation), as well as with other agents and discourses *as relays* (Bernstein, 1990), are controlled by the voice but are kept relatively open. The voice has been strengthened through the published text's reception in the public domain. A few critical articles on the publication have appeared in education reviews, and several invitations have been addressed to its authors to present the publication to wider audiences, mainly of teachers.

We should distinguish between this written text and the text produced in the course of the Scientific Support Group's distance and on-site support provision.[8] In the latter, voice is a matter of great significance and has methodological implications. However, in our present, tentative analysis we conflate these two texts as "transmitters' text" in relationship with teachers-as-acquirers-and-actors. Learning to practice the investigation activity is taken to be the same as actually practising it and potentially producing a series of changes internal to the teachers as pedagogic subjects and to the actual school context and activity.

The communicative context in the transmitters' text

In examining the principles regulating the communicative context in which the activity of acquisition/investigation is realised, we first examine the relations between the acquisition/investigation activity, on the one hand, and ordinary schooling activity, on the other, by briefly looking at their differences in content, in the modality of power relations within the activities, in their physical setting and institutional organisation. These differences between the two activities will be highlighted in order to provide a first image of the particular nature of the communicative context of the activity in question.

Classification and power relations

This acquisition/investigation activity is conceived as different in many ways from ordinary schooling activity and its sub-activities, such as teaching, administering, disciplining, and evaluating. Using the transmitters' text, let us first consider aspects of insulation/boundary (classification) between the two types of activity and related issues of power (Bernstein, 1990, 1996). Acquisition/investigation activity is intended to be a process of reflexive examination of the sub-activities outlined earlier, including teachers' meetings and other aspects of schooling, which are, to be conceptually, physically, and spatially kept apart, realised outside the required working hours and in unspecified spaces that may prove convenient for large and small group work; although some of the process, for example, peer observation, may occur partly in actual schooling time and space. Participation in such an activity is not mandatory and attendance by anything over two-thirds of the teaching staff involved is perfectly acceptable. The optional nature of this activity, both for the whole school and for every individual teacher, aims to underline its independence from the external hierarchical structure of power symbolised by the homogeneous imposition of school discourses and practices. In this activity, the ordinary power allocation and distribution scheme of the school does not hold. The head teacher may, from the purely administrative point of view, be responsible for the project in the school but the text does not give him/her an advantage of power and over power distribution in this activity. The same goes for the deputy head teacher or any other person in a statutory position of power/authority in the school, marking one important difference from the ministerial decree concerning school self-evaluation referred to earlier.

Students and parents have a rather ambiguous power status. Teachers, depending on the kind/modality of existing relationships with students and parents, may decide whether they may occupy a position in the activity more or less equal to their position in terms of power (through their representatives as subjects of the investigation) or inferior to their position (as data sources). The transmitters' text explicitly privileges and suggests ways of organising the former power position (PI, 1999, pp. 25, 131–135). Furthermore, the text introduces a few new roles: a school "co-ordinator" for the activity, sub-group co-ordinators and minutes recorders, and one or more school report compiler(s). They are to be elected among participating teachers and have procedural responsibilities. The need for vigilance is underlined by the text, so that their views or interests will not be imposed on the rest of the participants (PI, 1999, p. 27).

While recognising the variety of and conflict between equal or unequal authority/power positions, interests, "world-views", "representations", and "languages" among school actors, the text (PI, 1999, pp. 25–28) clearly projects and describes the shared commitment to the idea of democratic self-evaluation for change as being at the basis of a new solidarity among "willing" actors. This solidarity is realised by horizontal relations within the activity, aiming at replacing, or at least drastically reducing, vertical relations imposed and reproduced in ordinary school activity (PI, 1999, pp. 27, 133–134). Thus, the acquisition/investigation activity is an activity distinguished by strong boundaries from ordinary school activity and by explicit differences in power relations. The overall message is that "this is something different".

Framing

The transmitters' text provides a set of rules for the regulation of the communicative context and practices of the activity, of the relations between acquirers and transmitters, and of the relations among school agents.

Framing (external). Let us first consider the "external values of the strength of framing" *(Fe)*. *Fe* refers to the degree of control by transmitters and acquirers over what can be legitimate communication and what cannot (Bernstein, 1990, p. 37). In our study, we refer to control over what features of other communication contexts can be realised within the communicative context in question, as regulated by the transmitters' text. Here the concepts of reservoir and repertoire and horizontal and vertical discourse (Bernstein, 1996, 1999b) can be useful. The transmitters' text provides a privileged and privileging repertoire of knowledge and skills (embedded in a relevant regulative discourse) for practicing the activity of school-focused, sociologically informed educational "investigation", recontextualised from a broad reservoir composed of a set of social science discourses and research and evaluation practices. In other words, the transmitters' text is a repertoire of recontextualised (selected, made simple, made appropriate to the school context, recomposed, and so on) more or less vertical discursive resources. The acquirers (teachers in the IEP project) are expected to recognise the items/resources of this repertoire and draw from this repertoire in order to realise the activity.

Acquirers, in order to realise their ordinary schooling activity and its sub-activities, draw from a repertoire of knowledge and skills constituted from a variety of resources. As far as the acquisition/investigation activity is concerned, knowledge and skills for understanding, investigating, and discussing schooling activity may be drawn from a repertoire constituted from a variety of resources and experiences, sometimes including courses on research methodology attended during initial and/or in-service training, postgraduate research-based studies, the specialised press, and, more commonly, school experience itself, common-room talk with colleagues, and experiences in various political/professional groups and with the mass media. In other words, the repertoire available to the acquirers, other than that provided by the transmitters' text, is rarely formed by vertical discursive resources but more often formed by horizontal discursive resources. Thus, the question could be reformulated in these terms: What is the relation between the two repertoires; how strong is their insulation as defined by the transmitters' text?

The transmitters' text, on several occasions, notes the necessity to avoid staying enclosed in elements of horizontal discourse. In other words, it underlines the inappropriate character of the use of non-specialised discourse in the communicative context of the activity, stressing the need to keep the boundary between the two discourses rather strong. For example, "stereotypical generalisations", "oversimplifications", "phenomenal truths", "one-sided explanations", and "misinterpretations, myths and common-sense certainties" are to be avoided, in favour of "composite, sensitive, critical consideration of the multiple social, educational and cultural dimensions of the phenomena it investigates" (PI, 1999, pp. 27, 140). If the repertoire provided by the transmitters' text is not adequate, this suggests turning for assistance to the "scientific community", to vertical discourse resources and agents. Should the "technical difficulties" of the acquirers in realising the "investigation" be insurmountable, it suggests turning not only to the Scientific Support Group but also to the broader "scientific community", which may provide assistance and opportunities for further specialised training and eventually promote "the scientific and professional development of teachers" (PI, 1999, pp. 26–27).

It is important to note, additionally, that the written transmitters' text aims to involve research agencies and agents of the PRF in this and other potential projects of IEP, by inviting them to apply to become members of the Register of Collaborators, providing a specific form in the book for this, too, thus attempting to control and filter the assistance potentially provided, so strengthening the relatively weak voice they constitute. Here and elsewhere, the transmitters' text underlines the need to keep the communication context of this activity protected from input deriving from non-legitimate horizontal discursive resources but open (although there a is certain ambiguity here) to rather more legitimate vertical discursive resources.

Framing (internal). Let us now consider the "internal values of the strength of framing" *(Fi)* as defined by the transmitters' text (Bernstein, 1990, pp. 36–37). We shall refer to *Fi* as the principle regulating who has control over the selection, organisation/sequencing, pacing, and criteria of communication. In our study, we examine whether the rules set by the transmitters' text aim at retaining for the transmitters control over specific aspects of the communication context or at "delegating" control to acquirers, and to what degree. We deal with selection, sequencing, and pacing in turn.

Selection. First, the selection of the possible contents of communication is an issue the text pays some attention to. The thematic framework constitutes a message about what contents constitute legitimate communication and what do not. The framework, it is claimed, has embraced the most important aspects of school reality, including thematic categories that other frameworks often do not, such as central provision of resources or a national curriculum. The text goes into some detail to explain why this is so and what this means for the character of the investigation (PI, 1999, pp. 29–32). The text attempts to draw its legitimation from vertical discursive resources, as far as this selection of thematic categories is concerned, and claims to have taken critically into account research outcomes dealing with factors related to school quality and effectiveness, providing relevant bibliographical references which form part of its ideological message (PI, 1999, pp. 31, 135). However, the specific criteria for selecting from relevant vertical discursive resources, and for producing the specific framework of thematic categories by recontextualising these resources, remain implicit. In other words, the principles of the recontextualising are not made explicit in the text.

The text lays down some explicit rules for the selection of the contents of the communication by the acquirers. It demands from them inclusion of all thematic categories of the framework in the first phase of the investigation: Nothing should be left out, although acquirers are invited, in the first place, to review the categories and suggest possible modifications (PI, 1999, p. 132). In the second phase of in-depth investigation, the acquirers (the school's collective body of participating teachers and other school agents) may select the thematic categories they wish to look at in detail. However, the text focuses on several occasions on the criteria for this selection (PI, 1999, pp. 132, 135–136). The selection must refer to a wide range of issues and not only to central provision of resources, curricula, and staff (aspects of "input"). A selection that does not include aspects of processes and/or outcomes is considered to be inadequate. The transmitters' group (the Scientific Support Group) has the duty to control each school's selection of QIs, according to the criteria and to discuss them with the school. The QIs selected must not be just an array of issues but combine into a "working hypothesis" to tackle a specific question: "Which are the issues that in our school primarily may affect or determine the quality of education provided and its effects on learning and the development of students?"[9] (PI, 1999, p. 137).

As far as the selection of investigation techniques and instruments is concerned, the text suggests a wide range of possible investigation techniques and instruments from which acquirers may select, and examples are given in an additional file distributed to schools. The selection of the investigation instruments must correspond to the aim of the investigation, the questions set, the data required, and so on (PI, 1999, pp. 136–137, 153–

155). Acquirers are discouraged from using only techniques/instruments that they may be familiar with (for example, questionnaires as used by opinion polls and published in the media: see PI, 1999, p. 151). In other words, the transmitters' text strongly prompts the acquirers to adopt a wide but rigorously selected range of investigation techniques/instruments according to a set of research-like criteria. The need for the triangulation of data is also projected for this reason (PI, 1999, p. 153). Acquirers are expected to recognise the various rules and proceed to the realisation of their selection according to these rules.

Elements of the acquirers' repertoire drawing from more or less horizontal discursive resources, such as "empirical knowledge of the educational process" (PI, 1999, p. 135), are called upon as one basis of practice but are inadequate on their own to justify a selection of thematic categories or investigation techniques/practices. The appeal to rather vertical discursive resources, possibly already available to acquirers, remains unstated. Therefore, acquirers are oriented by the transmitters' text towards adopting selection criteria similar to the not unambiguously explicit criteria of the transmitters' text, by exercising practices of investigation (e.g., PI, 1999, p. 137) that more or less resemble practices of research, that is, drawing from and recontextualising vertical discursive resources. They must think and act in a way that is similar to the way researchers do, but adapted to the particular context of investigation in the school.

Sequencing. Next we consider aspects of *Fi* concerning the organization/sequencing of the contents and procedures of the communication as defined in the transmitters' text.[10] The *sequence of contents* in the framework of TAs and QIs are not to be reflected in the procedure of the investigation. During the first phase of the investigation, having briefly reviewed all the thematic categories, irrespective of sequence, acquirers are asked by the transmitters' text to set the categories in a new sequence. A sequencing criterion is given by the text. The criterion is a hierarchy of importance or rather a hierarchy of "problem weight" *for the specific school,* and the specific realisation of this criterion is left (or, rather, assigned) to the collective opinion of the acquirers. The transmitters, however, may control this criterion: Does *their* (the specific acquirers') new sequence actually reflect *their own* collective perception of *their* school's problems?

The QIs finally selected for the second phase of the investigation, according to the selection criteria discussed above, can be investigated in a sequence that the transmitters' text does not specify; for example, schools may choose to examine two or more QIs in parallel. However, once the data sources and the data collection techniques are selected by acquirers for the investigation of each selected QI, the sequence of contents is regulated by the order of the (vertical) research resources and practices. The transmitters' text (PI, 1999, pp. 151–160, and additional file) attempts to make this order visible, explicit, and *procedural*, by eliminating the theoretical context of the "research hypothesis". Thus, for the sequencing of the selected contents, the rules provided by the transmitters' text are rather explicit and the value of framing is rather strong.

Let us now turn briefly to the *sequencing of procedures* as such. The transmitters' text describes procedures in some detail, although it stresses in the relevant introduction that this is only for indicative reasons: These procedures draw legitimation from relevant bibliography, but schools are allowed to find the form and organisation appropriate for their specific condition (PI, 1999, p. 131). The detailed "indicative" procedures distinguish a first phase and a second phase. In the first phase, in particular, where a whole set of introductory procedures are to be performed, the text is quite explicit concerning the set of tasks, the number and sequence of different meetings (small group and plenary) for different tasks, and even the periods/intervals between meetings (PI, 1999, pp. 131–136). In the second phase, as already discussed, the sequencing of the investigation steps is, on the one hand, regulated by the internal order of each data collection procedure/instrument selected, as is made explicit by the text, while, on the other hand, the transmitters' text prescribes a series of actions and forms of grouping to be followed by acquirers during investigation (PI, 1999, pp. 136–138), irrespective of the specific technique or instrument deployed by acquirers. Therefore, despite their indicative nature, procedures are strongly and explicitly ordered in a sequence and controlled by the transmitters' text. Acquirers may have alternative realisation possibilities but the rules regulating these alternatives are explicit.

Thus, the transmitters' text defines framing, as far as the sequencing of selected contents and procedures is concerned, rather explicitly. In particular, control over criteria of sequencing is in some cases delegated to the acquirers (weak framing), while in other cases it is retained by the transmitters (strong framing). Control is retained by the acquirers in those cases that seem to be linked to the regulative aspects of the communicative context. As discussed below, this is crucial for the moral order of the activity and, ultimately, teachers' positioning in the discourse.

Pacing. Let us now turn to the value of *Fi* concerning the pacing of the communication. As Bernstein explains, pacing refers to the rate of expected acquisition of the sequencing rules (Bernstein, 1990, p. 52). The transmitters' text sets several fairly explicit rules concerning how much time may be devoted to each activity, and it allows for a considerable degree of variation. The external limits of each period of the activity are defined by the limits of the school year. The first phase should take place at the beginning of a school year and may vary from two to four weeks in length. The sequence of tasks must be completed in a limited number of meetings and a minimum of two. The second phase must start right after the report on the first phase has been completed, and submitted to and approved by the Scientific Support Group. The second phase may last for the rest of the school year, so long as there is enough time at the end to compile a demanding final report. In the second phase there can be two or three cycles of investigation, and each cycle may address one or two quality indicators, depending on the number of people in a school involved in the project. How much time will be devoted to a QI will depend on how demanding the investigation of the particular QI is and on what depth the group of acquirers want to go into, as well as on the capacity (knowledge and skills) of the group to realise an acceptable investigation procedure. However, the acquirers' group must decide upon these matters beforehand and draw up a clear programme. This is to be submitted to the Scientific Support Group as part of the report on the first phase and has the status of an "internal contract" and a "contract with the Scientific Support Group". Changes to this "contract" are allowed only if all the parties agree and may occur only at specific points in the procedure (PI, 1999, pp. 131–140).

Regulative discourse: The social and moral order of the activity

We have seen how the framing rules for the selection, sequencing, and pacing of the communication set by the transmitters' text regulate more or less strongly the investigation activity and communication. These rules draw from rather vertical discursive resources, though the text does not restrict itself to these resources. Activity and communication are, additionally, explicitly regulated by a strong "moral order".

We have seen already, when describing aspects of classification, the particular form of the social/power relations within this activity. The transmitters' text further insists on setting rules for the specification of appropriate social relations and attitudes that go, in many cases, far beyond the prerequisites of *proper* research/investigation in the school. It lays down rules for the participation of as many school agents as possible, including not only those with the appropriate actual or potential knowledge and skills but all those involved in the schooling process who have the appropriate attitude and "will". Research capacity is not an issue that can determine participation. Rules are also laid down for achieving consensus without eliminating differences, and particular processes have to be followed to achieve consensus and respect varieties of opinions. There are also rules for democracy. The activity has to provide "room" for all voices, particularly the weaker ones, to be heard, registered, and taken into account (PI, 1999, pp. 25–28, 131–140).

The transmitters' text emphasises the importance of research and of instructional discourse and its vertical resources, and this has implications for the regulative aspect of the communicative context and, therefore, for the pedagogical activity and relations. At the same time, we have identified an explicit regulative discourse, not necessarily compatible with the instructional discourse and its anticipated regulative consequences. There are real questions left unanswered. Will the efficiency of the investigation be sacrificed for the sake of achieving appropriate moral order, social relations, and attitudes? Are involvement, respect of others' voices, and "will for change" primary qualities for this project, while, for example, knowing how to conduct a good interview is not? Or is there a *tacit* assumption of the relation between ID and RD concerning the primary pedagogical relationship, as constituted in the text, its voice, power relationships, and principles of control?

Critical Reflections

In Bernstein's model, framing and particularly pacing rules regulate the economy of the transmission. Pacing regulates the temporal control over the selection and flow of pedagogic messages on the part of both transmitter and acquirer. The form the regulative discourse takes is itself a function of the pacing rules. The stronger the rule, the more likely it is that the control is positional and imperative; the weaker the rule, the more personal and interactive the form of control (Bernstein, 1990; Bernstein, personal communication, February 16, 2000). As shown in the preceding analysis, the framing rules in the transmitters' text are rather strong, especially the regulative aspects of ID, so that the RD is, in one sense, inscribed in the rules of framing of the ID. In addition, there is an explicit RD; the text stresses the importance, among other things, of co-operation, reflection, and democratic participation in decision-making processes and in achieving consensus. However, the "appropriate" meanings of such terms are likely to remain ambiguous, pointing simultaneously to their everyday meanings and to very specialised ones linked with the processes, procedures, and values of research practice. For example, is "reflection" to be understood as what we usually do when we decide, or are invited, to look back at what happens in a meeting? Or is it to be interpreted as a theoretical *reconceptualisation* of the relevant problem? Again, is democratic participation the same as what teachers do when they, by right, have their say in a staff or union meeting? Or is it the right and ability to *raise truth claims*, or to *contest the validity* of other actors' truth claims, through producing a *better*-documented *argument*?

In other words, are the criteria and practices recommended by the transmitters' text, implicitly, in the sense just indicated, regulated by the researchers' discursive practices and values, in which engaging in co-operative and collective action presupposes knowledge, skills, and research values? To put it differently, heavily distorting Habermas, is a specialised language essential "as the medium [...] of reaching understanding, in the course of which, participants to a world [of research] reciprocally raise validity claims that can be accepted or contested"? (Habermas, 1984, p. 99). Is this the implicit rule of the relationship between ID and RD?

This takes us directly to a significant issue that Bernstein's model helps us to raise, namely, the issue of the *tacit presuppositions* of a form of pedagogical practice. It is apparent that the tacit presuppositions of the form of practice, as constituted by the transmitters' text, provide tacit *criteria* for evaluating present or potential future applications of IEP in the school site. If our analysis is correct, the tacit criterion for teachers' products, within an IEP context, to be considered legitimate in public accountability debates is teachers' having and actually displaying research-specific knowledge, skills, and values. This is what the IEP model primarily requires for its application, but it does not offer any systematic provision of the required training. Therefore, even the suspicion that teachers' own representations for their school's context, activity, and product and their own projections of the image of their school might be assessed by this implicit criterion seems to us to suggest caution towards future applications of the IEP model, at least in conditions which are relatively unfavourable to teachers, such as public accountability exercises.

This is a rather unexpected conclusion that we, as co-producers of the model, co-authors of the transmitters' text, and potential agents of school reform initiatives, have been able to arrive at only by systematically employing the language of description that Bernstein's model makes available. It was also surprising to us to realise that the sensitivity, refined through sociological theory, that has made us distrustful and even dismissive of action research perspectives, with their under-theorised notion of teacher-as-researcher and their problematical vision of only school-based and teacher-initiated change, was not, in fact, enough to protect us from promoting an equally problematical model of pedagogic action and relationships. Thus, in avoiding the populist and radical-emancipatory modes of competence models (Bernstein, 1996), we have landed in an equally problematical mode, not very different from those others in its presuppositions, and not that far away, in its potential consequences, from the market-oriented models to be found in the effective-school discourses that are currently dominant.

A final word concerning Bernstein's use of discourse is relevant here. In various theories of discourse, the notion tends to be used indiscriminately in the analysis of social, cultural, and political identities. Restricting himself to the study of pedagogic discourse, Bernstein first asks sociological questions in his conceptualisation of the discourse. These concern the social basis of changes in the principles of distribution, recontextualisation, and evaluation constituting the discourse, in which the instructional is embedded in the regulative. Second, Bernstein provides very precise concepts to explore the nature of this embedding, as well as its consequences. This chapter aims to be a contribution towards an appreciation of this kind of approach and its tools of analysis.

Notes

* We wish to thank the members of the evaluation study team in Athens for their motivation and work, and particularly Anastasia Kotsira and Maria Tamboukou for providing us with data from school reports and interviews with teachers. We also thank Maria Tamboukou for her useful comments on an earlier draft of this chapter.

1. This project was designed as a 3-year pilot project (1997–2000). The object of the first two years (1997–1999) was mainly the experimental application of a school self-evaluation model that was still being formulated. The third year (1999–2000) was designed to focus on planning procedures practiced by the schools after self-evaluation. However, this was not achieved, like most experimental project proposals for 1999–2000, due to lack of resources. In 1997–1998 there were six secondary schools in the

project. In 1998–1999 there were eight schools, four secondary schools (two of which had also participated in the project in 1997–1998) and four primary schools. The numbers of teachers participating in the project were 155 in 1997–1998, and 148 in 1998–1999. The authors of this chapter participated in the design, realisation, and evaluation of the project.

2. These reports were to be produced by committees of five teachers (not including the head teacher but led by a deputy head teacher) and submitted to head teachers who would then write their own reports on teachers and schools. Both reports were then to be submitted to the inspector who would eventually evaluate the teachers, head teacher, and school using procedures that have not yet been specified. The legislation was meant to introduce procedures for school evaluation in primary and secondary education.

3. Notably, the model implemented in the 1997–1998 European pilot project on school-based self-evaluation described in MacBeath, Meuret, and Schratz (1997). Also see Schratz (1997), Altrichter and Specht (1998), and Popham (1993).

4. Though we cannot go into this issue in any detail here, we stress that this methodological decision is part of an attempt to maintain a tension in our study between a realist and a constructivist epistemology. Thus, we see the model as a device that, in some ways, affects practice. This fits into a realist epistemological frame and directs the inquiry towards choosing objective methods and procedures that will guarantee its validity and the validity of the research outcomes. But, at the same time, we see the research process itself as a distinct social activity, introducing and facilitating processes of reflexivity in the course of our study (cf. Pels, 1996, 1999).

5. As already suggested, one of the basic assumptions of our IEP model is that it contains a vision of productive change. This assumption presupposes a certain view of the processes of production and implementation of change through innovation. This is apparent in the central metaphor of the "game" often used among the research team members to conceptualise the creation of the model and its deployment in the pedagogical field. But our methodological choices allow us to experiment with a second metaphor in our textual analyses. According to this second metaphor, the model can be seen as a device or technology. Consequently, we are able in our analysis to make a comparison with an approach to the processes of production and implementation of an innovation, in terms of the concept of recontextualisation, as used by Bernstein, and in terms of the concept of translation as used by Grint and Woolgar (1997) and Latour (1987), and possibly from other theoretical perspectives. This directs the analysis not only towards teachers' (users') use of the model and the model's production, but also the whole process by which products are created, stabilised, and bounded. To put it differently, focusing on texts produced within the activities described earlier enables us to analyse them in terms of the principles of recontextualisation and the extent to which these have been recognised and realised by teachers. At the same time, it enables us to explore the textual strategies and rhetorical devices as part of, for example, boundary work, which constructs boundaries and fixes or creates fictions concerning the identities of subjects (such as teachers or researchers) and objects such as the IEP model,

thereby presenting them as pre-constituted entities. In other words, from a methodological point of view, we wish to draw parallels between and explore similarities and differences stemming from, on the one hand, Bernstein's core idea of the strength of boundary and, on the other, from the Social Studies of Science (Biagioli, 1999) approach, whose theoretical orientation focuses on boundary work accomplished within and by texts which serve to construct and sustain a social boundary.

6. Classification refers to relations between categories; for example, categories of discourse, agencies, and agents. In Bernstein's (1990) theoretical model, classification is linked to power, and the analysis of "voice" is part of the analysis of power relations.

7. All but one are not evaluation specialists but they receive the temporary identity attributed to them by the fact of being seconded to the Evaluation Department of the PI. The head and another key member of the authors' team are sociologists who were temporarily employed by the agency at the time when the model and material were constructed but who are permanently employed at the university.

8. Membership in the Scientific Support Group was regulated yearly by the head of the IEP project, the criteria being rather weak and referring to a minimum of research expertise, irrespective of discipline, knowledge of the school context, a certain communication capacity, and, above all, a strong "ideological commitment" to the model's principles.

9. This selection criterion was included only in the latest published version of the material.

10. Contextual features are explicitly given indisputable priority over the set of 20 thematic categories: "The whole of this analysis of the school's reality has no meaning unless it is examined in relation to [these contextual features]" (PI, 1999, p. 32).

Bibliography

Altrichter, H., & Specht, W. (1998). Quality assurance and quality development in education: International approaches and parameters, as applying to the Austrian school system. In J. Solomon (Ed.), *Trends in the evaluation of education systems: School (self) evaluation and decentralization; European workshop, papers, reports, discussion outcomes.* Athens: European Commission and Hellenic Ministry of Education.

Bernstein, B. (1990). *Class, codes and control: Vol. IV, The structuring of pedagogic discourse.* London: Routledge.

———. (1996). *Class, codes and control: Vol. V, Pedagogy, symbolic control and identity: Theory, research, critique.* London: Taylor & Francis.

———. (1999a). Official knowledge and pedagogic identities. In F. Christie (Ed.), *Pedagogy and the shaping of consciousness: Linguistic and social processes.* London: Cassell.

———. (1999b). Vertical and horizontal discourse: An essay. *British Journal of Sociology of Education, 20* (2), 157–173.

———. (2000). *Class, codes and control: Vol. V, Pedagogy, symbolic control and identity: Theory, research, critique* (Rev. ed.). Oxford: Rowman & Littlefield.

Biagioli, M. (Ed.). (1999). *The science studies reader.* London: Routledge.

Brown, A. J. (1999). Parental participation, positioning and pedagogy: A sociological study of the IMPACT primary school mathematics project. *Collected Original Resources in Education, 24* (3) (7/A02–11/C09).

Cooper, B., & Dunne, M. (2000). *Assessing children's mathematical knowledge: Social class, sex and problem-solving.* Buckingham, England: Open University Press.

Cousins, J. B., & Earl, L. M. (Eds.). (1995). *Participatory evaluation in education.* Bristol: Falmer Press.

Daniels, H.R.J. (1989). Visual displays as tacit relays of the structure of pedagogic practice. *British Journal of Sociology of Education, 10* (2), 123–140.

Davies, B. (1995). Bernstein on classrooms. In P. Atkinson, B. Davies, & S. Delamont (Eds.), *Discourse and reproduction.* Creskill, NT: Hampton Press.

Domingos, A. M. (1989). Influence of the social context of the school on the teacher's pedagogic practice. *British Journal of Sociology of Education, 10* (3), 351–366.

Dowling, P. (1998). *The sociology of mathematics education: Mathematical myths/pedagogic texts.* London: Falmer Press.

Ensor, P. (1999). *A study of the recontextualising of pedagogic practices from a South African university preservice mathematics teacher education course by seven beginning secondary mathematics teachers.* Unpublished Ph.D. thesis, University of London, England.

———. (forthcoming). *Producing a sociological analysis of mathematics teacher educator texts.*

Foucault, M. (1963). *Naissance de la clinique: Une archéologie du regard médical.* Paris: Presses Universitaires de France.

Grint, K., & Woolgar, S. (1997). *The machine at work.* London: Polity Press.

Habermas, J. (1984). *The theory of communicative action: Vol. I, Reason and the rationalization of society* (T. McCarthy, Trans.). Boston: Beacon Press.

Hopkins, D., Jackson, D., West, M., & Terrell, I. (1997). Evaluation: Trinkets for the natives or cultural change? In C. Cullingford (Ed.), *Assessment versus evaluation.* London: Cassell.

Latour, B. (1987). *Science in action.* Cambridge, MA: Harvard University Press.

MacBeath, J., Meuret, D., & Schratz, M. (1997). *Quality evaluation in school education: A practical guide to self-evaluation.* European Pilot Project, European Commission, Socrates Programme, Action III.3.1.

Morais, A. M., & Antunes, H. (1994). Students' differential text production in the regulative context of the classroom. *British Journal of Sociology of Education, 15* (2), 243–263.

Morais, A. M., Fontinhas, F., & Neves, I. P. (1992). Recognition and realisation rules in acquiring school science: The contribution of pedagogy and social background of students. *British Journal of Sociology of Education, 13* (2), 247–270.

Morais, A. M., & Miranda, C. (1996). Understanding teachers' evaluation criteria: A condition for success in science classes. *Journal of Research in Science Teaching, 33* (6), 601–624.

Morais, A. M., Neves, I. P., & Fontinhas, F. (1999). Is there any change in science education reforms? A sociological study of theories of instruction. *British Journal of Sociology of Education, 20* (1), 37–53.

Patton, M. Q. (1994). Developmental evaluation. *Evaluation Practice, 15* (3), 311–320.

Pedagogical Institute. (1999). *Internal evaluation and planning at the school unit* (J. Solomon, Ed.). Athens: Pedagogical Institute/Department of Evaluation.

Pels, D. (1996). Strange standpoints: Or, how to define the situation for situated knowledge. *Telos, 108* (Summer), 65–91.

———. (1999, January). *The critical quadrangle: Anti-essentialism in "science" and "common sense".* Paper presented at conference on "The Transformation of Knowledge", University of Surrey, England.

Popham, J. (1993). *Educational evaluation* (3rd ed.). Englewood Cliffs, NJ: Prentice Hall.

Schratz, M. (1997). *Initiating change through self-evaluation: Methodological implications for school development.* Dundee, UK: CIDREE Collaborative Project "Self-evaluation in School Development".

Tyler, W. (1995). Decoding school reform: Bernstein's market-oriented pedagogy and postmodern power. In A. R. Sadovnik (Ed.), *Knowledge and pedagogy: The sociology of Basil Bernstein.* Norwood, NJ: Ablex Publishing Corporation.

Worthen, B. R., Sanders, J. R., & Fitzpatrick, J. L. (1997). *Program evaluation.* New York: Longman.

Appendix

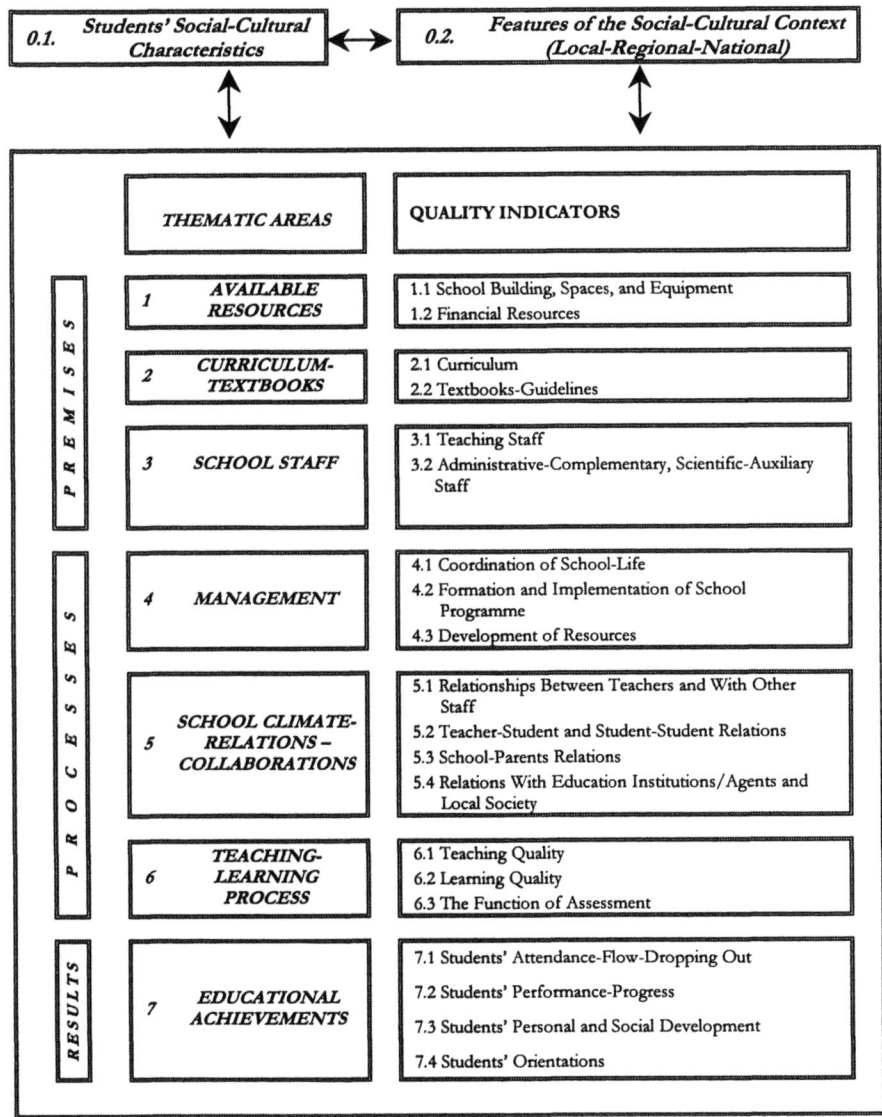

Framework of Thematic Areas and Quality Indicators
Source: PI (1999)

PART 4

Bernstein's Sociology of Education:
Looking Backward and Forward

Chapter 12

Classification Strength and Power Relations

Magnus Haavelsrud

In the classic contribution by Karabel and Halsey (1977), Bernstein was already seen as a "harbinger of a new synthesis" in terms of integrating micro and macro perspectives. Twenty years later his sociological theory of pedagogy has moved in the direction of a synthesis including explicit analysis of power relations. His contribution is therefore of relevance in the continued exploration of wholes in research on education.

It has been pointed out in the introduction to a festschrift in honour of Bernstein that this synthesis is characterised by continuities in his work since his early studies of language and social class (Atkinson, Davies, & Delamont, 1995). The editors see Bernstein's contribution to the study of language as constituting an initial phase. A second phase was introduced with the 1971 publication of "On the Classification and Framing of Educational Knowledge", whereas the third phase (from the early 1980s) attended to pedagogic discourse, educational transmission and pedagogic text. In what follows I review the three phases mentioned with a focus on the discussion of power relations. The concept of classification is a major tool in understanding these relations, in that strong classifications may signify relative autonomy between units whereas weak classifications may involve dominance and subordination between units.[1]

Language Codes, Class, and Power Relations

The first phase in Bernstein's contributions showed how children from the working class were socialised into a restricted language code characteristic of their social experience at home and in their community. This restricted code is adapted to the transmission of the deep meaning structure of the working class to its new members. But when working class children enter the school they are confronted with the elaborated code of the middle class. This meeting between a restricted and an elaborated code in the school is problematic in light of the ideal of equal opportunity, in that working class children are exposed to the discontinuity of having to learn a new code whereas middle class children enjoy the rewards of the fact that the elaborated code learned at home and in their communities is used as a standard of valid knowledge and ways of communicating in the school. The middle class meaning structures are then preferred and the working class children must leave their meaning structures behind and embark upon the task of learning new meaning structures and a set of social relations which privilege middle class children.

The solution to this problem has been debated by many. Some came up with the idea that working class children are restricted in the literal sense of this word. This interpretation leads to the argument of compensatory education for the purpose of learning the elaborated code in pre-school to be better prepared for competition in school with middle class children. Compensatory education is based on the understanding of working class homes as deprived in the cultural sense. This misunderstanding of Bernstein has been developed in many countries and has led to an attempt by Bernstein to distance himself from such policies which in a sense are based on a degrading of large segments of society as inferior to the middle class culture.

One reason for this misunderstanding might be the lack of explicit analysis of power relations in Bernstein's initial phase. In his comparisons between children's speech and the language practices required in school, Bernstein has demonstrated how an elaborated code is useful in transmitting the deep meaning structure of the middle class and how a restricted code is useful in transmitting the deep meaning structure of the working class. The class system limits access to elaborated codes by ensuring that schools are dominated by the meaning structure of the middle class. Thus, working class children are not in a position to enjoy equal opportunity with those whose meaning structure is institutionalised in the school. Bisseret (1979) shows how the early Bernstein ran into this epistemological difficulty when he adopted concepts such as innate intelligence/ability for generalising and understanding abstractions—concepts central to the essentialist theory of aptitude he was seeking to replace with a theory of how language codes could help explain scholastic success.[2] This failure to stay away from essentialist explanations broke with Bernstein's focus on the cultural. This point became even more important when his work was criticised for supporting the old ideology of aptitudes.

The dangerous adoption of essentialist concepts, coupled with the difficulty of staying away from giving value judgments, either on the two codes or on working class and middle class speakers and their cultures, resulted in some interpretations of Bernstein that alleged the deficient culture of the working class and the need for compensatory education at an early age to help working class children acquire the elaborated code of the middle class and the school. Bisseret shows how Bernstein distanced himself from such interpretations of his research by statements to the effect that although elaborated codes give access to alternative realities, they carry the potential of alienation of feeling from thought and of self from other. But Bisseret points to Bernstein's tendency to defend the restricted code not so much by emphasizing its explanatory and logical properties as by characterizing working class culture as warm and inclusive and powerful in its use of metaphors. Bernstein also values stylistic qualities such as simplicity, directness, vitality, and rhythm.

Bisseret questions Bernstein's idea that the elaborated code is the basic code for the objectification of human experience in light of his postulate that the code reflects, symbolises, and relates to the specific experience of a social class. How could it be that the code of one social class could be basic to the objectification of experience in another social class? Bisseret thinks that this contradiction stems from Bernstein's belief that the speech of the dominant class is a more perfected tool. Its linguistic property, such as its conjunctions and lexical forms, enables the speaker to make abstractions from concrete situations. Implicit meaning is transferred to explicit meaning. Bisseret argues that Bernstein continues to accept the dominant group's elaborated code and culture as the standard for explicit and formalised speech, and to accept that this code is more abstract, logical, and useful in developing rational thought. Access to this perfected tool is a central question in the class system. Bisseret points out that the elaborated code is reified by Bernstein in that he admits that it is less tied to a given or local structure and that it can be freed from its evoking social structure. Bisseret suggests that this could be a result of Bernstein's evolutionist view, that changes in the division of labour from a pre-industrial society with mechanic solidarity to the organic solidarity found in industrial societies with a high division of labour condition his reification of the elaborated code.

Bisseret admits that Bernstein is also aware of existing power relations in present-day class society, but she still argues that his real meaning is this:

> One thing is sure: he does not reason in terms of class antagonisms. In his mind, the dominant class does not seem to derive its class position from the existence of the others; it represents a superior degree attained in the course of the evolution of the human species, and each human group is called upon to achieve the same level. As the elaborated code supposedly expresses "the complex differentiated aims of the major society", and not the aims of the dominant class, each one should have access to it [...] he can envisage nothing but an egalitarian distribution of the elaborated code and of the meanings it expresses [...] he cannot imagine a better incarnation of human nature than the human beings of his own class; he remains convinced of the intrinsic superiority of his class's language. (Bisseret, 1979, p. 104)

Bisseret argues that Bernstein's attention is given, not to power relations but to psychologism and voluntarism in that for him the concept of "social structure" is taken to be equivalent to "interpersonal relations" and roles. The explanation for the use of different language codes in different classes does not include reference to dominance relations of age, sex, or class even though age roles, sex roles, and class roles, including language practices, are at least to some extent prescribed by these dominance relations. Bisseret argues that Bernstein's thesis that language practices can be explained with reference to learning different roles in the family is not, contrary to what Bernstein himself thinks, a sociological thesis but one derived from reductionist psychologism.

It seems that Bisseret has a point in her critique of how power relations were analysed in Bernstein's first phase, in that children's learning of an elaborated or restricted code at home is seen as dependent upon whether the parent's class position allows and encourages them to learn different speech systems in a person-oriented middle class family or whether their access is restricted because of the positional and rigid distribution of roles among working class family members. Bisseret argues that this focus on the social-psychological concept of role functions to mask power relations by focusing on explanations limited to interactions between units within the same analytic category. She argues that Bernstein agrees with her that he is "abandoning something of fundamental importance" (Bisseret, 1979, p. 106) when he expresses concern that his analysis "appears to separate the communication structure from the power relationships of society but this can be avoided if the same analysis can show the relationships between class structures and communication structure—which is where we began"[3] (Bernstein cited in Bisseret, 1979, p. 106).

Bisseret's diagnosis is that Bernstein's analysis never dealt with social structure as a whole, except in the evolutionist sense discussed above. And the major stumbling block in understanding power relations is that he studies each code and class in itself and not the relations between them. Bernstein's belief in producing the Truth in social science discourse is not seen as being countered by a realisation of how scientific activity in itself can be a value-laden affair. For instance, Bernstein asserts that restricted codes draw upon metaphors and elaborated codes draw on rationality. Based on this, how does Bernstein evaluate the contribution of metaphors in searching for the Truth as compared to rationality? Bernstein has also asserted that an elaborated code makes it more possible to understand the grounds of one's own socialisation and thereby enter a reflexive relationship to the social order, whereas a restricted code does not allow access to the grounds of one's own socialisation to the same degree, resulting in more limited reflexiveness (Bernstein, 1974, p. 176). Bisseret sees this as avoidance of analysing power relations and she states that Bernstein should have shown

> that class languages slowly took shape as an expression and instrument of social hierarchy in the making. During the whole of the nineteenth century the bourgeoisie forged its class identity and gradually defined itself as "subject", inasmuch as its practices as a whole, including its language practices, allotted to the dominated social categories an identity as objects. Scientific discourse on man has not escaped the grasp of the ideology secreted by the class in power. The breaking up of reality effectuated by the social sciences is no neutral activity: knowledge about man constituted itself by progressively accentuating the categorization and hierarchisation of human beings. A group of signifiers (for example "Aryan" and "Semitic" languages) and their syntactic organization progressively divided reality according to a system of similarities and differences, expressing and recreating at every instant concrete dominance relations. (Bisseret, 1979, p. 108)

In summary, these unresolved dilemmas stemming from Bernstein's early research are pointed out by Bisseret. Her *exposé* of Bernstein is clarifying and critical. She sees Bernstein's research as historic in that it is in the forefront of challenging the old theory that scholastic success could be explained solely by referring to the aptitude of pupils. But the early Bernstein operated as though the linguistic field was autonomous, in that he did not incorporate power relations into his theory:

> By always leaving power relations out of the analysis of linguistic data themselves, by referring them to a sphere outside linguistics, they fail to recognise an important point: class languages established themselves and continue to do so through a *relationship*, and in a manner which is neither relative nor arbitrary; language practices are a fundamental part of class identity, in the definition of which the system of symbolic perception of social relationships has often been omitted. (Bisseret, 1979, p. 91)

It is rather surprising that Bisseret's critical questioning of Bernstein's handling of power relations, his seeming preference for an elaborated code in scientific development, and his failure to see this code as infected by problematic power relations in society as a whole is not picked up by Bernstein commentators. There is no reference to Bisseret's analysis in the 20 contributions in Sadovnik (1995) and the 14 contributions in Atkinson et al. (1995). It is especially surprising to find Apple's (1995) analysis of Bernstein's relationship to the neo-Marxist or Gramscian sociology of education devoid of questions such as those posed by Bisseret. I find this surprising because any movement towards understanding power relations and the place of pedagogy in changing these power relations requires some kind of resolution to the questions posed by Bisseret.

Only in Atkinson (1985, pp. 98–100) have I found attention given to Bisseret's criticism. But this is only to rebut it. Atkinson presents a completely different reading of Bernstein in that he sees power and structural understanding, as opposed to a pluralist juxtaposition of class, ethnic, or regional cultures, as informing all of Bernstein's sociology. Atkinson admits, however, that this often is not recognised because in Bernstein, power is treated in a manner alien to mainstream sociology and because the treatment of power and structure are only implicit in the earlier essays. Thus, power relations emerge more clearly with more explicit structuralist analysis, especially in the theory of codes as explicated by Bernstein in 1981. Atkinson may be right in his argument that concepts of power and structure were implicit in Bernstein's first phase. On the other hand it seems that the criticism referred to above may have been a contribution to Bernstein's sharper focus on such questions in the further development of his theory. Bisseret's interpretation and critique raised some profound questions that might have been a valuable contribution to the evolving discourse about power relations at that time.

I agree with Atkinson that it is quite clear that Bernstein made class relations explicit when he wrote in 1981 that such relations

> refer to inequalities in the distribution of power and in principles of control between social groups, which are realised in the creation, distribution, reproduction, and legitimization of physical and symbolic values that have their source in the social division of labour. (Bernstein, 1981, p. 327)

But I do not find convincing arguments in Atkinson's (1985, p. 99) analysis to support his view that this framework underpinned Bernstein's earlier work on role systems in relation to positional and personal family types and its impact upon language learning. Given the lack of such arguments, it seems that Bisseret's criticism of Bernstein's earlier work should be recognised as a valuable contribution to the discourse. Also, it seems rather restrictive to admit that Bisseret might have an interesting question, but that it is not fit for translation "into an empirical specification in terms of modern descriptive linguistics" (Atkinson, 1985, p. 124). Arguments found in post-Bisseret criticism are irrelevant in terms of accepting or rejecting her criticism. If Bisseret had read Bernstein's important 1971 paper, "On the Classification and Framing of Educational Knowledge", her criticism would have been less relevant. But it seems that her criticism can still be seen as a valuable contribution to how power relations were treated in the first volume of *Class, Codes and Control* in Bernstein's initial phase. And her rather strong criticism may also have been valuable background for the 1981 paper in which Bernstein made the theory of codes more explicit.

Curriculum, Class, and Power Relations

As mentioned, it seems that Bisseret was not aware of the 1971 paper which signaled the second phase of Bernstein's contribution. In the paper it is demonstrated how power and control are transmitted from dominant classes in society via the school by the way the content is classified and the way interactions are framed. The principles of this classification and framing are derived from the meaning structure of the dominant classes and applied to all children in the school. This means that the selected principles have their power and control location in specific social classes or their fractions and are then applied to all. These new concepts were not only designed for the study of specific transmissions in the classroom; they were also useful in achieving an understanding of the organisation of the school as well as the relationships between macro actors in society. Selected principles were seen as fundamental in relaying the domination of middle classes over working classes. Elaborated codes could then be studied in the context of power and control at all levels of analysis, including the policy level at which certain principles were included and others excluded. The principles of classification and framing are decisive elements in Bernstein's concepts of collection codes and integration codes. The collection code is characterised by strong classification (insulation) between categories (discourses, agents, practices) and strong framing in the sense that interactions between teachers and pupils are highly restricted and controlled. The integration code is characterised by weak classification and framing, allowing for flexibility in mixing categories in a process of teaching/learning marked by a greater influence of teacher and pupil in classroom interaction.

The classification and framing analysis made it possible to generate various modalities of elaborated codes: a crucial feature of the theory missed by many critics. Thus, whether a code modality is a relay of class oppression is a question of its classification and framing values.

The Pedagogic Device and Power Relations

The third phase in Bernstein's theory is developed further in his last book, *Pedagogy, Symbolic Control and Identity* (1996). In this sociological theory of pedagogy, Bernstein focuses on the legitimate pedagogic text and how this text relates to the consciousness of the pupil. The legitimate text is defined as any realisation on the part of the pupil which attracts evaluation by the teacher. The legitimate text is the outcome of a pedagogic device which is a construction of utmost importance to the understanding of how the role of education is a construction of dominant forces. Thus, Bernstein has shifted his attention from the means by which given power relations were transformed to the transformator itself—called the pedagogic device. Previously he focused more on the message. In the last book his focus is on the medium or carrier itself. The construction of the pedagogic device is a product of specific rules on how knowledge is recontextualised in the school, how knowledge is distributed at various levels of the formal system of schooling, and how the attainment of this knowledge at the various levels is evaluated. Thus, the main conflicts about the pedagogic device in any society will centre around the rules of distribution, recontextualisation, and evaluation.

A basic feature of the pedagogic device is that the instructional component is always embedded in a regulative component defined by a preference for the values of a specific social order. Thus, the device functions ideologically to safeguard dominant power relations. This hidden characteristic of the device can more easily be detected if academic studies (pedagogic recontextualising field—PRF) is in a position to pursue its research independent of the discourse at the official policy-makers' level (official recontextualising field—ORF).

Bernstein proposes that there is a new arena of struggle to control the pedagogic device, in which there are four competing positions for launching and imposing pedagogic identities. In its retrospective aspect, the projected identity draws on grand narratives of the past (national, religious, cultural). In its prospective aspect, the identity draws on *selected* features of the past which can provide a basis for new motivations, dispositions, and values thought to be relevant to contemporary technological and economic change. These centring identities are contrasted with two opposed decentring positions, one projecting a neo-liberal market identity and the other projecting a therapeutic identity aimed at constituting a flexible and weakly specialised, co-operative participating identity. We have here a new pedagogic palette. Bernstein uses the same model to show the opposition between official identities and the new emerging informal identities arising under conditions of the weakening of identities with a strong collective base, for example, class, gender, and age. It seems that Bernstein has hit the nail on the head with the formulation that dominant pedagogic identity has embedded a retrospective pedagogic culture into a prospective management culture.

Bernstein's sociological theory of pedagogy focuses on the *privileged or legitimate pedagogic text* as any realisation on the part of the acquirer which attracts evaluation. The basic question is seen in reference to this text:

> Does a theory or approach focus upon the pedagogic subject's *relation* to this text in terms of his/her social class, gender, race attributes, or *any other discriminating attribute*, or does the theory/approach focus upon the internal constituents of the privileging text in the process of its transmission and acquisition at the level of the classroom or school (at the micro level) or educational systems (at the macro level)? (Bernstein, 1990, pp. 173–174)

In order to talk about reproduction, resistance, and transformation, it is, according to Bernstein, necessary to analyze the relationship between the "privileging text" and the consciousness of the pedagogic subject. In order to analyze this relationship, it is necessary to know what has been positively and negatively acquired. This implies that it is necessary to specify the rules regulating the construction, representation, and contextualising of the privileging text, that is, specifying the relations within (cf. Bernstein, 1990, p. 178).

Classification strength is the means by which power relations are transformed into specialised discourses, and framing is the means whereby principles of control are transformed into pedagogic relations which attempt to relay a given distribution of power. At the time Bernstein published the paper on classification and framing (in 1971), he was more concerned about the means by which *given* power relations were transformed. At that time the *transformator* was not made explicit. His 1990 paper on the pedagogic device focuses more on the medium—the carrier or the relay of power—than on its message or what is carried or relayed—or how power is translated:

> The theorizing of the pedagogic device enabled the integration of macro levels of analysis with institutional and interactional levels. The classification and framing analysis assumed what at the time was not available: the analysis of the construction of pedagogic discourse. While code modalities translated distribution of power and principles of control into forms of pedagogic communication and their contextual management, it was not entirely clear whose power and control was translated. (Bernstein, 1996, p. 3)

This new focus on the transformator itself may be seen as the "missing link" which might have been a basis for Bisseret's earlier criticism. The analysis of pedagogic discourse is basic in the construction of the pedagogic device. *Pedagogic discourse* is defined

> as a rule which embeds two discourses; a discourse of skills of various kinds and their relations to each other; and a discourse of social order [...]. From one point of view, pedagogic discourse appears to be a discourse without a discourse. It seems to have no discourse of its own. Pedagogic discourse is not physics, chemistry or psychology. Whatever it is, it cannot be identified with the discourses it transmits [...] pedagogic discourse is a principle, not a discourse. It is the principle by which other discourses are appropriated and brought into a special relationship with each other, for the purpose of their selective transmission and acquisition. Pedagogic discourse is a principle for the circulation and reordering of discourses [...]. We shall see later that this principle does give rise to a specialised discourse [...] *pedagogic discourse is a recontextualising principle.* Pedagogic discourse is constructed by a recontextualising principle which selectively appropriates, relocates, refocuses and relates other discourses to constitute its own order. (Bernstein, 1996, pp. 46–47)

One might well ask why Bernstein uses the word "discourse" when he actually means a rule or a principle. Would it not be better if he called it, for example, "the principle of reordering discourses"? A decisive question seems to be whether this principle or rule is explicitly formulated or whether it is hidden and implicit. It would seem that any principle can be made explicit, even that "recontextualising principle which selectively appropriates, relocates, refocuses and relates other discourses to constitute its own order". Another question is to what extent any given state tends to hide the secret formula for the construction of this ideological State apparatus (Althusser, 1971). The rules of distribution, recontextualising, and evaluation regulate the outcome of the device. The impact of the pedagogic device upon potential pedagogic meanings is decisive for what is relayed by the device. The device functions ideologically to safeguard dominant power relations. This leads to conflict about it and a possible outcome is "a form of communication which can subvert the fundamental rules of the device" (Bernstein, 1996, p. 42).

Basic to any pedagogic device is that the instructional discourse is embedded in the regulative discourse. This means that dominant preferences for social order are fundamental to the understanding of both hidden and explicit curricula. Empirical studies of how the instructional discourse is embedded in the regulative in different societies and contexts would contribute to the understanding of how power relations in a society are manifested in attempts at monopolising what Bernstein calls the *pedagogic discourse*. His point that the relationship between the official recontextualising field (ORF) and the pedagogic recontextualising field (PRF) is crucial to the question of autonomy of education is especially important at a time when it seems that the State in many countries attempts to monopolize the discourse. Already in his chapter on the "Aspects of the Relations Between Production and Education" (1977), Bernstein proposed that the relative autonomy of education from production would be characterised by strong classification between them and that the influence of production over education would be more possible when the classification is weak. Obviously, the latter is the case in recent developments demonstrated by the great interest of the economic sector in convincing the official recontextualising field, that is, the State, of selecting the pedagogic principles to be adopted in newly formed pedagogic devices (cf. the analysis of developments in Norway: Haavelsrud, 1996, pp. 287–294; Hovdenak, 1998, 1999, 2000; Wille, 1999).

This shift in official ideologies over the last 30 years from an ideology of competence to an ideology of performance can be understood as a change in the dominant ideology of the pedagogic device. The previous emphasis on the pupil's inner commitments and possibilities (dedications) has been replaced by short-term instrumentalities or short-termism, in which the formal school is seen as a contributor to modernisation and economic growth. In this quest for performance, a greater emphasis is placed on a new identity construction in which identities can be achieved through an explicitly entrepreneurial/vocational culture of the new rationality of the school. This is contrary to previous cultural punctuations in terms of ascribed identities such as age, gender, and age relations. These are now weak resources for stable, unambiguous, and lasting identities. The pedagogic device has therefore become an instrument of discontinuities from early socialization patterns—discontinuities that are based on the needs of transitional capitalism.

Thus, chapter 3 in Bernstein's 1996 book is an empirical illustration of the theory of how pedagogic discourse in the official recontextualising field (ORF) has shifted from *competence* (inner commitments and dedications) to *performance* (short-term instrumentalities or short-termism). The conflict about the pedagogic device both in the official and in the pedagogic recontextualising fields is a conflict related to the question of *pedagogic identities*:

> those identities which were given a biological focus (age, gender, age relation), "ascribed" identities, have been considerably weakened, are ambiguous and to some extent can be achieved. These cultural punctuations and specializations (age, gender, age relation) are now weak resources for the construction of identities with a stable and collective base [...] locational "achieved" identities of class and occupation have become weak resources for stable unambiguous identities. This weakening of stable, unambiguous, collective resources for the construction of identities, consequent upon this new period of transitional capitalism, has brought about a disturbance and disembedding of identities and so created the possibility of new identity constructions. (Bernstein, 1996, p. 76)

Power Relations and Relative Autonomy

It seems obvious that Bernstein's contribution to the understanding of how power relations are translated into pedagogic practice is a great contribution to understanding educational systems both at micro and macro levels. However, it would be helpful to the reader if investigations of the pedagogic device and the official and pedagogic recontextualising fields had foregrounded the analysis of hegemonic power and how a given power relates to its reproduction and translation in education. Related to this problem of analysing power is the question of utilising a possible relative autonomy in the pedagogic recontextualising field in which different modes of both competence and performance models can interact in such a way that peripheral and even oppressed voices can be heard in the pedagogic discourse.

As a supporter of the "radical mode" of the competence model, I had hoped that Bernstein in future work would be able to take a closer look at how new power relations could be created with the help of education or at least how knowledge could be *translated* into new power relations. Analysis is also needed of how pedagogic devices constructed in isolation from an autonomous pedagogic recontextualising field could become so hostile to the hidden message that the pedagogic device in a nation could, at least, contribute to the collapse of established power. This would mean that the *pedagogic device* could be a contributor to power creation and not only to its translation. Central to this analysis is the relationship between micro and macro in that power from below is obviously generated in micros. This means that an important research investigation would be one dealing with the conditions necessary for the development of an alternative pedagogic device. Such conditions would also have to be analyzed as a political problem in that the influence upon the State from social movements and political struggles would be decisive. In the research available there is not sufficient analysis of the function of the struggle between social groups and classes, that is, the political influence upon education, compared with the attention that has been given to the relationship between education and production. It seems that a focus upon the creation of priorities in political struggles may be a road to follow in the search for conditions for alternative pedagogic devices involving code modalities allowing for knowledge production rather than reproduction. Elsewhere (Haavelsrud, 1996, pp. 196–216), I have discussed the concept of democratic global governance. This concept belongs to the global discourse and it seems necessary to focus on the trans-national level in addition to the sub-national levels to find answers to conditions for new forms of pedagogy. As Giddens (1994) has pointed out, new forms of dialogic democracy involve both sub-national and trans-national levels. This implies that trans-national organizations with sub-national roots might become an even more important political force in time to come. This rather recent characteristic of political formations may underlie the recent interest of states in delving into questions of how even higher education can contribute to peace building, understood as non-violence, justice, and human rights.[4]

Bernstein (1990, p. 178) notes the possibility of placing any theory concerning the relationships between micro and macro in terms of what its concerns are and are not. His critique of Bourdieu includes his point that Bourdieu views education as a carrier of power relations external to education and that he does not subject the carrier itself, education, to analysis. I am not aware that Bourdieu has responded to this critique. If Bourdieu foregrounds power external to education and Bernstein analyses how power is translated in education, then a third contribution is needed, an analysis of how education translates into power external to it, that is, helps create new power relations (cf. McLaren, 1997, pp. 520–541). The question remains to what extent a pedagogic device could be dialogic and a source of change. It seems that a further development, of a possible synthesis incorporating education as liberation, would have to produce a better understanding of whether and under what conditions a pedagogic device could be constructed from within and how power could be generated from this device. It seems certain that one condition would be an active and powerful pedagogic recontextualising field, which in turn might be conditioned by a society characterised by dialogic democracy (Giddens, 1994; Haavelsrud, 1996, chaps. 9 and 13). This implies a solution to the problem of the strong classification between the inner and the outer and the dislocation of knowledge from the knower, which as Bernstein has pointed out is characteristic of educational systems in Western society. And it implies a relative autonomy of education, which means in Bernstein's understanding a strong classification between economic interests and educational discourse. It also implies a solution to the concept of inclusion in that its meaning would have to be extended to resolve the problem of the dominance of the new middle class[5] over symbolic control. These conditions for transformative or border pedagogy represent enormous challenges in many societies. On the other hand, the critical discourse available through social exclusion theories is there to stay, and the step into practice might not be too overwhelming, at least in some societies. It is of interest to note that Bernstein acknowledges oriental societies in the way the gap between the inner and the outer is bridged. It seems that comparative research might assist in revealing the differences across civilizations and religions in terms of some of these important concepts.

Bernstein (1996, p. 5) is concerned that his specialised focus shall remove to the background the larger concerns of education in terms of its relation to democracy. This new dimension in the contribution from Bernstein—describing a value for research—should be noted. This glimpse of the background of his research is greatly appreciated as it contributes to the wholeness of his contribution and it provides a foundation for that bridge that needs to be built between policy-driven research and policy-detached research. His description of democratic rights, as I read it, makes a meeting of minds possible about some items on the agenda of peace education and conscientisation (Haavelsrud, 1996, chaps. 2–8). He writes, about democratic rights, that enhancement has to do with boundaries and experiencing boundaries as tension points between the past and possible futures [...] it is the right to the means of critical understanding and to new possibilities [...]. The second right is the right to be included, socially, intellectually, culturally and personally. Now this right to be included is complex because to be "included" does not necessarily mean to be absorbed. Thus the right to be included may also require a right to be separate, to be autonomous. Inclusion is a condition for communitas and this right operates at the level of the social [...]. The third right is the right to participate [...]. Participation is not only about discourse, about discussion, it is about practice, and a practice that must have *outcomes*. (Bernstein, 1996, p. 7)

It is a great challenge to pedagogic research to become more involved in the construction of the pedagogic device, because it is decisive for the very idea and practice of democratic values. A State that attempts to exclude autonomous research on pedagogy, abandon such research, or co-opt it, has prepared the ground for monopolising the construction of the pedagogic device. This means that the State would be in a better position to regulate "the relationships between power, social groups, forms of consciousness and practice" (distribution rules), "regulate the formation of specific pedagogic discourse" (recontextualising rules), and also provide the criteria for evaluation (evaluative rules).

Combined with Bernstein's interest in democratic values is an explicit focus on *power relations*. His most recent formulations repeat the importance of understanding how classification strength

> is the means by which power relations are transformed into specialised discourses, and framing [...] is the means whereby principles of control are transformed into specialised regulations of interactional discursive practices (pedagogic relations) which attempt to relay a given distribution of power. (Bernstein, 1996, p. 3)

As it was not clear, from the analysis of classification and framing, whose power and control was translated, it became necessary to develop the theory of the *pedagogic device*. The pedagogic device cuts across levels and makes possible an integration of macro levels of analysis with institutional and interactional levels of analysis.

Bernstein's recent contribution is of great significance in guiding the development of both the official and the professional pedagogic discourse. Research is needed to determine whether and how the combination of retrospective and managerial identities is becoming increasingly important in school ideology (Brown, 1997, pp. 736–750; Hovdenak, 2000). How is consciousness going to be formed to fit what Brown calls the "flexible paradigm" as opposed to the obsolete "bureaucratic paradigm"? How will managerial principles manifest themselves in interactions in the classroom? This developing principle of flexibility should look for a code of conduct contrary to the one dominated by a bureaucratic paradigm: a personalized selection of job seekers, negotiated rule-making based on interpersonal cooperation, charismatic personalities, team work, and personalized and implicit rules in modes of social control and personal compatibility. The old paradigm was rule-following and inter-positional, its associated leadership style was command and control, and its mode of social control was impersonal and explicit. Authority was based on position and status. How would children from different social classes react to a school based on a reward system that gave preference to flexible managerial ideology? Which retrospective narratives are selected as valid knowledge in a world characterised by transitional capitalism based on the idea of equal opportunity to climb towards specific standards of true versus false knowledge, good versus bad values, and beauty versus ugliness? What are the characteristics of the common culture or standard compared with the variety of cultures found in multicultural society (McLaren, 1997)? As we know, also in reference to Bernstein's earliest research, the deep meaning structure of a culture is variable in the sense that different standards concerning knowledge, values, and aesthetics are present. It is my belief that Bernstein's 1996 book has contributed to the theory of how education can be understood in the context of the overall development of society in which equitable and democratic developments are at stake. I thank Bernstein for making more explicit his interest in democratic and fair development in which pedagogic devices become the center of discussion.

Notes

1. Code modalities vary with the strength of both classification and framing. Both of these vary according to the degree to which they are internally or externally influenced. The most recent discussion of the complexity of various code modalities is found in Bernstein (1996, pp. 17–38). In this chapter I focus mainly on the classification dimension and its external value. This means that I do not discuss the complexity of various combinations of degrees of internal and external influence in both classification and framing.

2. Bisseret was invited by Bernstein to give a seminar in the Department of the Sociology of Education at the University of London before the book was published, and he also

recommended that her book should be published (interview with Bernstein, 1997). In her book, Bisseret relates only to the early Bernstein, that is, to papers available in the 1968 publication, *Class, Codes and Control (Vol. I)*. I do not know why Bisseret has not taken a closer look at, for instance, the paper entitled "On the Classification and Framing of Educational Knowledge", which was first published in Young (1971).

3. A personal note: Three small episodes come to mind. My father used to tell us about the village doctor who greeted his fur coat. Comparing two different encounters with the doctor made him conclude this. In the first encounter my father appeared as a peasant and without his fur coat—in the second encounter he appeared as a local politician on his way to a municipal council. The doctor stopped to greet him only in the second encounter, namely, in the encounter when my father had his fur coat on. At a conference in Varanasi I was guided by a young Indian who showed me silk factories, the Holy Temple, and cremations of corpses along the River Ganges. He also pointed out castles and estates of kings and other rich people. When he pointed to yet another castle, I asked him if he ever talked to the people living there. No, he said, rich man talks to rich man, poor man talks to poor man. In a third episode, on an estate outside of Nairobi, I ended up in a bar one evening with the servants on the estate discussing, among other things, the problem of why some people primarily work with their heads and other people primarily work with their hands. On the way back to the estate, I was told by one of my, I thought, newly acquired friends, that tomorrow we do not know each other. Obviously, crossing the gap between far-away social realities could be threatening to them and their position in the structure in which they made their living. I do not know how the doctor would have told the story about greeting my father's fur coat (if he had known it at all), how the king of Nepal would have answered my question as to whether he ever talked to the poor man, and how the noble, white Englishman who owned the Nairobi estate would have valued my newly acquired friends. But all of these episodes are examples of interactions between centres and peripheries in which a meeting takes place between the strong and the weak, that is, they are examples of power relations. In all three of these episodes I was an observer or a third party. I *heard* my father tell me about his experience with the village doctor who greeted his fur coat. I *talked* with the poor Indian teenager who did not speak with the rich man, and I *talked* indirectly with the servants at the Nairobi estate about their relationship to their boss.

I do not discuss here my own experiences of power relations—partly because many of them are personal and confidential. I make one exception related to my education as a boy in a patriarchal, class society. One day I accompanied my peasant father to the village. Maybe I was 5, 6, or 7 at the time. On our way between offices and shops, we encountered one of the lawyers in this rather peripheral village. The lawyer spoke the centre language, had university degrees, and belonged to a different class. As a local politician my father knew him, and they talked. I was waiting for their conversation to end while displaying my peasant *habitus* by keeping my hands in my pocket. Then, suddenly, like lightning from clear skies, came the command from the lawyer whom I had never met before: "Get your hands out of your pocket!" As the reader will understand, this episode impressed me so much that I find reason to convey it 50 years later as an example of power relations at work. I think now it must have been an interesting blend of ageism, classism, and patriarchy. This was one of my first experiences of power relations in daily life involving someone outside my family. It was not the last. I continue to experience power relations every day even though they take new forms. I am not always on the losing side as in the example related. It could be of interest to others as well as myself to attempt a more thorough reflection on the sum total of such experiences.

4. A recent example is a conference in May 2000, at the University of Tromsø, Norway, on "Peace Building in Higher Education" *(www.peace.uit.no)*.

5. In 1977, Bernstein introduced the concept of the "new middle class" and since then this formation has been an important unit in the analysis of symbolic control as it varies with the "old middle class". In a recent discussion of the "new" and "old" middle classes as they relate to the development of the new flexible paradigm and the desired code of conduct in this new managerial ideology, Brown (1997, p. 745) overlooks this important contribution by Bernstein.

Bibliography

Althusser, L. (1971). Ideology and the ideological state apparatus. In B. Brewster, *Lenin and philosophy*. New York: New York Left Books.

Apple, M. W. (1995). Education, culture and class power: Basil Bernstein and the neo-Marxist sociology of education. In A. Sadovnik (Ed.), *Knowledge and pedagogy: The sociology of Basil Bernstein*. Norwood, NJ: Ablex Publishing Corporation.

Atkinson, P. (1985). *Language, structure and reproduction: An introduction to the sociology of Basil Bernstein*. London: Methuen.

Atkinson, P., Davies, B., & Delamont, S. (Eds.). (1995). *Discourse and reproduction: Essays in honor of Basil Bernstein*. Creskill, NT: Hampton Press.

Bernstein, B. (1971). On the classification and framing of educational knowledge. In M. Young (Ed.), *Knowledge and control* (pp. 47–69). London: Collier Macmillan.

———. (1974). *Class, codes and control: Vol. I, Theoretical studies towards a sociology of language* (2nd ed.). London: Routledge & Kegan Paul.

———. (1977). *Class, codes and control: Vol. III, Towards a theory of educational transmissions* (2nd ed.). London: Routledge & Kegan Paul.

———. (1981). Codes, modalities and the process of cultural reproduction: A model. *Language and Society, 10*, 327–363.

———. (1990). *Class, codes and control: Vol. IV, The structuring of pedagogic discourse.* London: Routledge.

———. (1996). *Class, codes and control: Vol. V, Pedagogy, symbolic control and identity: Theory, research, critique.* London: Taylor & Francis.

Bisseret, N. (1979). *Education, class language and ideology.* London: Routledge & Kegan Paul.

Brown, P. (1997). Cultural capital and social exclusion: Some observations on recent trends in education, employment, and the labour market. In A. H. Halsey, H. Lauder, P. Brown, & A. Stuart Wells (Eds.), *Education: Culture, economy, society.* Oxford: Oxford University Press.

Giddens, A. (1994). *Beyond left and right.* Cambridge: Polity Press.

Haavelsrud, M. (1996). *Education in developments.* Tromsø, Norway: Arena.

Hovdenak, S. S. (1998). *Pedagogic discourse as a hegemonic discourse.* Paper presented at conference on "Knowledge, Identity, Pedagogy", University of Southampton, England.

———. (1999). *Critical aspects of the Norwegian education reform process.* Paper presented at conference on "Does History Matter: Stability and Change in Education", Department of Education, Norwegian University of Science and Technology, Trondheim.

———. (2000). *90–tallsreformene: Et instrumentalistisk mistak?* Oslo: Gyldendal Akademisk.

Karabel, J., & Halsey, A. H. (1977). Educational research: A review and an interpretation. In J. Karabel & A. H. Halsey (Eds.), *Power and ideology in education.* Oxford: Oxford University Press.

McLaren, P. (1997). Multiculturalism and the postmodern critique: Towards a pedagogy of resistance and transformation. In A. H. Halsey, H. Lauder, P. Brown, & A. Stuart Wells (Eds.), *Education: Culture, economy, society.* Oxford: Oxford University Press.

Sadovnik, A. R. (Ed.). (1995). *Knowledge and pedagogy: The sociology of Basil Bernstein.* Norwood, NJ: Ablex Publishing Corporation.

Wille, T. (1999). *"Kringsatt av fiender": Utdanningspolitikk i klemme mellom pedagogiske idealer og næringslivets interesser?* Thesis written for major subject as part of the Cand. polit. degree, Institute of Education, University of Tromsø.

Young, M. (Ed.). (1971). *Knowledge and control.* London: Collier Macmillan.

Chapter 13

Crosswired: Hypertext, Critical Theory, and Pedagogic Discourse

William Tyler

> Cybernetics, in conjunction with language theory, discloses the real methodology by which a normalized society will be produced.
>
> [Kroker & Cook, 1984, p. 240]

Although computer-mediated learning appears to provide the potential for the most significant educational transformations of the coming century, pedagogic uses of the new information technologies are under-theorised in mainstream educational research (Thumlert, 1997, p. 1). Their advent has been greeted by one of two rather simplistic and unnecessarily polarised reactions. More generally, institutional response has been characterised by an optimism which, though technological and functionalist in origin, has affected many literary and educational theorists who see the communicative possibilities of the new media (particularly of hypertext) as potentially democratising, emancipating, and transformative. This response has been matched by a critical and reflective pessimism, common among social and cultural theorists within education faculties, who emphasise the new media's potential for deskilling and dehumanising teaching and learning, primarily as extensions of the neo-liberal impulse towards more efficient and mechanical forms of educational delivery. This chapter argues that both of these extreme positions may be avoided by a recognition of the convergence between the de-centring, deconstructive tendencies of contemporary culture and the recontextualising logic of pedagogic discourse, as delineated in Bernstein's later writings.

The following argument is intended, therefore, to open up a critical space that has not hitherto existed in sociological and culture-theoretical discussions of the pedagogical uses of the new media. The questions raised by this chapter are not new and can be found clearly articulated in many of the writings on media theory and pedagogy, as the following extract from a cultural studies web site attests:

1. How have pedagogical theories and strategies responded to (grown out of) post-modern theories of identity, authority, knowledge?

2. Where are the affinities, or convergences, between new pedagogies and the capabilities of new technologies? In what ways are process-centered, learner-centered models enhanced and enabled by distributive media?

3. What are some useful categories by which we can explore/test the convergences between distributive media and distributed learning? Are hypertext pedagogies the same or different from collaborative pedagogies? Is computer mediated communication (CMC) a substantively different pedagogical tool than constructive hypermedia pedagogies?

4. How does the issue of "knowledge" figure into the media/pedagogy relationship? What are some theoretical or methodological approaches that we can use to begin sorting out some of the possible relationships among knowledge/media/pedagogy? (Bass, 1996)

Compelling as the issues raised here may be, they have met with little original theoretical attention. This seems to be because they fall outside the scope of the available frameworks of cultural and critical accounts of digitalised culture (Valentine, 2000), which are not, in the main, concerned with the distinctive semiotic features of pedagogic discourse. The core of the argument developed here is that the polarisation of contemporary positions over educational uses of the Internet may be overcome by a recognition of the convergences and affinities that exist between the post-structuralist theories of hypertextuality and the recontextualising principle embedded in all forms of pedagogic discourse and its attendant devices and practices. This insight, which extends my previous applications of the social semiotics of pedagogic discourse to contemporary issues such as school reform (Tyler, 1995) and national curricula (Tyler, 1999), is based largely on a collection of papers by the late Basil Bernstein, published as *Class, Codes and Control, Vol. IV* (1990). It is argued that Bernstein's theory of pedagogic discourse provides a particularly valuable basis for generating a descriptive model not only of the applications of the virtualising technologies to educational contexts but also, reflexively, of the less explicit pedagogic processes of a digitalised culture.

This chapter develops the argument in the following way:

1. Setting out a context which draws on the author's experience of developing a widely used online educational resource on the World Wide Web;

2. Outlining the major theoretical responses to the challenge of hypertext-based learning which might be drawn from this experience;

3. Critically evaluating the relevance of Bernstein's theory of pedagogic discourse to the debates emerging from these interpretations, which have a bearing on contemporary educational issues; and

4. Developing a model drawn from Bernstein's recent writings on the regulative and instructional context of pedagogic discourse.

The concerns of this chapter are not those of mainstream sociology of education (the effects of class, gender, ethnicity, and race on educational processes and outcomes); they are unashamedly directed towards the task of generating descriptions of the distinctive internal features of pedagogic discourse. As Bernstein (1990) has put it: "Any theory of cultural reproduction must be able to generate principles of description of its own objects" (p. 171). In this instance, there are so many material issues of access, economy, and technology surrounding the educational applications of the new media that there is a danger that their truly transformative potential may be either obscured or misrecognised. This would be a great loss, not only because the discursive aspects of hypertextuality are at present poorly understood, but because a better understanding of pedagogic discourse may generate insights into the way virtualised forms of knowledge are produced, disseminated, and consumed through digitalised media. It is no accident, then, that Bernstein, in what was sadly to be his last paper (see this volume), spoke of the emergence of the Totally Pedagogised Society, prefigured in the triumphalism with which politicians greeted the electronic revolution. To the extent that society may be becoming "pedagogised" through the new media, the discursive dynamics of pedagogy deserve critical examination, if only to avoid the danger of their being absorbed in the void of their own simulacra.

Developing an Online Educational Resource: A Tertiary Education Example

Since any discussion of media is probably meaningless without some sense of context, my recent experience in creating an online educational site is offered as a basis for later discussion. This experience may then serve as a point of departure for critical reflection and theoretical interrogation.

At the Northern Territory University (NTU) in Australia, I co-ordinate a fairly large (300–400 students per annum) interdisciplinary course (called a "unit"), delivered in both face-to-face and flexible delivery (off-campus) modes. The unit, North Australian Studies, is one of several common units which are compulsory for all first year students. This course was, therefore, developed over several months, as the result of a management initiative, without any underlying pedagogic principle other than that its content should have regional relevance. It turned out to be something of an agglomeration covering a wide range of disconnected topics related to North Australia and the Northern Territory, in particular, political development, literary representation, physical geography, economic development (especially mining), law and order issues, Aboriginal culture, and state policies relating to Indigenous peoples, architecture, and the built environment—to name only the more prominent topics. Lectures are delivered and prepared by academic specialists from various faculties. Very little attempt was made to integrate or to thematise the topics across lectures or tutorial sessions.

To combat this fragmenting tendency in the structure and delivery of this course, I decided to develop an online resource on the World Wide Web which would be available to all students, on and off campus, and would integrate these topics. I found an integrative theme in a single issue—the proposed uranium mine development at Jabiluka near Darwin. This was and is an extremely controversial project, supported by both local and national governments, but opposed by the traditional Aboriginal peoples who own the land and by conservationist and ecological groups who object not only to uranium mining but to a development which has been excised from a world heritage site, Kakadu National Park, a unique wetland and escarpment wilderness area (made popular in the Crocodile Dundee movies). The peak of media interest in this issue came in 1998–1999 with a blockade of the site, a negative report from the UN World Heritage Committee, and a condemnatory motion from the European Parliament. The project has been the subject of several hundreds, if not thousands, of dedicated or closely related web sites produced by advocacy and governmental groups and agencies. It constituted a ready-made yet undeveloped resource for the North Australia unit, unifying as it did all of the topics dealt with in the unit—modernisation and Indigenous culture, economic developmental, ecological and conservationist, constitutional and political.

Using resources made available by the management for this online project, I clustered the many web sites under various topic headings and then layered each cluster in terms of its local, national, or international relevance. This produced a design which made access and exploration reasonably "user-friendly". The interconnectedness of these clusters was to some extent provided by the embedded links within the various sites themselves—Indigenous sites had reports countering official government agency impact statements; heritage sites had policy statements on mining; industry sites had Indigenous policy statements, and so on. However selective these may have been, and however polarised the position taken by the hosting agency or group, the individual sites provided a rich source of interrelationships which the student was enticed to explore.

To further counter the politicisation of the educational resource, I provided an online tutorial which presented a critical guide to both pro and anti perspectives. The site was developed with "state-of-the-art" graphics and internal links and put on the World Wide Web in February of 2000. The site has proven to be very popular with many students and lecturers at NTU. The site was subsequently used as a recruiting device by senior university management and has been given prominence among the home page links of Indigenous, green, and environmental education agencies. In the June 2000 issue of *National Internet Magazine* (*Internet.au*), the Jabiluka site (Tyler, 2000) was selected as the "Readers Site of the Month" and given a relatively rare five-star rating.

This limited experience of online education raises many important questions as to the pedagogic principles which underlie applications of the new technologies:

- Why was the translation from the primary or "real world" discourses of political debate, ecological and scientific knowledge, economics, and engineering and constitutional literatures into an educational resource (i.e., a pedagogic device) so apparently easy to achieve and so seamlessly produced? Was the availability of this wealth of material really so opportune, or did it contain hidden dangers and deceptions?

- How well did the thematic development of the issues achieve the pedagogic goal of course development and integration? Was the topical integration sufficient to induce the students to look for wider relationships between, say, Indigenous land rights and economic development, local and supra-national politics, the position of the nation state, the role of multinational companies in local economies, and the complexities of legal controls on the varied uses of uranium?

- How could one be sure that the checks and balances of impartiality in the representation of viewpoints and in the guided tutorial introduction would achieve a worthwhile educational outcome—that is, a critical consideration by the students of the arguments for and against the proposed mine, rather than a partial and ideological response which conformed to pre-existing prejudices—in other words, how would the material be read (if at all, in a conventional sense, rather than merely browsed)?

- Had this whole online project, in other words, merely been an exercise in the further fragmentation of the subject matter of this course, the increased polarisation of student viewpoint, the provision of further support for managerial controls over the production, development, uses, and marketing of academic output?

Open Textualities, Closed Technologies: Two Faces of Online Learning

These questions led me inevitably back to a reconsideration of the writings of Bernstein on the nature of pedagogic discourse, writings which have for so many years guided my own thinking about the nature of teaching and learning in practice, as well as about the theoretical understanding of the social and cultural influences and effects of teaching and learning. Coincidentally, the exercise of producing a web site came at the same time as I was choosing a topic for the Lisbon symposium, whose papers are the basis for this volume. My choice was driven by the fact that my own institution, despite making redundant several social scientists who had been delivering the internal program, was actively expanding, promoting, and funding the off-campus teaching and learning division. Was I confronting a defining moment in the future of higher education? If so, the understanding of this transformation assumed enormous significance which gave a particular edge to the usual critiques of neo-liberal tendencies in educational management, the diminishing role of the State in educational provision, and the deskilling of academic employment. As Peters asks,

> Who owns the Internet? What are the patterns of access and participation? What is the structure of multinational ownership in the new telecom monopolies? What is the relationship between the new telecommunications leviathans and the policies of deregulation? How will these developments impact upon the university and traditional concepts of knowledge and learning? (Peters, 1998, p. 85)

I turn, therefore, to consider the ordering principles of the virtualised forms of education produced by the online technologies, as they have been engaged in the existing literature. This review helps to define not only the deficiencies in this literature but also the particular challenges this form of the pedagogic device presents to Bernstein's own theory of pedagogic discourse.

To begin, I need to define and position the basic pedagogic device of web-based teaching and learning—"hypertextuality"—a feature which enormously expands and transforms the communicative possibilities of teaching and learning through the use of intertextual linkages. These open up possibilities which are radically different from the authored, linear, sequential, and stable textualities of print technologies and conventionally paced classroom learning and teaching. The complexity and structure of these linkages within and across texts facilitates a high level of interactivity between reader and text. At present, this interactivity is achieved at the navigational level but, in more sophisticated versions, it may also be achieved at the functional and adaptive level, where intertextual choices are attuned to the users' own preferences and tastes, and even their subjective goals and desires (Floridi, 1999).

The most significant literary and pedagogical definition of hypertext in other than purely technological language is to be found in Landow's seminal monograph, *Hypertext: The Convergence of Contemporary Critical Theory and Technology* (1992). Landow defines hypertext in terms of structuralist genealogies as the ideal form of textuality which draws heavily from literary theory:

> In *S/Z*, Roland Barthes describes an ideal textuality that precisely matches that which has come to be called computer hypertext—text composed of blocks of

words (or images) linked electronically by multiple paths, chains, or trails in an open-ended, perpetually unfinished textuality described by the terms link, node, network, web, and path: "In this ideal text," says Barthes, "the networks [*réseaux*] are many and interact, without any one of them being able to surpass the rest; this text is a galaxy of signifiers, not a structure of signifieds; it has no beginning; it is reversible; we gain access to it by several entrances, none of which can be authoritatively declared to be the main one; the codes it mobilises extend *as far as the eye can reach*, they are indeterminable [...]; the systems of meaning can take over this absolutely plural text, but their number is never closed, based as it is on the infinity of language"(emphasis in original; 5–6 [English translation]; 11–12 [French]). (Landow, 1992, p. 3)

The implications for teaching and learning of such a rupture of the traditional positioning of author and reader, as Landow argues, are quite radical and potentially emancipating:

One chief effect of electronic hypertext lies in the way it challenges now conventional assumptions about teachers, learners, and the institutions they inhabit. It changes the roles of teacher and student in much the same way it changes those of writer and reader. Its emphasis upon the active, empowered reader, which fundamentally calls into question general assumptions about reading, writing, and texts, similarly calls into question our assumptions about the literary education and its institutions that so depend upon these texts. (Landow, 1992, p. 120)

While Landow, like many other literary theorists (see Landow, 1994), views these developments optimistically, as emancipatory in their potential for destabilising the authoritarian relations assumed by traditional teacher and text-centred pedagogies, many left-critical theorists with strong institutional knowledge of recent educational reforms typically take a more cautious view. Peters and others (Peters & Roberts, 2000), for example, ground their critique of the uses of virtualising technologies in tertiary systems within a political economy paradigm informed by neo-Marxist readings of post-modernity and based on the experience of neo-liberal educational reform in Australia and New Zealand, seen against a background of changes in global capitalism. Their concerns are with the commodification of knowledge, the dissolution of academic authority, the repression of critical perspectives, and the triumph of utilitarian and managerial ideologies in the digitalisation and delivery of curriculum content. In other words, the shift from knowledge to information has the potential for obliterating the humanising, socially and culturally located fields of critical and reflective practices which have formed the core of institutionalised pedagogies in Western tertiary education systems. While this tradition is already being contested by the new managerialism as a form of "elitist nostalgia" (Gaita, 2000, p. 26), the potential for further undermining through the de-institutionalisation of teaching and learning is enormous. Peters concludes:

> To be provocative, one might say that the post-modern university, or the university in post-modernity, will come to exist solely in cyberspace with no need for large installations, campus buildings, libraries or lecture theatres. No need, perhaps, for large multicampus metropolitan universities. In the short term, each individual multicampus university may become functionally wired through the benefits of the new technologies, and universities in turn functionally wired through more effectively as a truly unified system of information flows and exchanges. In the intermediate term—and possibly twenty years hence—they may become outmoded and the concept of a university or even a national university system (in the longer term) simply another anachronism. By then we will, no doubt, have approached the fully, integrated, functionally wired, cybernetic society. (Peters, 1998, p. 89)

The polarisation of these perspectives, crudely put, between the literary/post-structuralist post-modernists and the Left-critical interpreters of the post-modern condition—may reflect the novelty of the challenges of hypertext. In Bernstein's terms, such a disjunction, between the possibilities of the instructional discourse and the constraints of the regulative, recalls a moment not unlike that confronted by sociologists in the early 1970s— between "interpretive" and "normative" perspectives: an unfortunate debate, which Bernstein's own writings did so much to resolve. Might Bernstein's theories be similarly applied to the present challenges of hypertextuality or do they need to be significantly rethought and recast to meet the communicative challenges of the new media?

Pedagogic Discourse and Post-modernity

At first blush, the new virtualising technologies have the potential to deconstruct, if not completely undermine, Bernstein's entire project of development of a theoretical framework of pedagogic discourse, that is, a bounded and distinctive field of knowledge transmission. This claim can be made on the following grounds, proceeding from the surface to the deeper structures of the theory:

- At the instructional and interactional levels, by dissolving the distinction between teacher and the taught, through the de-privileging of pedagogic authority, teachers could simply become machine minders rather than creative agents of the educational process. The communicative basis of instructional discourse is "de-authored".

- At the regulative and institutional levels, by effectively dissolving the institutional boundaries of the historical forms of educational organisation which have been the focus of so much of Bernstein's theorising—schools, colleges, and universities—along the lines suggested by Peters, to the point where we may approach the "fully integrated, functionally wired, cybernetic society". School systems might become simply integrated, multinational corporations, delivering educational products through the globalised methods of flexible production (usually typified as post-fordism). Society would then in a radical sense be ultimately "de-schooled", though not, of course, in the critical, emancipated sense advocated by Ivan Illich (1971).

- By making the class basis of knowledge transmission and acquisition become increasingly problematic. Although the outcomes of education may be shaped by inequalities such as access to informational technologies, the transformation of the school from an agency for imparting life and work-related skills to one which merely provides commodities for individualised consumption radically alters its position in the reproductive process. Learners and teachers become consumers, rather than producers and reproducers, of knowledge.

- By the immediacy and simultaneity of the hypertext form dissolving the distinctions between space and time which are the foundational categories of the classification and framing of knowledge and its contexts of transmission. If all knowledge is reduced by space-time compressions (the pedagogy of the compressed?) to processes of electronic storage and retrieval, accessible in indeterminate form, not only are the modernist enclosures of home and school, work and play, public and private rendered problematic or inoperable, but so too are the distinctions between the partitioning of knowledge (classification) and its sequencing (framing). While the space-time distinction, in Bernstein's descriptions, has always been a source of contention (Dowling, 1999), hypertext dramatises its fundamental instabilities.

- By the individualised market-driven logic of the new technologies eroding the specialised role of the school as an agency of moral regulation, as the most powerful reproducer of the ethical codes of modernity, the habits of work and sociality, as well as the cognitive forms which these sustain. Since Bernstein inherited this vision of the functions of the school from Durkheim, as the basis for any analysis of the moral crises of modernity, the relationships between pedagogy and the socio-economic order are thrown into disarray.

How can the changing forms of pedagogic discourse be a response to the moral crisis of late capitalism, if pedagogic discourse is so imbricated in this crisis itself? If the pedagogic device is based on an aesthetic rather than an ethical order, if knowledge is degraded to commodified packages of information, if teaching and learning are driven by the logic of seduction rather than by conceptual depth and intellectual integrity, then how can the pedagogic device sustain its relationship to the social, the moral, and the political which have defined its boundaries and its constitutive principles of order and control? Is the whole theoretical framework of pedagogic discourse merely a product of high modernity, attuned to and complicit with a particular age of mass-institutionalised and classroom-delivered instruction? Does the notion of pedagogic discourse itself have any meaning if it loses both its conventional face-to-face instructional core and also its embeddedness in the regulatory apparatus of educational bureaucracy?

In response, I argue that Bernstein's theory is not only well developed to meet with these challenges, but may also be central to an understanding of the dynamics of contemporary culture which have eluded so many of the prophets of the post-modern, cybernetic, and digitalised age. Undoubtedly considerable work needs to be done to theorise adequately the applications of Bernstein's theories to the challenges of the virtual classroom. However, the potential already exists within Bernstein's original formulations of the pedagogic device for recasting the relationships between pedagogic communication and virtualising technologies in terms of their similarity and convergence, rather than their erasure and rejection.

As I have argued elsewhere (Tyler, 1995, 1999), pedagogic discourse appears to exhibit the semiotic features that typify the virtualising culture of what has been called the post-modern condition (Lyotard, 1984). In fact, one might argue that many instances of post-modern culture, or rather what might be termed "post-culture" (Crook, Pakulski, & Waters, 1992), are infused by a de-institutionalised form of the invisible pedagogy, especially in its ludic manifestations such as the "leisure principle", "edutainment", and so on. This congruence appears to be mirrored in the fascination which educational practices hold for literary theorists such as Landow (1992), in the allegedly infantilising effects of contemporary American culture captured in Baudrillard's (1981) use of Disneyland, and in the affinities between Rorty's anti-representationalism and the pragmatic philosophies which underpin both the progressive educational writings of Dewey and the emerging media theories of the Internet (Sandbothe, 1998). Put another way, it would appear that an understanding of the social semiotics of pedagogic discourse may provide some powerful insight into the way in which the global, homologous, and virtual signifiers of cyberspace are realised within the diverse, localised contexts of subjective experience.

The convergence of education with the virtual world of hypertext as the intertextual play of signifiers that escape the strictures of representationalism is most strongly suggested by Bernstein's identification of the re-contextualising principle as constitutive of pedagogic discourse:

> Pedagogic discourse, then, is a principle which removes (de-locates) a discourse according to its substantive practice and context, and relocates that discourse according to its own principle and selective reordering and focusing [...]. Pedagogic discourse creates imaginary subjects [...] in this sense, it has no discourse of its own, other than a recontextualising discourse. We have now made the move from the distributive rules to the recontextualising rules which constitute pedagogic discourse. (Bernstein, 1990, p. 184)

When incorporated into an explicit pedagogic device, hypertext, therefore, invokes a secondary repositioning (or, more broadly, a secondary field of recontextualisation) with the digitalised objects of the virtualised field. While this insight raises the level of abstraction, it also provides the basis for a new transparency which may be the grounds for resistance, subversion, and rupture as well as an informed and critical basis for pedagogic practice. If educational applications of hypertext may be expected to exhibit the same indeterminacies, semiotic fractures, closures, and distortions of signification that typify the post-modern condition, conversely, one might be led to perceive the hidden pedagogic devices that underlie many, if not all, virtualised forms of contemporary culture.

These convergences and affinities between the semiotic field of hypertextuality and that of pedagogic discourse appear to provide a basis for a reflexive secondary reshaping of the recontextualised field of hypertext and for a creative reconstruction of the already virtualised and chaotic order of cyberspace. The convergences between the two orders of recontextualisation suggest a space for a creative exploitation of the informational sources of the Web as well as opportunities for critical repositioning of its materials in innovative pedagogical form. What remains is to specify the dimensions of this space in terms which are consistent with Bernstein's previous writings on pedagogic discourse in both the instructional and the regulative context.

Dimensions of the Virtual: Hypertext as Pedagogic Device

What is now required is a more specific model which can identify the positions and the dynamics of pedagogic communication under conditions of post-modernity. Such a model may at the same time reappropriate the semiotic order of post-modernity (such as floating signifiers, breakdowns in chain of signification), as indicated by post-structuralist theories, to a critical pedagogic purpose. Hypertext-based learning may have the potential (competence) for creating the ideal pedagogic device—one in which the ideal text (as suggested by Barthes) is located within what Habermas calls *the ideal speech situation*, as suggested by Ess (1994), which stresses the equality and freedom of each participant. However, the realisation of such an outcome in pedagogic discourse depends on (1) a critical exploration of the claims for the openness of hypertextuality against an analysis of its hidden communicative logic, its restrictions and distortions, or, in structuralist terms, its surface as opposed to its hidden features, in an environment characterised by information richness rather than information scarcity, and by a multiplicity of formalised voices and channels rather than a single pedagogic authority; (2) an exploration of the inter-relationships between the features of a hypertext-based instructional discourse and the dominant regulative discourses represented in the pedagogic identities and positions of contemporary educational policies and ideologies.

The "hidden curriculum" of hypertext

The claim that hypertextual documents represent an essentially open and indeterminate communication completely controlled by the reader (student) must be seriously questioned. Floridi (1999) challenges this notion as "the 'politically correct' fallacy" (pp. 123–125). He argues that this view (the reader's "liberation movement") confuses the physical and the conceptual levels of analysis and that the logical possibility that all hyperlinks may be equivalent relations (all connected, reflexive, symmetric, and transitive) is rarely realised in any one hypertext document. Almost all acquire a hierarchical structure based around a home page so that

> In practice the hypertext author can make one semantic universe available to the reader but certainly not every universe. The reader's navigation is *wilfully* constrained by the reader as well as by the writer around an axial narrative and it is usually very clear what is text and what is paratext (the footnotes, titles, etc). (Floridi, 1999, p. 125)

Floridi (1999) argues that the openness of the hypertext document is illusory, in that "the network of links is not meant to be alterable and only a selection of alternatives is allowed to the reader, whose degree of freedom is constrained by the author's original project and the cost/benefit ratio which determines the process of marking the whole set of documents" (p. 124). Since books are by no means uniquely linear or closed, it is more useful to see hypertext as anything but a "relational organisation of digital documents". Other critics, such as Thumlert, have seen a similar constriction which masks the political and economic forces shaping reader's choices:

> In this way, self-contained, educational CD-ROM products denied a wider, active "linking" interface may confer to the reader certain liberties in organizing information but may still circumscribe content and pre-ordain specific conclusions drawn from a given body of information, in effect, emulating "the work". Similarly, specialised educational search engines can, through specific programming algorithms, limit, filter and normalize the appropriate range of hypertextual discourse, in effect, emulating the "net-nanny", the hypertextual censor as benevolent patriarch. And central to educational concerns here, the broader and continuing organization of the Internet and the World Wide Web by corporate and private interests, information administrators, and digital technocrats jeopardizes (and poses important *classroom* questions about) the democratic and civil applications of information technologies. (Thumlert, 1997, p. 15)

While the hypertext document is socially constructed and, therefore, open to distortion, so too are the rules of interaction between reader, author, and text (as well as between readers themselves). Who can speak digitally—and to whom can one speak—are questions that provide as many possibilities of constraint by a hidden authority as do the internal, organised linkages of the text. Just as a text may be internally structured (linear/nonlinear) by the hidden hierarchies of links and choices, the possibilities for reader interactivity, the lines of communication and access are subject to rules which determine the varying levels of openness and closure to responses to the primary text. A rich source of possibilities for computer-mediated communication in education is provided by a survey of online learning by Paulsen (1995). Among others, Paulsen cites the Canadian study of McCreary and Van Duren (1987) which lists ten such configurations, ranging from the more conventional "structured seminar" through to the free-wheeling "inter-community networking".

The hidden principles which regulate the selection and configuration of the formalised (and therefore legitimised) channels of communication mirror those encountered in the structuring of the hypertext linkages in the published content. As these formerly unincorporated, implicit, occasional, and unstructured features of instructional discourse are mobilised and integrated into the formal possibilities of discourse, we confront an interactional or organisational equivalent of hypertextuality which may, however tentatively, be termed "hypervocality". This term is preferred to the more restrained Bakhtinian term, "multivocality", used by Landow (1992, p. 11) to reflect and capture the underlying principles of organization rather than its surface features of complexity. This feature of online learning may be defined as the apparently unconstrained and prodigious multiplicity of voices or formalised channels of communication, whose surface feature is that of an unrestrictive inclusiveness.

The regulative problematic here, as we shall see below, is the converse of the field of communicative regulation of conventional face-to-face teaching and presents a different kind of problematic as excess replaces scarcity: too much immediate information rather than too little, and the possibility of over-multiplication of vocality or formal channels of interaction—no longer the disciplinary problematic of asserting a single dominating voice (whether realised by the univocality of the printed text or the multivocal possibilities of an informal classroom). In this case, the organisation of communicative possibilities—How many voices are recognised? How are they "wired"? What ultimate status does each have?—are the objects for critical study. An analysis of the internal rules by which voices are formalised, connected to one another, and monitored may expose the covert forms of closure of hypertext-based pedagogy which, however seductive, may be only the appearances of informality, spontaneity, and inclusiveness.

While the surface features of hypertext and computer-mediated conferencing may offer the possibilities of ideal text embedded in an ideal speech situation, their regulative modalities present the perfect conditions for ideologically determined closure, however well disguised. The latent closures that may reside in any pedagogic device have, of course, been confronted before, in Bernstein's typologies of the invisible/visible pedagogies (1975), where overt permissiveness concealed performative closures that benefitted children of the new middle class. What distinguishes this form of the pedagogic device from invisible pedagogy, however, is not merely its level of abstraction but the indeterminacy of the boundaries which define its institutional location and internal organisational insulations. There appear to be two main dimensions to this distinction: (a) no longer do we have the home-school-work triplet of modernity which contained the sandbox environment of the invisible pedagogy within an insulated pedagogic space but, rather, a radical openness to the whole non-discursive environment, a permeability which embraces commercialisation and commodification of the pedagogic device just as the device can put up very little defence against the distortions of political activism, cultural nostalgia, or therapeutic promise; and (b) while the invisible pedagogy stood against the visible pedagogy, as a kind of modernist and stable binary, in any single hypertextual or virtualised device even these boundaries become blurred, as an authoritarian, lecture-centred course may be paralleled by a "user-friendly" and permeable conferencing and chat-room apparatus.

Pedagogic identity as regulative discourse

In the absence of walls, institutions, and stable boundaries and hierarchies between the teacher and taught, the home and the school, the classroom and the world, where can one find the regulative principles of pedagogic discourse in a virtualised learning environment? The beginnings of a particular model for theorising the interfaces between hypertext-based instructional modes and the regulative discourses of contemporary policy can be approached through modelling the four pedagogic identities as set out by Bernstein in several of his later writings (1995, 1996, 1999). I have argued elsewhere (Tyler, 1999) that "de-centred market" and "de-centred therapeutic" identities, on the one hand, and "retrospective" (e.g., fundamentalist, elitist) and "prospective" (reconstructed along lines of race, region, and gender) identities, on the other, are rarely found in their pure form and that regulation emerges from the dynamic interrelationships ("opposition and collaboration") or interchanges among them as they are incorporated into any one pedagogic device (e.g., a national curriculum, which may hold elements of all four identities in a particular discursive formation).

In my 1999 publication, I proposed a further opposition between the exchanges of two de-centred identity positions (i.e., market and therapeutic) and those which are associated with re-centring, through cultural and political processes. In Durkheimian terms, the first interplay could be identified with the process of organic solidarity (complexification) and the latter with the process of mechanical solidarity (cf. Baum, 1976). The full regulatory field is set out in Figure 13.1, which follows the structuralist logic of Bernstein's more general model of the macro-micro context of pedagogic discourse. In this adaptation, I loosely associate the temporalised (past/future) order of the re-centring positions with hypertextuality (i.e., the syntagmatics of how the text is to be read) and, by analogy, I associate the spatialised order of the de-centring positions with hypervocality (i.e., the paradigmatic configuration of legitimised voices). It must be emphasised, however, that these are merely suggestive lines of opposition for descriptive and analytic purposes and are not meant to restrict the range of possibilities of positional interchange in any empirical example.

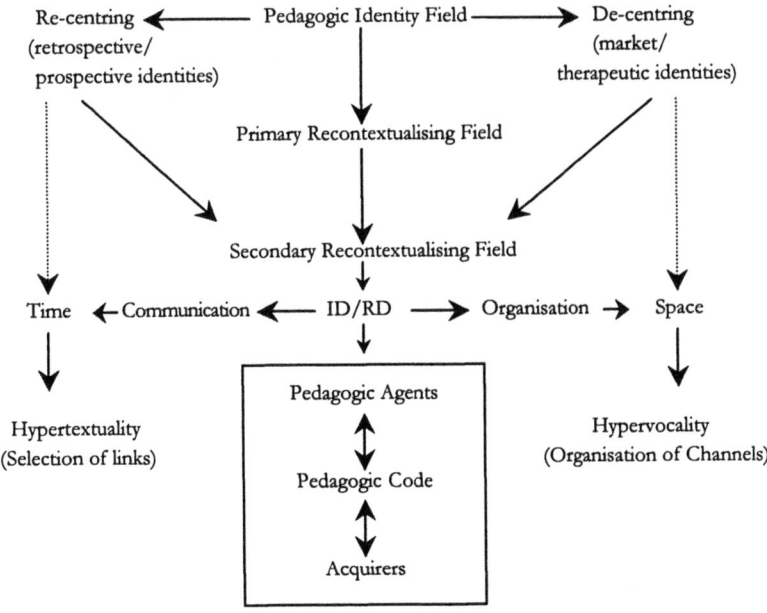

Figure 13.1—*The Discursive Field of Online Teaching and Learning (adapted from Bernstein's generic model of pedagogic discourse, 1990).*

The problematic posed by this descriptive model (Figure 13.1) is the nature of the interface between the pedagogic uses of hypertextuality and hypervocality on the one hand and the ideologically accented modalities of pedagogic identity on the other. What happens, for example, when different kinds of instructional modalities (variety enhancing, variety reducing) are positioned within different regulative fields which might be identified, as Bernstein has shown, in terms of four positions typical of contemporary educational ideologies and policy frameworks? An empirical question that might be explored through an application of the descriptions of the discursive processes set out in Figure 13.1 is: By what coding principles will the communicative possibilities of the new technologies at the instructional level (hypertextuality, hypervocality) be adopted by the regulative demands of various contemporary identity fields? Would an adherent of a more regressive identity position, for example, be more likely to adopt strategies which exhibit greater or less explicitness in the ordering and configuration of hypertext linkages?

While it is far too soon to argue on the basis of empirical evidence, one might speculate that there will be a degree of "elective affinity" or congruency between the variety-producing identity positions (instrumentalist, therapeutic) and those sites which project an appearance of transparency, openness, and evidentiality (such as a scientific government agency), although these are features which rely on covert bounded rules of exclusion and orchestration of vocalities. On the other hand, we might find that sites located in retrospective identity fields, those (elitist, fundamentalist) whose explicit interests are self-proclaimed and closed, are unexpectedly thrown open to questioning by the deconstructive potential of the medium itself. An analysis of the internal structuring of sites which present creationist and evolutionary perspectives in junior high school science courses would be an instructive test of the model.

Conclusion

It is clear, then, that Bernstein's theories of pedagogic discourse are not only adequate in providing a description of educational applications of hypertext under conditions of post-modernity but they also lay bare many of the latent dynamics and structures of the communicative features of the condition itself. This re-working of Bernstein's formulation of the recontextualising field illustrates the resilience of the fundamental categories of classification and framing, or temporality and spatiality, in contexts which seem at first sight to be far removed from their original modernist sites of development—home, classroom, and workplace. The insulations and hierarchies of these institutional forms may be seen to be reproduced in the communicative and organisational logic of the virtualised field and, therefore, to be open to the same kinds of critical enquiry which inform other interrogations of the processes of social and cultural reproduction.

It now remains to consider the situation of those authors/transmitters who wish to distance themselves from all of the positions of contemporary debate and merely use the vast resources of the infosphere to construct spaces which maximise critical thinking. Thumlert suggests a model for pedagogical uses of the Web grounded in critically informed structures:

> It must be emphasised, here, that a "grounding" does not take place in existing, monological structures of knowledge and truth-value, but through praxis. It is a "grounding" construed in terms of what Deleuze and Guattari call "nomadic centers": structures and reference points—they call them plateaus—that allow knowledge to cohere in unfinished, mobile patterns that remain, themselves, provisional and subject to critique; in effect, generated from the processes and activities of critique. (Thumlert, 1997, p. 18)

When this suggestion is interpreted through Bernstein's model of pedagogical communication, it would appear that the core pedagogical task would be to identify those cultural and political centres which might be the basis for a stabilisation of perspective (or corrective to a vertiginous fragmentation) without falling into the closures of "identity politics", moral panic, or nostalgic foundationalism. These dangers, as seen above, become all too obvious when dealing with a heavily contested topic such as the Jabiluka resource, with which I began this discussion—yet their value as a resource for critical departures is crucial. One should not be unaware, as I was, perhaps, in developing the Jabiluka site (Tyler, 2000), of the distortions of the pedagogical context itself, notably of the uses of management interests in exploiting the interdisciplinary and fluid structures of hypertext as a device for utilitarian "defragmentation", that is, the abolition of academic specialisms and disciplines through managerial or system imperatives rather than for intellectual and pedagogic integration.

The openness of hypertext and of the interactive potential that it holds for the remodelling of teaching and learning is enormous. However, unless its applications are informed by a critical theory of pedagogic communication, an awareness of its principles and dynamics which can locate its dynamics within patterns of complexity and stability, it risks being misappropriated by the distortions of ideological, political, and managerial interests, becoming the medium of an unreflective, de-centred, and de-historicised subjectivity and, as Valentine (2000) has warned, the instrument of a covert, intrusive, and ubiquitous governmentality.

Bibliography

Barthes, R. (1982). *S/Z*. Paris: Editions de Seuil. (R. Miller, Trans.). New York: Hill & Wang.

Bass, R. (1996). *A bigger place to play, or text, knowledge and pedagogy in the electronic age* [Online]. Available: *http://www.otal.umd.edu/~googie/bass/unit8.html* [December 12, 2000].

Baudrillard, J. (1981). *Simulacres et simulations*. Paris: Editions Galilee. (P. Beitchmann, Trans. *Simulations*. New York: Semiotexte).

Baum, R. C. (1976). Communication and media. In J. J. Loubser, R. C. Baum, A. Effrat, & V. M. Lidz (Eds.), *Essays in honor of Talcott Parsons: Vol. II, Explorations in general theory in social science*. New York: Free Press.

Bernstein, B. (1975). *Class, codes and control: Vol. III, Towards a theory of educational transmissions*. London: Routledge & Kegan Paul.

————. (1990). *Class, codes and control: Vol. IV, The structuring of pedagogic discourse*. London: Routledge.

————. (1995). A response. In A. Sadovnik (Ed.), *Knowledge & pedagogy: The sociology of Basil Bernstein*. Norwood, NJ: Ablex Publishing Corporation.

————. (1996). *Class, codes and control: Vol. V, Pedagogy, symbolic control and identity: Theory, research, critique*. London: Taylor & Francis.

————. (1999). Official knowledge and pedagogic identities. In F. Christie (Ed.), *Pedagogy and the shaping of consciousness: Linguistic and social processes* (pp. 246–261). London: Cassell.

Crook, S., Pakulski, J., & Waters, M. (1992). *Postmodernisation: Change in advanced society*. London: Sage Publications.

Dowling, P. (1999). Bernstein in frame: "Oh dear, is this a structuralist analysis?" [Online]. Available: *http://www.ioe.ac.uk/ccs/dowling/kings1999* [May 25, 2000].

Ess, D. (1994). The political computer: Hypertext, democracy, and Habermas. In G. P. Landow (Ed.), *Hyper/text/theory*. London: Johns Hopkins.

Floridi, L. (1999). *Philosophy and computing: An introduction.* London: Routledge.

Gaita, R. (2000). Truth and the university. In T. Coady (Ed.), *Why universities matter: A conversation about values, means and directions* (pp. 26–71). Sydney: Allen & Unwin.

Guay, T. (1995). *Web Publishing Paradigms* [Online]. Available: *http://hoshi.cic.sfu.ca/~guay/Paradigm/Adaptive.html* [December 12, 2000].

Illich, I. (1971). *Deschooling society.* New York: Harper & Row.

Kroker, A., & Cook, D. (1984). *The postmodern scene: Excremental culture and hyper-aesthetics.* New York: St. Martin's Press.

Landow, G. P. (1992). *Hypertext: The convergence of contemporary critical theory and technology.* London: Johns Hopkins.

———. (Ed.). (1994). *Hyper/text/theory.* London: Johns Hopkins.

Lyotard, J. F. (1984). *The postmodern condition.* Minneapolis: University of Minneapolis Press.

McCreary, E. K., & Van Duren, J. (1987). Educational applications of computer conferencing. *Canadian Journal of Educational Communication, 16* (2), 7–15.

Paulsen, M. F. (1995). *The Online report on pedagogical techniques for computer-mediated communication* [Online]. Available: *http://home.nettskolen.nki.no* [March 8, 2001].

Peters, M. (1998). Cybernetics, cyberspace and the politics of university reform. In M. Peters and P. Roberts (Eds.), *Virtual technologies and tertiary education* (pp. 74–92). Palmerston North, New Zealand: Dunmore Press.

Peters, M., & Roberts, P. (2000). Universities, futurology and globalisation. *Discourse: Studies in the Cultural Politics of Education, 21* (2), 125–139.

Sandbothe, M. (1998). Pragmatic media philosophy and the Internet [Online]. Available: *http://www.uni-jena.de/ms/pi.html* [June 24, 2000].

Thumlert, K. (1997). Hypertextuality and sociocultural contexts for education [Online]. Available: *http://home1.gte.net/grnjeans* [January 15, 2000].

Tyler, W. (1995). Decoding school reform: Bernstein's market-oriented pedagogy and posmodern power. In A. R. Sadovnik (Ed.), *Knowledge and pedagogy: The sociology of Basil Bernstein.* Norwood, NJ: Ablex.

———. (1999). Pedagogic identities and educational reform in the 1990s: The cultural dynamics of national curricula. In F. Christie (Ed.), *Pedagogy and the shaping of consciousness: Linguistic and social processes* (pp. 262–289). London: Cassell.

———. (2000). Jabiluka: An online educational resource. *Common units home page*. Northern Territory University, Darwin, Australia. [Online]. Available: *http://learnline.ntu.edu.au/commonunits/jabiluka*. Reviewed on Readers Site of the Month, *Internet.au* (Issue 56, June 2000, p. 102).

Valentine, J. (2000). Information technology, ideology and governmentality. *Theory, Culture and Society, 17* (2), 21–43.

EPILOGUE
Coda: Basil Bernstein Speaks

From Pedagogies to Knowledges

Basil Bernstein

I find myself in an unusual, if not difficult, position and certainly an embarrassing one. All of which may seem a singularly ungracious beginning. But I say this only to signal that I am not up to the responsibility of this final meeting. Clearly I should, whilst recognising the imaginative research contributions and their implications for development, address the central object of our meeting which is less my contribution to a sociology of pedagogy but more the nature and potential of a sociology of pedagogy. I would love to join in the discussion of the papers as another researcher responding to the work of others, but there has been very adequate discussion. So my contribution should be to furthering the discussion not of the papers but of a sociology of pedagogy. And that is where the difficulty and embarrassment begins. It begins because I have never felt, consciously at least, that I was working towards opening a new field of enquiry. I can remember that I used the description socio-linguistic to some of my papers, and happily went or gave seminars, not because of a commitment to a new field of study but because the title offered a temporary identity at a time when such a marker of belonging was very scarce. So it was a relief to be known by others as a something, yet my interest in language was essentially semantically driven. Language was the structuring interface by means of which a complex set of ordering and disordering processes were specialised by the social base of its speakers. What was paramount for me was the identification of origins of these ordering and disordering processes, their maintenance and change. Yet I could not have written this at the time when I was sheltering within this temporary identity. I can give another example of the quandary I find myself in today. I was appointed a professor in the University of London in the sociology of education in 1967 but I strenuously and successfully managed to avoid ever giving an inaugural lecture; a unique professional contribution, marked by an absence rather than a presence. I did not give an inaugural lecture because it is expected that it would reveal how the incoming professor regarded her/his field of activity and his/her trajectory within it. And this I knew was beyond me. It requires a general vision, a sense of the past, and the possibilities of its future, which I lack. So I always managed to avoid any general statements about fields, old or new. To do this I think requires a particular attitude and more importantly mode of engagement with the relevant field where the literature of that field is the crucial source of the professional identity and where the social interactions that flow from this mode of engagement reflect back and enhance this identity. I can offer as evidence for this absence of a field, or mode of engagement, the fact that I have written only one paper on the sociology of education itself. And I wrote that paradoxically to show the so-called new sociology of education was a spurious construction. I remember that the paper ended with "what is required is less allegiance to an approach but more dedication to a problem". I was very surprised later to be discovered as a structuralist and therefore operating within an approach. However, this marker included me in the sociology tribe at least by the back door of social anthropology but more likely by the Durkheimian orientation. Now Durkheim was an interesting case. He identified, or made explicit, a unique level of analysis, the sociological, and the procedures of its analysis, and through his empirical studies revealed the level of analysis in action, so to speak. Durkheim towers above us by the imaginative grandeur of his apparently diverse studies, yet connected to us I believe by his deep interest in and exploration of boundaries which certainly had a lasting influence on me or I brought it to my reading of his work.

So this introduction is a long apology for my inability to do what is expected here. In fact I am a little amazed that I have got as far as this. I think like Durkheim one can identify and make explicit the social base of the pedagogic relation, its various contingent realisations, the agencies and agents of its enactments. One can begin to formulate a language for the description of the production and reproduction of its discourses. At a more general level such a study connects with the maintenance and change of the knowledge base of society, and crucially with the maintenance and change of modalities of symbolic control, especially those implicated in the process of cultural reproduction. The pedagogic relation is that relation which normalises the intimacies of desire, and public aspiration, conduct, and its practices, through its shaping by macro structures. However, its discourses make available at the level of individual consciousness the means of disturbing such normalisation. If the pedagogic relation is so implicated in the knowledge base of society and its consequences, and the modalities of symbolic control often associated with the knowledge base, how is it that it has not been a crucial site of sociological analysis since Durkheim? Today we are told that we are entering a new societal mode brought about by the electronic revolution, and Castells has christened this new societal mode the Informational Society. It is very chic to run seminars, conferences, produce readers on Changes in the Knowledge Base of Society. But Blair's celebration of "Education, Education, Education" as the missionary position of New Labour is saying something quite different, although it appears in Blair's speech as a condition for the effective informational society and changing knowledge base. What is missing in the new discourse is the triumphant silence of the voice of pedagogic discourse as we move into the second totally pedagogised society; the first being that of the medieval period initiated by Religion. In the medieval period there was a seamless coordination of meanings, activities, and practices through the Catholic Church; a simple division of labour of symbolic control but all-pervasive in its functions, the realisation of a wholly coherent world and of place, position, and function within it.

Today in the United Kingdom there is growing evidence of the developments of T.P.S., that is, a Totally Pedagogised Society. New Labour is providing the agents and the Universities are providing the discourses, especially departments of education. Thus we now learn that every teenager is to have access to a counsellor to enable the adolescent to map an appropriate career; a rather strange choice of words when careers are being replaced by jobs. Teenagers are then to be positioned in flexible time which translates as being able to be re-positioned whenever and wherever external change requires. Family units, whatever form they take, are new sites for parenting skills. So another pedagogic translation is possible; family units become parenting skills. The world of work translates pedagogically into Life Long Learning and this is both the key and the legitimator of T.P.S. It is not difficult to see how the management of short-termism, that is, where a skill, task, area of work, or the like undergoes change, disappearance, or replacement, where life experiences cannot be based on stable expectations of the future and one's location in it, translates paradoxically into socialisation into T.P.S. via life long learning.

Now under these new conditions a vital new ability must be developed: trainability, that is, the ability to profit from continuous pedagogic reformations and so cope with the new requirements of "work" and "life". The concept of trainability places the emphasis upon "something" the actor must possess in order for the actor to be appropriately formed and re-formed according to technological, organisational, and market contingencies. This "something", the key to trainability, which is now crucial to the survival of the actor, crucial for the economy, and crucial for society, is the ability to be taught, the ability to respond effectively to concurrent, subsequent, or intermittent pedagogies. Cognitive and social processes are to be especially developed in the actor for such a pedagogised future. However, the ability to respond to such a future depends not upon an ability but upon a capacity. The capacity to enable the actor to project himself/herself *meaningfully* rather than relevantly or instrumentally into this future. It must be a *meaningful* projection if the past is to be recovered as a coherent past. The meaningfulness of time does not rest on an ability. In this sense, effective forming and re-forming rests upon something other than its own process. This capacity for meaningfulness is the outcome of a specialised identity. This identity cannot be constructed by lifting oneself up by one's bootstraps. It precedes the endless process of pedagogic forming and re-forming. It is not a purely psychological construction by a solitary worker as he/she undergoes the transition which she/he is expected to perform on the basis of trainability. This identity arises out of a particular social order, through relations which the identity enters into with other identities of reciprocal recognition, support, and legitimation, and finally through a negotiated *collective* purpose. The concept of trainability, the key to life long learning and life long learning itself, the mode of socialisation into the Totally Pedagogised Society, erodes commitment, dedications, and coherent time, and is therefore socially empty.

If the identity produced by trainability is socially empty, how does the individual recognise himself/herself and others? Such recognitions are by the materialities of consumption, by its distributors, by its absences. Here the products of the market relay the signifier whereby temporary stabilities, orientations, and evaluations are constructed. I have referred to the social emptiness of trainability, the condition for the pedagogy of the short-term. For Richard Sennett *The Corrosion of Character* is his translation of flexibility, short-terminism, when he asks, "How do we decide what is of lasting value in one's lives in a society which is impatient, which focuses on the immediate moment. How can long term goals be pursued in an economy devoted to the short term? How can mutual loyalties and commitments be sustained in institutions which are constantly breaking apart or continually being redesigned? These are the questions about characters posed by the new flexible capitalism" (Sennett, 1998).

However, in terms of the analysis here the focus is less on flexible capitalism but on its pedagogic expression and its management. And here the so-called weak state of the Global Economy is the strong state, for the T.P.S. is state driven and state funded, state focused and state assessed. Today the State through processes of centralised decentralisation, with its management strategies of resources following achieved targets, is making and distributing the possibilities of new pedagogic "knowledges" through a range of formal and informal agencies. Thus a new cadre of pedagogues, with their research projects, recommendations, new discourses, and legitimations, are being constructed. In turn this calls out new forms of training for these burgeoning positions and a flood of new journals assist in both professional specialisation and central assessment. Publishing houses are quick to ensure that these new professional discourses are served by a continuous supply of exposition, comment, criticism, evaluation, and of course international comparison. This benign circle of pedagogic inflation does not create autonomy for either the trainers or the trained, for both become subject to the targets set by the State. It would be a useful contribution simply to map the movements I have briefly described, the flowering of the discourses developed, the cost and patterns of recruitment.

More complex is the analysis of the contents and the recontextualising work the contents presuppose. From another point of view, the legitimations of the contents, that is, not simply the rationales for their existence, but also the effectiveness of the contents as treatments.

Is there now a common diagnostic language? An official diagnostic of the pathologies and therapies for the new period we are entering? To what extent is this language a preparation for, perhaps the means of, socialisation into new sets of expectations about our futures? We have now travelled some distance from a sociology of pedagogy.

I think now, looking forward, that a sociology of pedagogy does not indicate or suggest the conceptual development necessary to grasp the discursive culture for which we are being prepared. The term pedagogy has restrictive references, despite my attempt to expand its use. It also operates at too low a level of abstraction to serve as a macro-micro mediator. Neither does it point to the phenomena to be described. It is, however, crucial for one's understanding of the contextual management of transmission/acquisition and their code modalities.

What we require today is a conceptually generated systematic description through which the lower levels of past analyses can be integrated and projected on to the wide screen of contemporary change, imaginary and actual. I have lately been attempting what could be called a sociology for the transmission of knowledges.

Such a sociology would focus on the diverse sites, generating both claims for changes in knowledge forms and displacement of and replacement by new forms, creating a new field of knowledge positions, sponsors, designers, and transmitters. How real is the contemporary pedagogic panic? Is a segment of the economy setting up a generalised demand for new knowledge of "creativity", "adaptibility", on the basis of the imagined needs of a particular sector of the economy? Understanding I.T. is quite different from being programmed by it as the source of a new intellectual potential releasing the acquirer from the restricting boundaries, social and intellectual, of the old knowledges. How will this new diversity of knowledges map on to our present educational institutions? Which institutions are vulnerable to the new claims, to whom will the new knowledge forms be distributed? Will diversity more likely be found in the less privileging institutions, "whereas" the elite institutions will be more selective of their preferred knowledge, manner of transmission, and evaluation of staff and students? If this is the case then the diversity of knowledges with their target of weakening boundaries (social, intellectual, procedural) will not be distributed across institutions and students. On the contrary, the diversity will be filtered through the existing reproductive structures and so the present hierarchy of privileging institutions will be maintained. Plus ça change....

Bibliography

Castells, M. (1996). *The information age: Economy, society and culture: Vol. I, The rise of the network society.* Oxford: Blackwell.

———. (1997). *The information age: Economy, society and culture: Vol. II, The power of identity.* Oxford: Blackwell.

———. (1998). *The information age: Economy, society and culture: Vol. III, End of millennium.* Oxford: Blackwell.

Sennett, R. (1998). *The corrosion of character: The personal consequences of work in new capitalism.* New York: W. W. Norton.

Video Conference with Basil Bernstein

Lisbon, June 16, 2000

Basil – Hello, Brian.
Brian – How are you?
Basil – Fine. You are looking your usual jovial self. How is the wine there?
Brian – We're absolutely delighted and very grateful for you being willing to do this. We've had a very good three days, we sent you an e-mail earlier, and our notion was that maybe what would be the best thing to do would simply to be allow you to respond to that initially and have your way with us, as it were. Is that the right place to start for you?
Basil – At my age, it is difficult to have my way with 50 people…
(LAUGHTER)
Brian – You can try…
Basil – […] Well, first of all, Brian, I think that we really must congratulate Ana and Isabel for achieving this magnificent meeting. And I think that all the planning that went into it and the difficulties and the problems, these two are absolutely wonderful. Really wonderful. Wonderful.
(APPLAUSE)
[…]
Basil – Well, I thought about your questions and I thought I would freewheel on some of them and then they have to be opened up for a more general discussion. I think I'll be able to last more than an hour, if that's okay with you.
Brian – Basil, at anytime, if you're uncomfortable, if you had enough, please do tell us, and we'll be very happy with what you can manage.
Basil – Darling, you'll be the first to know!
(LAUGHTER)
I think that this question about the development of the theory is one [I have tried] to address on a number of different occasions but each time the recontextualising had been somewhat different and the papers which I se-

lected as being important, seemed to have changed. But I was thinking about this [...] and it occurred to me that one of the major reasons for changing the theory I've really never discussed before. It was as if some kind of denial system was operating at a crucial point in the realisation, and looking back I think it was this. Brian, I think, will remember the circumstances, which I am not going to go into in great depth, but I started the Sociological Research Unit in 1963, and it continued with about 15 to 16 people, sociologists, psychologists, linguists, for something, well I think, round about 1970-ish, but at that time an issue arose as to the direction which the SRU should take. I myself had been mightily disappointed by surrendering something like 8 years of my life to systematic, empirical research, only to see it dismissed without the proper attention paid to the principles that we had tried to elaborate. So I was really very fed-up, not so much with the Unit but with the whole empirical research scene, and so I discussed with the Unit that perhaps they should try to regenerate their own view of the world, their own research, what they wanted to do that would not be subjected to the authoritarian, hegemonising, repressive control of myself. So I went away, I think I went to Scandinavia for a fortnight. I think that's right, Brian, isn't it?

Brian – Yes.

Basil – And I left Brian and another member of the Unit to co-ordinate efforts to produce a new plan and a new direction. I had, by the way, already thought of one, but when I got back, to my great relief no new direction was forthcoming so it was then that I made the decision to disband the Unit, so the next 2 or 3 years I reduced the size of the Unit from 15 or 16 to 2 or 3. I think this was a crucial move of my part, because after that time, through being involved with the daily necessities of empirical research on a vast program I really had no time to think and what I did think was very short pieces on schools like "Consensus and Disaffection in Education", "Ritual in Education", "Open Schools, Open Society" so that was very little systematic work done outside the socio-linguistic work. I was also very frustrated by the theorising of the socio-linguistic framework and my main belief is that the only good thing that came out of the SRU was a long friendship with Ruqaiya Hasan and Michael Halliday. Is Ruqaiya about?

Brian – Yes, she is…

Basil – Ruqaiya is there, isn't she?

Ruqaiya – Hello, how are you Basil?

Basil – Hi Ruqaiya, stay cool girl!

(LAUGHTER)

So really, I think it was the fact that I was basically disappointed with the inability to properly conceptualise the code theory that made me move on, but moving on also had other implications and that was, although I always took research students because I was no good at lecturing, I find that extremely difficult to do, very anxiety making and not worth the trouble. And also I smoked too much during lectures so that after I virtually reduced the Unit to two or three people, so was more or less self functioned without me, I took on a lot of students and from then on these research students and myself, I think, were responsible for the move that took place in the development of the theory. There's no way in which I could have possibly have developed whatever I have developed without the counsel, aid, support, criticism, spontaneity, enjoyment, excitement of the vast number of research students I had enormous pleasure working with, many of whom are at the conference. So, I owe them a very great debt indeed. So that, sociologically speaking, it was a shift in the location that produced a shift in the nature of the discourse that I produced.

Now, if I look at the discourses, it is going to take me another five minutes, Brian?

Brian – That's all right.

[...]

Basil – If I look at the discourse itself, then it is clear that with the virtual disbanding of the SRU the early work that had been done on schools crystallised in the "Classification and Framing" paper which, I think, I gave in 1971. And that was, for me, a great breakthrough, because I was able to free myself of the imperfections of the socio-linguistic theorising, make distinctions between power and control which I thought were absolutely invaluable and necessary, and show that you could have modalities of elaborated codes, so the question was what were the principles selecting, why a particular modality was institutionalised for particular groups of children. This insight, I'm afraid, was never discovered by anybody in the literature, so you've got it here for the first time. There's a great silence about these matters, I notice, in the literature; elaborated codes are very middle class oriented, etc., etc., etc., all that old nonsense, these are for people who not only won't read but can't read. So I consider that a crucial paper, obviously, but I think probably the most important paper in the whole set was one which everybody told me was totally unreadable, which to my mind, was the most elegant paper I have ever written, because to me to get elegance in a paper is crucial and to get conceptual elegance is to me absolutely exciting. So, it is not so much the political implications of what I do is important, but the elegance of the formulation and the generative power of the concept for empirical description. But the paper which I think I like is the "Codes Modalities and the Process of Cultural Reproduction: A Model" which I think was 1981. It took 10 years from classification and framing to the code modality paper, and that code modality paper looked back and produced a much more formal theorising of codes and it looked forward to the pedagogic device. So many of the terms that we use later appear in that paper. I suppose that the next one would be 1985, 1986, which was the pedagogic device which was published in a reader by, I think, a man called Richardson, an American, and I think that paper is an interesting paper, although I think the version in the last book is much better, is much more elegant. And finally, I think the vertical and horizontal discourse paper, I think also is important. Now, the shift that took place between 1970s and the vertical and horizontal discourse paper, that shift was signalled in the introduction to the pedagogic discourse paper, pedagogic device paper, in Richardson's book. In the introduction of the paper, I try to distinguish my work from Bourdieu, because at that time, they were always going on about Bernstein and Bourdieu and we are very different and in many senses, in certain senses, complementary, but in other senses, theoretically very opposed and my opposition to Bourdieu was based upon his dogmatism. I had always found it very uncomfortable to be told by a theorist what I may or may not discover, or what I may or may not conceptualise. I find this a kind of academic arrogance that... I simply can't take it, but unfortunately is endemic in our game: once you've got your own way, you make certain nobody else can play that way. Could be an epitaph for many of us or an epigram if you're clever. Or an obituary, if you're not. Have three for the price of one, Brian.

Brian – Yes, absolutely.

Basil – Absolutely! So, the ... Yes! in the introduction, I've made a distinction between "relation to" and "relations within", the idea being it is very, very important what everyone does, to look at X or Y's position with respect to something. And to look also at "relations within" that something, by that something it is constituted, produced, reproduced, and changed. In other words, it is very important to put together "relation to" and "relation within". Bourdieu's theory is very powerful but it's basically, a relativity theory, it is concerned, basically, with "relation to"... I don't want to get into it in great detail. Now, in order to do that, really, I think of the apparatus to show the "relation to", so the next 10 years were concerned with the "relationship within" and the first major attempt at "relationship within" was the pedagogic device in order to show how pedagogic discourse was itself constructed. And then this was followed, there was still something missing, because though that paper showed, or at least, attempted to show in principle, at least conceptually, what pedagogic discourse was, how it was organised, how it was produced and reproduced and changed ... it didn't actually, [...] do everything, [...] it didn't actually show the nature of pedagogic discourse. It showed how it was put together but it didn't show its nature; it did actually show its distinguishing features and the vertical and horizontal discourse paper was a complex paper which aimed to show the distinguishing features of these two very powerful modes of discourse. It's also ironic that I couldn't stand the romanticising of everyday language, anymore than I can stand the romanticising of the working class, or anymore than I could stand, you know, the double indemnities of the middle class. So, all this is just radical chic that I can't be bothered with. So that I think [...] that vertical and horizontal discourse enabled me to show the importance of "relations within" and "relation to", to show how the internal structure of discourse affected the positions and social relationships which produced the discourse itself and I took sociology an example of that. So, roughly, that's my notion of development as I see it. Basically and summarising: I think the crucial change was the classificatory change, a change in the classification of me as a director of research, that is, giving up the Sociological Research Unit. I never knew at the time how important that it was. So that's roughly a discussion of your first question. Would you like me to see if there's any comments on this, before I go on to the second bit? What would you like? I'm entirely in your hands, metaphorically, darling!...

(LAUGHTER)

Brian – I think Basil, what we'll do if we may, it's to go through the questions and then have a discussion afterwards.

[...]

Basil – Now, [...] oh yes, totally pedagogised society... I've been very interested lately in the diversity of knowledges which are becoming available and so I was quite fascinated by Bill Tyler's paper. Bill, where are you?

Bill – Hello! Here!

Basil – Hi, Bill!

Bill – Hello, how are you doing?

Basil – Doing work at the moment.

Bill – I picked up, great minds think alike, Basil, because you and I raised just the same issues. You know, I haven't spoken to you, I haven't had an e-mail response from you for 4 years, since our conference in Melbourne, at Fran Christie's; it's very reassuring for me to find that the sort of issues that you address in your small paper were the ones that I, on my own sweet ownsome, tried to give a response to in the terms of your theory in my independent, spontaneous, initiative on that...

Basil – Independent, authentic, integrated, post-modern...

Bill – Oh, no, no... sorry...

Basil – Don't worry. I was interested in Bill's paper, and of course from different points of view, Joe Muller's paper, because they both introduce very fascinating possibilities. I think it might be worth spending a little time on hypertext, which I think the interesting thing, at least from my point of view about hypertext, is, first of all, to find out something about the modes of its distribution, not only its production and creation, but the mode of its distribution. Who is going to receive hypertext and who is not. And my bet is that hypertext and the various software that are being created will be only directed at the less able degree students, the less able, in the more marginalised institutions in higher education. I cannot see hypertext going either to Oxford or Cambridge, Durham or London or Edinburgh, neither can I see it happening in the natural sciences. If I can go on. Now the interesting thing about hypertext seems to me, of course, where do you find the recontextualising field which was a very, very important point that you've made, where the hell is it, and the point is it's become local. In fact, one can make a proposition which would go like this: the more open the discourse available to the inquirer, the greater the contextual support necessary to ensure a vertical orientation or navigation. The crucial thing about the Internet, about hypertext, is how you navigate and how you navigate is orientation, and how do you orientate to this open discourse, and I think that the only way in which you orientate effectively, that is, to acquire the criteria, because the criteria for effectively navigating are the criteria for successful evaluation, and I think the way in which this is done, it's what I would call a segmental pedagogy, so what you would find, and you give examples of this in your paper, you note that the modes of intervention that are recommended are 11 by one academic, these are contextual interventions...

Bill – Yes, yes...

Basil – ...where specialised competences are made available in disconnected segments. It's not fragmentation, Bill, it's segmentation, I think, and secondly, and another, so what you've got it's a very extensive contextual social support in which a vertical discourse will play... a very important part in shaping what I would call the navigational gaze, which is very similar to the pedagogic gaze that the acquirer, the recontextualising principle in the school becomes a pedagogic gaze of the acquirer, if you follow what I mean. In this way, I think that this contextual support, one, it makes it a very expensive transmission, very expensive; secondly, it requires considerable organisation; thirdly, it may be the most effective way of organising hypertext from the point of view of the acquirer, it's through an integrated code from the point of view of transmitters because how do you ensure across the segments that all these competences are going to be kept with each other? If you got seven or eight different contexts in which specialised competences are being required, how do you ensure some kind of ideological integration across these segments? Unless, of course, the move towards hypertext is initially moralised. So I think that if I was looking at it, I would be looking at navigation, I would be looking at the principle whereby the student will be able to negotiate this endless sea of on the whole quite worthless discourse. And so I think this whole area is a very, very crucial area for further development. And I think that, you know, between us, I think you have opened it up beautifully descriptively but I feel that I would be looking not so much at macrostructures but much more at the navigational principles that acquirers are expected to acquire. So that's about that paper.

Bill – Thank you Basil, that was very helpful. Do you... What did you think of the concept of hypervocality as an organising principle for access to the pedagogic device or the secondary field that I tried to sketch out there? Did you find that that was a helpful way of looking at the reconstruction of the spatial within a virtualised field? That is, the proliferation of the voice of structure?

Basil – I have difficulty with terms like hypervocality, because (this is basically a difference between us, it's not a crucial difference, I think its almost a difference of temperament) I cannot deal with things like proliferation, I need... if it's hypervocality, then some voices are more vocal than others. I think many of these terms, Bakhtin-derived terms, produced a spurious differentiation, a spurious lack of differentiation, a spurious lack of hierarchy. To me, wherever there is pedagogic there is hierarchy. What is interesting, it's the language of description that we use, because the language of description masks hierarchy, whereas the language of description should attempt to sharpen its possibility of appearance. So that's the only reason. However, in the end, the value of a concept is how we use it, and I'm sure that there'll be no problems about the value of your use of the term, it's just... I would find difficulty in using this language, but I think that maybe, they may even

be differences of approach that we both have.
Bill – Thank you very much, Basil.
Basil – Brian, come back, Brian. I have now dealt with all your questions that you've got here unless you'd like one on the totally pedagogic society. Do you want that one?
Brian – Yes, please.
Basil – Okay. How is it going at your end?
Brian – Sorry, Basil?
Basil – How is it going at your end, if you can still remember that you have one?
(LAUGHTER)
Brian – Our ends are all in sight, Basil.
Basil – No means, then.
Brian – No, no means.
Basil – No means... Oh, dear, I am lost, no means, only ends, what a way to go... Now, I think that what struck me, after reading through three volumes of Castells, and you got to have a constitution for that, you really have, especially the appendices that nobody, I am sure, reads except me, I've been through it, and it occurred to me that there are one or two little lacunae in that vast tract which I think is probably one of the most important bibles, modern bibles, that we've got in sociology. It is a magnificent achievement, whatever one may say about it here and there, but what it misses, it's this: On the one hand, it's clear that we've got a weak global state, but if we look at the State as the pedagogic state, we never had a state as strong as the pedagogic state, as the State we have now and that we are going to see. So we have this contrast between inside and outside, inside strong pedagogic state, outside weak global state. And the weaker the global state the more likely that the EU would have immense power over the internal orderings of the European states. Now, in Portugal, there was, I think about a month ago, there was a Lisbon conference, which was convened by the President of the EU, who was... Portugal holds the presidency now. They produced something like 200 pages of documents and policy which I had the good fortune to read. Much of it is about life long learning. Much of it is producing the new adaptability, flexibility, creativity. Isn't this now a common language of diagnosis, and also a common solution, in that pedagogy is seen as no more than the technology? Life long learning, no problems, we've got all this data and we can construct life long learning, principles and practice, in exactly the self-same way we can construct any technology. The notion that pedagogy is always inadequate, the why of at

the moment it is always ineffective, doesn't seem to have any effect whatsoever and I'm talking about, I would not like to be repeated about this at the moment, but the basic thing is the way in which the State is moving to ensure that there's no space or time which is not pedagogised. And this is new, the only other time in which we had a totally pedagogised society was in the medieval period, when the Catholic Church created this seamless, coherent, systematic society, in which people's positions and powers were known and understood and developed. So we have this notion now... The question is: Who are these totalising pedagogues? Where are they coming from? How are they constructing this technology which the State takes for granted? Can we actually create it with no problems whatsoever? Could the pedagogy be just the technology? And it isn't just the technology. It isn't. It's a moralising ruler and without that knowledge there will be real problems in creating anything at all, in my own view actually, and that's why I really think I am not even certain that we've got pedagogy any more. [...] So that I will need time to think more deeply about this, but if any seed ... in the end there will be all the departments of education and colleges of education, both formal and informal agencies getting money; you will see research councils offering vast sums for developing questions, stupid ideas. For example, as Brian has said when he saw me, some kind of typology of teachers from novice to expert, as if somehow you could do, carry out such a study, that teaching can be decontextualised that you could abstract its practice from the context in which it is realised. Along this route lies madness, so I think that [what] we're experiencing now is a pedagogic panic which is masking the moral panic, a deep moral panic in the society, about what is and where is it going, and this is a period of the pedagogic panic. And it's the first time that pedagogic panic has masked the moral panic.

Brian – Basil, thank you very much. What we agreed to do at this end, at this point, was to allow people...

Basil – Have champagne!

Brian – Yah, yah... how I was saying to you last Monday, it is difficult to underestimate the mess in a world where people are asking—in Britain, anyway—the government for a million pounds to do the sort of novice to expert typology of teaching as if nobody had ever thought of, or invented, or noted the importance of the regulated and the importance of context in these matters. Basil, I want to give other people an opportunity to ask you questions. First of all, I'll ask Ruqaiya if she has a question.

Basil – She'll have 20 questions! Ruqaiya will have 20 questions and not one!
(LAUGHTER)

Ruqaiya – No, at the moment, I was only going to ask one question. Basil: I was wondering about the word recontextualisation, and being a linguist, paying a good deal of attention to the *re*, and so wondering whether every time one says recontextualising, whether there is a sense of any originary contextualising, one that is authentic, and if so is there any way of characterising that particular contextualising?

Basil – No, I don't think that... recontextualising does not presuppose a lower text. But it does presuppose a primary text and one can distinguish between a primary text and a lower text. The primary text itself, it's primary in the sense it's maybe the first time it had been used for recontextualising purposes. So, for example, Piaget was a primary text for progressive recontextualising. But Piaget itself is not a lower text. In other words, you can only understand Piaget by looking at other theories of child development to which he was opposed. So the short answer is no, there was no lower text. However, to say there is no lower text, it's not to deny, I must not deny that there are primary texts; part of the problem in avoiding essentialism is that you throw the baby out with the bath water. I think it's very important to hold down to the notion of primary text. So I think one can talk about a primary text with reference to recontextualising and then one can talk about a secondary text because after Piaget came Vygotsky, and Vygotsky brought in Bakhtin, and Harry Daniels can tell that story better than I can. So I think it is useful to look historically at primary and secondary text which had been subject to recontextualising, often by the same people, oddly enough.

Brian – Harry, do you want to put something after that?

Harry – Well, I was... You know what I'd like to talk about. Can you hear me, Basil?

Basil – Yes. Yah.

[...]

Harry – You've often written about the extent to which those early Luria lectures that you went to in the sixties had an impact on you.

Basil – Yes, they did, changed my whole mind.

Harry – Can you go a little bit further than that statement, which is the one I heard you say before?

Basil – Well, if you actually go to an art gallery and you see a painting which changes the way in which you see the world, what more can you say? And I think the impact... Marion is sitting next to me, we both went to those six lectures, which were astounding. Remember, here was Luria talking about language in a way that the Brits have never talked about language. Using experimental methods which were absolutely darlings to listen to. And, being centrally... the regulative function of speech, and I took up that notion of the regulative function and it has begun everything I've done since. So I think, and he was such a wonderful man, Luria. After lectures we used to go and have a drink with him, [to Marion] do you remember? It was a long time ago, it must have been... in the early sixties. We used to go to a pub with Luria, and he was just such a wonderful, generous, spontaneous man, who talked for hours in a very open, beautiful way. So the whole notion of the regulative function of speech which was both positive, which was both enabling and disabling, was very important. Also the study of twins. I didn't read his neurological work there. It was the early work, it was really the work that was very much connected with Vygotsky, it was that part of Luria's work which had strongly influenced Vygotsky that intrigued me. Could he provide an experimental base which Vygotsky never had?

Harry – Have you never thought why those two in the thirties never did what you've done in the seventies, eighties, and nineties?

Basil – Well, I don't think there was any need for them to do it, because they had Marxism. You see, they wouldn't have been allowed to develop a macro-structure theory that was not Marxist. I mean, Vygotsky took for granted the Marxist framework. I mean, they took it for granted. For example: language as a tool, which is straight Marx, so that it wouldn't have been possible for them to do it, I don't think. I don't know who would have done it, I don't know. I'm not certain with the Durkheim..., I really don't know, I really don't know. I think my engagement has been really quite an obsessional engagement with one problem, which is unusual in my subject, and I found it very exciting of course, but much more so because of the research students. As you well know, Harry, in our many discussions...

[...]

Brian – Basil, we've got no prearranged order of questions to you, but I know many people want to ask you many things, so... there's only time for a few people to have the opportunity. Can I ask Mario, now, as one of your most eminent ex-students, to speak to you?

Mario – Hello, how are you?

Basil – Hello Mario!

Mario – I'm going to ask a short question, not 99 pages as you say, eh?

(LAUGHTER)

When Bill Tyler finished his paper, I became very unoptimistic about the pedagogic situation in modern society, and I concluded for myself two points: Pedagogy has invaded all the more intimate spirits of everyday life, the first one and the second, there is no way to escape from pedagogising in modern societies. I find this very related with what you say in the way you say to the symposium, and this is why I want to ask you: Is this related to the triumphant silence of the pedagogic voice discourse as we move in the totally pedagogised society?

Basil – Can you repeat the last sentence, Mario, for me?

Mario – Are these two points I bring out related to what you say in your paper, "The new discourse is the triumphant silence of the voice in the pedagogic discourse", as we move to the second totally pedagogised society?

Basil – Yes, the short answer is yes. I think that only by systematically revealing the voice of this silence can we actually make this pedagogy enabling rather than disabling. I'm not against pedagogy itself, that would be stupid, but I'm against the way, the technologising of the pedagogic, I'm against the ludicrous way in which it is used in this attempt to control. I'm against any kind of pedagogy which leaves the self empty and this is what I fear most of all, the emptying of the self, and the role of pedagogy in such evacuation, and I think we have to mount a critique but not the stupid critique of the seventies, that was completely... that did nothing. But a critique which enables us to show how pedagogic discourse works. How it's produced, how it's distributed and particularly looking at... you see, its effectiveness is often assumed and we have to ask ourselves when it is effective, what are the conditions that have made it effective, and what does effectiveness [...] actually mean with respect to whatever has been acquired? [...] I'm afraid that wasn't a very good answer to your question. I can try to reformulate it. [...] One, my opposition to what is going on, it's because pedagogy is simply seen as a technology, that a group of people can now put together a discourse aimed at producing changes in individual experiences, knowledges, and competency, in a quite, almost mechanical way. This pedagogy they produce is completely decontextualised from the rest of the acquirer's life span. The notion that pedagogy must be meaningful, not simply relevant, how to combine relevance and meaningfulness, I think, is the challenge of pedagogy and to put these two together, relevance and meaningfulness, means that you can not actually design a pedagogy without making explicit the regulative discourse which generates it. [...] This is my objection.

Mario – Thank you very much.

[...]

Brian – Basil, we've almost come to the end of this transmission and there's still lots of people who would like to say hello to you. Is there anybody you

would like to shout at? Is there anybody who you like to speak to?
Basil – No, all of them.
Brian – You've got a wide choice here.
Basil – All of them. They're given up 3 days of their lives.
[…]
Brian – I'm going to give people one last opportunity to come in. Alan Sadovnik wants a word, Basil.
Alan – Hi, Basil.
Basil – Where are you?
Alan – Can you see me? Next to Harry, Basil. I was struck at the similarity between the ending of your "Social Class and Pedagogic Practice" paper in '87 with the ending of this brief paper. At the end of "Social Class and Pedagogic Practice" you suggest that despite their egalitarian rhetoric, what was then the new market-dependent pedagogics of the eighties or what you called a new pedagogic Janus, which you saw as furthering the older inequalities, and then you conclude that the price for democracy in education was perhaps too high. At the end of this short statement, the one that we've read, you seemed equally sceptical about the potential of the new information technology, by saying: "On the contrary, the diversity will be filtered through the existing reproductive structures so that the present hierarchisation of privileging institutions will be maintained". And then: "The more the things change, the more they remain the same". Do you have any optimism about any democratic possibilities within the next period? Or do you continue to be equally sceptical as you were in the late eighties?
Basil – Well, first of all, there is some evidence for my scepticism. Elite institutions do not have to change their discourse in order to maintain their privileged positions. They do not have to change their discourse because they have very large sums of money available to them. These large sums of money can be used to buy in experts, to buy in the leaders of research in many fields. As a consequence, one may expect less change in the structure of the discourse of elite universities. However, if you belong to a modernised higher education institution, the only weapon that you've got to maintain your market situation is your discourse. And therefore, you will change your discourse in order to optimise your market niche. And by changing your discourse in order to optimise your market niche you make yourself vulnerable to the new claims. And when you have the new claims on change in higher education, which will then be some kind of legitimation for, on the whole, not a very effective activity. So that you will find more diversity for those unique specialisations and more specialisation for those

unique diversities. So the empirical evidence for that statement would be what I just said. As far as democracy, I never can understand how we continue to talk about democracy in education. We need to do our best to put them in separate sentences. I mean, education is a state-generated activity and any attempt to make changes in the system can only be done with the approval, in the end, of the State and its various agents and agencies. The State now has put all education in a very tight box, through announcing hundreds and hundreds of targets for institutions to reach. It basically can control both input and output. I think if I was going to talk about democracy in education, I would put my faith in an area which so far very few people have really bothered with, and then I would be looking at informal education, I would be looking at adult education, I would be looking at popular education. And I think in those areas, of informal education outside of the State, there's a possibility for change and initiative, and that's where I would be looking, and that's what I would like to see developed. As is being done, because the other view is even more pernicious, and that is to withdraw your children from the State schools and it's happening wholesale in the States. And that is even more conservative, that's even more conservative a move. What do you think about that, Alan?

Alan – I think that you're right on target with that, and I think that, clearly, the patterns that you've just generally described are patterns that are existing in the States as well, certainly both in higher education, where precisely those processes that you've described are occurring differently in elite institutions than they are in the non-elite institutions. And I think you've really put your finger on it, and in terms of democracy, I would agree wholeheartedly that in the States probably more so than elsewhere that has been a flight from state schools precisely for the reasons that you have suggested and certainly in ways that have been far or less democratic than 10 years ago. So, I would agree that there's reasons for concern and scepticism.

Basil – What we're doing really is replacing the word democracy by the word opportunity, so, what we're really doing is by saying oh, well, we can open our elite institutions and our medical schools to marginalised members of our population, this is democracy: it isn't. You mustn't confuse opportunity with democracy. And this is the problem.

Brian – Basil, we've got to close: the transmission time is up. And won't begin to try to thank you for what you've contributed to us. Can I close by underlining our thanks here, repeating what you started your transmission with, our thanks to Ana and Isabel and the people here who've put this conference together, and at your end for Marion to getting you as far as the couch and into shape for speaking to us. [...] I mean, you and I have known for a long time, but it's a question of the sublime to the ridiculous, that's life and a chance would be a fine thing. I wish you a path towards the sublime, this evening, tomorrow and in the immediate future.

Basil – I really am very happy that we've been able to arrange this meeting, and I'm delighted to in fact, being able to have this joint, open discussion. And I apologise for a certain wildness in my speech but I'm not very good at spontaneity and I'm only a contrived man, sorry, person!

(LAUGHTER)

So, take care all of you, and I'm glad the conference has been such a great success.

[...]

(APPLAUSE)

[...] text omitted

... pause

Contributors

HARRY DANIELS is Professor of Special Education and Educational Psychology and co-director of the Centre for Sociocultural and Activity Theory Research at the University of Birmingham, UK. He is currently working on a number of projects concerned with marginalisation and exclusion, and cultural transmission.

School of Education, University of Birmingham
Edgbaston, Birmingham B15 2TT, UK
Phone: (44) 121 414 6482
E-mail: H.R.J.Daniels@bham.ac.uk

BRIAN DAVIES is Professor of Education at the Cardiff School of Social Sciences, Cardiff University, Wales. His recent research has included work on PE, sport and nationalism in Wales, the links between vocational preparation and the needs of SMEs in Wales and Westphalia, the effects of National Curriculum testing in mathematics and mentoring in pre-service nurse education.

Cardiff School of Social Sciences, Cardiff University
Glamorgan Building, King Edward VII Avenue, Cardiff CF10 3WT, Wales, UK
Phone: (44) 292 087 4848
E-mail: wbdavies@ntlworld.com

MARIO DIAZ is Professor at the Institute of Education, Universidad del Valle, in Cali, Colombia. He is currently an external consultant of the National Institute for the Improvement of Higher Education in Colombia (ICFES) and advisor to some universities in the country. His recent research includes the examination of the pedagogic codes of academic culture in higher education, and of the institutional recontextualising field of higher education in modernity and post-modernity.

Carrera 68 13B-61, Apto 1003 Torre B, Cali, Colombia
Phone/Fax: (57) 2 331 4011
E-mail: mardiaz@calipso.com.co

MAGNUS HAAVELSRUD is Professor at the Institute of Education, Norwegian University of Science and Technology, Trondheim. He has mainly worked within the fields of educational sociology, peace research, peace education, and development education.

Institute of Education, Norwegian University of Science and Technology
N-7491 Trondheim, Norway
E-mail: Magnus.Haavelsrud@svt.ntnu.no

RUQAIYA HASAN is Emeritus Professor of Linguistics at Macquarie University, Australia. Having worked with Bernstein in the late 60s, she has maintained a keen interest in the relations of the semiotic and the social. Her main research interests are stylistics, discourse analysis, semantics, and socio-semantic variation.

Macquarie University
14/133 Sydney Road, Fairlight, NSW 2094, Australia
Phone/Fax: (61) 2 9949 4547
E-mail: rhasan@LAUREL.ocs.mq.edu.au

KARL MATON, of St John's College, University of Cambridge, is currently writing up his doctoral thesis, which develops a dynamic epistemological sociology of knowledge through a case-study of the institutionalisation of cultural studies in post-war English higher education.

St. John's College, University of Cambridge
Cambridge CB2 1TP, England, UK
Phone: (44) 116 220 1066
E-mail: karl.maton@ntlworld.com

CONTRIBUTORS 387

ROB MOORE is Reader in Sociology of Education, Homerton College, University of Cambridge. He is currently researching youth transitions and higher education in the UK and has written on various aspects of education and the economy and theories of knowledge and the curriculum.

Homerton College, University of Cambridge
Hills Road, Cambridge CB2 2PH, England, UK
Phone: (44) 160 366 3046   Fax: (44) 122 350 7120
E-mail: robmoore@bc.internet.com

ANA MORAIS is Professor of Education and co-ordinator of the ESSA group—Sociological Studies of the Classroom—at the School of Science, University of Lisbon, Portugal. Her recent research includes a number of projects particularly centred on the primary and secondary classroom and on curriculum, in the sciences. Both instructional and regulative contexts are objects of study and intervention.

Department of Education, School of Science, University of Lisbon
Campo Grande, C1-1, 1749-016 Lisbon, Portugal
Phone: (351) 21 750 0114   Fax: (351) 21 750 00 82
E-mail: amorais@fc.ul.pt

JOHAN MULLER is Professor of Education and Head of Department at the University of Cape Town. He teaches sociology of knowledge and curriculum and has published widely in these areas.

Department of Education, University of Cape Town
Private Bag, Rondebosch, 7700 Cape Town, South Africa
E-mail: jpm@education.uct.ac.za

ISABEL NEVES is Assistant Professor of Education and co-ordinator of the ESSA group—Sociological Studies of the Classroom—at the School of Science, University of Lisbon, Portugal. Her recent research includes a number of projects particularly centred on the primary and secondary classroom and on curriculum, in the sciences. Both instructional and regulative contexts are objects of study and intervention.

Department of Education, School of Science, University of Lisbon

Campo Grande, C1-1, 1749-016 Lisbon, Portugal
Phone: (351) 21 750 0114   Fax: (351) 21 750 00 82
E-mail: ineves@fc.ul.pt

PARLO SINGH is Associate Professor and Director of the Centre for Language, Literacy and Diversity at the Queensland University of Technology, Australia. She is currently working on a number of research projects that deal with the negotiation of cultural identities as students acquire pedagogic discourses in culturally diverse secondary school, higher education, and workplace contexts.

Centre for Language, Literacy and Diversity, Queensland University of Technology
Kelvin Grove Campus, Queensland 4059, Australia
Phone: (61) 7 3864 2111   Fax: (61) 7 3864 3988
E-mail: p.singh@qut.edu.au

JOSEPH SOLOMON is Assistant Professor of Sociology of Education at the University of Athens. His interests focus on the analysis of modes of school organization, evaluation, and resistance. Since 1987, he has collaborated with Professor Bernstein on a number of projects.

Department of Early Childhood Education, University of Athens
10 Anghelou Vlahou Street, 105 56 Athens, Greece
Fax: (30) 61 993 437
E-mail: Jsolomon@ath.forthnet.gr

ANNA TSATSARONI is Assistant Professor in the Department of Early Childhood Education, University of Patras, Greece. Her research interests are in the sociology of scientific knowledge, the sociology of school knowledge, and theoretical issues in social science. Currently, she focuses on the analysis of pedagogical texts.

Department of Early Childhood Education, University of Patras
265 00 Patras, Greece
Phone: (30) 61 997 875   Fax: (30) 61 996 310
E-mail: tsatsaro@upatras.gr

WILLIAM TYLER is Associate Professor of Sociology and Associate Dean of Humanities and Social Sciences at the Northern Territory University in Darwin, Australia. Apart from his continuing applications of the sociology of Basil Bernstein, his current interests include post-modern criminology and the changing socio-cultural conditions of Indigenous peoples.

Faculty of Law, Business and Arts, Northern Territory University
Darwin, 0909 Australia
E-mail: WillTyler@msn.com.au

PHILIPPE VITALE is Lecturer in Sociology at the Department of Sociology, Université de Provence, Aix-en-Provence, and member of the Mediterranean Laboratory of Sociology, Maison Méditerranéenne des Sciences de l'Homme, Aix-en-Provence. He recently completed his thesis on the teaching of sociology in Europe.

Département de Sociologie, Université de Provence
29 Avenue Robert Schumann, 13621, Aix-en-Provence, Cedex 1, France
Phone: (33) 4 4295 3356
E-mail: philippevitale@hotmail.com

GEOFF WILLIAMS is Senior Lecturer in English at the University of Sydney, Australia, where he teaches courses in child language and literacy development and systemic functional linguistics. His current research includes work on semantic variation, children's language play, and children's use of metalanguage as a metasemiotic tool.

Department of English (A20), University of Sydney
Sidney 2006, Australia
Phone: (61) 2 9351 2276
E-mail: geoffrey.williams@english.usyd.edu.au

Index

A

Adventures in the Skin Trade, 55
Afonso, M., 189, 190, 204
Aggleton, P., 213
Alexandria, 171
Althusser, L., 4, 93, 329
Alvarez, A., 100
American Sociological Association, xiv
Anstey, M., 264, 274
Antunes, H., 189, 190, 295
Apple, M. W., 324
Arithmetica, 171
"Aspects of the Relations Between Production and Education", 329
Assemblies of God, 256
Athens, 291
Atkins, P., 137
Atkinson, P., 319, 324–5
Australia, xv, 11, 20, 257, 262, 342–3, 346
 see also Queensland
Axel, E., 102

B

Bakhtin, N., 135, 353, 375, 378
Barthes, Roland, 345–6, 351
Bass, R., 340
Baudrillard, J., 350
Baum, R. C., 355
Bazerman, C., 102
Beck, J., 159
Belgium, 124
Benjamin, W., 131
Berkeley, xv
Berlin, I., 174

Bernstein, Basil, xiii–xvi, 1–12, 18, 19, 34, 37, 38, 40, 48, 49–50, 61–2, 66, 68, 70, 71, 72, 73, 83–94, 99, 105, 106–9, 115–19, 122, 123, 125, 138–42, 145, 153–61, 166, 171, 175, 177, 178–9, 185, 186, 187, 188, 195, 198, 206, 210, 213, 215, 223, 225, 226, 252–5, 259, 260, 261, 287–8, 289, 294–6, 297, 299, 300, 302, 303, 307, 308, 309–10, 319–334, 339, 340–1, 344–5, 347–51, 354, 355–7, 363–8, 369–83
Bernstein, Francis, xv
Bernstein, Marion, xv, 378, 379, 383
Bernstein, Saul, xv
Bisseret, N., 3, 320–5, 328
Blair, Tony, 365
Bloomsbury, xiii
Bluehills State High School, 256, 263–71, 277
Booker, Christopher, 167
Bordeaux, University of, 115
Borges, J. L., 130
Botelho, A., 190
Boudon, R., 120
Bourdieu, P., 8, 48, 84, 138–9, 140, 141–2, 170, 331–2, 372
Bowles, S., xii
Breier, M., 142
Bricmont, J., 142
Britain, see United Kingdom
British Sociological Association (BSA), 4
Brown, A. J., 298, 333–4
Bruner, J. S., 25, 49
Buci-Glucksman, C., 131
Bull, G., 264, 274
Burke, E. 172

Butt, D., 60, 74
Byrce, Ms., 271–6, 278

C

Cairney, T. H., 37
Cali, 9
Callon, M., 138
Câmara, M. J., 189, 190, 199, 201
Cambridge, 9, 172, 174, 374
Canada, xv
Cape, the, 9
Cape Town, 132, 142
Castells, M., 84, 365, 376
Catholic Church, 365, 377
Cazden, C., 262
Christie, Fran, 102, 276, 374
City Day College, Shoreditch, xiv
Class, Codes and Control, xv, 1–2, 5, 107, 325, 340
Classical Mainstream Programme (CMP), 120
"Classification and Framing", 4, 371
Cloran, Carmel, 49, 50, 55, 62, 63, 68
"Code, Modalities", 4, 89, 372
Cole, M., 100, 103–4
Colombia, 9
complex cognitive competence (CC), 229–31
complex socio-affective competence (CSA), 229–31
computer mediated communication (CMC), 340
"Consensus and Disaffection in Education", 370
Cook, D., 339
Cooper, B., 295
Corrosion of Character, The, 366
Coulthard, M., 75
Cousins, J. B., 293
Coxon, E., 256
Crook, S., 350
Curriculum and Democracy, 113

D

Daniels, Harry, xiii, xv, 5, 8, 99–109, 213, 295, 378–9, 381
Darwin, 342
Davies, Brian, xiii, xvi, 1–11, 121, 295, 319, 369–73, 376–3
Davydov, V. V., 101
Del Rio, P., 100
Delamont, S., 319
Deleuze, G., 129, 357
Derrida, J., 87, 145
Dewey, John, 350
Diaz, Mario, 5, 8, 83–95, 379–80
Diophantus, 171
direct pedagogic practice (DPP), 206–7
Disneyland, 350
Domingos, A. M., 296
Donaldson, M., 49
Dowling, P., 187, 295, 297, 348
Dunne, M., 295
Durham, 374
Durkheim, Emile, 4, 7, 8, 84, 113, 114, 115, 116, 130, 132–8, 139, 140–2, 143, 144, 146, 349, 355, 364–5, 379

E

Earl, L. M., 293
Edinburgh, 144, 374
"Education and Production", 4
Edwards, A. D., 73, 267
Elam, M., 134
Elementary Forms of the Religious Life, The, 132
Ellsworth, E., 251
Emotionally and Behaviourally Disturbed (EBD), 8
Engestrom, Y., 8, 99, 100, 103–5
England, 9, 172
English language, 20, 256, 263–4, 265–6, 272, 273, 276, 278
Enlightenment, the, 129
Ensor, P., 295, 296, 297
Entwhistle, N., 140, 144
Ess, D., 351

European Parliament, 342
European Union, 124, 376
Évolution Pédagogique en France, L', 113, 116
"Experimental Study of Concept Formation", 106

F

family instructional discourse (FID), 206–7
family regulative discourse (FRD), 206–7
Fermat, Pierre de, 171, 174
Fermat's Last Theorem, 171–2, 174–5
Ferreira, L., 189, 200
Figiel, S., 259
Firth, J. R., 57
Fitzpatrick, J. L., 293
Floridi, L., 345, 352
Floud, Jean, 2
Foliaki, L., 256
Fontes, A., 238
Fontinhas, F., 189, 199, 200, 228, 295
Ford Foundation, 2
Forman, E. A., 103
Forquin, J. C., 114–15
Foucault, M., 4, 84, 86, 87, 92, 93, 135, 295
France, 115, 124, 171
Franco, R. W., 256
Frazer, J. G., 133
Freud, Sigmund, 130
Freidson, Eliot, xv
"From Pedagogies to Knowledges", 252–3
Fuller, S., 137
Fullner school, 256

G

Gaita, R., 347
Gateway/Maintown, 18
Gee, J., 141, 143, 144
Geertz, C., 132
Gellner, E., 178
General Approach Plane (GAP), 117–8, 120, 122

general regulative discourse (GRD), 229, 239
Gibson, D., 142, 143
Giddens, A., 130, 331, 332
Gintis, H., xiv
Giroux, H., 129, 251, 252
Goldman-Eisler, Frieda, 2
Gore, J., 251, 252
Graham, Ronald, 173
Gramsci, Antonio, 93, 324
Graves, N. D., 256
Graves, T. D., 256
Great Divide, the, 130, 131, 136–7, 138, 141, 142
Greece, 10, 288–310
Grillo, R. D., 141
Guattari, Felix, 357

H

Haavelsrud, Magnus, 3, 5, 10–11, 319–34
Habermas, J., 136, 309, 351
Hacking, I., 133, 139, 142, 144
Halliday, Michael, 5, 19, 29, 34–35, 48, 370
Halsey, A. H., xiv, 319
Hasan, R., 5, 6, 7, 18, 19, 25, 26, 29, 35–6, 47–75, 370, 377–8
Hawaii, 262
Heath, S. B., 17, 18, 19, 20, 141, 143
Hendricks, Migiel, 142–4, 145–6
Hickling-Hudson, A., 252
higher autonomy and power (HAP), 18, 19, 21–2, 34, 37, 39, 40, 42
History of Schools and Schooling, xiii
Hoffman, P., 171, 173, 175
Hoggart, R., 167
Holdaway, D., 23
Holland, J., 201, 213
Hopkins, D., 293
Hovdenak, S. S., 329, 333
Hughes, M., 19, 20, 28, 33
Hunter, I., 255
Hu-pei, Kathryn, 262
Hypertext: The Convergence of Contemporary Critical Theory and Technology, 345–6

I

ID/RD, *see* instructional discourse, regulative discourse
Ignatieff, Michael, 170
Illich, Ivan, 348
indirect pedagogic practice (IPP), 206–7
Informational Society, the, 365
Institute of Education, London, xiv, 2
instructional discourse (ID), 6, 253, 295–6, 299, 308–9, 355
Internal Evaluation and Planning at the School Unit (IEP), 10, 287–310
Internal Evaluation and Planning at the School Unit (PI, 1999), 291–3, 295, 298, 300–7, 308
Ivic, I., 103

J

Jabiluka, 342–3, 357
Jackson, D., 293
Jameson, Ms., 264–72, 275, 277
Jardine, D. W., 129
Jones, A., 256, 262
Jordan, Cathie, 262

K

Kakadu National Park, 342
Karabel, J., xiv, 319
KEEP project, 262
Kermode, Frank, 168–70
Klein, Melanie, 215
Knorr Cetina, K., 137
Koïnè, 122–5
Kozulin, A., 99
Kroker, A., 339
Kuhn, T., 162, 163, 168

L

Labov, W., 3
Landow, G. P., 345–6, 350, 353
Lather, P., 129
Latour, B., 137, 138, 140, 142, 146

Lave, J., 100, 102
Leibnitz, G. W., 131
Lemke, J. L., 102, 263
Lepa, Ana, 257–8
Lepa, Josia, 256–8
Levi-Strauss, C., 142
Life Long Learning, 365, 376–7
Lisbon, xiii, xv, 344, 369, 376
London, xi, xiii, 6
London School of Economics, xii
London, University of, 363, 374
Lopes, A., 234
Lourenço, A., 234
lower autonomy and power (LAP), 18, 19, 20–1, 22, 26, 34, 37, 39–40, 42
Luce, P., 256
Luke, C., 251, 252
Luntley, M., 177
Luria, A. R., 4, 105–6, 378–9
Lyotard, J.-F., 132, 349

M

Maastricht, Treaty of, 114
MacBeath, J., 292
Macquarie group of researches, 62–3
Maher, F. A., 251
Manchester United, 174
Mara, D., 256
Marx, Karl, 84, 379
Marxism, 4, 84, 158, 324, 379
Maton, Karl, 5, 9, 153–79, 252
Matos, M., 189–90
Matthews, J. M., 252
Mau, R. Y., 256
McCarthy, T., 136
McCreary, E. K., 353
McLaren, P., 129, 251, 252, 332, 334
McRae, Donald, 5
Mead, G. H., 4, 84
Medeiros, A., 228
Melbourne, 374
Mercer, N., 73, 267
Metamorphosis, 55
Methodist church, 256
Meuret, D., 292

Minick, N., 103
Miranda, C., 189, 202, 295
Montessori, Maria, 215
Moon, B. C., 17
Moore, Rob, 5, 9, 153–79, 252
Morais, Ana, xiii, xvi, 5, 10, 185–217, 223–44, 295, 369, 382
Mormon church, 256
Muller, Johan, 5, 8–9, 129–46, 163, 168, 252, 374
Munsie, L., 37

N

Nascimento, T., 234
National Internet Magazine, 343
Nedelmann, B., 114, 121
Network for Educational Information, 293
Neves, Isabel, xiii, xvi, 5, 10, 185–217, 223–44, 295, 369, 382
New Directions, 4
New Labour, xv, 365
New Literacy Studies (NLS), 131, 141–6
New Sociology of Education (NSE), 113, 115, 153, 156, 162, 178
New York University, xiv
New Zealand, xv, 256, 259, 260, 262, 346
Newell school, 256
Ninio, A. Z., 25
North Australian Studies unit, 342–4
Northern Territory, 342
Northern Territory University (NTU), 11, 342
Norway, 329
Nuffield Foundation, 2

O

Official Pedagogic Recontextualising Field (ORF), 289, 290, 291, 294–5, 298, 326, 329, 330
Olson, D. R., 100
"On Pedagogic Discourse", 4
"On the Classification and Framing of Educational Knowledge", 4, 319, 325
"Open Schools, Open Society", 370

Oxford, 174, 374

P

Painter, C., 48
Pakulski, J., 350
Parsons, Talcott, 84
Passeron, J. C., 117, 122
Patton, M. Q., 293
Paulsen, M. F., 353
Pedagogic Recontextualising Field (PRF), 298, 303, 326, 329
Pedagogical Institute, 287, 289, 290–1, 293
Pedagogy, Symbolic Control and Identity, xv, 326
Peneda, D., 228
Penthouse, 269, 270, 271
Peters, M., 345, 346–7, 348
Piaget, Jean, 1, 378
Pierce, C., 132
Pires, D., 189, 190, 191, 206
Pollner, M., 136
Popper, K., 48, 153, 176
Portugal, 223–5, 226–44, 376
Poulantzas, N., 93
Primary Socialisation, Language and Education, 2
Prinsloo, M., 142
Proust, Marcel, 170

Q

Quality Indicators (QIs), 291, 292, 293, 304, 305–6, 307
Queensland, 10, 20, 252, 256, 263; Samoan community, 10, 255–78; *see also* Samoa, Samoan language

R

Ramognino, N., 119–20, 121–2
Ratner, C., 106
Règles de la Méthode Sociologique, 114
regulative discourse (RD), 253–4, 295–6, 299, 307–9, 355
rhetorical unit (RU), 55, 56

Ringer, F., 134
"Ritual in Education", 370
Roadville, 18
Roberts, P., 346
Robitaille, D., 243
Rocha, C., 190, 193, 195, 199, 204
Rorty, R., 135, 136
Rose, D., 253
Rosenberg, Harold, 168, 169
Rousseau, J. J., 1
Rowe, G., 213

S

sabir, 122–3
Sadovnik, Alan, xiii–xvi, 324, 381–2
Salazar, A., 224
Saljo, R., 103
Salomon, G., 100
Sam, I. A., 256
Sam, S., 256
Samoa, 257, 259, 262
Samoan language, 256, 260
Sandbothe, M., 350
Sanders, J. R., 293
Sanunder State High School, 256, 263–4, 271–6, 277–8
Schooling in Capitalist America, xiv
Schools for the Implementation of Experimental Education Projects (SIEP), 289, 290
Schratz, M., 292
Schutz, A., 132
Scientific Support Group, 293, 298, 299, 303, 304, 307
Semel, Susan, xiii, xv
Sennett, Richard, 366
Sense of an Ending, The, 168
Seventh Day Adventist church, 256
Shapin, S., 130, 131, 133, 134
Shotter, J., 135
Simmel, Georg, 129–30
Simon, B., 136
simple cognitive competence (SC), 229–31
simple socio-affective competence (SSA), 229–31

Sinclair, J. McH., 75
Sinclair, M., 256
Singh, Parlo, 5, 10, 170, 251–78
"Social Class and Pedagogic Practice", 381
Sociological Research Unit (SRU), 2–4, 370–1, 373
Sokal, A., 142
Solomon, Joseph, 5, 10, 287–310
South Africa, xv, 142
Spain, 224
specific instructional discourse (SID), 229–31
Specific Problem Plane (SPP), 117–18, 120, 122
specific regulative discourse (SRD), 229–31
Stepney Settlement Boys' Club, xiii–xiv
Stinky Cheeseman and Other Fairly Stupid Tales, The, 40
Stone, C. A., 103
Stone, M., 265
Street, B. V., 141, 143
Sydney, 20, 21, 50, 72
Sztompka, P., 114, 121

T

Taiwan, xvi
Terrell, I., 293
Tester, K., 130, 131
Thatcher, Margaret, xv
Thematic Areas (TAs), 291, 293, 305
Thinking and Speech, 101, 109
Thompson, K., 132, 133
Thompson Tetreault, M. K., 251
Three Little Pigs, The, 7, 19, 21, 22–34, 273, 275
Three Little Wolves and the Big, Bad Pig, The, 39, 40
Thumlert, K., 339, 352, 357
Tiatia, J., 259
Tizard, B., 19, 20, 28, 33
Torr, J., 48
Torrance, N., 100
Totally Pedagogised Society (TPS), 252–3, 341, 365, 366, 367, 376–7, 380
Towards a Sociology of Pedagogy, xiii

Trackton, 18
Tradition of the New, The, 169
Tsatsaroni, Anna, 5, 10, 287–310
Tudge, R. H., 105
Turner, S., 131
Tyler, William, 5, 11, 289, 339–58, 373–6, 379

U

United Kingdom, xv, 5–6, 153, 224, 252, 365, 377
United Nations World Heritage Committee, 342
United States of America, xv, 224, 256, 382
Uniting church, 256
University College, London, xiv, 2

V

Valentine, J., 340, 358
Van Duren, J., 353
Vasquez, O., 103–4
Veiga Simão reform, 224
"Vertical and Horizontal Discourse", 5, 8
Vico, G., 135
Vineta, N. A., 256
"Visible and Invisible", 4
Vitale, Philippe, 5, 9, 113–25
Vygotsky, L. S., 8, 47, 48, 49, 58, 84, 99–103, 104, 105–6, 108–9, 185, 378, 379

W

Waters, M., 350
Weber, M., 84, 121
Wells, C. G., 17, 19, 20
Wells, G., 102
Wendt, A., 259
Wertsch, J., 99, 100
West, M., 293
Westgate, D. P. G., 267
Westminster College of Education, xiv
Whitty, G., 213
Whorf, B. L., 55–6

Wiles, Andrew, 172, 174, 175
Wille, T., 329
Williams, G., 5, 7, 17–42, 63, 68
Winterhoff, P. A., 105
Wittgenstein, L., 135
World War II, xiii
World Wide Web, 343, 350, 351, 352, 357
Worthen, B. R., 293
Wrong, D. H., 130
Wyndhamn, J., 103

Y

Young, Michael F. D., 4, 113, 146, 153

THIS SERIES EXPLORES THE HISTORY OF SCHOOLS AND SCHOOLING in the United States and other countries. Books in this series examine the historical development of schools and educational processes, with special emphasis on issues of educational policy, curriculum and pedagogy, as well as issues relating to race, class, gender, and ethnicity. Special emphasis will be placed on the lessons to be learned from the past for contemporary educational reform and policy. Although the series will publish books related to education in the broadest societal and cultural context, it especially seeks books on the history of specific schools and on the lives of educational leaders and school founders.

For additional information about this series or for the submission of manuscripts, please contact the general editors:

Alan R. Sadovnik
Rutgers University-Newark
Education Dept.
155 Conklin Hall
175 University Avenue
Newark, NJ 07102

Susan F. Semel
The City College of New York, CUNY
138th Street and Convent Avenue
NAC 5/208
New York, NY 10031

To order other books in this series, please contact our Customer Service Department:

800-770-LANG (within the U.S.)
212-647-7706 (outside the U.S.)
212-647-7707 FAX

Or browse online by series at:

www.peterlang.com

www.ingramcontent.com/pod-product-compliance
Ingram Content Group UK Ltd.
Pitfield, Milton Keynes, MK11 3LW, UK
UKHW021850210426
5322IPUK00022B/581